The 2000s

A Decade of Contemporary British Fiction

Titles in *The Decades Series*

The 1970s: A Decade of Contemporary British Fiction,
edited by Nick Hubble, John McLeod and Philip Tew

The 1980s: A Decade of Contemporary British Fiction,
edited by Emily Horton, Philip Tew and Leigh Wilson

The 1990s: A Decade of Contemporary British Fiction,
edited by Nick Hubble, Philip Tew and Leigh Wilson

The 2000s: A Decade of Contemporary British Fiction,
edited by Nick Bentley, Nick Hubble and Leigh Wilson

The 2000s

A Decade of Contemporary British Fiction

Edited by

Nick Bentley, Nick Hubble and Leigh Wilson

Bloomsbury Academic
An imprint of Bloomsbury Publishing Plc

B L O O M S B U R Y
LONDON · OXFORD · NEW YORK · NEW DELHI · SYDNEY

Bloomsbury Academic
An imprint of Bloomsbury Publishing Plc

50 Bedford Square	1385 Broadway
London	New York
WC1B 3DP	NY 10018
UK	USA

www.bloomsbury.com

BLOOMSBURY and the Diana logo are trademarks of Bloomsbury Publishing Plc

First published 2015
Reprinted 2016
First published in paperback 2017

© Nick Bentley, Nick Hubble, Leigh Wilson and contributors, 2015, 2017

All rights reserved. No part of this publication may be reproduced or transmitted in any form or by any means, electronic or mechanical, including photocopying, recording, or any information storage or retrieval system, without prior permission in writing from the publishers.

No responsibility for loss caused to any individual or organization acting on or refraining from action as a result of the material in this publication can be accepted by Bloomsbury or the author.

British Library Cataloguing-in-Publication Data
A catalogue record for this book is available from the British Library.

ISBN: HB: 978-1-4411-1215-6
PB: 978-1-3500-0542-6
ePDF: 978-1-4411-7549-6
ePub: 978-1-4742-6274-3

Library of Congress Cataloging-in-Publication Data
A catalog record for this book is available from the Library of Congress.

Series: The Decades Series

Cover design: Eleanor Rose

Typeset by RefineCatch Limited, Bungay, Suffolk

Contents

Contributors		vii
Series Editors' Preface		ix
Acknowledgements		xii
	Introduction: Fiction of the 2000s: Political Contexts, Seeing the Contemporary, and the End(s) of Postmodernism *Nick Bentley, Nick Hubble and Leigh Wilson*	1
1	Literary History of the Decade: Fictions from the Borderlands *Martyn Colebrook*	27
2	Special Topic 1: Subcultural Fictions: Youth Subcultures in Twenty-first-century British Fiction *Nick Bentley*	53
3	Special Topic 2: Translating Neuroscience: Fictions of the Brain in the 2000s *Laura Salisbury*	83
4	Postcolonial and Diasporic Voices: Contemporary British Fiction in an Age of Transnational Terror *Lucienne Loh*	115
5	Historical Representations: Reality Effects: The Historical Novel and the Crisis of Fictionality in the First Decade of the Twenty-first Century *Leigh Wilson*	145
6	Generic Discontinuities and Variations *Daniel Weston*	173
7	International Contexts 1: The American Reception of British Fiction in the 2000s *Ann Marie Adams*	199
8	International Contexts 2: From Multicultural Enthusiasm to the 'Failure of Multiculturalism': British Multi-ethnic Fiction in an International Frame *Ulrike Tancke*	223

Timeline of Works	245
Timeline of National Events	253
Timeline of International Events	261
Biographies of Writers	269
Index	281

Contributors

Ann Marie Adams is a Professor of English at Morehead State University, where she teaches graduate and undergraduate courses in British literature, film and gothic studies. Her scholarly work has appeared in *The Kentucky Philological Review*, *The Journal of the Midwest Modern Language Association*, *Yeats Annual*, *Papers in Language and Literature*, *Modern Drama*, *Critique*, *Callaloo*, *LIT* and *Contemporary Literature*.

Nick Bentley is Senior Lecturer in English literature at Keele University in the UK. His main research interests are in post-1945 British literature and literary and cultural theory, and especially in intersections of postmodernism, postcolonialism and contemporary fiction and culture. He is author of *Martin Amis: Writers and Their Work* (Northcote House, 2015); *Contemporary British Fiction* (Edinburgh University Press, 2008); *Radical Fictions: The English Novel in the 1950s* (Peter Lang, 2007); and editor of *British Fiction of the 1990s* (Routledge, 2005). He is currently working on two books: one on *Contemporary British Fiction: The Essential Criticism* (Palgrave, 2016); and one on the representation of youth subcultures in fiction and film 1950–2010. He is also co-editor of *The 2000s: A Decade of Contemporary British Fiction* in The Decades Series (Bloomsbury, 2015).

Martyn Colebrook is an independent researcher. He completed a PhD focusing on the novels of Iain (M.) Banks at the University of Hull (2012). He co-edited the first collection of scholarly essays on Banks, *The Transgressive Iain Banks* with Katharine Cox (McFarland, 2013) and has published individually and collaboratively within the field of twentieth-century fiction with chapters including 'Contemporary Scottish Crime Fiction and Terrorism', '*The Wasp Factory*, the Gothic and Mental Disorder', 'Paul Auster and Alienation' and 'Gordon Burn, *Somebody's Husband, Somebody's Son* and the Yorkshire Ripper'. Additionally, he has organized conferences focusing on, among other topics, 'Representations of 9/11', 'Millennial and Apocalypse Fiction', 'Michael Moorcock' (with Mark Williams, University of Mainz) and 'Angela Carter'.

Nick Hubble is Reader in English at Brunel University, London, UK. Nick is the author of *Mass-Observation and Everyday Life: Culture, History, Theory* (2006;

second edition 2010); co-author of *Ageing, Narrative and Identity* (2013); and co-editor of *The Science Fiction Handbook* (2013), *The 1970s: A Decade of Contemporary British Fiction* (2014) and special issues of the journals *EnterText*, *Literary London* and *New Formations*. Nick has published journal articles or book chapters on writers including Pat Barker, Ford Madox Ford, B.S. Johnson, Naomi Mitchison, George Orwell, Christopher Priest, John Sommerfield and Edward Upward.

Lucienne Loh is Lecturer in English Literature at the University of Liverpool, UK. She has previously taught at the University of Wisconsin-Madison, Brunel University and Royal Holloway, University of London. She is author of *The Postcolonial Country in Contemporary Literature* and has published a number of articles on postcolonial literature and theory as well as on contemporary British literature. She helped to establish the Postcolonial Studies Association in 2008 and is an Associate Editor for the *Journal of Postcolonial Writing*.

Laura Salisbury is Senior Lecturer in Medicine and English Literature at the University of Exeter. She is the author of *Samuel Beckett: Laughing Matters, Comic Timing* (2012) and co-editor of *Other Becketts* (2002), *Neurology and Modernity: A Cultural History of Nervous Systems, 1800–1950* (2010) and *Kittler Now: Current Perspectives in Kittler Studies* (2014). She has also written numerous articles and chapters on Beckett.

Ulrike Tancke has held a position as Junior Professor of English Literature at Johannes Gutenberg-Universität Mainz. She has studied and worked at several British and German universities (Universität Trier, Lancaster University, Johannes Gutenberg-Universität Mainz, Brunel University) and has published on both contemporary and early modern writing, including two monographs entitled *'Bethinke Thy Selfe' in Early Modern England: Writing Women's Identities* (Rodopi, 2010) *and Deceptive Fictions: Narrating Trauma and Violence in Contemporary Writing* (Cambridge Scholars, 2015).

Daniel Weston is Lecturer in Twentieth-Century English Literature at the University of Hull. He has published articles or chapters on Ciaran Carson, Philip Larkin, D.H. Lawrence and W.G. Sebald. He is currently writing a monograph titled *Contemporary Literary Landscapes: The Poetics of Experience*.

Leigh Wilson is Reader in Modern Literature at the University of Westminster. She is the author of *Modernism and Magic: Experiments with Spiritualism, Theosophy and the Occult* (2013) and co-editor of *The Edinburgh Critical Edition of The Selected Works of Andrew Lang* (2 vols, 2015).

Series Editors' Preface

Nick Hubble, Philip Tew and Leigh Wilson

Contemporary British fiction published from 1970 to the present has expanded into a major area of academic study in the last twenty years and attracts a seemingly ever-increasing global scholarship. However, the very speed of the growth of research in this field has perhaps precluded any really nuanced analysis of its key defining terms and has restricted consideration of its chronological development. This series addresses such issues in an informative and structured manner through a set of extended contributions that combine wide-reaching survey work with in-depth research-led analysis. Naturally, many older British academics assume at least some personal knowledge in charting the field of the contemporary, but increasingly many of these coordinates represent the distant past of pre-birth or childhood not only for students, both undergraduate and postgraduate, but also for younger academics. Given that most people's memories of their first five to ten years are vague and localized, an academic born in the early to mid-1980s will only have real first-hand knowledge of less than half these forty years, while a member of the current generation of undergraduates, born in the mid-1990s, will have no adult experience of the period at all. The rather self-evident nature of this chronological, experiential reality disguises the rather complex challenges it poses to any assessment of the contemporary. Therefore, the aim of these volumes, which include timelines and biographical information on the writers covered, is to provide the contextual framework that is now necessary for the study of the British fiction of these four decades.

Each of the volumes in this Decades Series emerged from a series of workshops hosted by the Brunel Centre for Contemporary Writing (BCCW) located in the School of Arts at Brunel University, London, UK. These events assembled specially invited teams of leading internationally recognized scholars in the field, together with emergent younger figures, in order that they might together examine critically the periodization of contemporary British fiction by dividing it into its four constituent decades: the 1970s symposium was held on 12 March 2010; the 1980s on 7 July 2010; the 1990s on 3 December 2010; and the 2000s on 1 April 2011. During these workshops, draft papers were offered and discussions ensued, with the aim of exchanging ideas and ensuring both continuity and also fruitful interaction (including productive dissonances) between what would become chapters of volumes that would hopefully exceed the sum of their parts.

The division of the series by decade could be charged with being too obvious and therefore rather too contentious. In the latter camp, no doubt, would be Ferdinand Mount, who in a 2006 article for the *London Review of Books* (LRB) concerned primarily with the 1950s, 'The Doctrine of Unripe Time', complained 'When did decaditis first strike? When did people begin to think that slicing the past up into periods of ten years was a useful thing to do?' However, he does admit still that such characterization has long been associated with aesthetic production and its relationship to a larger sense of the times. As Frank Kermode so influentially argued in *The Sense of an Ending: Studies in the Theory of Fiction*, published in 1967 just before the period covered by this series began, divisions of time, like novels, are ways of making meaning. And clearly both can also shape our comprehension of an ideological and aesthetic period that seem to co-exist, but are perhaps not necessarily coterminous in their dominant inflections. The scholars involved in our symposia discussed the potential arbitrariness of all periodizations, but nevertheless acknowledged the importance of such divisions, their experiential resonances and symbolic possibilities. They analysed the decades in question in terms of not only leading figures, the cultural zeitgeist and socio-historical perspectives, but also in the context of the changing configuration of Britishness within larger, shifting global processes. The volume participants also reconsidered the effects and meaning of headline events and cultural shifts such as the miners' strike of 1984–5, the collapse of communism, Blairism and cool Britannia, 9/11 and 7/7, to name only a very few. Perhaps ironically, to prove the point about the possibilities inherent in such an approach, in his LRB article Mount concedes that 'For the historian ... if the 1950s are famous for anything, it is for being dull', adding a comment on the 'shiny barbarism of the new affluence'. Hence, even for Mount, a decade may still possess certain unifying qualities, those shaping and shaped by its overriding cultural mood.

After the symposia had taken place at Brunel, the individuals dispersed and wrote up their papers into full-length chapters (generally 10,000–12,000 words), revised in the light of other papers, the workshop discussions and subsequent further research. These chapters form the core of the book series, which, therefore, may be seen as the result of a collaborative research project bringing together twenty-four academics from Britain, Europe and North America.

Each volume shares a common structure. Following the Introduction, the first chapter of each volume addresses the 'Literary History of the Decade' by offering an overview of the key writers, themes, issues and debates, including such factors as emergent literary practices, deaths, prizes, controversies, key developments, movements and best-sellers. The next two chapters are themed around topics that have been specially chosen for each decade, and that also relate to themes of the preceding and succeeding decades, enabling detailed readings of key texts to emerge in full historical and theoretical context. The tone and context having been set in this way, the remaining chapters fill out a complex but comprehensible picture of each decade. A 'Postcolonial Voices' chapter addresses the ongoing legacy of Britain's Empire and the rise of globalization, which is arguably the most significant long-term influence on contemporary British writing. 'Historical Representations' is concerned not just with historical novels but with the construction of the past in general, and thus the later volumes will be considering constructions of the earlier decades so that a complex multilayered account of the historicity of the contemporary will emerge over the series. The chapter on 'Generic Discontinuities' highlights the interaction between the socio-cultural contexts, established in earlier chapters, and aesthetic concerns. The 'International Contexts' chapters allow the chosen international academics allocated them to write about the key international aspects of the British fiction of the particular decade they are focusing on. This might variously concern how the fiction relates to international ideological, aesthetic and other relevant movements and/or how the fiction influenced international fiction and/or international reader reception. Each decade is different, but common threads may emerge.

In the future it is hoped to expand the Decades Series by adding to the first four planned volumes others that extend the period of 'Contemporary British Fiction': both by covering subsequent decades as they complete their course and also by featuring precursory decades, extending the focus of study backwards in time to cover the British fiction of the modern and post-war periods.

Works cited

Kermode, Frank. *The Sense of an Ending: Studies in the Theory of Fiction*. Oxford: Oxford University Press, 1967.

Mount, Ferdinand. 'The Doctrine of Unripe Time'. *London Review of Books*, 28:22 (16 November, 2006): 28–30. Available online: http://www.lrb.co.uk/v28/n22/ferdinand-mount/the-doctrine-of-unripe-time (accessed 30 May 2015).

Acknowledgements

We would like to thank all our contributors for their expertise, patience and generosity when responding to our queries and guidance as this book has gradually taken shape. We have enjoyed excellent support throughout from the editorial team at Bloomsbury, especially David Avital and Mark Richardson, who have been instrumental in bringing this book to fruition.

We gratefully acknowledge the support of the Brunel University Research and Knowledge Transfer Committee for providing the funding that enabled the Brunel Centre for Contemporary Writing to host the 'Contemporary British Fiction Decades Seminar Series' during 2010 and 2011, which has led to the publication of the volumes in this book series. Without the support of administrative and catering staff at Brunel these events could not have taken place. We would also like to thank all the academics and postgraduate students who attended and contributed to the discussions at these events.

We would also like to mention the staff at Brunel University Library, the British Library, the National Library of Wales and other research libraries who have provided support to the contributors to this volume.

Introduction: Fiction of the 2000s
Political Contexts, Seeing the Contemporary, and the End(s) of Postmodernism

Nick Bentley, Nick Hubble and Leigh Wilson

As Big Ben finished chiming midnight on New Year's Eve 1999, London welcomed in the new century with fireworks and a 'River of Fire' pyrotechnic display on the Thames. Earlier that evening, the opening ceremony of the £758 million Millennium Dome had been attended by an audience of 10,000 including the Queen and the Prime Minister, Tony Blair. It was a particularly triumphant night for Blair as he also officially opened the London Eye and then signified a new confident, successful, classless Britain by joining hands with the – somewhat uncomfortable looking – Queen in singing 'Auld Lang Syne'. Blair's 'New Labour', which had ended eighteen years of Conservative Party rule when they swept to power in the landslide election victory of 1997, were no longer constrained by their pledge to adhere to the previous Government's spending figures for the first two years of their term and were therefore set to increase public spending. They were expected to repeal the notorious Conservative 'Section 28' law in place since 1986, which outlawed the 'promotion' of homosexuality, and to further extend equal rights legislation generally. They had successfully introduced devolved government in Scotland, Wales, and – following Blair's support for the 'Peace Process' – Northern Ireland; and were looking to extend this to English regions. Furthermore, many were optimistic that they would also start the process of allowing Britain to share in the new European currency due to be introduced in two years' time. The 1990s had seen the final collapse of the Communist Bloc and the seeming advent of a 'new world order'; now there was the prospect of a more diverse and inclusive Britain emerging under New Labour politicians, who, unlike Margaret Thatcher, believed there was such a thing as Society but were none the less comfortable with individual aspiration and personal freedom.

Viewed in retrospect, this optimism now seems, at the very least, misplaced and yet to regard the feeling at the turn of the millennium as simply the product of false consciousness is to misunderstand the significance of what actually happened during the decade. The strange thing was that rather than political failure leading to demoralization, the Labour Government were in fact successful beyond any realistic expectation. By the end of the decade, in which they remained constantly in power by comfortably winning the General Elections in 2001 and 2005, they had completed much of the progressive programme outlined above by repealing 'Section 28' in 2003, passing the Equality Act (which came into force in 2010) and investing heavily in the public sector, especially in Education and Health. Despite the setback of Northern England rejecting regional assemblies in a 2004 referendum, devolution proved to be a popular success in Scotland and Wales. The respective elections in 2007 of a minority Scottish National Party (SNP) Government, with Alex Salmond as First Minister, in Scotland and of Plaid Cymru into a power-sharing coalition with Labour in the Welsh Government, seemed to fulfil the aim of providing nationalist voices with a degree of autonomy without undermining the cohesion of the UK. It was only after 2011, when the unanticipated election of a majority SNP Government led to the 2014 referendum on Scottish Independence, which was rejected by 55 per cent of the Scottish electorate, that the potential constitutional questions thrown up by the 1997 Devolution Act suddenly became a major public issue. However, both the resultant debate and the referendum itself can be seen as reinvigorating democratic participation and therefore as a good outcome in itself. The irony of this is that, despite enabling this process, the Labour Party has been the biggest political loser as its levels of support in the immediate aftermath of the referendum plummeted in Scotland, where it had won fifty-six of the seventy-two parliamentary seats in 1997. However, that trajectory was not apparent at the end of 2009.

Some of Labour's failures even proved fortuitous, both to them and the country. The five key economic criteria that were announced in 1997 as the preconditions for triggering a referendum on membership of the Euro were never met and quietly around about that time the Government abandoned the planned 2006 referendum on acceptance of the new European Constitution, which national opinion polling showed to be unpopular. Not joining the common currency turned out to be advantageous as it spared the UK from the devastation of Eurozone economies such as Spain, Ireland and Greece during the global recession in the closing years of the decade. Instead, Labour under Gordon Brown, who had taken over as Prime Minister from Blair in 2007, was successful in averting the collapse of major banks and had brought the country out of recession before the decade's end. On balance, therefore, one might have expected a positive national mood at the end of a decade marked by public investment, devolution, social liberalization and the formal end of the British Army's 38-year deployment in Northern Ireland, following the Provisional IRA's decommissioning of its weapons and the establishment in 2007 of a power-sharing government between the Democratic Unionist Party and Sinn Féin in the newly reinstated (following its suspension in 2002 and nearly five years of direct rule from London) Northern Irish Assembly.

That the decade was not experienced in this positive light is due mainly to two sequences of events that happened in the United States but which had global consequences. The first of these took place on 11 September 2001, when the terrorist group Al-Qaeda hijacked four passenger airliners and crashed three of them into, respectively, the North and the South Towers of the World Trade Center, and the Pentagon. The fourth plane, United Airlines Flight 93, crashed into a field as the passengers attempted to overwhelm the hijackers. The attack left nearly 3,000 people dead, including sixty-seven British citizens, and led to the US President, George W. Bush, declaring a War on Terror within days. On 7 October 2001, US, UK and other allied forces from NATO invaded Afghanistan to overthrow the Taliban regime, who were harbouring elements of Al-Qaeda. At peak involvement, nearly 10,000 British troops were deployed and their final withdrawal from Afghanistan was not until 2014, by which point 453 British military personnel had died. On 20 March 2003, US and UK forces invaded Iraq in order to topple the regime of Saddam Hussein – an aim that was quickly achieved – but remained for 'peace-keeping' purposes amidst what had effectively become a civil war. British troops were based in the Southern city of Basra before their eventual withdrawal in April 2009, during which time 179 military personnel died.

The Iraq war was never popular with the British public. Between one and two million people marched through the streets of London on Saturday 15 February 2003 in opposition to the war that was then seen to be pending, and opinion polls that week showed 52 per cent of the population opposed and only 29 per cent in favour (Travis and Black). While near universal support from the political parties and the media did lead to a brief swing in public opinion during the early weeks of the invasion, there was always a large minority in opposition. Following the overthrow of the regime, the Iraq Survey Group were unable to find any Weapons of Mass Destruction (WMD) in Iraq – the pretext on which the war was fought – and public opinion turned decisively against the War and Tony Blair. A YouGov poll taken to mark the tenth anniversary of the invasion found that 53 per cent of the public thought the war had been wrong and that 50 per cent thought that Blair had deliberately misled Parliament about the existence of WMD: figures that echoed those recorded in October 2004 when the news of the non-existence of the WMD was first confirmed (Farmer). The experience of the Iraq War and its ongoing legacies have left a bitter aftertaste to the memory of Blair's premiership.

The other key external event that influenced Britain during the decade was the financial crisis of 2007–8 and the subsequent global recession. The roots of the crisis lay in a combination of factors stemming from the collapse of the US housing market in 2006 and the related subprime mortgage crisis. The knock-on effects of devalued assets, which threatened the collapse of large financial institutions in the US and globally, were only contained by the use of public funds to bail out the banks – a process that was initiated in Britain by the Brown Government. The subsequent global depression lasted until 2012 and the consequences in terms of the increased national debt levels of many Western countries are very much ongoing. In Britain, the crisis and recession were marked by a succession of crisis points such as the 'run' on the Northern Rock Bank in the autumn of 2007, which resulted in its nationalization the following spring; the huge bailout of the high street banks, Lloyds and the Royal Bank of Scotland, in October 2008; and the collapse of a number of well-known shopping chains in the run-up to Christmas 2008, including Woolworths, MFI and Zavvi (which had previously been known as Virgin Megastores). By the end of the decade, Britain was back out of recession officially but the negative experience of many of the public, and the awareness that the huge increase in national debt incurred by the bank bailout would result in cuts in public services and job losses in the public sector, contributed to the sour mood that would see Labour ejected from office in May 2010.

However, the disillusionment was not simply caused by the experience of the financial crisis from 2007 but also the realization that many of the problems revealed in this period were actually the consequence of longer underlying trends. In 2014, the Credit Suisse Global Wealth Report revealed that 'the UK was the only country in the G7 to have recorded rising inequality in the 21st century' (Treanor). This was not, as the report makes clear, just as a result of the recession at the end of the decade adversely affecting those on lower incomes but a steady process of rising inequality across the whole period. In fact, the trend dated back to the rule of the Thatcher Government in the 1980s, as the sociologists Richard Wilkinson and Katie Pickett were to make clear in their influential 2009 book, *The Spirit Level*:

> Long before the financial crisis, which gathered pace in the later part of 2008, British politicians commenting on the decline of community or the rise of

various forms of anti-social behaviour, would sometimes refer to our 'broken society'. The financial collapse shifted attention to the broken economy, and while the broken society was sometimes blamed on the behaviour of the poor, the broken economy was widely attributed to the rich. Stimulated by the prospects of ever bigger salaries and bonuses, those in charge of some of the most trusted financial institutions threw caution to the wind and built houses of cards which could stand only within the protection of a thin speculative bubble. But the truth is that both the broken society and the broken economy resulted from the growth of inequality. (5)

Back in the late 1970s, under the Labour Government of Jim Callaghan, Britain had been one of the most socially equal countries in the world, registering its lowest ever levels for the Gini co-efficient recording income inequality and for the proportion of individuals below the poverty line, as well as registering its highest ever level of social mobility (see Beckett, 409–10). What the Financial Crisis demonstrated, therefore, was how much the social fabric of the country had declined since then despite the prosperity and optimism that had appeared to characterize the country from the mid-1990s to the beginning of the new millennium. It is recognition of this decline that has formed the backdrop to the subsequent rise of a lack of faith in the political class – exacerbated by the MPs' expenses scandal of 2009 – and public support for political parties, such as the Greens, the SNP and the United Kingdom Independence Party (UKIP), which offer alternative approaches to the mainstream parties.

Therefore, it is tempting to look back at the Financial Crisis and view it as providing a harsh intrusion of real life, which punctured the illusory nature of social life as it was lived and understood in Britain for most of the 2000s. However, what we should also consider is the way that such a mode of thinking resembles much of the social and cultural response to 9/11 earlier in the decade, which was, as Slavoj Žižek argues in *Welcome to the Desert of the Real* (2002), to view it similarly as a dose of reality exposing the illusions and complacency of western society. Against this position, Žižek argues that:

> We should ... invert the standard reading according to which the WTC explosions were the intrusion of the Real which shattered our illusory sphere: quite the reverse – it was before the WTC collapse that we lived in our reality, perceiving Third World horrors as something which was not actually part of our social reality; as something which existed (for us) as a spectral apparition on the TV screen – and what happened on September 11 was that this fantastic screen apparition entered our reality. It is not that reality entered our image: the image

entered and shattered our reality (i.e. the symbolic co-ordinates which determine what we experience as reality). (16)

Žižek's argument is based on the fact that 9/11 was uncannily prefigured by the catastrophe sequences in many American disaster films, including science-fictional portrayals of the future such as *Escape from New York* (1981), *Independence Day* (1996) and *The Matrix* (1999) – this latter film providing his book's title in the scene where the hero, Neo, is made to see the world as a post-holocaust landscape of burnt-out ruins to which 'the resistance leader, Morpheus, utters the ironic greeting: "Welcome to the desert of the real"'(15). Žižek explains that the fact that Americans fantasize about this kind of spectacular destruction is fully in keeping with the insights of psychoanalysis: the maintenance of our everyday reality comes at the costs of suppressing numerous desires and drives with the potential for destruction; these types of anxiety fantasy parasitically appeal to such destructive urges and give expression to the unconscious wishes for society to end in catastrophe. But this does not mean, he argues, that what psychoanalysis is supposed to do is liberate us from these fantasies so that we can confront reality as it really is. In fact, these fantasies are part of the structure by which 'reality' is maintained as they provide an outlet for destructive desires that cause no harm to actually existing society. Therefore, in order to really engage with reality it is necessary not to free oneself from fantasy but to identify with it fully in the manner of Jacques Lacan's notion of 'traversing the fantasy':

> In our daily existence, we are immersed in 'reality' (structured and supported by the fantasy), and this immersion is disturbed by symptoms which bear witness to the fact that another, repressed, level of our psyche resists this immersion. To 'traverse the fantasy' therefore ... means *fully identifying oneself with the fantasy* – namely, with the fantasy which structures the excess that resists our immersion in daily reality. (17; emphasis in original)

Only by fully identifying with the fantasy, can we structure our resistant excess differently so that it is not perpetually sublimated, as in the experience of watching Hollywood blockbusters, but enabled to function as an alternative core of our identity. Instead of having to make sense of the world from within the constrained, timetabled and prescribed routines that constitute our daily 'reality', identifying with the fantasy offers an alternative point of view and therefore a genuine perspective on 'reality'. In the context of 9/11, identifying with the fantasy does not mean identifying with the terrorists but with the insight that our 'reality' was shattered on that day by the influx of the fantastic. What was revealed as the irreducible core of that 'reality' was the non-identity of our conscious understanding of the world with our unconscious structuring of the world. In other words, one way in which we consciously chose to believe the world worked was revealed to be at odds with another way in which we knew it worked but chose to ignore. This is not, as Žižek points out, a postmodern argument in which we are being told that 'reality' is merely a symbolic fiction that we have misperceived – indeed, in these kinds of formulations, the utterly conventional thinking of postmodernism is revealed as precisely no more than the commonsense rejoinder not to confuse fiction for reality. Rather, the ultimate lesson concerning representation to be learnt from 9/11 is the exact opposite of postmodern mantra: '*we should not mistake reality for fiction* – we should be able to discern, in what we experience as fiction, the hard kernel of the Real which we are able to sustain only if we fictionalise it' (19; emphasis in original).

In other words, Žižek is arguing for an aesthetic response to the crises of the decade that treats them as eruptions of the fantastic that allow us to grasp some sense of the otherwise hidden realities that are actually shaping our social experience. In Britain, examples of such a response that reference 9/11 directly include Pat Barker's *Double Vision* (2003), J.G. Ballard's *Millennium People* (2003) and Ian McEwan's *Saturday* (2005). The latter, in particular, typifies a broader movement of the decade away from postmodernism as a literary and aesthetic mode, which is discussed later in this Introduction. First, however it is instructive to consider the ways in which we might approach the relationship between fiction and the events of the period in which it is produced. This is particularly pertinent in this collection of critical essays published only a few years after the object of their study. The issue of critical distance is always a concern in the field of contemporary literary criticism, and in this sense it is necessary to consider the notion of the 'contemporary'. At the beginning of their preface to the edited volume *Mourning Diana: Nation, Culture and the Performance of Grief* (2002), Adrian Kear and Deborah Lynn Steinberg quote from the preface to another academic work, like theirs investigating the cultural and social significance of the death of Princess Diana in August 1997, but unlike theirs appearing in the same year as her death. From what they call this 'unusually rapidly produced academic collection', titled *Planet Diana: Cultural Studies and Global Mourning* (Re:Public, 1997), they quote the editors' argument that academic work needs to engage with its own present:

Academics are generally slow and late; often too late, in their response to public matters that matter now, not tomorrow. Beaten by the immediacy of journalism, their seriously theorized but nonetheless on-the-spot insights do not often get the opportunity to enter into the public arena until everyone else has moved on. (v)

Kear and Steinberg distance their collection from this call to the academy to get with it, and their challenge to this position centres on the relation between scholarship and the moment. While journalism is 'produced *in* the moment', scholarship, in its commitment to the future, not just to an endlessly repeated 'now', strives to produce a properly historicized 'now'. In contrast to the 'immediacy' of journalism held up as a model in the quote above, Kear and Steinberg claim that their collection 'is an attempt to respond to the critical imperatives and renewed perspectives of hindsight' (x). However, for all their resistance to the remade 'now time' of the Re:Public collection, their own collection was published a mere five years after Diana's death, suggesting that even hindsight is a sped up, almost instantaneous thing in our contemporary.

As well as the relatively short distances between event and its scholarly consideration, what also distinguishes the two collections is the different – although central for both – place given to figures of sight in thinking about the relationship between the contemporary and reflection on it. The two collections bifurcate in part at least around the different implications of 'insight' and 'hindsight'; the former implying proximity, a piercing of the surface of something that is close by the vision of an observer that has a special and rare perspicacity; the latter implying distance, and a coolness of vision dependent upon the extent of the gap between observer and observed. Such figures of sight – so crucial for so long to European attempts to articulate understanding and knowledge – have become particularly salient and particularly fraught in debates about our ability to understand our present and in thinking through the construction of the period of 'the contemporary' itself. At the beginning of his *Twenty-First-Century Fiction: A Critical Introduction* (2013), Peter Boxall describes the problem attending any attempt to define or describe the contemporary as being 'that the time we are living through is very difficult to bring into focus, and often only becomes legible in retrospect' (1). At the same time, though, for Boxall our contemporary suffers from specific failures of sight, the clarity lacking not in the eye of the observer but in the thing observed. He argues that the last decades of the twentieth century were dominated by a sense of lateness or belatedness, 'a vast historical gloaming, a gathering agedness' (23) and that as a result the new century *as* new suffers from a lack of visual clarity:

> Cultural experience in the early decades of the new century suffers as a result from a peculiar double vision, a sense at once of being extraordinarily old, and impossibly young, stranded somewhere between the end of one world order and the beginning of a new one, bereft of a clear sense of our own age. (23)

This sense of a specific problem of vision attendant on the contemporary indicates too the extent to which it has been increasingly distinguished from other contemporaries. While the word 'contemporary' was in general use as a description of the present, and was used to describe novels in particular, from the beginning of the twentieth century (as in Elizabeth Drew's *The Modern Novel: Some Aspects of Contemporary Fiction*, from 1926 or Philip Henderson's *The Novel Today: Studies in Contemporary Attitudes* from 1936 or Frederick Robert Karl's *A Reader's Guide to the Contemporary English Novel* from 1963), what is of much more recent origin is the idea that the 'contemporary' denotes not just every present but the particular present of the early twenty-first century. As part of this, the use of the term has shifted from its function as an adjective (contemporary fiction, for example, as in the Elizabeth Drew book cited above) to its dominant use as a noun, 'the contemporary'. This intense focus on the present has certainly led to questions of temporality dominating much work in the humanities through the early twentieth century, with David Woods, in his *Time After Time* (2007) arguing that the period will be seen in the future as exhibiting not the linguistic turn so often ascribed to the early twentieth century, but a 'temporal turn (or return)' (129). Indeed, some critics have argued that the rise to dominance of 'the contemporary' as a central organizing principle of both our period generally and of so much recent work in the humanities is a result of the discrediting of 'postmodernism' and its breezy way with chronology. The contemporary then covers an increasing number of sub-terms used to name and analyse our current state, such as Zygmunt Bauman's 'liquid modernity', Gilles Lipovetsky's 'hypermodernism' and Vermeulen and van den Akker's 'metamodernism', all of which foreground the particularities around our temporal moment in terms of a problematizing of the idea of time itself. In particular, many of these terms claim that, or are symptomatic of the idea that, the central characteristic of the contemporary is a failure to acknowledge, create or take into account the particular temporal moment of the future (see Peter Osborne, *The Politics of Time*). If this is the case, the concentration on *seeing* the contemporary, or how the contemporary should be seen, comes to be rather differently inflected. It becomes possible that such anxiety of sight masks the disappearance of what precisely cannot be seen – the future.

In one of the most powerful and influential accounts of late capitalism over the last few decades, this temporal crisis is linked in important ways with the debate about sight, with the figures of proximity and distance so often used to think about the present. For Fredric Jameson, most recently articulated in his *The Antinomies of Realism* (2013), the periodizing force in late capitalism, the result of its anxious sundering of productive relation with the past and its reifying vision of the future, focuses on the surface of a time – 'a world dated by costume and fashion, haircuts and coiffures, hit songs, popular music, the yearly make of the automobile and the occasional distinctive building style' (299) – privileging, inevitably, pure visibility over the interpretative act or any sense of the complex dynamics of change. As Jameson argues, this is true not just for the present's relation to the past, but for our relation to our own time: 'The present as history nowadays requires us to turn it into just such a named period, and to endow it with a period style, on which we look back' (299). Here, we distance ourselves from the present in order to see it as surface; the strong sense of the contemporary as a period is then for Jameson not so much an indication of our desire to understand and wrestle with its particular situations and problems but rather of a reifying process, which in the end asserts the situation of the present as given rather than made through the dynamics and imbalances of power. The ability to 'see' the surface of the period, then, acts as a persuasion that the period exists *as* a period, and that it could only ever be the way it is and no other.

These questions of temporality, vision, proximity and distance are at stake in one of the most influential critical interventions in the idea of the contemporary since the turn of the millennium, and indeed in critical responses to it. At the beginning of his essay, 'What is the contemporary?', based on the inaugural lecture of a seminar series given in 2006/7 and originally published in Italian in 2008, the philosopher Giorgio Agamben asks the question 'What does it mean to be contemporary?' Agamben's first indication of an answer is from Friedrich Nietzsche via Roland Barthes: 'The contemporary is the untimely' (40). This sense of untimeliness, of time being out of joint, the phrase from *Hamlet* so influentially at the heart of Jacques Derrida's argument about history following the collapse of Communism in his *Specters of Marx* (1993), dominates Agamben's answers to his initial questions. This may seem to be paradoxical – the etymology of 'contemporary' (with/together in time) would seem to suggest a togetherness, a cohesion, a moment of homogeneity in time, rather than the fractured divisions suggested by Agamben and Derrida. However, summarizing Nietzsche's position in his *Untimely Meditations* (1873–6), Agamben claims that those who:

are truly contemporary, who truly belong to their time, are those who neither perfectly coincide with it nor adjust themselves to its demands. They are thus in a sense irrelevant [*inattuale*]. But precisely because of this condition, precisely through this disconnection and this anachronism, they are more capable than others of perceiving and grasping their own time. (40)

This out of timeness, Agamben is quick to point out, does not however allow a nostalgia, a fantasy of living in a time other than the actual present. The true contemporary is aware of the time in which they live, and that it is the only time for them, but at the same time maintains a distance from it. At the heart of Agamben's definition of the contemporary, the person who is truly contemporary in their anachronistic sundering from their time, is the question of how to *see* one's own time. The inhabitant of the present who is not a true contemporary fails because they are too close to it to see it clearly, 'they are not able to firmly hold their gaze on it' (41). As Agamben goes on to argue, however, the gaze of the true contemporary is not straightforward. Whereas conventionally the ability to see is linked to figures of light and clarity, for Agamben the true contemporary sees not light but darkness; what the true contemporary perceives in their time is not clarity but obscurity (44). Darkness then does not denote a non-seeing, but a special kind of seeing. Using current theories about why the sky at night is dark, Agamben suggests that the darkness perceived by the contemporary is in fact a different kind of light, a light that has not yet/cannot arrive in time. To be a contemporary is: 'to perceive in this darkness a light that, while directed toward us, infinitely distances itself from us. In other words, it is like being on time for an appointment that one cannot but miss' (46).

One of the things the contemporary perceives through this distanced vision in the present is the past: 'Only he who perceives the indices and signatures of the archaic in the most modern and recent can be contemporary' (50). What the true contemporary recognizes about the present is the particular and forceful presence of the origin within it. This origin, this pastness in the present, is that in the present which is unlived: 'And to be contemporary means in this sense to return to a present where we have never been' (51–2). It is only the contemporary who is able to transform time, to put 'it in relation to other times' (53), and to see in the present that which others, together in the same moment of time but not true contemporaries because of their failures of vision, cannot.

It is just this assertion of the need for a clear vision predicated on distance, however, that prompts Pedro Erber's critique of Agamben's essay. For Erber, Agamben's argument has at its base an unacknowledged and unproblematized 'primacy of vision as a mode of relating to the present' and, as Erber goes on to say, seeing 'requires necessarily a certain degree of detachment, since there is no vision without distance' (38). This distance reproduces rather than critiques the central assumptions of European culture since the Enlightenment – the relation between truth and distance, the privileging of the subject over the object – assumptions that have fuelled Europe's assurance of its primacy over its non-European 'others'. Erber sees Agamben's essay as an anxious symptom of the way that globalization has reversed the dynamics of colonialism, so that Europe is now experiencing itself as 'colonised' and its presumed distinction (as the locus of reason, of democracy and of the universally 'human') is put under pressure. In the end, the failure of Agamben's essay for Erber is the failure to acknowledge that our contemporary 'has become inextricable from the increasing contemporization of difference – to the extent that, denying the latter, it is the present itself that one refuses to recognize' (43–4). What is most crucial in the contemporary for Erber and what Agamben fails to acknowledge is that 'the same word names today the historical period in which we supposedly live and the very impossibility of historical periodization, insofar as the unity of its putative subject unravels itself in singularities irreducible to generalization' (44). The link made by Erber here between the contemporary and globalization – indeed the assertion that 'the contemporary' is problematically predicated on the circumstances and effects of globalization – inevitably politicizes the debate. As quoted by Erber, the anthropologist Marc Augé has argued that 'a generalized situation of cultural circulation' has forced a situation within anthropology where the 'other' must be recognized as our contemporary (Augé, 50). In distinction to Agamben's distanced insight, this acknowledgement of contemporaneousness forces the 'subject of knowledge' (Erber, 34) – the anthropologist here, but more generally the European academic – to recognize their object as not the other but themselves.

In the area of literary studies, these questions of vision, proximity and distance, of the relations between the 'subject of knowledge' and their object are apposite too. Since the turn of the century a number of things have led to a far closer relation between literary criticism and its objects; that is, writers and literary texts. This has produced both a criticism that acknowledges its own assumptions and its own implication in the moment of the present, as urged by Erber, but risks, too, a certain cosiness between the academy and its one-time 'others' that accommodates the demands of consumer capitalism in the ways identified by Jameson. This doubling effect can be seen in a number of areas. First, the contemporary as a privileged period of criticism and study has gradually been established since 2000, and can be seen in the large number of undergraduate and postgraduate modules now offered on it. While in one way this could be seen as literary criticism's overdue recognition of the legitimacy of the present, another cause could be a less welcome effect of the increasing marketization of higher education through the period, in which demand from students (now seen as 'consumers') for courses on the contemporary, supposedly less demanding because of the 'familiarity' of the content, is quickly acceded to. Second, writers and academic literary critics are increasingly more proximate through the presence of creative writing courses in English departments, and the increasing presence on these courses (since the economic crisis of 2007 caused remuneration from publishers to plummet) of writers as teachers. Third, an awareness that the 'empire' has been 'striking back' for at least three decades now, while being seen as a cause of the revival of the fortunes of the British novel in the 1980s, is also in danger of flattening differences, such that the term 'the British novel', used predominantly by critics in Anglophone studies (such as this one), begins itself to colonize and make proximate locations and identities – Indian, Pakistani, Irish, Caribbean and so on – whose difference would be a challenge. In these works, which have begun to trouble the distinctions between 'hindsight', 'insight' and self-reflection, as the point of disagreement between Agamben's and Erber's essays shows, the results of such shifts are by no means uncontentious.

In addition to considering the relationship between the producers of fiction and the socio-economic and political concerns of the period in which they are writing, novelists are also acutely aware of the aesthetic and stylistic forms in which they operate, as well as their relationship to a series of literary and critical heritages against which they locate their own literary practice. In terms of literary form perhaps the style that continued to loom over the first decade of the twenty-first century was postmodernism, despite most commentators agreeing that the heyday of postmodern fiction and art peaked around the 1980s and 1990s in Britain. Indeed, an exhibition at the Victoria and Albert Museum in London in 2011 was very specific about dates in its title: 'Postmodernism: Style and Subversion 1970–1990'. Although this exhibition covered a range of aesthetic practices from architecture to pop music the sense was that postmodernism could now be seen as a late-twentieth-century set of cultural practices in much the same way as modernism has come to represent an early-twentieth-century movement. However, many writers in the first decade of the twenty-first century have continued to engage with narrative techniques, styles and approaches that speak in varying ways with (and against) postmodernism. It is possible, then, to think of the 2000s as a decade in which novelists and cultural critics examine the end, or indeed, ends of postmodernism. This can be approached in (at least) three ways here.

First, in a purely chronologizing sense, then perhaps the events of 9/11 can be seen as a representative historic marker. Martin Amis, for example, in an article first published in the *Guardian* a week after the event, described the collapse of the twin towers of the World Trade Center as the 'apotheosis of the postmodern era' (5) suggesting it represented both a culmination and moment of breaking with a certain way of thinking about contemporary society and politics – 'a worldflash of a coming future' (5). 9/11 has taken on a cultural significance similar to the way in which Virginia Woolf cited the first Post-Impressionist Exhibition at the Grafton Galleries in London in December 1910 as the moment when 'human character changed' (320) heralding the arrival of modernist sensibilities, or when Charles Jencks referred to the demolition of the Pruitt-Igoe housing project on the 16 March 1972 as 'the day Modern architecture died' (9). These identifications of specific events as representing paradigm shifts in cultural movements are, of course, provocative and mask the complexities of the relationship between historical moments and the literary and aesthetic practices undertaken by writers and artists. Nevertheless, as suggested earlier with respect to Žižek's interpretation of 9/11 as an eruption of the fantastic, they can act as useful markers in our sense of the movement of literary history.

Second, we might think about the end of postmodernism in terms of its limits in a philosophical sense. If postmodernism has to do with a sense of a radical scepticism towards all systems that claim totalizing narratives whether that be to the idea of truth, individual identity or the production of meaning, or a defining set of ideological parameters, then many writers in the 2000s began to think beyond that limit. As Adam Kelly (2011) has argued (although mainly in the context of North American writers), many of the novelists coming to prominence in the late 1990s and 2000s grew up with postmodernism as the dominant aesthetic form. Any claim for its avant-garde status therefore could be said to be undermined by its apparent ubiquity in the last decades of the twentieth century. Indeed it is possible to identify the 1990s as the period of popular postmodernism in that it became embedded in mainstream culture in a way that undercut any sense of radical alterity. This can be seen, for example, in the number of films in the 1990s that offered postmodern challenges to the concept of a verifiable reality; films such as *Total Recall* (1990), *Forrest Gump* (1994), *Pulp Fiction* (1994), *Twelve Monkeys* (1995), *Scream* (1996), *Trainspotting* (1996), *Pleasantville* (1998), *Sliding Doors* (1998), *The Truman Show* (1998), *The Matrix* (1999), *Fight Club* (1999) and

The Blair Witch Project (1999). These films were mostly box office successes and despite a certain cult status many of them gained, they can hardly be seen as part of a radical avant-garde bound on shaking up mainstream or bourgeois sensibilities. The 1990s was also the decade in which postmodern experimenters in fiction could be said to have firmly established themselves as the new literary establishment in Britain: Martin Amis, Julian Barnes, A.S. Byatt, Angela Carter, Ian McEwan, Salman Rushdie and Jeanette Winterson were no longer radical upstarts but the go-to writers for broadsheet editorials on the novel and stock-in-trade for university courses on contemporary fiction. Historiographic metafiction and self-reflexive parody became the dominant literary practices during the 1990s, and the writers and artists emerging after this period were faced with either a sense of exhaustion and boredom with its oft-repeated pronouncements, or the need to continue to push its fracturing and relativistic outlooks. The attempt to cast off the formal legacies of the previous generation can be seen for example in the collection of short stories edited by Nicholas Blincoe and Matt Thorne called *All Hail the New Puritans* published in 2001. This volume is introduced with a ten-point New Puritan Manifesto that rejects the textual obfuscations and complexities associated with postmodernism. Point 4, for example, states: 'We believe in textual simplicity and vow to avoid all devices of voice: rhetoric, authorial asides'; while the following point insists 'In the name of clarity, we recognise the importance of temporal linearity and eschew flashbacks, dual temporal narratives and foreshadowing' (i). This end of postmodernism then can be seen in the sense that perhaps its main ideas had become widely accepted thus achieving any aesthetic, philosophical or political goals it might have had. (Although given its relativism it is problematic to speak of intended goals.) It is illuminating in this context to turn to Jean-François Lyotard's definition of postmodernism as a mode that unlike modern aesthetics 'puts forward the unpresentable in presentation itself; [but] which denies itself the solace of good forms' (81). By the 1990s, however, a certain amount of easy recognition of the ludic qualities of postmodernism meant that for most interested parties postmodernism was now just part of the cultural wallpaper and, as Jameson has argued in *Postmodernism, Or, The Cultural Logic of Late Capitalism*, had contributed to its own 'waning of affect' (10).

This connects with a third way of thinking about the end of postmodernism, in the sense of its ends and means as a set of cultural practices. As many commentators from Jameson to bell hooks have noted, postmodernism can be read not as a radical disruption of totalizing narratives with the potential liberatory space that that opens up, but in fact the appropriate aesthetic practice to go hand-in-hand with late capitalist and neo-imperialistic practices as pursued by Western nations. The embracing of postmodernism then in the academies and in popular culture can be seen as a component of cultural imperialism that exports ethical relativism to subaltern and marginalized groups, making it difficult to ground an oppositional politics in any set of agreed ideologies such as the class struggle, feminism or resistant postcolonialism. The end of ideology thus becomes an acceptance of the inevitability of the shifting grounds of the market economy. This became increasingly significant after the collapse of communism in the Soviet Union and Eastern Europe in the early 1990s. Francis Fukuyama's identification of the end of history thus dovetails neatly with Jameson's identification of the lack of historicity in postmodernism's tendency to sweep over specific historical fact as inevitably contributing to unverifiable grand narratives of official history. The prominence of neo-historical fiction in the 2000s as noted by critics such as Alan Robinson (2011) and Ann Heilmann and Mark Llewellyn (2010) is significant in this context, albeit with a recognition of history as a narrative bound up with discourses of political and ideological power, rather than the debilitating postmodern rejection of historical facts. Writers such as Jane Harris, John Harwood, Hilary Mantel and Sarah Waters emerged (or came to prominence) in the 2000s and developed narrative strategies that disrupt certain official histories whilst not rejecting the possibility of establishing a grounded sense of the past. As Alan Robinson has argued, there has been a recent move by novelists towards constructionist approaches to historical narratives, for whom 'the past is only accessible in mediated form, through mainly textual representations, but [who] presume that these representations correspond to and thus enable some knowledge of a once-existent reality' (15). The historical novel of the 2000s forms the focus of Leigh Wilson's chapter in this volume.

It is, then, with a sense of a break with dominant literary and cultural forms of the previous decade that several writers discussed in this volume establish themselves. Postmodernism, of course, was always an awkward compound word, but there is a sense in which the awkwardness has been extended by a series of post-postmodernisms. Several terms have emerged in the literary/critical field in the last ten years or so that attempt to register this extension/rejection of the postmodern including post-postmodernism (Nealon), beyond postmodernism (Stierstorfer), after postmodernism (Potter and López), altermodernism (Bourriaud), metamodernism (Vermeulen and van den Akker), digimodernism (Kirby), the new puritans (Blincoe and Thorne) and the new sincerity (Kelly), amongst others. As mentioned earlier, some of these terms problematize the idea of time itself, but the sheer range of them suggests something of the broad desire in literary and cultural criticism to move beyond the postmodern, while recognizing its continuing importance as a critical shadow cast over the first decade of the twenty-first century. As Potter and López note, in the new century, 'it is impossible to avoid considering postmodernism' (3). The desire to interrogate the legacies of postmodernism is mirrored in the work of several British novelists in the 2000s and can be identified in three strands: those novelists who continue to use narrative techniques associated with postmodernism but who have reintroduced a set of grounded ethical positions; those who have attempted to return (or continue) to work in a broadly realist mode as an implicit rejection of postmodernism; and those who have self-consciously returned to modernist techniques as a way of return to a pre-postmodernist aesthetics. These categories overlap and as often with the attempt to shoehorn writers and their work into a particular modal framework, much depends on the critical lens applied to aspects of their work. In the first category, however, it is possible to include writers such as Nicola Barker, A.L. Kennedy, Hari Kunzru, Toby Litt, Tom McCarthy, David Mitchell, Ali Smith and Will Self who have all continued to use the self-reflexive and metafictive complexities associated with postmodernism in their fiction, but have also tried to come out of the other side of the relativism this implies with an alternative sets of ethical positions appropriate to the new millennium. David Mitchell's novels, for example, operate in textual worlds in which characters reappear and themes crisscross various geographical locations and historical settings. His complex intersection of nine historical periods and specific modes of writing in *Cloud Atlas* (2004), for example, offers the basis of a postmodern playfulness with historicity; nevertheless, it also attempts to arrive at some defined and concrete sense of human values that tie the periods and forms together. Similarly, the search for meaning in *Number9Dream* (2001) negotiates the symbolic frameworks and consumerist surfaces of contemporary Japan, but the novel as a whole establishes the sense that the search for meaning is still a worthwhile endeavour, thus rejecting the scepticism of such a quest in much postmodern thinking. A desire to stitch together fragments instead of allowing them to float apart is implied in his fiction and represents a significant shift from postmodernism's logical negativism. Similarly, Ali Smith, in novels such as *Hotel World* (2001) and *The Accidental* (2005), has also presented her exploration of contemporary culture in modes that are often described as postmodern in their presentation of fragmented forms and multiple character perspectives. Nevertheless, the implicit political commentary in her examination of contemporary frameworks of gender and class finds grounding in a set of ethical and political positions. Many of these novelists, then, offer a kind of complicitous critique, to use a concept developed by Linda Hutcheon, of postmodernism itself. Postmodernism for these writers is no longer simply a mode that deploys parody of past styles but itself often becomes the object of the parody. For some, this Mobius-strip reflection on its own status may simply be a confirmation of postmodernism's love of paradox. However there is a clear sense that it becomes no longer the ideal form from which parodies of previous grand narratives and styles are launched, but itself becomes the butt of the joke and the source for parodic reworking. In addition, many writers who were associated with postmodernism in their early careers have perhaps stepped back from its more extreme philosophical relativism whilst retaining in their 2000s fiction broadly experimental approaches, including Martin Amis, Julian Barnes, Jim Crace, Alasdair Gray, Ian McEwan, Salman Rushdie, Iain Sinclair and Jeanette Winterson.

A second category that eschews the relativism, fragmentation and ludic outlook of postmodernism could be described as a re-engagement with realist modes of writing. Peter Boxall, for example, identifies certain twenty-first-century novelists as engaged in looking for new realisms: 'There is, in the fiction of the new century, as well as in a very wide range of other disciplines and intellectual networks, a strikingly new attention to the nature of our reality' (10). Similarly, Philip Tew identifies the fact that there is a 'new sense of reality' emerging in the work of several novelists of the new millennium (29). Realism, in its philosophical sense, implies the possibility of arriving at a set of truth claims about the nature of reality and the human condition, and although many writers of this new realism have used techniques that extend far from the definition of classic realism on the nineteenth-century model as identified by critics such as Catherine Belsey and Roland Barthes, they are nevertheless genuinely engaged in trying to represent authentic experience in their fiction. Many novelists associated with the expression of marginalized positions in British society, especially in terms of ethnicity, have continued to work in what is predominantly a realist form. For example, Monica Ali's *Brick Lane* (2003), Andrea Levy's *Small Island* (2004), and Caryl Phillips' *A Distant Shore* (2003) operate primarily in the realist mode in their attempt to record the authentic experience of migration to Britain in the postwar and contemporary period. Many of the expressions of subcultural affiliation in the fiction of this decade also tend towards the realist mode, as can be seen in the work of John King, Courttia Newland and Alex Wheatle, although as Nick Bentley shows in Chapter 2 of this book, others, such as Gautam Malkani and Stewart Home, have used unreliable narrators, and metafictional and self-reflexive frameworks in their evocation of fictional subcultures. Zadie Smith's *White Teeth* was famously described by the critic James Wood as 'hysterical realism' indicating the tension between postmodern play and realistic portrayal where, 'the conventions of realism are not being abolished but, on the contrary, exhausted, and overworked' (n.p.). In Chapter 6 of this volume, Daniel Weston shows how some of Smith's critical writing argues for a rejection of the debilitating opposition of experimental and realistic forms of writing.

A third response to the waning of postmodernism in the 2000s can also be identified in those novelists, including Smith, who have consciously returned to modernist forms of writing. Ian McEwan in *Atonement* (2001), despite its metafictional twist, examines the modes of writing associated with modernism in its deployment of a style that self-consciously deploys the interior monologues and free-indirect discourse associated with one of the novel's key literary references, Virginia Woolf. This is extended in his 2005 novel *Saturday*, which is significantly set in that most modernist of locations, Bloomsbury, and offers the interior speculations and world view of brain surgeon Henry Perowne on a single day in 2003, the very day of the demonstration in London against the War on Terror mentioned earlier. Other modernist precursors have garnered the attention of novelists in the 2000s. Zadie Smith, for example, used E.M. Forster's *Howards End* as a key intertext in her 2005 work *On Beauty*, while Alan Hollinghurst has attempted to engage with the modernistic styles of Henry James in his Man Booker Prize-winning novel of 2004, *The Line of Beauty*. (Perhaps the search for beauty in both these novels is an indication in itself of a rejection of postmodernism's scepticism towards such essentializing qualities.) The trend for reinvigorating modernism has continued in Smith's *NW* (2012) and in Will Self's *Umbrella* (2012) and *Shark* (2014), which all consciously evoke and deploy modernist styles in their attempt to capture contemporary and historical London. This renewed interest in modernist writers and techniques has led David James and Urmila Seshagiri (citing, as examples, Julian Barnes, Ian McEwan, Will Self and Zadie Smith) to argue that, 'At a moment when postmodern disenchantment no longer dominates critical discourse or creative practice, the central experiments and debates of twentieth-century modernist culture have acquired new relevance to the moving horizon of contemporary literature' (87–8).

It is in this climate of pushing forward new forms while continuing a dialogue with the immediate and longer literary past that the chapters in this book contextualize the fiction of the 2000s. Martyn Colebrook's introductory chapter (Chapter 1) describes the emergence of regional fictions and regional frictions during a decade in which Britain experienced both the effects of devolved national government and the consequences of globalization on a hitherto unprecedented scale. He explores these fictions and frictions by examining the representation of Yorkshire, Wales and London in, respectively, key novels by David Peace, Niall Griffiths and Gautam Malkani. By also including the Ireland of Patrick McCabe, Colebrook draws attention to the temporal as well as geographical nature of borders within Britain and the fact that the boundaries of the British State are not set in stone but subject to the shifting sands and tides of history. What characterized the decade, overall, was the speed by which narratives that could apparently be dismissed as counter-cultural contestations of mainstream values at its beginning, came to be seen by its end as speaking, as Shaw says, 'profoundly to the world of the new millennium' (3).

Colebrook's chapter is followed by two Special Topic chapters that identify aspects of fiction during the decade that have been particularly significant. In the first of these (Chapter 2), Nick Bentley discusses the way in which fiction interested in youth subcultures has become a prominent feature of contemporary British fiction, suggesting that writing about youth subcultures provides a rich ground for discussing aspects of British society and culture more broadly. He identifies two main ways in which subcultural fiction operates during the period: novels that look at contemporary youth subcultures as a way of engaging with wider debates in the culture and society of the 2000s; and novels that form a critically nostalgic look at past subcultures, offering a revisionist account of British society and culture of the postwar period. In the first category Bentley offers close analysis of Gautam Malkani's *Londonstani* and John King's *Skinheads*, which offer an interesting contrast of differing youth subcultures in the suburbs of contemporary West London. He goes on to discuss fiction by Alex Wheatle and Stewart Home who use contrasting forms and modes in their engagement with subcultures of the 1980s and 1960s respectively.

In the second of the Special Topic chapters, Laura Salisbury (Chapter 3) focuses attention on the rise of the 'neuronovel' in British fiction as a response to the shifting perceptions of the brain and mind in contemporary scientific and medical research. As her chapter demonstrates, fiction that attends to this topic represents a:

> significant subgenre of literary fiction of the 2000s – one that explicitly works through the implications of the cognitive revolution for what the literary novel, since the nineteenth century, has considered a privileged mode of working: the penetration of consciousness, the exploration of the workings of the human

mind, and the mapping of a subjectivity that could both bear the weight of, and act as a lodestone for, the autonomous, liberal, perhaps even moral individual. (84–5)

In this way she shows how the neurological turn represents a broader suspicion towards the psychoanalytical models that dominated twentieth-century fiction. Her chapter goes on to look closely at three novels that have the neurological as a central theme: Ian McEwan's *Saturday* (2005), Sebastian Faulks' *Human Traces* (2005) and Tom McCarthy's *Remainder* (2005).

In the next chapter (Chapter 4), Lucienne Loh identifies the continuing importance of postcolonialism as a literary-critical practice in the 2000s, albeit with new resonances and directions. She argues that this is partly to do with the impact of the 9/11 attacks both globally and for writers and critics working in Britain. As she argues, the contemporary task of postcolonial criticism is 'to suggest on-going but different modes of resistance seeking to overcome forms of prejudice faced by minority groups within Britain' while recognizing that 'some groups have been affected more than others by the repercussions of 9/11' (120). She goes on to examine the distinct categories of 'Black British' and 'Asian British' writing in this context before offering readings of a range of fiction produced in Britain in the 2000s including Martin Amis' 'The Last Days of Mohammad Atta' (2006), Ian McEwan's *Saturday*, Chris Cleave's *Incendiary* (2005), Nadeem Aslam's *Maps for Lost Lovers* (2004), Leila Aboulela's *Minaret* (2005) and David Dabydeen's *Molly and the Muslim Stick* (2008).

In Chapter 5, Leigh Wilson examines how the historical novel, following a steady increase in respectability during the closing decades of the twentieth century, has emerged in the 2000s as the dominant, prize-winning, form of mainstream British fiction. Arguing that historical novels represent an attempt to smuggle realism in by the back door in the wake of postmodernism, she employs Roland Barthes' concept of the 'reality effect' to analyse key texts such as Ian McEwan's *Atonement* (2001) and Hilary Mantel's *Wolf Hall* (2009) and *Bring Up the Bodies* (2012), in which techniques originally developed by the modernists have become the new reality effects: 'Where the modernists privileged the representation of interiority in order to question and destabilize the question of reality, to make the familiar unfamiliar, and to thin the boundaries between real and representation, the contemporary writer of the historical novel uses them to *secure* the real' (154). While the effect of Mantel's novels being restricted to the limits of Cromwell's consciousness is to imply that the individual mind and its perceptions are the truest connection we have to the real, this relationship is acknowledged to be more problematic by McEwan. However, Wilson argues, although the narrator of *Atonement* is ultimately revealed to be in bad faith, this does not equate to John Fowles' breaking of the fictional framework at the end of *The French Lieutenant's Woman* (1969), and McEwan remains a defender of realism. In contrast, an extended reading of David Peace's Red Riding Quartet (1999–2002) serves to demonstrate how 'it is only through the practice of fictionality that the real can be properly, ethically experienced and interrogated' (165).

In Chapter 6, Daniel Weston begins with Zadie Smith's essay from 2008, 'Two Paths for the Novel', and her reading of the situation of the contemporary novel as one of bifurcation – between what Smith calls a 'lyrical realism' and an experimental rejection of the conventions of realism. The entrenched opposition this implies offers, for Smith, a poor prognosis for the future of the novel. Weston argues, however, that the novels of the 2000s are more nuanced and complex in their intermingling of realism and experiment than Smith's essay allows. While acknowledging that the very idea of experiment shifted through the decade, in his reading of novels by Ian McEwan, Jon McGregor, David Peace, Ali Smith, Tom McCarthy, John Burnside and Zadie Smith herself, he argues that, rather than bifurcation and opposition, 'an awareness of these issues' underlies such work 'in submerged and subtle ways' (176). The last two chapters (Chapters 7 and 8) focus on British fiction of the 2000s in an international context, both how it has been received internationally, and how it engages with transnational concerns and issues. Ann Marie Adams focuses on the North American context and identifies the way in which British writers have increasingly been seen to transcend their national identities, at least with respect to American critics and reviewers, and have become part of a general category of world writing. This is despite the success of British novelists in America such as Zadie Smith, Ian McEwan and J.K Rowling. Adams argues that this lack of attention to the national context of British writers is due primarily to the attention given in American criticism to an ongoing conversation with literary modernism, to which she suggests contemporary British literature has an 'uneasy relation' (203). In this context, Adams goes on to discuss the way in which the novels by British authors that have proved popular with American readers tend to be those celebrated for their accessible storytelling and those that offer (neo-)historical accounts of a pre-modernist world. In this context, she discusses the critical reception in the United States of a number of British writers including A.S. Byatt, Kazuo Ishiguro, Hilary Mantel and Alan Moore.

In the final chapter of the volume Ulrike Tancke examines the shifting perspectives on multiculturalism in Britain and Europe across the first decade of the twenty-first century. In particular she identifies the use of the term in political rhetoric and a shift from the Blairite celebration of the term to suspicion towards its effects by David Cameron towards the end of the decade. Tancke shows how the complex social and political relationship with multiculturalism is a significant aspect of contemporary British fiction and its engagement with national and international politics. In this sense she argues that certain novelists present an 'unease about the multicultural ideal . . . but position their critique of multiculturalism within a new, universalist agenda that takes the constants of human nature as its point of reference' (226–7). Her chapter goes on to explore these issues with respect to three novels of the decade: Zadie Smith's *White Teeth*, Monica Ali's *Brick Lane* and the less well-known *The Curry Mile* (2006) by Zahid Hussain.

Overall, the collection of chapters contained in *The 2000s: A Decade of Contemporary British Fiction* aims to contribute to, and develop, our understanding of the literary climate of a decade that is still within our immediate experiences and memories. It hopes to open up debates and readings of fiction that will continue to attract critical attention in the coming decades. It is difficult to establish a canon of contemporary fiction, as this field of literary studies is continually shifting in ways that are different from and more acute than other periods of literary study; nevertheless, we hope the volume will encourage readers to consider the ways in which certain writers, novels, themes and concerns will begin to emerge as indicative of the body of fiction that attempted to come to terms with a decade that saw seismic shifts in political and economic contexts in Britain and globally.

Works cited

Agamben, Giorgio. 'What is the Contemporary?' In *What Is An Apparatus? and Other Essays*. Trans. by David Kishik and Stefan Pedatella. Stanford: Stanford University Press, 2009.

Ali, Monica. *Brick Lane*. London: Doubleday, 2003.

Amis, Martin. *The Second Plane*. London: Jonathan Cape, 2008.

Augé, Marc. *An Anthropology for Contemporaneous Worlds*. Stanford: Stanford University Press, 1999.

Ballard, J.G. *Millennium People*. London: Flamingo, 2003.

Barker, Pat. *Double Vision*. London: Hamish Hamilton, 2003.

Barthes, Roland. 'The Reality Effect'. *The Rustle of Language*. Trans. Richard Howard. Oxford: Blackwell, 1986. 141–8.

Bauman, Zygmunt. *Liquid Modernity*. Cambridge: Polity, 2000.
Beckett, Andy. *When the Lights Went Out: What Really Happened to Britain in the 1970s*. London: Faber and Faber, 2009.
Belsey, Catherine. *Critical Practice*. London and New York: Routledge, 1988.
Blincoe, Nicholas, and Matt Thorne, Eds. *All Hail the New Puritans*. London: Fourth Estate, 2001.
Bourriaud, Nicholas. *Altermodern*. London: Tate Publishing, 2009.
Boxall, Peter. *Twenty-First-Century Fiction: A Critical Introduction*. Cambridge: Cambridge University Press, 2013.
Derrida, Jacques. *Specters of Marx: The State of the Debt, the Work of Mourning and the New International*. New York and Abingdon: Routledge, 2006 [1993].
Erber, Pedro. 'Contemporaneity and its Discontents'. *Diacritics* 41:1 (2013): 28–48.
Farmer, Andrew. 'Majority Say Iraq War was Wrong'. Available online: https://yougov.co.uk/news/2013/03/14/majority-think-iraq-war-was-wrong/ (accessed 30 May 2015).
Fukuyama, Francis. *The End of History and the Last Man*. London: Hamish Hamilton, 1992.
Heilmann, Ann, and Mark Llewellyn. *Neo-Victorianism: The Victorians in the Twenty-First Century, 1999–2009*. Basingstoke and New York: Palgrave Macmillan, 2010.
Hollinghurst, Alan. *The Line of Beauty*. London: Picador, 2004.
hooks, bell. 'Postmodern Blackness'. *Postmodern Culture* 1:1 (1990): 1–7.
Hutcheon, Linda. *The Politics of Postmodernism*. London and New York: Routledge, 1989.
James, David, and Urmila Seshagiri, 'Metamodernism: Narratives of Continuity and Revolution'. *PMLA* 129:1 (2014): 87–100.
Jameson, Fredric. *Postmodernism, Or, The Cultural Logic of Late Capitalism*. London and New York: Verso, 1991.
Jameson, Fredric. *Antinomies of Realism*. London: Verso, 2013.
Jencks, Charles. *The Language of Post-Modern Architecture*. New York: Rizzoli, 1984.
Kear, Adrian, and Deborah Lynn Steinberg, Eds. *Mourning Diana: Nation, Culture and the Performance of Grief*. London: Routledge, 2002.
Kelly, Adam. 'David Foster Wallace and the New Sincerity in American Fiction'. *Consider David Foster Wallace: Critical Essays*. Los Angeles and Austin: Sideshow Media Group Press, 2010. 131–46.
Kelly, Adam. 'Beginning With Postmodernism'. *Twentieth-Century Literature* 57: 3 & 4 (2011): 391–422.
Kirby, Alan. *Digimodernism: How New Technologies Dismantle the Postmodern and Reconfigure Our Culture*. London: Continuum, 2011.
Levy, Andrea. *Small Island*. London: Review, 2004.
Lipovetsky, Gilles. *Hypermodern Times*. Cambridge: Polity, 2005.
Lyotard, Jean-Francois. *The Postmodern Condition: A Report on Knowledge*. Trans. Geoffrey Bennington and Brian Massumi. Manchester: Manchester University Press, 1984.

McEwan, Ian. *Atonement*. London: Jonathan Cape, 2001.
McEwan, Ian. *Saturday*. London: Jonathan Cape, 2005.
Mitchell, David. *Number9Dream*. London: Sceptre, 2001.
Mitchell, David. *Cloud Atlas*. London: Sceptre, 2004.
Nealon, Geoffrey T. *Post-Postmodernism: or, The Cultural Logic of Just-in-Time Capitalism*. Stanford: Stanford University Press, 2012.
Nietzsche, Friedrich. *Untimely Meditations*. Cambridge: Cambridge University Press, 1997 [1873–6].
Osborne, Peter. *The Politics of Time: Modernity and Avant-garde*. London: Verso, 1995.
Phillips, Caryl. *A Distant Shore*. London: Secker & Warburg, 2003.
Potter, Gary, and José López. *After Postmodernism: An Introduction to Critical Realism*. London and New York: Athlone Press, 2001.
Re:Public (Ien Ang, Ruth Barcan et al., Eds). *Planet Diana: Cultural Studies and Global Mourning*. Kingswood, New South Wales: Research Centre in Intercommunal Studies, University of Western Sydney, Nepean, 1997.
Robinson, Alan. *Narrating the Past: Historiography, Memory and the Contemporary Novel*. Basingstoke: Palgrave Macmillan, 2011.
Self, Will. *Umbrella*. London: Bloomsbury, 2012.
Self, Will. *Shark*. London: Bloomsbury, 2014.
Shaw, Katy. 'Introduction' in *Analysing David Peace*. Newcastle: Cambridge Scholars Press 2011.
Smith, Ali. *Hotel World*. London: Hamish Hamilton, 2001.
Smith, Ali. *The Accidental*. London: Hamish Hamilton, 2005.
Smith, Zadie. *White Teeth*. London: Hamish Hamilton, 2000.
Smith, Zadie. *On Beauty*. London: Hamish Hamilton, 2005.
Smith, Zadie. *NW*. London: Hamish Hamilton, 2012.
Stierstorfer, Klaus. Ed. *Beyond Postmodernism: Reassessments in Literature, Theory and Culture*. Berlin: Walter de Gruyter, 2003.
Tew, Philip. 'A New Sense of Reality? A New Sense of the Text? Exploring Meta-Realism and the Literary-Critical Field'. *Beyond Postmodernism: Reassessments in Literature, Theory and Culture*. Ed. Klaus Stierstorfer. Berlin: Walter de Gruyter, 2003. 29–50.
The Matrix (film). Directed by The Wachowskis. USA. Warner Brothers. 1999.
Travis, Alan, and Ian Black, 'Blair's Popularity Plummets', *Guardian* 18 February 2003. Available online: http://www.theguardian.com/uk/2003/feb/18/politics.iraq (accessed 30 May 2015).
Treanor, Jill. 'Richest 1% of people own nearly half of global wealth, says report', *Guardian* 14 October 2014. Available online: http://www.theguardian.com/business/2014/oct/14/richest-1percent-half-global-wealth-credit-suisse-report (accessed 30 May 2015).
Vermeulen, Timotheus, and Robin van den Akker. 'Notes on Metamodernism'. *Journal of Aesthetics & Culture* 2 (2010): 1–14.

Victoria and Albert Museum (V&A) (exhibition). Postmodernism: Style and Subversion 1970–1990. 2011–12. Available online: http://www.vam.ac.uk/content/exhibitions/postmodernism/ (accessed 14 May 2015).

Wilkinson, Richard, and Katie Pickett. *The Spirit Level: Why Equality is Better for Everyone*. London: Allen Lane, 2009.

Wood, James. 'Human, All Too Inhuman'. *The New Republic* 30 August 2001. Available online: http://www.newrepublic.com/article/61361/human-all-too-inhuman (accessed 13 January 2015).

Woods, David. *Time After Time*. Bloomington, Indiana: Indiana University Press, 2007.

Woolf, Virginia. 'Mr. Bennett and Mrs. Brown'. *Collected Essays:* Volume 1. Ed. Leonard Woolf. London: The Hogarth Press, 1966, 319–37.

Žižek, Slavoj. *Welcome to the Desert of the Real*. London: Verso, 2002.

1

Literary History of the Decade
Fictions from the Borderlands

Martyn Colebrook

The fiction of the 2000s under discussion in this chapter is notable for its response to contemporary 'moments' with three of the novelists in this chapter emerging for the first time into the public consciousness and establishing reputations that would see their critical profile increase markedly during the decade. Niall Griffiths, David Peace and, latterly, Gautam Malkani, came to write novels that have been critically received as responding to specific political or social trends. The unifying themes of Griffiths' fiction are related, principally, to revenge and to linguistic innovation and their relationship between the extremities of 'characters' psychology' (Holcombe, n.p.). Additional to this, and most relevant as the unifying theme between each novelist in this chapter, is the presentation of a nuanced authenticity through the 'performance' of the demotic voice as articulated through the disenfranchised voices of a sequence of twenty-somethings who are desperately seeking to find some connection to the world around them. As Lea explains, 'The idea of the authentic as a quality of the material world has been current throughout British postmodern writing. It is an engagement that is identifiable, in different ways and for different reasons, in texts as diverse as Zadie Smith's *White Teeth* (2000), Niall Griffith's *Sheepshagger* (2001), Andrew O'Hagan's *Be Near Me* (2006), Rachel Cusk's *The Bradshaw Variations* (2009) and Monica Ali's *Untold Story* (2011)' (Lea, 461). Notions such as Badiou's 'passion for the real' (32) and Shields' 'reality hunger' have come to be applied to the dislocation that permeates individual lives through the heavily mediated dissemination of mass culture, the dulling and throttling of the ability to 'feel' or 'experience' and a great emphasis on the ways in which individuals construct their identity in relation to the society that surrounds them.

For Peace, the dominant themes in his fiction emerge from the quintet of novels embracing the gothic Yorkshire noir that infuses the Red Riding Quartet and *GB84*: 'together they constitute a secret history of a decade of corruption and upheaval which redefined British society, politics and culture, and which continues to influence – and to limit – the way we live now' (Hedgecock, n.p.). The obsessive focus is on the effect of the contemporary retreat from politics and spiritual belief which in turn creates a pernicious and more unstable world for us to inhabit. Peace also presents his world through the medium of stylistic innovation, a repetitive and intense recreation of the occult histories underpinning the political, social and cultural conflicts of the 1970s and the 1980s.

For Gautam Malkani, *Londonstani* (2006) is his only novel to date and represents the contribution to this discussion of fiction of the 2000s made by a novelist based in London. With his depiction of 'rude-boys' and desis, Malkani's energetic and fizzing novel became part of a broader debate about the 'publishing industry's promotional culture – in which pundits are complicit, however much they protest their critical distance' (Graham, n.p.) – and 'marketing multiculturalism', which began in earnest with the publication of *White Teeth*.

Grits, Griffiths' debut in 2000, was enthusiastically taken up by the now obligatory quote-merchant, Irvine Welsh, which led to the inevitable comparisons with *Trainspotting* (1993), given Griffiths' judicious ability to 'throw his voice'. As Griffiths himself has stated on his profile on the British Council website (Holcombe, n.p.), such labels are 'lazy', while Holcombe claims 'a more accurate word would be obvious' (n.p.). Holcombe suggests further: 'If there is any writer who can take over Welsh's mantle as the primary chronicler of life lived away from the Working Title Home Counties version of Britain, it is Niall Griffiths' (n.p.).

To this effect, the coverage of regional Britain, and the borders, invokes the fourth novelist in this quartet, Patrick McCabe, who continued to maintain his marked interest in the darker side of contemporary culture with a novel that dissected the construction of contemporary Irish masculinity through a peculiarly Ballardian sensibility. Herein lies the contention at the heart of this chapter – the four novelists in question are connected through their depiction of 'regional fictions' and 'regional frictions'.

The cultural context, which provides the framework for this chapter, and the fiction under discussion here, is one in which Britain became fragmented and the impact of globalization started to become translated into the fictions being produced. As Morrison explains '[w]hat is necessarily true of contemporary fiction, like all literature, is that it needs to be read as a product of the cultural conditions from which it emerges' (7) and that what makes such fictions significant is 'their ability to locate themselves in the interstices – the spaces between national cultures, genders and histories' (7). These 'spaces between' are an appropriate metaphor for the initial cracks and then full-scale fragments that emerge from the breakup of Britain and from within these fissures the new regional voices and experiences began to emerge, eventually gathering momentum into a cascade of contemporary fictions. Through the statutory granting of powers to the respective administrative bodies, communities within these regions gained more autonomy and with that emerged more confident and vocal voices in artistic terms. A further contributing factor that informs the production of these fictions is globalization and the processes of performance and performativity through the process of transnational exchange. To this effect, when examining the recent fiction of Patrick McCabe and Malkani's debut, it becomes apparent that these are authors who are responding to globalization and its effects, as well as the specific British context of a globalized culture.

Moving back to the idea of regional fictions, the rise of David Peace is significant in that his early fiction emerged under a Blairite Government, which went to war in Iraq, and then received its major shot in the arm after David Cameron's Conservative Government introduced policies that invoked the worst socially deleterious effects of Thatcherism. Highlighted in Granta's Best of Young British Novelists list of 2003, Peace shot to prominence with the publication of the Red Riding Quartet (1999–2002) through Serpent's Tail – Peace has subsequently moved to Faber, a marked departure from the rather rebellious and oppositional force that his former publisher espoused but significantly a move to a publisher with a significant reputation for maintaining and endorsing the 'literary culture' from which Peace's novels have attracted much attention. The tetralogy, beginning on the cusp of the noughties – *Nineteen Seventy-Four* (1999), *Nineteen Seventy-Seven* (2000), *Nineteen Eighty* (2001) and *Nineteen Eighty-Three* (2002) – is inspired by the Yorkshire Ripper murders and through its 'visceral and unflinching' (Holcombe, n.p.) approach demands that the reader 'think[s] about the horror of decaying institutions [and] what terrors may be inflicted in the name of the maintenance of power' (n.p.). Set against the political backdrop of Thatcher's Government, Peace presents an irredeemable view of Yorkshire as a microcosm for the political turbulence and conflict that marked the decades with a bleak and unrelenting despair inherent in his fiction.

GB84 (2004), which was awarded the James Tait Black Memorial Prize, franked the form in terms of Peace's credentials and his exposure was firmly guaranteed with the publication of *The Damned Utd* (2006), filmed in 2009, and the television adaptations of the Red Riding novels for Channel 4 (2009). Therefore, it was 2009, as the decade drew to a close, that saw an explosion of interest in his work from academics and the reading public as a whole. Katy Shaw suggests that 'the "Year of Peace" marked the intersection of a specific set of circumstances that conspired to propel the author and his work into a wider global consciousness' (2). Despite the novels' emphasis on significant decades throughout the twentieth century, 'readers quickly found that the novels of David Peace also speak profoundly to the world of the new millennium. Read in the UK in 2009 – a year of industrial disputes, spending cuts and political movement to the Right – the worlds of Peace's novels seemed particularly resonant' (3).

On a more pragmatic level, the themes of transgressive identity and masculinity which bookend the fiction of Peace, while also attracting attention for his presentation of gender, are also pertinent to this chapter as a whole as the fiction of the decade demonstrated how the fragmentation of both trade unions and political unions impacted on individuals. All of the texts are thematically linked through their discussion of regional presentations of conflict through the communities and individuals who are affected. From a structural perspective, this chapter addresses each of the four novelists in turn, beginning and concluding with a globalized response to contemporary Britain from fiction in Ireland and Hounslow. In between we move, geographically, from Wales to Yorkshire, effectively gaining closer proximity to the London powerhouse that these fictions are reacting to. However, we begin in Southern Ireland where the globalized limina that pervade the country are interrogated and considered by Patrick McCabe.

Caravan on the borderland: Patrick McCabe's *Call Me the Breeze*

The oeuvre of Patrick McCabe is defined by the social fantastic, a mode that fuses the depiction of people performing the everyday minutiae of life with the surreality or irreality of social life in the country. The title of *Call Me the Breeze* (2003) references Lynyrd Skynyrd and Eric Clapton (amongst others, I suspect). The text addresses the blurring of the respective spaces configured by art and biography, as well as the public and the private. As my own title suggests with its echoes of 'House on the Borderland', in McCabe's work this rural area functions as a liminal space in which subversions and transgressions are able to take place, revelling in the Bakhtinian carnivalesque potential afforded to them. The country has become an arguably problematic yet recurrent trope for representing a national consciousness split and divided; the country also provides an environment in which such fictions can operate, producing the hybridity that would reflect the fictional wanderings likely to occur if you fused the surrealism of David Lynch and urban oddness apparent in the fiction of Alan Warner.

Call Me the Breeze is the tale of Joey Tallon, a minor celebrity living in the small, close-knit town of Scotsfield where dread and death sit comfortably alongside their companions, hilarity, absurdity and abandon. The readers are drawn into a narrative where Boye Henry, Hoss and their companions come to symbolize local hardline enforcers, earning their wealth and status through brutality and corruption, a line of work that eventually leads to respectable recognition. Joey too is a figure in transition, having been sacked as a barman and factory production line operative, he proceeds to engage in the process of 'total organisation', becoming a seeker after truth, a self-appointed messianic figure and a Dostoyevskyan holy fool who determines to assuage the community's guilt for its violent deaths. His transformation is initiated by his love for and obsession with Jacy, a beautiful blonde-haired girl who is of such stereotypically Californian appearance that she may well be Joni Mitchell's double. Joey has a desire for everyone to know and hear the truth but his reputation as a kidnapper, fantasist and jailbird undermines people's belief in his ability to tell these truths with honesty. Seeking the true story of what actually happened to Campbell Morris, who was found dead in the reservoir, and Detective Tuite in the animal pit, Tallon is impeded at every opportunity because Boye Henry and Hoss, formerly men of violence, are now the proverbial pillars of the community – prosperous, entrepreneurial but still harbouring a virulent streak of violence and a propensity for revenge.

As readers, we are never actually introduced fully to Joey Tallon, the protagonist in a novel composed of epistolary fragments which are found in a suitcase within the caravan that Tallon inhabits. This structure lends itself to the reading I want to provide. It is difficult to identify particular codes of masculinity and homogeneity within this text, given that McCabe undermines each framework he creates, and thus to interrogate a particular type is counterproductive to the thematic concerns of this text. Each fragment is a remnant of a letter timed and dated from the 1970s, which details Tallon's particular musings and thoughts, his aspirations and ideals, his loves and losses. This is the narrative of self-disclosure, the fragility of a prose-constructed pose. The structure is that of a postmodern pastiche, a collage, as evidenced by the opening pages:

> The End is in the beginning – that's what the ancients say anyway.... You can't be a famous writer and go throwing your papers around you like that.... As soon as

I finished writing anything, I'd just shove it into a bag. A leather holdall to be precise.... I've had a really good time going through it. And if I was any kind of writer at all, I'd have made something worthwhile out of it, instead of just sitting here rambling half the night, filling up pages with discursive nonsense. I mean it's not as if enough didn't happen. Particularly during the seventies, when the old leatherette holdall found itself very much favoured, particularly by anonymous men who had a predilection for leaving it behind them in a crowded public place. (2)

Tallon's collection of letters demonstrate an identity and, the primary point of this paper, the formation of an Irish masculinity, which is informed by the polydiscursive media to which he is exposed. He watches Robert de Niro play the anti-hero avenger, Travis Bickle, in *Taxi Driver*, models himself on the lead singer of a punk bank, identifies with Charles Manson and the Family, and is influenced by such texts as Herman Hesse's *Steppenwolf*. The fragmentation of his own narrative imitates the fragmentation of an identity and masculinity constructed by the hegemonic heteronormative masculinities performed throughout Hollywood and this leads to a possible postcolonial reading of Tallon as a media-produced construct, informed and fractured by the dominant, globalized formulations of popular culture. He essentially becomes an individual based on existing paradigmatic structures, a consumer of stereotypes and a performer and aspirational celebrity as defined by those who have fulfilled these roles. Tallon is also the characteristically unreliable narrator, a star player in his own tableaux vivant, his drug-inspired testaments flitting and flirting with the boundaries between that which may be believable and that which may be false. The permeability and flexibility of his narrative evidences the different influences on his own self-idealized status as he swiftly moves from hero to truth teller to terrorist to kidnapper to inmate and finally to celebrity. In this respect he acts in opposition and counterpoint to Hoss and Boyle who come to suggest a historical legacy of Ireland that has moved from violence to a more incipient and institutionalized set of codes.

Part of this construction includes his life within Mountjoy prison during which time his colleague Bonehead and he establish a prison reading group in which they devour the works of Beckett, Hesse and Joyce, despite Joey's admission that he hasn't actually read them before. There is a particular posturing in the ability to seem well read without having actually read the novels in question. This pose represents a further development of Tallon's own image, the bringer of culture to those who have been incarcerated and the self-appointed guardian of values.

It's about what has happened in our hearts (emph), and how it really is possible for art to act as a mirror to the soul, to become a powerful agent for transformation and rebirth! If not outright absolution [...] I suppose in a sense I want to act as a symbol for Ireland and for what has been going on here these past years. (265)

Although stated with what would seem to be the utmost satirical intent, McCabe here posits Tallon in a tradition imitating the role of the artist in society, the influential maker of culture in a small town. He aggrandizes his own position, wishing to act as a symbol for the national consciousness and proposing the idealist vision of art as a tool for social change; the artist as an agent of influence in a culture saturated by the proliferation of multiple artistic platforms and opportunity.

By writing his memoir and successfully selling it to a publisher in Literary London, Tallon thus becomes blessed with the ability to exploit a personally determined propensity for self-propagating verbophilia and mythomania. The validation of his own posturing by such a bastion of contemporary publishing almost represents a colonialism of a different type where the male artist must obtain recognition from existing power structures in order to try to memorialize his experience, albeit one that is both unreliable and functions as a vehicle for his own self-promotion.

Due to his failure to court Jacy successfully, Tallon's main sexualized relationship is with a plastic doll, parodically re-enacting a range of different psychoanalytical constructs and theorizations that have come to characterize the study of masculinity as a fluid, amorphous set of existing codes that contribute to the negotiation of the 'male' in the contemporary, postmodern landscape. This is further reinforced by Joey's kidnapping and imprisoning Jacy (leading to his arrest and imprisonment) as though to further demonstrate different extremities of behaviour.

Tallon's performance of identity means he comes to embody the renegotiation of masculine codes in relation to the postcolonial othering. Drawing from a globalized media, he acts out the expectations conferred upon him by the media in which he immerses himself. By allowing his self-validation to be conferred upon him through the dominant cultural entities of Literary London and Hollywood, Tallon becomes a subject of the postcolonial gaze, albeit one who is satirized by virtue of McCabe's send-up of the Dostoyevskyan holy fool. His distinction from Hoss and Boyle acts as an ongoing counterpoint to historical expectations of the Border State as embodied in the gangsterish activities they engage in. With this in mind, we move on to consider Niall Griffiths' presentation of another outsider, Ianto, disenfranchised from the State and articulating his objections.

An articulate anger: Niall Griffiths' *Sheepshagger*

Regarded as a disturbingly lyrical 'hymn both ancient and modern' (*Independent*) that is 'haunting and intensely imagined, layered with chilling humour and charged with linguistic energy' (A.L. Kennedy), Niall Griffiths' *Sheepshagger* (2001) is a startling examination of revenge, feral savagery and liminal geography that combine as imperatives for an individual to murder, violate and ravage the English middle-classes whom he perceives as being responsible for his cultural and familial disinheritance.

In the figure of Ianto, a chimera, there exists a necessary anti-hero who, in Griffiths' words, 'is a skeletal, rawboned force of nature shaped by the deprivations of his childhood' (2). Griffiths' exploration of the familiar tropes of childhood emasculation, violation and alienation creates 'a timeless parable of violent revenge', which is as much a meditation as an outraged scream, imbued with the hallucinatory invective that characterizes his characters' lurid visions and expletive-ridden vernacular.

After the critical success of his debut novel, *Grits* (2000), Niall Griffiths garnered a reputation for representing an equivalent to the Scottish cult novelist, Irvine Welsh. Although understandable, Griffiths' prose and his capacity to perceive and engage with the *terra firma* he knows suggest that critics could identify points of comparison other than the immediately evident. The sublime terror of William Blake, the wrathful and blood-soaked Biblical orators, a touch of Greek tragedy, as well as more recent writers such as D.H. Lawrence, Hubert Selby Jnr. and Alexander Trocchi all echo through texts which explore the spiritual power that manifests itself at the limits of the human experience.

Regional portrayals of male dysfunctional behaviour by writers such as McCabe and Duncan McLean, whose *Bunker Man* (1998) represents the highly disturbing tale of a school janitor's obsessions with the social panic over a paedophile and his transgressive affair with a young student, are also precedents for this novel and, as Tebbs and Bagnall suggest, 'Griffiths' language has a genuine lyricism, and Ianto's humanity lurks deep and damaged, his actions almost understandable'.

To surmise, *Sheepshagger* is narrated retrospectively through, in the first instance, a series of post-binge conversations involving Ianto's friends who are divided in their condemnation and sympathy with his acts. Interspersed in these conversations are sequences (that may be dreams) involving Ianto and then the reader is led through a series of different events, from a rave to a violent storm on a mountainside, before the onset of a violent, tragic conclusion. In terms of plot, Griffiths addresses the plight of a virtually mute teenager, Ianto, whose ancestral home, a dilapidated lair in the West-Wales mountains, has been turned into a weekend retreat by a group of young English middle-class professionals. When his grandmother dies during an eviction prior to the house conversion, Ianto vows revenge upon the Colonialists and anyone else whom he perceives as having wronged him. For the reader, the acts of revenge they witness involve a sequence of ritualized, highly visceral murders whose victims are a Borstal inmate and two English backpackers. However, it is not until the denouement of the novel, where I will begin my analysis, that further revelations afford the opportunity for a significant change of perspective. Since his childhood, Ianto has roamed wild in the Welsh countryside, existing in a grey area between human and animal. On one particular occasion he encounters an English hitchhiker who verbally abuses him before sexually assaulting him, biting his member and rendering it permanently deformed.

I want to avoid a gender-based reading of this text and instead approach this moment as an apparent expression of the recognized trope of the emasculated male as a metaphor for a country that is being progressively colonized: the 'body politic' being violated in the physical transactions and economic exchanges, symbolizing physical and geographical conquest present within the narrative.

On an intertextual level, *Sheepshagger* shares thematic and narrative concerns with an earlier novel of political significance, *Complicity* (1993), by Iain Banks. Described by the *Guardian* as 'his livid comment on Thatcherism and the 80s zeitgeist' and a compelling, impassioned 'exploration of the morality of greed, corruption and violence, venturing fearlessly into the darker recesses of human purpose' (x), *Complicity* combines the frenetic narrative pace of a thriller with an overwhelmingly powerful dose of drugs, betrayal, sexual intrigue and retribution. Instead of focusing on one protagonist, Banks' novel examines the relationship, friendship and conflict between two males; one an underdog-championing journalist named Cameron Colley and the other, a morally righteous serial killer named Andy Gould. Andy Gould's decision to carry out a series of murders whose victims have been involved in a variety of public scandals is partly motivated by his own experiences of disillusionment with the ruling establishment in his previous career, the British Army and a vicious childhood sexual assault enacted by a man claiming to be a policeman.

Both Griffiths' and Banks' novels address a multitude of similar themes in their respective representations of past and contemporary political alienation; both protagonists suffer sexual assaults in their respective childhoods and choose murder as their preferred form of revenge against oppressors; both novels seem to be protests against exploitation and savagery. At once a subtle political critique and a contemporary rendering of the chemical generation, Griffiths' work cannot be comfortably placed within a genre. Instead, he joins a list of writers such as Rachel Tresize, Irvine Welsh and Duncan McLean whose novels address the rage and fury about social structures, the equation between wealth (or lack of) and entrapment, and the stability of identity in the postmodern, contemporary landscape. Indeed, violence seems to represent an expression of the deep rage his characters feel at the futility of human striving, a rage that he expresses with Blakean and Biblical wrath. The pertinence of Banks' essentially Thatcherite context informs Griffiths' own interpretation of the social context of Blairite Britain. Blair himself expressed his admiration of Margaret Thatcher and through this articulation of her views, 'New Labour' embarked on a programme that embraced her free-market ideology. Policies such as deregulation, privatization of significant national industries, diluting the powers of Trade Unions and the administration of a labour market that was defined as 'flexible' simply intensified her legacy whilst masquerading under the guise of an alternative to Conservatism.

In *Sheepshagger*, epigraphs from Friedrich Nietzsche's *Thus Spake Zarathustra* and Psalm 58 preface the narrative and suggest Ianto has the persona of one who is vindicated in his decisions to kill and violate those who have enacted such acts against him. Indeed, as well as articulating a debate regarding the politics of the period, Griffiths incites an intriguing argument regarding the social acceptance or abhorrence that greets Ianto's actions. Indeed, the first page of the novel read thus:

> –Hell of a boy, Ianto, wasn't he.
>
> –Hell of a boy's right, aye. Straight from-a-fuckin place he was if yew ask me, like.
>
> –Nah, he wasn't. No demon him, mun. He wasn't put yer on this earth fully formed as a murderer, like, he –
>
> [...] Hundreds, no fuckin millions-a people have a shitey upbringing and they don't turn into killers, do they?
>
> [...] No, Griff's right, mun. Under fuckin' Thatcher? Major? The poverty, the repossessions? All that shite? New fuckin' Labour's no bastard better, either. So, fuck, by yewer reasoning, Danny, we'd all be fuckin murderers. Awful fuckin lot uv shitey upbringings in-a past couple-a decades, mun. (1)

At the novel's inception, this opening chorus of voices provides one of the major debates in the narrative, whether Ianto's actions are those of one influenced by nature or nurture. His friends argue that if his nationalism and violence were justified then the entirety of the Welsh nation would be murderers, whilst they are confronted with the suggestion that he was not born as an evil individual and it is the social conditions that have caused his demise. In later conversations this argument will extend to the philosophizing Danny who argues that 'We're all blank canvases when we're born' (158), 'Nothing natural can ever be evil' (120). Coupling these quotations with the epigraphs allows for the recurrent confused stabs at concerns about abuse, culpability and nature versus nurture.

Our first encounter with Ianto takes place during a dream sequence as he finds a lamb whose eyes have been pecked out by predatory birds on the Welsh mountainside. Ianto attempts to restore sight by placing two pebbles into the bloodied eye sockets but as the lamb begins to bleat, Ianto realizes that there was 'Something within him but not without. Something in him dashed against the ancient world' (5). Despite the starkness of this scene, there is a tenderness to the act that Ianto attempts and this dichotomy between the ancient and the modern has a resonance through the text:

> With the immense world-cupping knowledge comfort of living on and in his ancestral land his feet on the same soil his far forefathers dug in [...] Which they can't feel that here, these new owners, ignorant of the particular preterite here, its knowledge and possible belonging, they can't feel that connection in their blood: although, which burns in Ianto more, they behind the double-glazing [...] don't seem at all perturbed or attenuated or even bothered by this lack. (22)

In this respect, Ianto physically and mentally embodies the named geography of Griffiths' Wales. A key word here may be use of 'preterite' (denoting a verb tense used to express past action, belonging to the past), which establishes the house as a structural feature of the overall narrative. By identifying this as a grammatical feature, *Sheepshagger* then becomes oriented around the moment when this object is removed from its owners and transferred to people whom Ianto regards as 'other' or those who have no inherited right to ownership. Indeed, the preterite is mentioned before the formative Celtic mythologies, histories, the primitive, feral and unformed landscape blood-sodden and battle-torn in its infancy, all of which inform the 'knowledge' and 'belonging' that come to differentiate Ianto from the owners. The idea of lack within this quotation characterizes Ianto; he is 'defined by no date or place of birth nor lineage nor pedigree' (38), he exists outside of all formal structures, he is rootless and wandering yet unfettered and therefore free.

As Ianto confronts the owners of the house, he is told that the land is 'private property' and therefore exclusive, enclosed and encompassed within specifically defined domestic borders. Ianto's rage at his exclusion is not the anger of one who desires such domesticity, it is the frustration at what he perceives as a colonizing of his history, the civilizing of his nature.

After being chased from the house, Ianto hides in a nearby bog:

> Before Ianto was this was, forming and flowering and forever waiting its wearer. And almost as proof, jack-o'-lantern shows himself in the middle of the mire, rises made from the rancid aftermath of some battle long forgotten, some steel-hewn bone leaching its mulch, the compost of long-forgotten warriors. This bog is a wet necropolis for man and for beast. The heat of corruption and that of the earth's innards themselves the searing scorched genesis of this delicate and fragile pale flame, which as Ianto watches sputters and worms itself into some soft substance. [...] Ignis Fatuus, floating phantom lantern guiding Ianto up on to the drier land he mounts as if triumphant, arms spread in the drizzle. (26)

The bog, 'a necropolis for man and for beast' suggests it is a site of fusion. Such words as 'genesis' and 'fragile pale flame' connote a spiritual or religious image to this passage and if you consider that the 'pale flame' is a product of 'the heat of corruption' and 'some long forgotten battle' and that it led Ianto out of the bog then I would contend that this is the moment at which Ianto's quest becomes spiritual. In the same passage, the narrator observes: 'marvel at what dreams may rise from blight and canker, from putrefaction and decay. His perpetual grin in the always rain which is mirrored in the moon' (27) and one newspaper review commented that, in the context of the book's protagonist, this is 'a sick irony, Ianto is no one's dream' (Tebbs and Bagnall, n.p.). I would disagree with this statement, given that iconography of a 'pale fire', the genesis of 'man and beast', the symbolism of the moon is irony, it is a dangerous hybrid, equating the moon and madness with a human undertaking a spiritual quest, his perpetual grin giving him the appearance of a 'lunate-tic'. That the bog is waiting for a wearer projects the figure of Ianto as being composed of many layers; a skeletal form wearing the history of a nation, framed by the ancient and the modern, capable of abhorrent violence and innocent tenderness.

At this point, the reader anticipates Ianto proceeding on his journey into the mountains as the avenging angel infused with warlike Celtic myths, particularly given that the march into the mountains and call of the hills is a recurrent symbol of Nationalism. However it is in the conclusion where the denouement is revealed, suggesting a somewhat scathing analysis of the society surrounding Ianto. After realizing that he is responsible for the series of murders that have taken place, Ianto's friends lure him to the mountains and kill him, claiming that they will be heroes for murdering a 'sicko and a pervert' (237). This does not represent a call to arms or for vigilantism. The narrative is told retrospectively and the debate over Ianto's actions has veered between sympathy and condemnation for nearly 270 pages. Consider the first image in the dream: Ianto is the narrative's blind wandering sheep leading by his instincts who society has tried to restore sight to, to civilize. He is the ancient clashing against the modern, his violence is juxtaposed against his humanity, but the conclusion strikes me as a critique of a society that Ianto rejects, the society that criticizes its political oppressors yet murders one who chooses to act, albeit futilely against the dominant order. Irrespective of the political metaphors, symbols that may be employed within *Sheepshagger*, it is significant that the narrative is always character focused, that Ianto's damaged humanity and structures haunt the readers long after the page is turned and his actions remain almost understandable.

Having deservedly achieved a reputation for articulating the transgressive and the controversial, Niall Griffiths' oeuvre represents an important part of contemporary Welsh writing and his work is signified by 'prose of extraordinary strength and depth . . . that seeks out the charged glories of unfettered experience' (Evans, n.p.). He is writing about a society that exists fundamentally on a history of broken promises, betrayals, cultural invasion and disillusionment. However, aside from the fervent, necessary, demotic, firebrand style, Griffiths' novels remain a valuable tool for the analysis and critique of the frustrations of a young Welsh underclass whose heritage and identity is threatened through invasion and oppression.

Through Ianto, Griffiths comes to depict a process of regional frictions chafing in extremely violent form against the dominant centre. With the presentation of Ianto's mistranslating his own history and language – those aspects which typically inform the presentation and expectations placed upon the Border State – Griffiths is able to subvert the view of the colonizers. As Peddie argues, 'in its titular reappropriation of a term used by the English to denigrate the Welsh, *Sheepshagger* advances an adversarial politics chiefly through the presence of the remarkable Ianto' (116) and through this resistance from the borderlands, Griffiths comes to consider the deeply contested battlegrounds of identity and politics, as well as identity politics through an exemplary regional fiction. We now move from Wales to Yorkshire and the Midlands and to the roots of Thatcherism in David Peace's fiction.

'An aggrieved act of witnessing': David Peace's *GB84*.

It is appropriate to begin with two extracts from *Nineteen Eighty-Three*, the final novel in David Peace's Red Riding Quartet and the year immediately before *GB84*:

> *In your dreams, you see things* –
>
> > The Mid stinks of damp, full of punks and students from the Tech, a couple of blokes from the Labour club who want to talk politics until it's obvious state you're in you can't, not that it stops you taking the piss out of Thatcher in this morning's *Post* with her vision of a return to the values of the Victorian era, ruling Britain into the 1990s, until she gets another bomb from the Yorkshire Republican Army that is, and that's you that is, the YRA. (*1983*, 49)

The direction of Peace's language here is telling, positioning the 'you' of the extract between the Yorkshire Republican Army and the YRA equates regional identity with the individual, with the personal, with the person who will be sending the bomb. The slippage between YRA and their phonologically similar counterparts emphasizes this further, aligning two individual groups whose focus is the preservation and protection of a specific area under threat. Peace's obsessive eye for detail is important, the 'Mid' just as easily a pub name as a possible region, 'the Tech' pointing to a specifically (post)industrial area with the added 'punks' and 'students' highlighting the temporary cessation of local conflicts for solidarity in the face of a greater threat. The emergence of these plans from 'dreams' suggests the creation of a regional consciousness, that once more the individual identity comes to embody and represent the region in the wider narrative concerns.

In the apocalyptic conclusion of *Nineteen Eighty-Three* the final sequence marks out the territory Peace will address in *GB84*:

> *No hope for Britain*[. . .]
> You get in the bath. You lie in the bath in your wings –
> The water is warm.
> You see the scenes; see the scenes as you could not at the time –
> The shadows in your heart, the fear and the hate –

> *The hate and the fear.*
> You put all your fear and all your hate together and get:
> *Yorkshire, England, 1983.*
> You pick up the razor blade from the side of the bath:
> *My county, my country, right or wrong.*
> Four tears trickle down the sides of your nose.
> But it's all right, everything is all right, the struggle is finished –
> The water red.
> You write three last words on a piece of damp paper. (*Nineteen Eighty-Three*, 405)

Directly before the bleak '*No hope for Britain*' are relentless repetitions of 'The Hate' intersected with the intonations of rectifying errors, righting wrongs and generating hope from despair, creating an atmosphere of persecution, paranoia and intent aimed specifically at the region. The retrospective view of the 'scenes' suggests reconsideration and a new form of understanding, with the 'shadows' of the heart intensifying this connection with location. In a culmination of 'hate and fear' the result is the sequence of region, nation and date contrasted with the collision between the choice of 'county' or 'country'. That the water is red reveals not only the terminal decision made but also, one suspects, a particularly politicized conclusion, which Peace then goes on to illustrate in *GB84*.

The tensions between realism and aesthetics in Peace's work are reflected in his poetic prose, the cadences and syntax of grim despair, the incantations that create unsettling disruptions and interruptions. The rhythms and repetitions echo the poetry of Iain Sinclair, a novelist for whom David Peace expresses great admiration. Maintaining the intersections between region and identity, 'Mapping his-story onto existing spatial and temporal frameworks, Peace offers an antithetical presentation of order and disorder, carving into old landscapes which penetrate and strain under his new creations and renovations of the recent past' (Shaw, 6).

The themes and characteristics of Peace's writing evidence specific and dense layering within each narrative, schisms and ruptures are piled upon one another as characters endure the nightmarish brutality meted out by institutions such as the West Yorkshire Metropolitan Police, and Peace's acute diagnosis of the power generated by the manipulation of social forces and its wider impact upon the events during 1984 is just one of the different structures explored in this novel.

GB84 adopts a more sophisticated and formal organization of material that underpins the narrative structure of two striking miners, Martin and Peter, whose accounts are interspersed between the wider chronology of the novel.

Joseph Brooker suggests in his essay 'Orgreave Revisited': '[t]oo many dates, too much diaristic information, threaten to broach the border between fiction and fact, the novel and the documentary – and this disturbance of the aesthetic is just the effect of Peace's temporal framing. This aspect of the book gives it an unusual intimacy with written and recorded history' (Brooker, 40).

The 'intimacy' Brooker identifies corresponds with the uncomfortable proximity Peace seeks to establish between reader and subject matter, the same 'ethical function' he ascribes to crime fiction. It is little surprise that the excess threatens to 'broach the border between fiction and fact' since the recurrent themes of Peace's novels and the levels of complicity they establish between historical fact and contemporary fiction demonstrate that the act of writing is also an act of recovery and commemoration, a simultaneous explosion and exposition. As McNeill suggests, 'In labouring to transform data like Richards' into fiction, *GB84* carries out a work of political excavation. Memory, in this social or political sense, "has a built in utopian function" where "past memories will have a constitutive role in the forging of present and future perceptions"' (93).

Peace's intense regionalization of the conflict exploits the powerful juxtaposition of the Government's mindset against the resilient determination on a local basis to resist this assault. In keeping with the subject matter here, individual regions *coal*esce in their formation of a united 'national front'. I am persistently reminded of these formulations by this brief but powerful illustration of one aspect of the Thatcher project on a wider scale: 'Groups of nations put together artificially will not have sufficient identity for them to stay together and they will collapse' (Margaret Thatcher, 16 November 1991).

At the centrality of *GB84* is a 'nation' in the process of fragmentation and breakdown, a region in the process of solidification and the persistent Government-sanctioned incursions to expose and exploit the faultlines in the regional seam. This is evident from the beginning of *GB84* when Martin's narrative commences with the rumblings of revolution and uprising, Peace echoing the occultist tones that Iain Sinclair brings to his own London-based wanderings: 'The dead brood under Britain. We whisper, we echo. The emanation of Giant Albion' (2). The invoking of 'whisper' and 'echo' suggests solitude and isolation but also cycle and repetition, the beginning of another conflict and the exhumation of those from the past into a highly relevant present where 'Giant Albion' suggests both historical power and formidable size. Its Celtic undertones point to the mythic or the mythopoetry of region as opposed to nation, the politicization of groups in defence of a regional identity, a regional heritage, a regional lineage and a regional livelihood from the pernicious threat of invasion and destruction. 'Echo' also suggests a degree of incongruency and uncanniness, that there will be differences in this conflict from those which have passed.

The emphasis on history, lineage and inheritance in relation to the formation of a regional identity in communities whose economy is founded upon the continued presence of traditional industry and labour is highlighted in the call to arms issued by The President:

> The President talked about the secret December meetings between the Chairman and the Prime Minister. He talked about their secret plans to denationalize the coal industry. Their secret nuclear, electric dreams. Their secret hit lists –
> Their open and savage schemes to butcher an industry. *Their* industry –
> For then the President spoke of history and tradition. The *history* of the Miner. The *tradition* of the Miner. The legacies of their fathers and their fathers' fathers –
> The birthrights of their children and their children's children –
> The essential battles to come. The war that must be won. (7)

The repetition of 'secret' here exposes the atmosphere of conspiracy and paranoia that is pervasive throughout Peace's oeuvre and hints at the intention to systematically destroy a Union founded to operate as both one and many in their protection of workers. 'Essential battles' emphasize the necessity of combating the threat and the continuation through 'children's children' reinforces the familial aspect to this identity, the following in relatives' footsteps out of economic necessity (which is often fetishized as tradition?). There is also a significant tension in the use of 'denationalize', which invites readings of the negotiations between regional and national priorities for a specific economic community – the underpinning factor is class and the opposition is to disenfranchisement through wealth from the heart of the nation's capital, *the* Imperial trope against which the areas that Peace and Griffiths represent, given their simultaneous Othering and embracing by (Literary) London. As Thatcherism reaches its peak through these 'End of Days' battles against the Union of Mineworkers, and Yorkshire comes to represent a militant regional State against the might of Westminster, Peace's fiction hits its peak audience at a time when the most open reinvigoration of Thatcherite policies is undertaken in the UK. In the face of industrial militancy, attacks on the public services and the brazen antagonism of professions in the face of completing the Thatcher project, the air of GB2010 is not dissimilar from that of the Peace project.

We now move from the 1980s and into urban Hounslow where the global and the material are fused in Gautam Malkani's *Londonstani* and histories are articulated with an equally powerful militancy but from a different perspective.

The metropolitan men: Gautam Malkani's *Londonstani*

A novel of the moment and one of the most talked about debuts in 2006 following the bookworld and publishing clamour that surrounded its appearance, *Londonstani* (2006) is a vibrant, savagely funny text which responds to many different facets of life in teenage multicultural Britain, specifically the region of Heathrow feed roads in Hounslow.

Anticipated as one of the publishing highlights of 2006 and yet received with a range of mixed reviews, *Londonstani* is an audacious, messy and inventive tale, which is of, about and set in the contemporary moment with its execution, language, typology, narrative and subject matter. Challenging stereotypes and subverting expectations throughout, Malkani's novel is an immediate and urgent response to the sociocultural challenges and cross-cultural melange that has come to comprise and compromise London. Robert McCrum summed up the overlaps between 'a culture in thrall to the marketing departments of "big business" and driven by publicity hype' (McCrum quoted in Graham, n.p.) and his post mortem about the novel's failure gathered more pace: 'If it had been published,' he writes, 'as its author once intended, as a teen novel, it might have found a secure place as a contemporary classroom cult' However:

> Once Fourth Estate, hungry to cash in on the *White Teeth* and *Brick Lane* market, had paid an advance in excess of £300,000, the die was cast. Thereafter, *Londonstani* had to be 'the literary novel of the year'. Like a Fiat Uno entered for Formula 1, after a squeal of brakes and a loud bang, *Londonstani* was reduced to a stain of grease, and some scraps of rubber and tin, on the race track of the 2006 spring publishing season. In Borders or Waterstone's, *Londonstani* is already being airbrushed from history. (n.p.)

James Graham questions McCrum's rather sweeping dismissal of the novel's failure when aligned with the critical and commercial successes of *White Teeth* (2000) and *Brick Lane* (2003), inquiring as to whether it is the first case of 'multiculturalism being mis-marketed' (n.p.). In the case of *White Teeth* there are a multitude of other contributing factors to its success, including the significant championing and marketing frenzy that was undertaken by the *Guardian* in advance of its publication. If we consider this complicity between media outlets and the canon-makers, there is the impact, until 2011 when it was cancelled, of the 'inexorable rise in influence on the literary field of production by "The Richard and Judy Book Club" since its introduction to their daily talk show in 2004' (n.p.).

Londonstani begins with Hardjit, the ringleader of a gang who are violent in their actions but somewhat obtuse in their ethos, delivering a vicious assault to a white boy who may or may not have verbally abused him. Throughout this ritualistic performance, fusing gangsta/desi/rudeboy rap and patter with the delusions of a biography worthy of a noir crime novel, Malkani then proceeds to explore the lives of Hardjit's peers, Ravi, Amit and Jas, the latter representing a figure who has joined the gang to gain his friends' approval and esteem but finds his bookish ways a hindrance to the posturing he must undertake as the gang terrorize their small suburban surroundings and find themselves embroiled in criminal activities beyond their capabilities.

Londonstani focuses on the effects and consequences of intergenerational conflict and expectation amongst ethnic diaspora and the struggle of individuals who are trapped in a space between cultures and nationalities. The use of language as an agent for differentiating and thus preserving identity operates as a strong thematic concern within *Londonstani* and Malkani's ear and eye for dialogue is, at times, striking in its ability to capture the fiercely vibrant and kinetic patter that his protagonists employ.

When considering contemporary literature and film from the South Asian diaspora in Britain, 'of utmost importance is the diasporic figure's call for "new figurations, for alternative representations and social locations for the kind of hybrid mix we are in the process of becoming" within the context of an increasingly postmodern, postcolonial world' (Braidotti 2, cited in Pervez, n.p.). As the work of Salman Rushdie, Hanif Kureishi, Meera Syal, Monica Ali, Suniti Namjoshi and Gurinder Chadha indicates, South Asian diaspora writers and filmmakers in Britain have a tendency to 'reject the centre', deliberately refusing the collectively singular identity with which they are traditionally affiliated or saddled. With this sense of 'eschewing the centre' and challenging existing categories of labelling, the term 'postcolonial' already seems clunky, inward looking and problematic. So when we consider the revolutionary potential that may or may not exist at work below these texts, it does come as something of a surprise that Malkani opens *Londonstani* thus:

– Serve him right he got his muthafuckin' face fuck'd, shudn't b callin me a Paki, innit'.

After spittin his words out, Hardjit stopped for second, like he expected us to write em down or someshit. Then he sticks in an exclamation mark by kickin the white kid in the face again. – Shudn't b callin us Pakis, innit, u dirrty gora. (1)

Niall Griffiths, writing in the *Daily Telegraph*, suggests that this opening challenges, unsettles and proves nothing. According to Griffiths it's the 'Vanilla Ice' of conventional beginnings. By comparison, I would argue that Malkani is aggravating and provoking any existing expectations or positions. These sorts of rhythms and extended, elongated and lyrical syntactical structures and grammar recur throughout *Londonstani*, here they are used to fulfil an emphatic and explosive beginning to the novel. Whereas the vernacular is no stranger to readers of contemporary fiction, the use of text-speak is. Confronting your reader with such an opening sequence of sentences is the first shot in what becomes a long, drawn out tactical fight. This is the act of using language as an oppositional, transgressive and aggressive force and establishes early on the intelligence that Malkani brings to the rest of the novel, his cultural assault, or indeed his assault on culture. By using the usually highly inflammatory language of the racially prejudiced, projecting it onto the lips of the typically white, male monocultural troglodyte and then having his subject dish out the characteristic beating normally reserved for the boots of an oppressive force, he quite deliberately forces the reader to confront their own fears and concerns. That said, it is this direct and distinctly confrontational approach which contributed to the novel's commercial failure. As Graham suggests: 'Despite the evidence that suggests – in fact precisely because – the non-realist narrative and linguistic techniques have made this novel unpalatable to this audience, I suggest it presents a valuable alternative vision of multiculturalist society to that currently inscribed within the dominant discourse' (n.p.).

Whereas Smith's and Ali's works present a form of media-friendly 'authenticity' with the mellifluous tagline 'she's young, Black and British', Malkani challenges this particular 'hurdle', claiming 'the characters in *Londonstani* are basically defined by their differing levels of inauthenticity – that's kind of the point, it's about performance and pretence – so the whole authenticity test that the media kept applying to me becomes even more ridiculously meaningless' (quoted in Graham, n.p.).

In this respect:

> the poetics [of British Asian literature] bespeaks a type of literature, or art in general, as a production machine that operates as an open multiplicity, transmitting the flows and intensities inherent in lines of flight that are opened and closed during the process of identity formation. More importantly, such a minor poetics is 'immediately social and political, affected by a high level of linguistic deterritorialization and expressive of a collective assemblage of enunciation'. (Bogue, 59)

In other words, in order for a minor culture to represent itself, it must subvert a major language by deterritorializing that language and imbuing it with a minor tradition. *Londonstani* is about expressing the anxiety, expression and performance of a rising urban youth culture, the complicity of the demographic within this culture, the hypermasculine responses to a growing insecurity of identity amongst teenage males, the refusal or inability to assimilate and the searing commentaries on those who do so, when joining another 'group' or 'scene', who perform assimilation whilst maintaining their own existing cultural heritages. That *Londonstani* started life as a sociological thesis is evident, given the range of topics and thematic engagements covered within its narrative and plot. As Malkani puts it in an article for the *Financial Times* on the eve of the novel's publication, 'the more demotic desi subculture gives kids a more porous identity. It is derivative in a positive sense that fosters social cohesion and inclusiveness'.

Although this text does, indeed, address the protagonists' perception of some intergenerational failure and shift that has allowed the maternal and paternal roles to flux and change within the domestic sphere, it may be that this also exists as an overarching motif for the parents of the current generation to act as a reasoning for perpetuating the racial violence that still exists between rival gangs and cultures. Later on in this opening sequence, Hardjit ups the stakes against his helpless and hapless rival:

> – U cussin ma mum? an the less venacular, – U b disrespectin my mother [...] None a us dared argue, an Hardjit'd found a reason to kick the white kid in the face again, an again, an again, this time punctuating the rapid-fire beatin with, – U fuckin gora, u cuss'd my mum, an then adding variations like, – U cuss'd my sister an ma bredren. U cuss'd my dad, my uncle Deepak, u cuss'd my aunty Sheetal, my aunty Meera, ma cousins in Leicester, u cuss'd ma grandad in Jalaandhar. (10–11)

Notice the shift here. Malkani's use of the vernacular and different stylistic innovations works. The definition of a regular beat to the beating adds impact, 'the specifically linguistic mechanisms that Malkani uses to explore these themes perform the very kind of disruptive (disrespectful, even) subcultural articulations he is interested in' (Graham, n.p.). Notice the deliberate and quite styled manner in which Hardjit justifies his actions now, the familiar familial motivations making it apparent he views the personal insult as one that is also aimed at his relatives, his heritage throughout the different generations. For all these are the lost generation of the twenty-first century, willingly trapped in a no-place of inter- or intracultural conflicts, they are still aware of and protective of the family traditions and rituals.

The intolerance for those who enact and perform a different approach to this cultural assimilation is made evident by the group's highly insular attitude and Othering of those they refer to as 'coconuts' – brown on the outside but white on the inside:

> You think you better than your own kind cos you is so white n you read some poncey books n newspapers? [...] Wat business you got goin? Readin fuckin batty books? [...] Wat's wrong wid your own bredren, brown boy? Look at us. We's b havin a nice car, nice tunes, nuff nice designer gear, nuff bling mobile. But no, you wanna b some gora-lovin, dirrty hippie wid fuckin Radiohead playin in your car. Look at ma man Jas here. Learn some lessons from him. (22–3)

This is 'The disenfranchised generation of Asian youth attempt[s] in this novel to counter what they perceive as a problematic ghettoization of their parents' lives, through the creation of a London subculture that calls into question not just mainstream middle class white British life, but also the lives of Asian immigrants pegged into particular social roles' (Pervez, n.p.), but the quotation has multiple functions in relation to the agenda and foci Malkani expresses through his narrative. The scathing comments concerning 'poncey books n newspapers' (23) and the perceived assumption of a cultural privileging, and thus superiority, that derives from this choice of lifestyle is the initial target for the group's mockery, the suggestion that their target is aiming for self-improvement as a way of ensuring he can distinguish himself from such people as Hardjit and Jas is the source of aggravation. Evidence of the hypermasculinity at work within the narrative comes to the fore – reading newspapers and having bookish tendencies draws the homophobic insult 'batty boy', a charge all too often laid on for Jas. The perception that reading and education are effeminizing points to this recurrent destabilization of cultural normalizing at work within the narrative, the rejection of a paradigmatic value system predicated on self-improvement through the espousing of predominantly middle-class values concerning education and learning. This is further emphasized by the accusation that the subject of this tirade ought to 'Look at us [your own bredren]. We's b havin a nice car, nice tunes, nuff nice designer gear, nuff bling mobile', questioning his process of apparent Othering and differentiation from the culture and ethnicity of his birth. The emphasis on the car, music, clothes and technological possessions points to the onset or reconfiguration of an already existing consumer rhetoric and lifestyle that is part of the process of self-definition each character must go through in order to assume the acceptability of their peers. This is the language of the new youth urban culture, of the sizeable disposable income and its distribution on luxury goods, of the name making the individual, the importance of being seen in the fashionable restaurants and the nightclubs. In opposition to the previous generational values, this is the process of simultaneously creating an identity different from those around you but also gaining access to the higher echelons of the existing social strata from which exclusion has been enforcement, never an option.

To conclude, there exists a corpus of 'British Asian writers and filmmakers [who] are engaged in a collective process of enunciating a unique minor literature that is gradually carving out a more flexible space within which to negotiate the diverse particularities of Britons everywhere, diasporic and otherwise' (Pervez, n.p.). *Londonstani* is a striking contribution to this body of work; its multi-thematic focus and innovative typology taps into a kinetic and vibrant substrate at work within contemporary culture and through Malkani's comprehensive survey. Suffice to say that the minor literature's position on the margins is prominent enough for the artistic operating space on offer to be exploited successfully and with as much vibrancy as this vital, relentless and uncompromising novel.

Through the presentation of four different regional responses to globalized Britain and the conflicts that came to inform and then follow the subsequent devolution of power to regions, this chapter has discussed themes such as language and identity and how they have come to be articulated through a collection of novels that embody this epoch in contemporary fiction.

Significantly, three of the authors have been brought into the canon of contemporary fiction from a position of relative obscurity – whether through the lack of visibility associated with their initial publishers or their own personal profile. The author who gained notoriety for the spectacular overestimation of sales is Malkani, which demonstrates the manner in which sales figures and the commercial bottom line come to define, for the publishers at least, the respective success or failure of a novel. It is such a numerically deterministic approach that demonstrates the complicity between return on investment and those who are the arbiters of 'cultural success'. While the regional novel is still a market that offers food for political thought, it has not had the rising stars of the 1990s and the 2000s to mark fiction after 2010.

In response to the desire for authenticity and the search for the 'real', discussed earlier in this chapter, contemporary fiction has moved on at the end of the decade into realms whereby the medium of the novel has become both the subject of fiction and attempts to transgress the physical boundaries imposed upon it. Tom McCarthy's *Remainder* (2005) and Steven Hall's *The Raw Shark Texts* (2007) were both, effectively, metafictional tales about amnesia and memory that had two markedly different routes: McCarthy was rejected by many UK publishing houses on the grounds of commercial viability before being published by Metronome in France, and then the independent Alma Books in the UK, while Hall's book was released to a hail of plaudits from Canongate. In both cases, the complicity between the reviewers and the market place dictated the process of coming to into the public consciousness.

Works cited

Badiou, Alain. *The Century*. Cambridge: Polity Press, 2007.
Banks, Iain. *Complicity*. London: Abacus, 1993.
Bogue, Ronald. 'Minor Writing and Minor Literature'. *Symploke* 5:1 (2005) 99–118.
Brooker, Joseph. 'Orgreave Revisited: David Peace's GB84 and the Return to the 1980s'. *Radical Philosophy* 133 (2005) 39–51.
Evans, Gareth. 'More Sheepshagging'. 3 June 2001. Available online: http://www.3ammagazine.com/buzzwords/2002_mar.html (accessed 16 May, 2015).
Graham, James. 'An Interview with Gautam Malkani: Ealing Broadway, 6th November 2007'. *Literary London: Interdisciplinary Studies in the Representation of London*, 6:1 (2008).
Graham, James. '"this in't Good Will Hunting": *Londonstani* and the market for London's multicultural fictions'. *Literary London: Interdisciplinary Studies in the Representation of London*, 6: 2, September 2008. Available online: http://www.literarylondon.org/london-journal/september2008/graham.html (accessed 3 June, 2015).
Griffiths, Niall. *Grits*. London: Jonathan Cape, 2000.
Griffiths, Niall. *Sheepshagger*. London: Jonathan Cape, 2001.

Griffiths, Niall. 'Shudn't b calling us Pakis, innit'. *The Telegraph*, 7 May, 2006. Available online: http://www.telegraph.co.uk/culture/books/3651965/Shudnt-b-calling-us-Pakis-innit.html (accessed 16 May, 2015).

Hedgecock, Andy. 'David Peace interviewed by Andy Hedgecock'. Black Static, 12 March, 2009, TTA Press. Available online: http://ttapress.com/582/david-peace-interviewed-by-andy-hedgecock/ (accessed 3 June, 2015).

Holcombe, Garan. 'Niall Griffiths'. British Council website. Available online: http://literature.britishcouncil.org/niall-griffiths (accessed 3 June, 2015). 2005.

Holcombe, Garan. 'David Peace'. British Council website. Available online: http://literature.britishcouncil.org/david-peace (accessed 3 June, 2015). 2013.

Independent. Book review on the back of Griffiths, Niall, *Sheepshagger*. London: Vintage. 2002.

Kennedy, A.L. Book review on the back of Griffiths, Niall, *Sheepshagger*. London: Vintage. 2002.

Lea, Daniel. 'The Anxieties of Authenticity in Post-2000 British Fiction'. *MFS Modern Fiction Studies* 58:3 (2012): 459–76.

Malkani, Gautam. *Londonstani*, London: Fourth Estate, 2006.

Malkani, Gautam. 'What's right with Asian boys'. *The Financial Times*, 21 April, 2006.

McCabe, Patrick. *Call Me the Breeze*, London: Faber, 2003.

McCrum, Robert. 'Has the novel lost its way?' *The Observer*, 28 May, 2006.

McNeill, Dougal. 'Sheffield Year Zero: The Ends of GB84'. *Critical Engagements* 2:2 (2008), 71–97.

Morrison, Jago. *Contemporary Fiction*. London and New York: Routledge, 2003.

Peace, David. *Nineteen Seventy Four*. London: Serpent's Tail, 1999.

Peace, David. *Nineteen Seventy Seven*. London: Serpent's Tail, 2000.

Peace, David. *Nineteen Eighty*. London: Serpent's Tail, 2001.

Peace, David. *Nineteen Eighty Three*. London: Serpent's Tail, 2002.

Peace, David. *GB84*. London: Serpent's Tail, 2004.

Peace, David. *The Damned Utd*. London: Faber and Faber, 2006.

Peddie, Ian. 'Warmth and Light and Sky: Niall Griffiths in Conversation'. *Critical Survey*, 20:3 (2008): 116–27.

Pervez, Summer. 'Londonstani' presented at *Literary London* Thursday 3rd July, Brunel University, 2008.

Shaw, Katy. 'Introduction'. In *Analysing David Peace*, Newcastle: Cambridge Scholars Press, 2011.

Shields, David. *Reality Hunger: A Manifesto*. New York: Knopf, 2010.

Tebbs, Paul and Nicolas Bagnall. Book review of *Sheepshagger* by Niall Griffiths. *The Telegraph*, 23 March, 2002. Available online: http://www.telegraph.co.uk/culture/4727546/Paperbacks.html (accessed 16 May, 2015), 2002.

Welsh, Irvine. *Trainspotting*. London: Secker and Warburg, 1993.

2

Special Topic 1
Subcultural Fictions: Youth Subcultures in Twenty-first-century British Fiction

Nick Bentley

Two spates of inner-city rioting in Britain bookend the first decade of the twenty-first century, both of which were largely reported in the press as being fuelled by youth gangs. In the summer of 2001, in Oldham, Bradford, Leeds and Stoke-on-Trent, Asian youths (predominantly) were blamed for inciting clashes with the police and for causing criminal damage to property. Ten years later, the shooting of Mark Duggan in Tottenham in August 2011 sparked a number of nights of inner-city violence in London, Manchester and Birmingham. Added to this are reports of individual incidents in which youth gangs have been involved in violent clashes and gang-related deaths (Huq *On the Edge*; Tyler). Media rhetoric of 'hoodies', ghettoization and urban youth street gangs continues to be a staple of the British press' love affair with moral panics around youth subcultures (Robinson). Partly in an attempt to understand the underlying causes of violence amongst youths, but also sometimes reinforcing the sense of moral panic, several novels of this period have offered representations of subcultural groups, several of which will be discussed in this chapter. This fiction sits aside a number of films that have explored subcultural contexts, including: *Fishtank* (2009), *Four Lions* (2010), *Green Street* (2005), *Kidulthood* (2006) (and its sequel *Adulthood* [2010]), *Neds* (2010), *Sweet Sixteen* (2002) and *This is England* (2006). (This trend seems far from abating as we move into the second decade of the twenty-first century with films such as *Ill Manors* and *Soul Boy* and TV dramas such as *Top Boy*.) Most of these novels and films, in addition to their emphasis on youth violence, criminality and promiscuity, also acknowledge the importance of subcultural affiliation in the lived experience of characters growing up in contemporary Britain.

A significant influence on this trend can be attributed to the success in the 1990s of fiction and film that identified youth subcultures as the basis for the exploration of bildungsroman narratives alongside critical commentary on contemporary British society and culture. Perhaps two novels in particular are important here: Hanif Kureishi's *The Buddha of Suburbia* (1990), which details the main character, Karim Amir's experiences of a racially prejudiced Britain in the 1970s set against his involvement with various subcultures from the tail end of the hippy movement through Bowie-influenced space rock to punk; and *Trainspotting* (both Irvine Welsh's 1993 novel and Danny Boyle's 1996 film adaptation), which explored skagboy subculture in 1980s' and early 1990s' Edinburgh. These novels can be seen as having reinvigorated the trend for subcultural British fiction that stretches back to (at least) the 1950s and both were clearly influential in the rise of the genre in the 2000s. In the 1950s, novels such as Colin MacInnes' *Absolute Beginners* (1959), Alan Sillitoe's *Saturday Night and Sunday Morning* (1958) and Keith Waterhouse's *Billy Liar* (1959) amongst others can be seen to be initiating this kind of novel in a British context. This is an aspect of literary studies that has not received much critical attention, yet it was certainly an important area of literary production in the first decade of the twenty-first century. This chapter identifies a range of novels published during the decade that explore the social and political importance of contemporary and historical youth subcultures in British society. It will identify the range of approaches taken in this body of work, put forward factors fuelling this trend, and offer discussion of individual novels by Stewart Home, John King, Gautam Malkani and Alex Wheatle, as well as referring to other relevant fiction.

Before looking at the novels, however, it is useful to examine the place of fictional representations of youth subcultures in relation to subcultural studies more generally during the period. Studies of youth have traditionally identified subcultural expression either in terms of aesthetic practice – pop/rock music, fashion, artwork (album covers, posters, etc.) or as sociological categories of youth, in opposition to parent, mainstream or dominant culture. This approach established itself in two main movements: the Chicago School that broadly speaking followed a sociological and ethnographic approach; and the Birmingham School, associated with the Centre for Contemporary Cultural Studies (CCCS) at Birmingham University, that tended to pursue theoretical, ideological and, from the later 1970s onwards, semiotic analyses.[1] After this period, however, there was a move away from the focus on the theoretical, semiotic and ethnographic study of 'classic subcultures', and several critics began to challenge and critique some of the assumptions of those earlier approaches:

writers such as Gary Clarke, David Muggleton, Steven Redhead and Sarah Thornton began to think in terms of post-subcultures and emphasized the fluidity of subcultural construction and association, and the self-reflexive aspects of collective belonging. This move drew on postmodern models of identity and signification, and began to challenge both the identification of subcultures as revealing in imaginary forms aspects of ideological frameworks of class out of which the 'classic' subcultures emerged, as in Cohen's 'Subcultural Conflict and Working Class Community' (1972), and the utopian potential offered by the resistance of subcultural style, for example in Dick Hebdige's *Subculture* (1979). As Weinzierl and Muggleton suggest in the introduction to an important 2003 collection of essays in this context, *The Post-Subcultures Reader*: 'The era seems long gone of working-class youth subcultures "heroically" resisting subordination through "semiotic guerrilla warfare". Both youth cultural activities and the research efforts in this field seem nowadays to reflect a more pragmatic approach compared to the romanticism of the CCCS, whose authors saw a radical potential in largely symbolic challenges' (4).

Post-subcultural theories also suggest a shift away from the ideological and spectacular aspects of youth to an emphasis on their textual construction, which makes the articulation and rendering of them in literature especially significant. In this chapter, I am particularly interested in the way in which fiction in the 2000s has been involved in the construction (rather than representation or recording) of subcultural identity, and how selected novels utilize other forms of cultural expression, for example, popular musical forms and references, fashion and subcultural spaces. Before looking at specific examples it is informative to identify three aspects of cultural theory that have importance for the analysis of the fiction, and have been influential in the development of post-subcultural approaches over the last fifteen years or so.

The first of these can be demonstrated by the emphasis on the importance of performance for members of subcultures. Clearly drawing on and adapting the theories of Judith Butler, approaches that stress performativity emphasize the way in which an individual's consumption of, and affiliation to, subcultural identity is fluid and dependent on context, rejecting the idea that individuals are, or ever were, permanently attached to discrete subcultures. This concept of performativity resonates with corresponding notions of postmodern identity as fluid, unstable, constructed and often self-aware and ironic. This connects to a second theoretical perspective that has become increasingly influential in subcultural studies – that associated with the French sociologist Michel Maffesoli. Maffesoli is working in a Marxist tradition, but has identified what he sees as a trend in postmodern capitalist economies towards 'urban tribes' as a way of identifying a fragmentation of the notion of the 'masses' in traditional Marxist discourses. His identification of tribes does not reject issues of class, but it problematizes the model of class affiliation through horizontal stratification within working-class culture and society. Rob Shields succinctly sums up Maffesoli's approach: 'The "little masses" of Maffesoli's analysis are heterogeneous fragments, the remainders of mass consumption society, groups distinguished by their members' shared lifestyles and tastes. *Tribus* are thus not "tribes" in the traditional anthropological sense, for they do not have the fixity or longevity of tribes. Nor are they neo-tribes; they are better understood as "postmodern tribes", or even pseudo-tribes' (x). The third theoretical development in subcultural studies in the last two decades relies heavily on Pierre Bourdieu's notion of cultural capital and, in particular, Sarah Thornton's development of this concept into what she calls 'subcultural capital', which:

> confers status on its owner in the eyes of the relevant beholder.... Subcultural capital can be *objectified* or *embodied*. Just as books and paintings display cultural capital in the family home, so subcultural capital is objectified in the form of fashionable haircuts and well-assembled record collections (full of well-chosen, limited edition 'white label' twelve-inches and the like) ... subcultural capital is embodied in the form of being 'in the know', using (but not over-using) current slang ... both cultural and subcultural capital put a premium on the 'second nature' of their knowledges. (11–12; emphasis in original)

As Thornton stresses in her example, music and fashion are crucial elements in the articulation of subcultural capital and knowledge about music in particular creates a cultural hierarchy amongst affiliates of the subculture. Thornton also emphasizes the importance of the media as a 'primary factor governing the circulation of subcultural capital', which has resulted in a new self-awareness and self-reflexivity in the articulation and representation of subcultural identity in a range of media, including fiction.

In a British context, the post-subcultural focus on the individual's consumption of (youth) culture and the critique of traditional models of subcultures as monolithic collectives of identity challenged aspects of the earlier theories, most notably those derived from the Contemporary Centre for Cultural Studies that dominated British subcultural studies from the 1960s to the 1990s. As a result of this debate (with a few notable exceptions such as Ken Gelder, Rupa Huq, Paul Hodkinson and William Osgerby) the focus on British subcultures appears to be on the defensive in sociology and cultural studies in the 2000s although there is evidence of a resurgence in the field since 2010.[2] This chapter argues, however, that the interest in youth subcultures did not disappear and fiction that engages with subcultural identity appears to have had a renaissance in Britain during the first decade of the twenty-first century, filling the gap, to a certain extent, left by sociology, ethnography and cultural studies.

The subcultural novel of the 2000s can be categorized into three broad types: (i) novels that look back at previous recognized subcultures such as rastas or hippies from the position of the twenty-first century; (ii) fiction that focuses on contemporary youth subcultures; and (iii) novels that offer an examination of group dynamics more generally without a distinct label attached to the group. Some novels, of course, offer narratives that combine two or more of these characteristics and inevitably there is overlap of the categories in this typology.

The first kind of novel presents youth cultures from the past, and identifies a reengagement with a variety of subcultures from the 1950s to the 1990s. There is often an element of nostalgia in this kind of novel although this could be termed a 'critical nostalgia' in that the group ethics, and ideological and everyday practices of the subculture, are interrogated as much as they are celebrated. They also offer an examination of the specific historical contexts in which the subculture emerges, offering a dynamic relationship between individual characters, the subculture, and the parent and dominant cultures to which the subculture stands in opposition. In this way, the contemporary subcultural novel appears to be attempting to reclaim older models of collective affiliation that coalesced around youth identities – fashion, style, spaces and behaviour – whilst at the same time revealing something of the anxieties in contemporary British culture around the continued fragmentation of socially cohesive groups. Novels in this category would include Jonathan Coe's *The Rotters' Club* (2001); Stewart Home's *Tainted Love* (2005); Alex Wheatle's *East of Acre Lane* (2001); and certain sections of John King's *Skinheads* (2008). Jonathan Coe's novel details the growing up of a number of mainly white youths in Birmingham in the 1970s and traces the transition from prog rock to punk as a cultural setting for their bildungsroman narrative. This is set alongside an examination of the effects on individuals of two key political concerns of the decade: the IRA bombings in Birmingham and trade union activity. Wheatle's novel is set in Brixton in the early 1980s and examines the experiences of a number of characters who are part of the reggae and dub subculture, while Home's *Tainted Love* offers a critical exploration of the impact on individuals and society of the hippy and drug counterculture in Britain in the 1960s. King's novel, as we will see, in part recalls the originating, late 1960s' moment of the skinhead subculture, as well as its revival in the late 1970s and early 1980s and its continuation into the 2000s. Hanif Kureishi's *Gabriel's Gift* (2001) might also be included here, as although it is set in the contemporary moment it looks back critically to the utopian and idealistic ideas embedded in the hippy and glam rock subcultures as they manifested themselves in a British context in the late 1960s and early 1970s.

The second kind of subcultural novel of the decade is set in contemporary Britain and engages with social, political and cultural issues in a subcultural context. These novels address a range of contemporary social and cultural concerns, from the perennial identification of youth culture with criminality, anti-social behaviour and promiscuity, to concerns specific to the decade such as the politicization of youth in terms of class, race and/or racism and terrorist activity in the wake of 9/11, 7/7 and the wars in Afghanistan and Iraq. Novels that address some of these issues include Monica Ali's *Brick Lane*, Courttia Newland's *Society Within* (1999), Alison Miller's *Demo* (2006), Zadie Smith's *White Teeth* (2000) and *On Beauty* (2005), Gautam Malkani's *Londonstani* (2006), John King's *Skinheads* and Alex Wheatle's *The Dirty South* (2008). In Monica Ali's *Brick Lane*, for example, the group called the Bengal Tigers that the character Karim joins can be seen as a youth subculture as, although it includes members of all ages, it is especially attractive to younger members of the Asian community growing up in Tower Hamlets following the 9/11 attacks. This group is established to resist the 'Lion Hearts', an alternative group in the area that represents a broad subculture of far right British youth that are planning 'A March Against the Mullahs' in response to 9/11. There is an element of misguided inauthenticity in Karim's involvement that seems at odds with his background as a second-generation son of Bangladeshi parents who has never left Britain. The novel suggests that his attraction towards Nazneen, an immigrant from Bangladesh, is part of his attempt to connect himself with a sense of Bangladeshi and Islamic rootedness from which he feels his upbringing in Britain has excluded him. However, the description of this group takes on new meaning when considered in light of the 7/7 attacks in London two years after the publication of Ali's novel to the extent that the ironic tone can seem somewhat inappropriate to readers after 2005.

As a different kind of response to the international politics of the 2000s, Alison Miller's *Demo* is a bildungsroman that tells the story of sixteen-year-old Clare's journey from her family home in Glasgow to Florence to take part in an anti-capitalist demonstration. The novel describes the outlook, utopian ideals and some of the short comings of the anti-capitalist subculture that includes a mixture of (mainly white) rastas and new age hippies. This category might also include J.G. Ballard's *Kingdom Come* (2006), which includes a subculture of sports fans who wear shirts emblazoned with the St. George cross and pursue what one of the characters in the novel describes as 'soft fascism' in their celebration of an English nationalism that threatens ethnic minorities deemed not to belong to their perception of an authentic Englishness (168).

The third category of subcultural novel is more tentative and identifies a trend in recent novels for the depiction of loosely connected individuals whose sense of affiliation is less fixed, but nevertheless manifests itself in a group identity in which an untitled and imagined subculture is constructed. In this sense, the social group portrayed is marginalized and offset from mainstream society, but its internal cohesion is either more difficult to categorize, or is used as a metaphor for broader concerns about the marginalization of subaltern groups. This category includes, for example, Kazuo Ishiguro's *Never Let Me Go* (2005), an alternative reality/science fiction novel in which a group of young adult clones are effectively farmed to provide replacement organs for the mainstream public, or 'normal' people as the novel's narrator calls them. Other examples would be Nicola Barker's *Behindlings* (2002), where a collection of disparate characters of differing backgrounds and ages are connected in their unspecified 'following' of a central character Wesley; and Niall Griffiths' *Grits* (2000), in which a diverse group of underclass drop-outs and loners gather in a small Welsh village and engage in debate about the harm done to them by contemporary society and the meaning of life more generally. Set in the mid to late 1990s, *Grits* represents a kind of come down from the hedonism of the summer of love. Joe Stretch's debut novel *Friction* (2008), which can also be placed in this category, offers a hyperreal exploration of some of the excessive behaviours indulged in by a group of twenty-somethings who frequent both the mainstream and underground clubs in Manchester's university quarter. Stretch's writing in this novel conveys rapidity and is supercharged to a level that neatly frames his portrayal of a series of hedonistic characters that mix post-millennial scepticism with an increasingly disillusioned romanticism. In Stretch's Manchester, subcultures are part of the scene but the sceptical individualism of the wily characters enables them to negotiate those subcultures without committing. In Gwendoline Riley's *Sick Notes* (2004), also set in Manchester, the main characters encounter 'rock kids' in Piccadilly Gardens (117) and the 'student crowd' for whom 'the boys are rickets thin, the girls have doughy stomachs' (90), but subcultures as coherent youth groups or scenes are seen as outmoded; a group of teenage Mods, for example, is described as 'lean boys in shiny suits and girls in shift dresses and white tights, stamping and shivering, frowning while they tweak their hairdos in the window' and are ultimately positioned by the novel's main character Esther as 'Timecops ... the reason they look like they're from 1965 is that they are from 1965' (87). What replaces this tie to group sociality is tentative, suspicious but nevertheless longing relationships with others encapsulated for Esther by a reference to Linder Sterling's description of her walks with Morrissey as 'very intimate but very separate at the same time' (80).

This displacement of the currency and cohesion of classic subcultures can also be seen in the rise in the 1990s and 2000s of cyberpunk and steampunk novels by British writers, including Ken MacLeod, China Miéville, Jeff Noon, Philip Pullman and Philip Reeve. Miéville's *Kraken* (2010), for example, projects a world that is organized into competing underground groups that the main character, Billy Harrow, encounters in his quest to solve the mysterious disappearance of a giant squid from the British Museum of Natural History where he works. This science fiction scenario offers a metaphorical presentation of the way in which contemporary London can be seen to be organized into various gangs or subcultures. This last group of novels suggests a move towards the idea of post-subcultures, a concept that was beginning to be theorized in the 1990s and 2000s as an extension of, and often reaction to, some of the approaches adopted in classic Birmingham School analyses of subcultures. This is an interesting group of novels, but given restrictions of space the following discussion will concentrate on examples from the first two categories identified above.

Gautam Malkani, *Londonstani* (by way of Zadie Smith's *White Teeth*)

Malkani's debut novel *Londonstani* describes the relationships and behaviour of a group of middle-class, West London teenagers who coalesce into a subculture that combines British-Asian and black American pop cultural contexts. It picks up on a group first identified, in fictional terms, in Zadie Smith's *White Teeth*, in which Smith describes the new subculture of Raggastanis: 'It was a new breed, just recently joining the ranks of the other street crews: Becks, B-Boys, Indi kids, wide-boys, ravers, rude-boys, Acidheads, Sharons, Tracies, Kevs, Nation Brothers, Raggas and Pakis; manifesting itself as a kind of cultural mongrel of the last three categories. Raggastanis spoke a strange mix of Jamaican patois, Bengali,

Gujarit and English' (231). Smith represents this group as part of a competing range of subcultural identities at the beginning of the 1990s and reflects the acceleration and plurality of groups in the period identified in the theory referred to above as post-subcultural. Smith also registers the hybrid cross-fertilization that goes towards the creation of this 'new breed':

> Their ethos, their manifesto, if it could be called that, was equally a hybrid thing: Allah *featured*, but more as a collective big brother than a supreme being, a hard-as-fuck *geezer* who would fight in their corner if necessary; Kung Fu and the works of Bruce Lee were also central to the philosophy; added to this was a smattering of Black Power ... but mainly their mission was to put the Invincible back in Indian, the Bad-aaaass back in Bengali, the P-Funk back in Pakistan. (231–2)

The rhetoric of breeds and hybridity is part of an extended metaphor in Smith's account of a multicultural Britain coming to terms with postcolonial migrations and new ethnicities and the plethora and melding of subcultural affiliations seems to be part of this identification. The tone in this novel produces an ironic distance and gently mocks the aspirations of this group of teenagers coming to terms, in their own way, with the prejudices felt by the South East Asian second generation youths growing up in London in the last decades of the twentieth century.

Smith's novel is noticeably pre-9/11 (and pre-7/7), unlike Malkani's book, which, although it retains some of *White Teeth*'s comic evaluation also provides a harder-edged description of violent acts and criminality in which a similar (although later) group engages. Unlike the distanced narrative of Smith's novel, *Londonstani* displays the language of the subculture in its use of the first-person narration of Jas, a teenager who represents himself as part of a rudeboy or desi subculture in the West London suburbs. Jas finds affiliation to this subculture necessary in order to connect with his peer group at school and the novel makes it clear that the subculture operates in response to a feeling of marginalization from mainstream society experienced by the group. One of the distinctive features of this novel, however, is a self-awareness of the way in which subcultural identity is performed:

> I still use the word rudeboy cos it's been round for longer. People're always tryin to stick a label on our scene. . . . Anyway whatever the fuck we are, Ravi an the others are better at it than I am. I swear I've watched as much MTV Base and Juggy D videos as they have, but I still can't attain the right level a rudeboy authenticity. If I could, I wouldn't be using poncey words like attain an

authenticity, innit. I'd be sayin I couldn't keep it real or someshit. An if I said it that way, then there'd be no need for me to say it in the first place so I wouldn't say it anyway. After all, it's all bout what you say and how you say it. Your linguistic prowess an debating dexterity (though whatever you do don't say it that way).[3]
(5–6)

The desire for Jas to be included within the group is clear, however much of the focus is on the excruciating tangles he gets himself into with respect to the notion of authenticity. Authenticity is located not in organically belonging to an area or a natural internalized response to an environment but in learning a set of mediated behaviours and forms of expression. Paradoxically, then, authenticity is reframed as something to be learned and performed. The markers of attainment are judged against globalized and commodified forms of the subculture as exemplified for Jas in MTV Base and Juggy D videos. Much of the ironic drive of Jas' narrative comes out of this paradox – the need for him to construct for himself a level of authenticity that will allow him to be respected by the group. This cultural knowledge then feeds into behaviours undertaken by the group in a passage that describes Jas' involvement in the beating up of a white youth who, it is claimed, has used racist abuse towards the group, and who we later learn is one of Jas' old school friends:

> I had to redeem myself after my gimpy remark bout spellin Paki with a capital P. After all Ravi had spotted the white kid in the first place an Amit's helped Hardjit pin him against the brick wall. But me, I hadn't added anything to either the physical or verbal abuse a the gora. To make up for my useless shitness I decided to offer the following carefully crafted comment: – Yeah, bredren, knock his fuckin teeth out. Bruck his fuckin face. Kill his fuckin ... well, his fuckin, you know, him. Kill him.
>
> This was probly a bit over the top but I think I'd got the tone just right an nobody laughed at me. At least I managed to stop short a sayin, Kill the pig, like the kids do in that film *Lord a the Flies*. It's also a book too, but I'm trying to stop knowin shit like that. (9)

Jas' involvement here is on the periphery and his violence remains verbal rather than physical; nevertheless, the relationship between cultural influence and actual lived experiences is foregrounded. Note here the distinct change in register between Jas' articulation of his behaviour to his textual audience (the reader) and the report of his actual speech to the group. Malkani's approach, although in the first person, is similar to Smith's combination of the comic with the serious. The account of the violence if taken on its own terms is clearly worrying and plays into notions of criminality and deviance that are stock-in-trade in the representation of youth cultures. It is interesting to note, however, that the critical and commercial success of Smith's novel was not achieved by *Londonstani* despite a similar focus on youth in West London. Of course one of the reasons for this might be their respective historical contexts and precisely the fact that *White Teeth* is pre-9/11 and 7/7, whereas Malkani's novel was published later. The comic tone with which the group of South-East Asian youths are treated in *Londonstani* did not seem to play into the contemporary shifts in representations of Muslim youths in the wake of revelations about the 'home-grown' nature of the 7/7 terrorists. In a review for the *Guardian*, for example, Kamila Shamsie opined 'the problem with Jas' narration is that too often the slick superficiality of his life becomes the slick superficiality of the novel'.

Jas' comment in the second paragraph of the quotation also identifies the importance to the group of what Sarah Thornton defines as subcultural capital. Although Jas can relate his situation to the film adaptation of William Golding's *Lord of the Flies*, this cultural knowledge has become useless in the environment in which he finds himself. Jas recognizes that this kind of knowledge has to be replaced by that which is respected within the group. It is in this context that the novel, through Jas, makes references to specific artists respected by the desi subculture: Usher, DMX, The Panjabi Hit Squad, Panjabi MC and RDP (Rhythm, Dhol and Bass). This combination of Black American, British Asian and South-East Asian musical influences sits alongside references to other cultural signifiers valued within the group, for example German cars, European fashion, and Japanese and Scandinavian 'fones' such as Sony Ericsson, Samsung and Nokia. As well as revealing the globalized nature of contemporary subcultural consumption, this list identifies the way in which it embraces rather than challenges mainstream products. This aspect of the text corresponds to the key aspects of post-subcultural analysis where the affiliation to a potentially subversive range of subcultural practices (as identified for example in some of the CCCS approaches) is seen to be outmoded.

This reduction in the radical potential of subcultural membership is also manifest in the novel's focus on the importance of business for the group, appropriating, but not challenging, dominant capitalist practices into the subcultural context:

> The bredrin [Davinder] was our best customer, you see, an if a good desi knows anything, it's how to look after their best customer.
>
> I don't even want to know where Davindr'd got all his merchandise from, but it kept us in business an you can't be a businessman if you in't in business, innit. Our business is reprogramming mobile fones, which basically means unblocking

them or unlocking them so they can be reconfigured.... We're businessmen innit. (40–2)

Like many twentieth-century subcultural fictions, an element of underground, semi-legal, if not outright illegal behaviour is emphasized. Discourses of criminality and deviancy are often glamorized and exoticized in subcultural texts and *Londonstani* is no different in this respect. What is perhaps distinctive in this novel is the emphasis on the capitalist paradigms that drive mainstream society, are also followed by the subculture. Jas, for example, utilizes his economics GCSE in developing the underground 'fone' unblocking network, which is really just a form of competition with his father's 'legitimate' mobile phone business. Jas' subculture does not subvert mainstream economic parameters in the drive for underground or countercultural social and economic relationships; rather it tries to mark out its own territory within the prevailing economic system.

The novel, then, represents a complex mix of celebrating and critiquing the lived ideologies of the rudeboy/desi subculture of the late 1990s/early 2000s. This balance is effectively achieved through the narration, which, by its manipulation of register and style, formally dramatizes many of the paradoxes within the subculture. This is perhaps shown most dramatically in the awkward revelation at the end of the text that Jas, whom the reader has been encouraged to believe is of Indian, Pakistani or Bangladeshi ethnicity, turns out be a white, middle-class kid whose full name is Jason Bartholomew-Cliveden. This may (or may not) be a surprise for the reader, but the implication is that subcultural identity in the 2000s has become a matter not of belonging to an 'authentic' social or ethnic group as it might have been in classic subcultural studies and fiction, but is manifest in a framework in which youth identities are more clearly subject to media construction and performance.

John King, *Skinheads* (2008)

John King's fiction provides an interesting comparison to Malkani's novel. King's 2008 *Skinheads*, in particular, shares a similar west London setting to *Londonstani* (and indeed *White Teeth*). King's novels typically focus on white, working-class subcultures: his 1990s' fiction tended to look at football fans and hooliganism (*The Football Factory* (1997), *Headhunters* (1998) and *England Away* (1999)), while his 2000 novels have focused more on music subcultures, although the two are seen to be entwined. His 2000 novel *Human Punk* describes the exploits of punk teenagers in the 1970s and, like *Skinheads*, is set in the Slough area. Part of King's aim is to reclaim some sense of realism and social justification from the uncritical moral panics surrounding youth subcultures in the news media. *Skinheads*, in particular, attempts to offer access to the thoughts, relationships and outlooks of individuals associated with this most maligned of subcultures, although the political ambiguities and contradictions of some of its associations with right (and left) wing politics is registered. In many ways, King aims to write back to the series of novels produced by Richard Allen in the 1970s that typically re-enforced the negative images of the skinhead subculture, especially its racist elements. Whereas Richard Allen (pseudonym of the Canadian journalist and pulp fiction writer Peter Moffat) was in his forties when he wrote *Skinhead* (the first novel in the series) in 1970 and had no first-hand experience of skinhead culture, King can claim greater personal knowledge of the subcultures he chooses to write about. (Richard Allen's subsequent novels in the 1970s include *Suedehead* (1971), *Skinhead Escapes* (1972), *Skinhead Girls* (1972) and *Skinhead Farewell* (1974).) This does not necessarily make them more authentic, but there is the impression that King is writing out of a milieu he knows well. The difference between King's relationship to the subculture he writes about and Allen's is similar to the distinction in subcultural ethnography between participant observation, where the cultural researcher has been (and often continues to be) an active member of the subculture, and 'slumming' research, in which the researcher joins the subculture for a limited time, without ever committing to its views and behaviours (Gelder, 32–7). In fact, against the privileging of experience as achieving representational authenticity, the relation between Allen's novels and the groups they depict demonstrates the circulation between the lived ideologies of a subculture and their representation in fiction. This meant that Richard Allen's highly popular series in the early seventies was influential in the right-wing political tenor taken by some members of the skinhead revival in the later 1970s and early 1980s. As William Osgerby (2012) writes, framing Allen's novel within the series of subcultural novels produced by the New English Library (NEL):

> while *Skinhead* and its sequels certainly resonated with the 1970s rhetoric of chaos and conflict, it would be a mistake to see the books as a straightforward 'reflection' of their historical context. Rather than being a touchstone for the 'real' social and political climate, the NEL novels should be understood as actively framing the social world. Conjuring with images of subcultural savagery, they did not simply reproduce but actively contributed to a wider discourse which presented Britain as beset by crisis. (232)

John King's *Skinheads* then extends that sense of circulation in that it also registers the place that other fiction (directly Allen's) has in this process, and indeed a friend of Terry English, one of the main characters in King's *Skinheads*, carries the nickname Hawkins in honour of the main skinhead character in Richard Allen's novels, Roy Hawkins. One section of the novel details the way in which the skinhead as a demonized figure is objectified by an imagined gaze of authority: 'he was the face in *American History X* and *Romper Stomper* and *Skinhead*, he was the thick fat man in hundreds of dramas and sitcoms and documentaries and cheap undercover TV movies' (230). King's aim is to open up and deconstruct this media-constructed stereotype, first by allowing access to the inner consciousness of characters and second, by showing the variety of ideologies and ethical considerations within the homogenized and popularly mediated figure of the skinhead.

The novel has three main characters, each of which references different moments in the historical development of the subculture. Terry English is the eldest and represents the original skinhead movement of the late 1960s that developed out of the Mod subculture and was influenced by the Jamaican ska and rudeboy music that was exported to Britain from the Caribbean during the period. Terry's cousin Ray is more associated with the skinhead revival in the late 1970s and early 1980s and has a much more politically aggressive outlook. Ray's politics are complicated and mix socialist elements with right-wing and nationalist sentiments. The third main character is Lol, Terry's son, who has inherited his father's love of ska, but negotiates the cultural outlooks and ideologies it promotes in a contemporary youth setting. The novel is narrated in the third person, but focalizes through each of these main characters in different chapters and although all the characters are presented as living in the 2000s, the use of memories in some of the interior monologue sections takes the reader back to earlier moments in the 1960s, 1970s and 1980s, and offers a kind of critical nostalgia for previous manifestations of the skinhead subculture and indeed for the social and cultural atmosphere of Britain during those periods.

Much of the novel is concerned with a debate over what represents the authentic skinhead culture between the two phases represented by Terry and Ray. As the novel is keen to emphasize: 'For Terry English being a skinhead is all about the boss sounds coming out of Jamaica – the pumped up beat and stripped down vocals of reggae music' (53). Terry's resistance to dominant culture represents what Laclau and Mouffe (1985) call 'a chain of equivalence' between marginalized identities and politics, whereby subaltern groups are encouraged to make connections across class, gender and ethnicity in a common struggle against prevailing systems of power. Terry's love of early ska and rudeboy music reflects his own assertion that he is not overtly political, however it also reveals his acceptance of the diversity of multicultural Britain. This contrasts with his cousin Ray and in many ways the debates around multiculturalism in the novel are expressed implicitly in the varieties of skinhead culture to which each of these characters holds allegiance. One of King's aims is to give space to the lived ideologies of white working-class culture – an ethnicity that several critics and cultural commentators have argued has been misrepresented in contemporary culture (Collins; Jones; Tyler).

Ray's politics are more complicated and evade conventional notions of left and right. The novel tells us of his belief in 'the welfare state and core socialist values' (96), but he is also angered by 'how the England-haters further up the ladder had slagged off the army for caning the fascists and liberating the Falklands. It was the same with Afghanistan and Iraq' (123). Formally, the sections that focus on Ray's memories use stream-of-consciousness techniques to reveal the interior thoughts and philosophizing of a character that is normally objectified in the mainstream press as ignorant and unthinking. One chapter, for example, details the impact on Ray of reading George Orwell's *Nineteen Eighty-Four*, which connects with him in ways he did not expect:

> as soon as he finishes reading *Nineteen Eighty-Four*... he knows it links up with Oi, in a way, the real skinhead approach, because street punk has told him it's okay to be proud... that he's allowed to think for himself, to refuse bribery, to be proud of his Englishness and his culture, and all the pretence and bullshit is shaved away, right back to the bone, he juts out his jaw and clenches his fists and isn't going to let the intellectuals or money-grabbers or fake patriots take his flag away from him, that's how he feels and it's all there in Orwell's writing. (247)

This is part of a long stream-of-consciousness section that details Ray's further exploration of literature that he feels speaks directly to his situation: Ray Bradbury, Albert Camus, Aldous Huxley, Alan Sillitoe and Aleksandr Solzhenitsyn. The organic, autodidactic development of Ray's reading at this point is emphasized and this self-education replaces, to a certain extent, his love of music, and indeed helps to temper his previously angry feelings, 'keeping his mind active so he doesn't go mad about things like he did before, and he has to admit, if he's honest, that he's never felt better in his life' (250). In his rendering of Ray, King avoids the patronizing tone that often attends middle-class presentation of working-class figures in fiction. It also rejects the level of ironic distance that is a prominent feature of Malkani's novel.

However, this section is set in 1984 and represents a maturing Ray who has reached a certain stepping back from his more extreme political views. Earlier flashbacks detail his involvement in racial violence, most notably in the chapter 'Running Riot in '81', which describes what the tabloid press (especially the *Daily Mail*) at the time dubbed a 'race riot' in Southall on 14 July 1981, where a number of skinheads and members of the Southall Asian community were involved in clashes on the high street and around the Hambrough Tavern where a gig with two Oi bands (4-Skins and The Business) was taking place. In part, Ray's narrative is keen to address what he considers to be the misrepresentation of the events of that night in the popular press and suggests that rather than starting the violence, the skinheads were attacked on their way to the gig. Ray's narrative, however, in its replication of the racist language used on the night seems to undermine the claim of innocence he makes for the skinheads.

The novel, then, sets in opposition two versions of the skinhead culture as represented by Terry and Ray, and it is in the figure of Terry's son Lol that this opposition is played out in 2000s' Britain. King identifies the way in which, through his upbringing, Lol has been forced to negotiate the learned ideologies from his familial influences: 'being born into a skinhead family you didn't have much choice about how you grew up – the music you liked – he had been raised on his mum and dad's ska records – Ray's Oi – and Lol was the place where it all collided' (61). Lol has shortened his name from Laurel, the name given to him by Terry after the Jamaican ska artist Laurel Aitkin, and this ownership of his name represents a claim for an independent identity although it is still framed by a received cultural reference. Lol's cultural affiliations are reflective of a post-subcultural hybridity of previous styles and he is linked to the contemporary group his uncle Ray notices emerging in west London called the BB-Boys: 'This new wave of kids pissed all over the acid-house rave brigade. Things were looking up. The Nineties had belonged to the children of the hippies, drugged-up flower-power babies charging top dollar for peace and love. The offspring of the skins and punks and football hooligans were claiming the new century' (69). Lol is more interested than Ray and Terry were in forming his own band and taking ownership of the music that forms a crucial part of the subcultural identity. Lol's narrative is more typical of the subcultural novel in that it represents the typical bildungsroman, however, in Lol's case this is not a conflict with the parent culture, but a continuation of that culture against the mainstream. This offers a new kind of articulation of subcultural identity than that marked out in classic studies of subcultures from the Birmingham School, for example in Phil Cohen's 'Subcultural Conflict and Working Class Community', and John Clarke's 'The Skinheads and the Magical Recovery of Community'.

King's narrative style is to show not tell and the authenticity of the various positions and outlooks represented in the intersection between Terry, Ray and Lol forms a commentary on white working-class culture in Britain from the 1960s to the present. Although the novel at times appears to present an uncritical account of racist ideologies, especially in the figure of Ray, it does so in a way that encourages the reader to challenge them and shows how they are embedded in broader cultural relations. It also complicates the way in which this particular subculture is unfairly identified in the mainstream media as inevitably right wing.

Alex Wheatle, *East of Acre Lane* (2001)

Although also set in London, in contrast to King's *Skinheads*, Alex Wheatle's fiction focuses on African-Caribbean ethnicities. Wheatle produced two novels between 2000 and 2010 that engage with the representation of youth subcultures: *East of Acre Lane* (2001) and *The Dirty South* (2008). These follow on from his late 1990s' debut novel, *Brixton Rock*, which explored the Rastafarian subculture in South London in the early 1980s. While *The Dirty South* is set in the 2000s, *East of Acre Lane* continues Wheatle's interest in reassessing the subcultural environment of the early 1980s, a period of course that was charged with community tensions around Brixton and other south London suburbs culminating in the riots of 1981. The novel is focalized through Biscuit (real name Lincoln), an eighteen-year-old who, because he finds it difficult to gain legitimate employment, carves out a living by selling drugs and engaging in other low-level criminal exploits. When the text opens he has transgressed one of the unwritten laws of the subculture by inadvertently burgling an apartment that turns out to belong to the girlfriend of the brother of Nunchaks, 'the Brixtonian crime lord' (1). By the time he discovers his mistake, he has sold the goods on and much of the plot revolves around him trying to get the property back in order to stave off a beating from Nunchaks and his gang. As with much of Wheatle's writing, however, the plot is not necessarily the primary function of the novel. As with many subcultural novels, Wheatle's aim is to provide an accurate description of the lifestyle, language and outlook of the subculture on which the novel focuses. Alongside Courttia Newland, Wheatle is one of the first writers to convey this particular inner-city culture in fiction and *East of Acre Lane* contains a certain amount of reportage. The novel, however, avoids some of the clunkiness that can be found in early subcultural novels such as the sections in Colin MacInnes' *Absolute Beginners* where the interpretation of the teenager's environment is delivered with a foresight that seems closer to MacInnes' forty-year-old sensibility than that of the teenager that is supposed to be telling us the story. Wheatle's documentary impulse is more subtly embedded in the (often comic) scenes and passages of dialogue it offers, and references are made in the various conversations between Biscuit and his friends and other members of the subculture – Coffin Head, Sceptic, Yardieman and Frank – that reveal the events and political contexts concerning them in the first few months of 1981. Several references are made to the killing of Blair Peach by the police at an anti-racism rally in 1979 and to the tensions between the police and black and Asian youth in Brixton. One of the novel's aims is to offer an authentic, street-level account of the riots in Brixton in April 1981 and to counter the reporting of the events in the mainstream press. The inter-subcultural violence and concerns encountered by the main characters in the first parts of the novel slip away in the face of the riots as the police become the common enemy, and the various factions within the subculture unite against them. This form of subaltern representation is inevitably partial but offers concrete, everyday causes for the release of violence at this particular historical juncture. The politicization and aggression apparent during the riots are thereby firmly located in a narrative of cause and effect with the events and climate in the months and years preceding them, including high levels of unemployment amongst South London youth, poor housing conditions and resentment over the unfair targeting of Black and Asian people by the police through the hated 'sus' laws. These laws allowed the police to stop and search any person suspected (without concrete evidence) of being involved in criminal activity. As the Lord Scarman Report into the 1981 Riots in Brixton found, these laws were often used unfairly by the police to target African-Caribbean youth, and in part contributed to the outpouring of violence on the London streets.

Part of the development of the novel's recording of subaltern identities is to create a sense of belonging within an authentic description of the subcultural world evoked by reference to music, fashion and lifestyle. Music in particular is used to glue together the sense of scene and plot development and musical references track the feelings and outlook of the characters. This produces a form of pathetic fallacy, as often the music is part of the environment in which the characters move. For example, in a scene in which Biscuit talks to Frank Huggins about his desperate attempts to find a job, they overhear someone playing UB40's 'One In Ten' in the block of flats where they live: '"They got it right, innit", commented Frank. "One in ten *are* unemployed. How much is that in the whole country" / "Bout five million", answered Biscuit' (101). One memorable scene relating to musical knowledge and identity involves Biscuit being asked what appears as the equivalent of a bank's security questions when he visits a new dealer to score some 'collie'. The questions are all based on an intimate knowledge of the local DJs, clubs and sound crews, which Biscuit shows he can name with ease. As with *Londonstani*, this indicates the way in which subcultural capital and knowledge allows an individual to gain legitimacy within the subculture.

The use of music to parallel the politics of the situation can also be seen after another character, Coffin Head (Everton Beckford), is arrested, taken to an unknown police station and beaten up by six officers in an attempt to get him to provide the names of people dealing heroin and cocaine in the area. Afterwards, when he visits Biscuit, he hears Burning Spear's 'Jah A Guh Raid' and 'he couldn't help but concentrate his ears on the haunting lyrics' (121). These lyrics return to the refrain, 'Some one gots to pay/Jah A Guh Raid', matching Coffin Head's desire to get revenge in some way for the beating he has received, and anticipating the anger against the police revealed in the riots that are presented later in the novel. Coffin Head becomes increasingly politicized, reading up on Eldridge Cleaver and the Black Panther movement, and consequently buys an illegal gun from a white skinhead in a pub in Rotherhithe, identified as 'National Front country' (145). He intends to use the gun on a policeman in revenge for the beating he received in the cells. As he explains to his friend Sceptic, 'It seems you forget wha' dem did to you an' me Friggin pigs dem, all dey do is jus brutalise us. Why do we affe tek it, man?' (246). Sceptic's unspoken response to Coffin Head's question reveals a more pragmatic approach to the realities of racist attitudes to black youth endemic in the policing of London in the early 1980s: 'Sceptic looked upon his friend with concern, wondering why Coffin Head couldn't just complain to his brethrens about the police beatings he received, rant about it, then accept it as part of life for a black youth living in the inner city' (246). It is the context of this breakdown of relations between the police and the black and Asian communities that forms the backdrop for the detailed ground-level description of the violence that erupts on the streets of Brixton in April 1981, and in which Coffin Head is heavily involved, although he chooses not to use his gun as he originally intended.

Although Coffin Head, Biscuit and their immediate friends do not get involved in organized political action, *East of Acre Lane* provides an understanding of the way in which the characters negotiate a set of lived ideologies. An important figure in this context is Jah Nelson, whom Wheatle uses as a spokesman for the political (and spiritual) aspects of Rastafarianism. Jah Nelson listens to Burning Spear and in his flat 'the ancient map of Africa looked down from the wall' (155). When Biscuit visits him, Nelson instructs him in the history of the Rastafarian movement and the reasons why it represents a discourse of resistance against racist ideologies in Britain. Nelson is blind in one eye, which is either an indication that his political and religious outlook does not see the whole picture in the context of Britain in the early 1980s, or that he appears as a kind of seer, a modern-day Tiresias whose special vision can see the actual ideological contexts behind the false consciousness attending many in the subculture. As Nelson explains because of his travels and acquired (political) knowledge, 'My eye dem are fully open now, albeit jus' de one' (163). The name Nelson, of course, is also reminiscent of another heroic figure with one eye, Horatio Nelson.

Like many good subcultural novels, *East of Acre Lane* succeeds in portraying the range of nuanced feelings, motivations and ethical outlooks that exist within a subculture and that are often overlooked in the media presentation of a homogenized construction of deviant youth. The novel, then, is clear in its political agenda, although it avoids the polemical in its representation of the everyday lives of those living in the Brixton area during the period of the riots in 1981. In its description of petty (and sometimes more serious) criminality, it can be accused of reproducing stereotypes, to a certain extent, about youth from African-Caribbean ethnicities in London, nevertheless it also offers an authentic set of the ideological contexts against which that behaviour can be understood.[4]

Stewart Home, *Tainted Love* (2005)

As with Alex Wheatle's aim to produce an authentic portrayal of growing up in South London in the early 1980s, Stewart Home's *Tainted Love* also claims fidelity in its presentation of the excesses of Britain's counterculture of the 1960s. Whereas Wheatle's and King's fiction draws on a tradition of British working-class realism, Home is more influenced by surrealist experimentation as established in the early to mid-part of the twentieth century and avant-garde writing developed in the period that forms the main setting for *Tainted Love*. The novel claims to be the authentic account of Jilly O'Sullivan, purportedly based on the life of Home's real mother, Julia Callan-Thompson. There is a framing device at the opening of the text, in which Jilly's son, Lloyd O'Sullivan, explains in a note dated 2005 that what constitutes the text is his mother's notes towards her autobiography, which Lloyd has edited.[5] Jilly's narrative is also presented through other kinds of material including a fictional interview with the real-life psychedelic psychiatrist R.D. Laing, whom Jilly counts as one of her friends, and a film script written by Lloyd based on aspects of his mother's life.

In terms of the representation of a subculture, then, Home's novel is of the second type mentioned in the introduction of this chapter, in that it looks to the past. Given that rose-tinted spectacles are a feature of the 1960s, it is somewhat telling that Home's novel certainly sheds these in his representation, through Jilly, of the hedonistic and ultimately self-destructive lifestyle of those associated with the counterculture during the decade. Home's conceit is that Jilly is at the heart of the development of this counterculture in 1960s' London, and her life maps the variety of cultural and subcultural transitions of that decade. To do this, he presents Jilly as meeting, and often having intimate relationships with, a series of figures that have become central to the public consciousness of the period. She claims as her friends and acquaintances Ronnie and Reggie Kray, Philip Rachman, R.D. (Ronnie) Laing, Alexander Trocchi, Michael Reeves, Colin MacInnes, Michael de Freitas (Michael X), John Lennon and several others who are crucial to Britain's cultural revolution in the 1960s. Her life during the decade maps popular cultural history as a series of transitions: the novel begins with her early involvement and then rejection of the CND movement, attachment to beatnik culture, association with the hippy movement in the mid-1960s (including the stereotypical trip to India to find spiritual enlightenment), and then the darker turn the decade takes in conventional accounts in the later 1960s and into the early 1970s, ending with descriptions of the arrival of punk, reggae and skinhead revival subcultures in the mid-1970s.

In this way Jilly is used as an embodiment of popular cultural history in a way that is reminiscent of Woody Allen's *Zelig*, who happens to be present at key moments of the twentieth century. In Home's novel, Jilly is 'seventeen years old in the summer of 1961' (15) and is on the borders of the beatnik and hipster scene in the early 1960s, although this cultural milieu is also shown to dovetail with London's criminal underground. Jilly acts as an escort and prostitute, placed eventually in the employ of the Kray twins. She becomes pregnant during this period, and although she does not disclose the father, J.F. Kennedy is rumoured as a possibility. To cover for Reggie Kray's homosexuality, which he feels undermines his gangster image, she is paid to lose a paternity suit against him. As she describes the Krays: 'On the surface the Krays appeared impressive but underneath they were complete phonies their image had no more substance than the Hollywood gangster movies on which they modelled themselves' (14). This interweaving of real-life individuals with fictional characters and situations sets the pattern for the rest of the novel. In this way it draws on a number of literary conventions from the bildungsroman and eighteenth-century picaresque to the semi-pornographic pulp fiction that came to prominence in the postwar period (see Osgerby, 2012). Whether Home is parodying that kind of novel is difficult to determine and his reported celebration of Richard Allen's series of Skinhead novels in the 1970s suggests that the form is more a 'complicitous critique', to use a term coined by Linda Hutcheon, if not a wholehearted homage to that kind of popular pulp novel (1989). It could also be described as a type of fiction that evokes what Hutcheon in *A Poetics of Postmodernism* calls 'historiographic metafiction', although it is clear that in Home's novel the fiction outweighs the historical accuracy or the concern with theoretical problems of representing the past in Jilly's lurid account of the 1960s' counterculture. Indeed, Home quite often self-consciously writes against the kind of literary novel that is usually described by Hutcheon's term, and historical accuracy is not part of his aim. Home's involvement in anarchist politics involves a radical disruption of what he sees as the conventions of established literary culture in Britain, and his comments about Richard Allen's work should certainly not be seen as aping the political sentiments of the earlier writer's fiction.

Behind the underground exoticism and exaggerated encounters with the decade's heroes and anti-heroes, Home offers a social critique of aspects of British culture during the period. For example, in the fourth chapter, 'Mother of Shame', Jilly details the attitudes to unmarried mothers in the early 1960s. After becoming pregnant, Jilly tries to get assistance from several social bodies and is eventually given an interview with Sister Wesson, a 'moral welfare worker' who offers to help her but only under strict caveats: 'As I left Sister Wesson told me not to return unless I was ready to move into accommodation that was suitable for an unmarried woman' (37). Jilly is eventually forced to put her baby up for adoption. (This baby is Lloyd.) As Jilly shows: 'In 1962 it really wasn't acceptable for a girl to keep a baby born out of wedlock. Even in the beatnik circles I moved in it wasn't easy to bring up a child outside of marriage' (32). There is a similar critique of the aggressive and racially coded rental practices in London in the period, focused through the figure of Peter Rachman, although the text makes it clear that Rachman became the most notorious example of a widespread practice amongst greedy landlords during the period.

Alongside the social critique, Home aims to counter the fashionable reconstruction of the 1960s in the public consciousness and to undercut the hero status that many cultural commentators and pop historians have proffered to key figures. In one scene, for example, John Lennon is presented as being masturbated by Jilly (who is projecting as his mother) while tripping on LSD and heroin. The racial politics of Michael de Freitas, Britain's most important Black Power figure in the 1960s, is also sent up in the narrative: at one point Jilly reports Michael's comments:

> 'You know, Jilly, I'm sure glad you an Alex is Celtic, because once this race war gets going we're all gonna be offing whitey.'... Michael carried on in this vein for the entire journey, stressing among other things that John Lennon, who we were going to visit, could trace his roots back to Ireland.... He needn't have worried about this. Everyone knew the Beatles were an easy touch, since to use a phrase that Michael was fond of applying to any potential sponsor, they had money falling out of their assholes. (90–1)

Here, Home clearly determines that any political or idealistic motivation in the 1960s is at base embedded on an exploitative system of acquiring money.

There is a particularly dismissive account of Colin MacInnes, who is described by Jilly as 'mad for black rough trade, mad to break with the key values of the adult world which he had never properly joined, but above all mad to meet characters that might bring his rather contrived novels to life' (69), and who is reported as saying 'I'm drunk on cool. I'm so cool so cool I don't feel the heat. I'm the Jesus of cool. A man who absolutely refuses to repeat himself' (77). MacInnes, of course, is interesting in the context of this chapter, as he is probably the first novelist in the postwar period concerned with detailing the daily lives of youth subcultures. In his ground-breaking *Absolute Beginners*, MacInnes offers descriptions of teenagers (as a specific subculture), Ted culture, jazz fans (Mod and Trad), beatniks and Marxist folk fans providing contemporary readers with representations of the diversity within the media-constructed images of deviant youth or teenagers (as a broad group), although it has to be said that MacInnes' representation of Teddy Boys reproduces rather than interrogates the moral panic surrounding this particular subculture in the 1950s (see Bentley, 2010). However, Home, through Jilly, decides to focus on what are perceived to be MacInnes' ulterior motives in focusing on youth, African-Caribbean and gay subcultures in his London Trilogy of novels. In comparison with Alexander Trocchi, another important countercultural writer of the period, Jilly dismisses MacInnes with the following: 'MacInnes continued to churn out pot-boilers long after his brief and undeserved moment in the limelight had passed. In sharp contrast my genuinely gifted friend Alex Trocchi ceased publishing fiction when he had nothing left to say' (71).

This distinction between the two novelists is illuminating in terms of placing Home's formal influences. Trocchi, in contrast to MacInnes, was author of a number of subcultural texts in the 1950s including *Young Adam* (1957) and *Cain's Book* (1960), which are a mixture of anarchist accounts of heroin abuse and avant-garde, surrealist experimentation, and it is in this tradition that Home appears to want to place his own fiction. In political terms this kind of anarchism eschews practical political commentary under the veneer of an exotic and surrealist performance of subversion. I agree with Home that Trocchi is the better writer, however, despite his reported ulterior motives MacInnes offers a set of practical (although perhaps simplistic) subversive sentiments and genuinely anti-racist feeling, unlike Trocchi's (and Home's) rather individualistic and self-destructive form of anarchism. In the latter chapters of the novel Jilly describes the later 1970s' subcultural scene, with one section detailing a riot between punks, rastas and skinheads at a Rock Against Racism event. Any genuine political engagement is underplayed as the singer in the reggae band that's performing at the gig explains, 'These anti-racist benefits always end in disaster.... Them Socialist Worker school-teachers say they want reggae band for Rock Against Racism, so I say it cost them £120' (222). Here, mutual pecuniary exploitation is deemed more important than political commitment. Jilly concludes this chapter: 'Thatcher attaining power is a symptom and not the cause of the things that are wrong with London' (224), a statement that registers her ambiguous relationship to the political dichotomies of Left and Right during a decade for which a politics of ambiguity was rarely an option for many working-class people.

Of course, this reading of the text's political positioning is based on how far Jilly's accounts and views are deemed reliable (factually and ideologically) and whether Home is, in fact, indicating a level of ironic distance towards her narrative, as he does in his performance art.[6] It is popularly said that if you remember the 1960s, then you weren't there, however Jilly's account is significantly detailed, especially given her experimentation with most of the available drugs of the period and her eventual heroin addiction. Towards the end of the novel she comments, 'One of the things I'd learned long ago was that in order to lie successfully the best approach is to mix outrageous fabrications with concrete details from factual material one knows inside out' (212), and this might be applied to her accounts throughout the novel, and indeed to Home's approach to fiction generally. It is possible, of course, that this is Home's point; that the cultural memories of a period are inevitably filtered through a haze of nostalgia and/or misremembering, or have been deliberately adjusted for effect. Jilly's accounts of her meetings with key figures of the period, however, are presented as authentic and, although the debilitating effects of drug misuse on her physical and mental health are reported, the veracity of the descriptions of her encounters is not challenged by Lloyd the editor, or by the text as a whole. Characters in novels are, of course, fictional creations, nevertheless they are used as vehicles to transmit ideological positions and the reader is obliged to weigh up their own (political) responses to the sentiments presented. Despite a certain level of ironic distance, readers of *Tainted Love* are encouraged to interpret the various characters Jilly meets (Lennon, Michael X, MacInnes) in the same way that she (and presumably Home) reads them. By extension, then, the text encourages the reader to adopt Jilly's anarchic ambivalence towards recognized political positioning.[7] This emerges as perhaps the final judgement the novel offers of the 1960s, in that the radical promise of the early part of the decade is ultimately snuffed out in the darker drug excesses of the later 1960s and 1970s.

Conclusions

At least two conclusions can be drawn from this survey of novels that address aspects of subcultural life in Britain in the first decade of the twenty-first century. First, the genre is healthy and seems to be growing, both in the sense of critically nostalgic portrayals of previous subcultures and as a way of recording contemporary concerns and anxieties for and about youth. Whether this is related to a market for this kind of work, or whether this reveals a genuine reflection about the way in which social groups organize themselves in contemporary society is debatable. In many ways the construction of smaller, subcultural friendship groups could be indicative of the way in which older forms of affiliation around class have been pushed to the background, or at least manifest in different ways: if class consciousness has waned, as many have argued, then subcultural consciousness still seems to carry weight. Although the older, Birmingham School type of subcultures seems to be outmoded, there is clearly still a sense in which youth internally divides itself into recognized cultural groupings. It is more difficult to label these than it may have been in the past, but the labels themselves were always problematic. A second conclusion relates to the way in which urban youth and perhaps urban culture more generally can be seen to be operating in relation to what Michel Maffesoli identifies as urban tribes. Most of the novels discussed in this chapter take place in London, however, they reveal intimate social worlds, which in many ways seem to be isolated from each other, despite the fact that their concerns around class, ethnicity, gender and age are very similar.

Notes

1. See the work of John Clarke, Phil Cohen, Chas Critcher, Jenny Garber, Stuart Hall, Dick Hebdige, Angela MacRobbie, Paul Gilroy and Paul Willis. The collection *Resistance Through Rituals: Youth Subcultures in Post-War Britain* is a grounding text of the CCCS work on subcultures. See also Ken Gelder's excellent critical overview of the group in 'Subcultures and Cultural Studies: Community, Class and Style at Birmingham and Beyond'.
2. There have been three academic conferences in Britain since 2010 that have focused on youth subcultures: 'Subcultures, Popular Music and Social Change', London Metropolitan University, September, 2011; 'Teenage Kicks: Representations of Youth Subcultures in Fiction, Film and Other Media', Keele University, July 2013; and 'Here by the sea and sand: A symposium on Quadrophenia', University of Sussex, July 2014. The first of these also saw the inauguration of the Subcultures Network: The Interdisciplinary Network for the Study of Subcultures, Popular Music and Social Change.
3. In the original hardback version of this novel, Malkani uses the word 'finesse' instead of 'authenticity' in this passage. The quotation here is taken from the Harper Perennial paperback version of 2007.
4. For a discussion of the Alex Wheatle's *Brixton Rock* in comparison with fiction by Courttia Newland and other postcolonial British writers, see Upstone.
5. Stewart Home's real name is Kevin Llewellyn Callan, and the use of the name Lloyd as Jilly's son, clearly echoes Home's real middle name.
6. In the 'Mission Statement' on the Stewart Home website, the author stresses '"Stewart Home" is a construction'. Available online: http://www.stewarthomesociety.org/mission-statement.htm (accessed 18 August, 2014).
7. This is not to say Home's politics are ambivalent, as can be seen by his engagement with anarchist politics over the last thirty years or so.

Works cited

Adulthood [film]. Dir. Noel Clarke. Pathé Pictures International, 2008.
Ali, Monica. *Brick Lane*. London: Black Swan [2003], 2004.
Allen, Richard. *Skinhead*. London: New English Library, 1970.
Allen, Richard. *Suedehead*. London: New English Library, 1971.
Allen, Richard. *Skinhead Escapes*. London: New English Library, 1972.
Allen, Richard. *Skinhead Girls*. London: New English Library, 1972.
Allen, Richard. *Skinhead Farewell*. London: New English Library, 1974.
Ballard, J.G. *Kingdom Come*. London: Fourth Estate, 2006.
Barker, Nicola. *Behindlings*. London: Flamingo, 2002.

Bentley, Nick. 'The Young Ones: A Reassessment of the British New Left's Representation of 1950s Youth Subcultures'. *European Journal of Cultural Studies* 8:1 (2005): 65–83.

Bentley, Nick. '"New Elizabethans": The Representation of Youth Subcultures in 1950s British Fiction'. *Literature & History* 19:1 (2010): 16–33.

Burning Spear. 'Jah A Guh Raid' [song]. *Hail H.I.M.* UK. Radic, 1980.

Butler, Judith. *Gender Trouble: Feminism and the Subversion of Identity* London: Routledge, 1990.

Clarke, John. 'The Skinheads and the Magical Recovery of Community'. In S. Hall and T. Jefferson, Eds. *Resistance Through Rituals: Youth Subcultures in Post-war Britain*. London: Hutchinson, 1976, 99–102.

Coe, Jonathan. *The Rotters' Club*. London: Viking, 2001.

Cohen, Phil. 'Subcultural Conflict and Working Class Community'. In Ann Gray, Jan Campbell, Mark Erickson, Stuart Hanson and Helen Wood, Eds. *CCCS Selected Working Papers, Volume 1*. London: Routledge [1972], 2007.

Collins, Michael. *The Likes of Us: A Biography of the White Working Class*. London: Granta, 2004.

Fishtank [film]. Dir. Andrea Arnold. BBC Films, UK Film Council, IFC Films, 2009.

Four Lions [film]. Dir. Chris Morris. Optimum Releasing and Drafthouse Films, 2010.

Gelder, Ken. *Subcultures: Cultural Histories and Social Practice*. Abingdon and New York: Routledge, 2007.

Gelder, Ken. 'Subcultures and Cultural Studies: Community, Class and Style at Birmingham and Beyond'. *Subcultures: Cultural Histories and Social Practice*. Abingdon and New York: Routledge, 2007, 83–106.

Green Street [film]. Dir. Lexi Alexander. Universal Pictures, 2005.

Griffiths, Niall. *Grits*. London: Jonathan Cape, 2000.

Hall, Stuart, and Tony Jefferson, Eds. *Resistance Through Rituals: Youth Subcultures in Post-War Britain*. London: Hutchinson & Co Ltd, 1976.

Hebdige, Dick. *Subculture: The Meaning of Style*. London: Methuen & Co., 1979.

Hodkinson, Paul. *Goth. Identity, Style and Subculture*. London: Berg Publishers, 2002.

Hodkinson, Paul, and Wolfgang Deicke, Eds. *Youth Cultures: Scenes, Subcultures and Tribes*. London and New York: Routledge, 2007.

Home, Stewart. *Tainted Love*. London: Virgin Books, 2005.

Huq, Rupa. *Beyond Subculture: Pop, Youth and Identity in a Postcolonial World*. London: Routledge, 2006.

Huq, Rupa. *On the Edge: the Contested Culture of English Suburbia*. London: Lawrence and Wishart, 2012.

Hutcheon, Linda. *A Poetics of Postmodernism: History, Theory, Fiction*. London and New York: Routledge, 1988.

Hutcheon, Linda. *The Politics of Postmodernism*. London and New York: Routledge, 1989.

Ill Manors [film]. Dir. Plan B. Revolver Entertainment, 2012.
Ishiguro, Kazuo. *Never Let Me Go*. London: Faber & Faber, 2005.
Jones, Owen. *Chavs: The Demonization of the Working Class*. London: Verso, 2011.
Kidulthood [film]. Dir. Noel Clarke. Revolver Entertainment, 2006.
King, John. *The Football Factory*. London: Jonathan Cape, 1997.
King, John. *Headhunters*. London: Jonathan Cape, 1998.
King, John. *England Away*. London: Jonathan Cape, 1999.
King, John. *Human Punk*. London: Jonathan Cape, 2000.
King, John. *Skinheads*. London: Jonathan Cape, 2008.
Kureishi, Hanif. *The Buddha of Suburbia*. London: Faber and Faber, 1990.
Kureishi, Hanif. *Gabriel's Gift*. London: Faber and Faber, 2001.
Laclau, Ernesto, and Chantal Mouffe. *Hegemony and Socialist Strategy*. London: Verso, 1985.
MacInnes, Colin. *Absolute Beginners*. London: MacGibbon & Kee, 1959.
Maffesoli, Michel. *The Time of the Tribes: the Decline of Individualism in Mass Society*. Translated by Don Smith. London: Sage, 1996.
Malkani, Gautam. *Londonstani*. London: Fourth Estate, 2006.
Malkani, Gautam. *Londonstani*. London: Harper Perennial [2006]2007.
Miéville, China. *Kraken*. London: Macmillan, 2010.
Miller, Alison. *Demo*. London: Penguin, 2006.
Neds [film]. Dir. Peter Mullan. E1 Entertainment, 2010.
Newland, Courttia. *Society Within*. London: Abacus, 1999.
Osgerby, William. *Playboys in Paradise: Masculinity, Youth and Leisure-Style in Modern America*. Oxford: Berg/New York University Press, 2001.
Osgerby, William. *Youth and the Media*. London: Routledge, 2004.
Osgerby, William. '"Bovver" Books of the 1970s: Subcultures, Crisis and "Youth-Sploitation" Novels'. *Contemporary British History* 26:3 (2012): 229–331.
Riley, Gwendolen. *Sick Notes*. London: Vintage, 2004.
Robinson, John. 'The social construction of deviant identities: the devil wears a hoodie'. In Derek Kassem, Lisa Murphy and Elizabeth Taylor, Eds. *Key Issues in Childhood and Youth Studies*. Abingdon and New York: Routledge, 2010, 125–35.
Shamsie, Kamila. 'How many a us bredren b here?' Review of *Londonstani* by Gautam Malkani. *Guardian*. 6 May 2006.
Shields, Rob. 'Foreword: Masses or Tribes'. In Michel Maffesoli, Ed. *The Time of the Tribes: the Decline of Individualism in Mass Society*. Translated by Don Smith. London: Sage, 1996.
Sillitoe, Alan. *Saturday Night and Sunday Morning*. London: W.H. Allen & Co Ltd, 1958.
Smith, Zadie. *White Teeth*. London: Hamish Hamilton, 2000.
Smith, Zadie. *On Beauty*. London: Hamish Hamilton, 2005.
Stretch, Joe. *Friction*. London: Vintage, 2008.
Sweet Sixteen [film]. Dir. Ken Loach. Icon Film Distribution, 2002.
This is England [film]. Dir. Shane Meadows. Optimum Releasing, 2006.

Thornton, Sarah. *Club Cultures: Music, Media, and Subcultural Capital*. Cambridge: Polity Press, 1995.
Top Boy [TV programme]. Dir. Yann Demange (Series 1) and Jonathan van Tulleken (Series 2). Channel 4, October 2011–September 2013.
Trainspotting [film]. Dir. Danny Boyle. Channel Four Films, PolyGram Filmed Entertainment, 1996.
Tyler, Imogen. *Revolting Subjects: Social Abjection and Resistance in Neoliberal Britain*. London: Zed Books, 2013.
UB40. 'One in Ten' [song]. *Present Arms*. DEP International, 1981.
Upstone, Sara. 'Postcolonial Voices'. In Nick Hubble, Philip Tew and Leigh Wilson, Eds. *The 1990s: A Decade of Contemporary British Fiction*. London: Bloomsbury, 2015, 123–48.
Waterhouse, Keith. *Billy Liar*. London: Michael Joseph, 1959.
Weinzierl, Rupert and David Muggleton. 'What is "Post-subcultural Studies" Anyway?' In David Muggleton and Rupert Weinzierl. Eds. *The Postsubcultures Reader*. Oxford: Berg, 2002, 3–23.
Welsh, Irvine. *Trainspotting*. London: Secker & Warburg, 1993.
Wheatle, Alex. *Brixton Rock*. London: BlackAmber Books, 1999.
Wheatle, Alex. *East of Acre Lane*. London: Fourth Estate, 2001.
Wheatle, Alex. *The Dirty South*. London: Serpent's Tail, 2008.
Zelig [film]. Dir. Woody Allen. Warner Bros., 1983.

3

Special Topic 2

Translating Neuroscience: Fictions of the Brain in the 2000s

Laura Salisbury

In 1990, the forty-first President of the United States used Proclamation 6158 to designate this decade without the Berlin Wall or the Iron Curtain as the inauguration of something new:

> Now, Therefore, I, George Bush, President of the United States of America, do hereby proclaim the decade beginning January 1, 1990, as the Decade of the Brain. I call upon all public officials and the people of the United States to observe that decade with appropriate programs, ceremonies, and activities. (n.p.)

One can imagine the surprise or even scorn that would have been poured on Bush had he hailed a decade of the liver or the kidneys, or had someone determined that the 1990s might be thought of as the decade of the stomach. The decade of the brain, however, has both logic and gravitas because contemporary Western culture is insistent that the human brain is determinedly singular – the organ of the mind and place where flesh and those seemingly immaterial aspects of subjectivity are inextricably entwined. Bush's proclamation, of course, addresses the extraordinary impact of the 'cognitive revolution' of the second half of the twentieth century, in which scientific attention was refocused on to the structural workings of mental processes within the material brain rather than the behaviours they produced. Using approaches developed in the fields of artificial intelligence and cybernetics in the 1950s, computer science, neuroscience, psychology, anthropology and linguistics all went on to develop accounts of the relationship between brain and mind as products of evolutionary biology – of biochemical genetics and Darwinian natural selection. By the 1990s, an extraordinary scientific consensus had emerged on the subject of the human mind: that mental life and the very sense of subjectivity itself are somehow produced by the workings of an evolved neurological substrate, even if more nuanced scientific accounts have been careful to insist that mental life cannot simply be reduced to the neuronal. Indeed, it is perhaps rather clearer now in the 2010s, after decades of mapping projects and attempts to translate neurobiology into psychological correlates, that mind, though dependent on a singular brain, is not simply an epiphenomenon of it, and that personhood cannot quite be reduced to that baggy but still discursively dominant category of mind. Even if there has been a temptation to assert that 'we are our brains', as reductionists would have it – that there is and can be no *deus* outside of the *machina* – many producers and readers of neuroscience are still seeking to press on the fact that it remains unclear precisely how neuronal processes work within the brain and extended nervous system and how they interact with an environment to realize specific aspects of subjective experience.

Despite the application of various forms of critical brakes to the neuro-turn, we nevertheless remain firmly within a historical moment in which '"the social," and "life" itself have ... undergone a refashioning as a result of the new life sciences in general and neurobiology in particular' (146), as Roger Cooter has recently put it. This is a turn that has seen internalized psychological notions of personhood and identity apparently ceding their dominance to what Fernando Vidal calls, in his 'Brainhood, Anthropological Figure of Modernity', the 'cerebral subject', or Nikolas Rose, in an essay from 2003, the 'neurochemical self'. With the self reframed as a property of the brain's neural architecture, networks, neurotransmitters, and even its genes, in the 1990s and 2000s there was a strong sense of a new terrain opening up that might require the remapping of our epistemologies and ontologies. While the clear purpose of Bush's proclamation was to insert government into this as yet to be fully determined space through 'programs aimed at introducing Members of Congress, their staffs, and the general public to cutting-edge research on the brain and encouraging public dialogue on the ethical, philosophical, and humanistic implications of these emerging discoveries' (n.p.), one might argue that these are exactly the areas the novel has traditionally seen as its home turf. And in 2009, as the decade of the brain was drawing to a close, Marco Roth suggested that the novel had not been idle in staking its claim, as he coined the term 'neuronovels' for a striking set of fictions that explored the

> cultural (and, in psychology proper, a disciplinary) shift away from environmental and relational theories of personality back to the study of brains themselves, as the source of who we are. This cultural sea change ... began with the exhaustion of 'the linguistic turn' in the humanities, in the 1980s, and the discredit psychoanalysis suffered, around the same time. (n.p.)

It is indeed possible to mark out neuronovels as a significant subgenre of literary fiction of the 2000s – one that explicitly works through the implications of the cognitive revolution for what the literary novel, since the nineteenth century, has considered a privileged mode of working: the penetration of consciousness, the exploration of the workings of the human mind, and the mapping of a subjectivity that could both bear the weight of, and act as a lodestone for, the autonomous, liberal, perhaps even moral individual.

2005 functions as a peculiar *annus mirabilis* for British literary fictions of the brain. It is the year that Ian McEwan publishes *Saturday* – a novel that directly explores the biological basis of mental life and human personality through the experiences and musings of a brain surgeon who comes into violent contact with a man who has Huntington's Disease. Sebastian Faulks publishes *Human Traces* in the same year, turning his central focus of attention from the experience of war, which for him and so many authors of literary fiction in the late 1980s and 1990s had become a synecdoche for exploring trauma and its attendant reshaping of body and mind, to a teasing out of the relationship between psychiatric disorder and neurological dysfunction and damage. Faulks explicitly follows the emergent discipline of late nineteenth- and early twentieth-century neurology and the split between neurobiological and psychoanalytic accounts of disordered selfhood as an occasion for exploring the point where soma somehow becomes translated into psyche. Although it was written in 2001, 2005 also saw the publication of Tom McCarthy's first novel, *Remainder*, which uses the subject of a traumatic head wound to explore a world denuded of a subjectivity freighted with the emotional continuities and perceptions of contained transcendence that somehow anchor it to a sensation of reality. Broadening one's focus from 2005, one finds David Lodge's *Thinks . . .* (2001), a campus novel focusing on the thoughts, feelings and writings of a professor of cognitive science and a novelist teaching creative writing. There is also Mark Haddon's *A Curious Incident of the Dog in the Night-time* (2003), which uses a narrator, usually taken to have a neurological disorder that forms part of the autistic spectrum, to produce an effect of estrangement that roughens up and renders opaquely revealing the capacities and oddities of its imagined neuro-typical readers. McEwan returns to neurological damage in the figure of a mother living with the psychological discontinuity produced by a head-wound in *On Chesil Beach* (2007), while Michael Nath's debut novel, *La Rochelle* (2010), uses the first person perspective of a neurologist to thicken, rather than to reduce, an account of how lives might be enmeshed in complex networks of psychological attachments and resistant matter.[1]

Following Roth, one might read the neurological turn in British fictions of the 2000s as something that mirrors an increasing suspicion of psychoanalytic accounts of mind within the discipline of psychology. As science refocused its attention on the putative solidity and empirically testable 'reality' of a psychology linked to neurological functioning, maybe culture simply followed. If much fiction in the 1990s was dominated by accounts of mind that emerged from and worked to reproduce what Roger Luckhurst, in *The Trauma Question*, calls 'trauma culture', a significant strand of fiction in the 2000s did turn its attention from psychological wounding, so central to psychoanalytic accounts of selfhood, to the extraordinary, though seemingly 'mindless' reconfigurations and displacements of so-called 'normal' subjective experience that attend neurological damage or dysfunction. Novels such as McEwan's *Atonement* (2001) and Faulks' *Birdsong* (1993) specifically entangle the intolerable experiences of war with the psychic fault lines psychoanalysis suggests are the inevitable sequelae of the production of a sexual identity, emphasizing the centrality of psychological damage both to their narrative content and to their form. Both novels, at least partially, shape stories and modes of narration that mime a psychoanalytically inflected notion of subjective splitting along the line of a psychic wound.[2] In *Saturday* and *Human Traces*, however, there is a clear movement towards the startling contingency of neurological disorder. A fault in the sequencing of one's genetic coding, one particular configuration of neuroanatomy, a blow to the head, or an internal 'cerebral accident' like a stroke, are all it takes to break both the realist and the psychoanalytic narrative of personality apart.[3]

In *The New Wounded: From Neurosis to Brain Damage*, the philosopher Catherine Malabou asks explicitly what aesthetic might be consonant with the absolute break in psychic continuity that can be the result of neurological damage. '[W]hat rhetoric could possibly account for the breakdown of connections, for destructive metamorphosis. And who would write the aphasic's novel?' (55), she wonders. She reaches for Samuel Beckett and his stylistic 'figures of interruption, pauses, caesuras – the blank spaces that emerge when the network of connections is shredded' (55), but why not the neuronovels of the 2000s? One simple answer is that these novels rarely mime the disintegrated psychic fabric of neurological disturbance, either through a sustained or explicit use of the disruptive formal resources of modernism, or by reconfiguring the shape of the human according to unrecognisably new, scientized topographies. *Remainder* does render palpable the flattened affect, the loss of depth, that Malabou finds distinctive of the neurologically disrupted – those 'new wounded' who, for her, mime the psychical mood of a late capitalism dominated by the persistent breaking of social contracts and connections. In *Saturday*, however, the narration works towards modelling a self undergirded by a significant phenomenological attention to feelings of subjective experience that invoke a reasonably continuous psychological self. Though not allergic to all modernist technique – and we will explore later the significance of free indirect style in *Saturday* – McEwan persistently lays emphasis on aesthetic modes that work to support a sense of a thick, deep, and recognizably 'real' psychology over the lacunae and impenetrable resistances of subjectivity that some modernist forms foreground. As such, networks of connection are made and remade rather than shredded; and what is broken is gathered up in the implicit humanism of a particular novelistic version of psychological realism.

In this chapter, I will explore the ways in which neuronovels of the 2000s ask questions of the status of subjective, phenomenal experience, and of the kind of affective landscape one finds the self inhabiting, when, as Nikolas Rose puts it in *The Politics of Life Itself*, 'the deep psychological space that opened in the twentieth century has flattened out' (192). This represents a major thematic and sometimes also a formal shift from the emphasis on psychological trauma, fractured memory, and depth psychological models of subjectivity of the 1980s and 1990s, with neuromaterialism frequently functioning as a strong attempt to anchor reality and subjectivity to forms of matter and evidence that might resist the vagaries – those slippings and slidings – of representation associated with modernism and postmodernism. And yet, despite a repeated insistence on the seemingly irrefragable connection between neuronal activity and mental life, the concentration in these texts on phenomenological experience and affective bonds also offers up a sense that mind, and indeed subjectivity (which may not simply be coterminous with mind), might exceed what is located within the head. Paradoxically, though the neuronovel of the 2000s uses the authority of neuroscience to subtend a commitment to a material reality of human subjectivity that takes the novel behind modernism's angsty subjective aporias, and the games of representation that mark literary postmodernism, it nevertheless finds itself exploring modes of linguistic and literary representation that implicitly redistribute and sometimes even critique the localized territory of the cerebral self.

Seeing is believing

A man looks through a window on to a square below and asks himself a question:

> if I look out of the window and see men crossing the square, as I just happen to have done, I normally say that I see the men themselves. . . . Yet do I see any more

than hats and coats which could conceal automatons? I *judge* that they are men. And so something which I thought I was seeing with my eyes is in fact grasped solely by the faculty of judgement which is my mind. (Descartes, *Meditations*, 43–5)

In Descartes' famous thought experiment in the Second Meditation, this scene is used to trace out epistemological limits, or the shapes of what can be known. In this account, however, it becomes clear that one can never really know without the encroachment of doubt's shadow; instead, one can judge. There *is* an external world with its own qualities to be found, but it cannot be grasped directly – only through our perceptions, representations, ideas, memories, concepts; in other words, it can only be accessed through the structures of consciousness. Of course, the Second Meditation also contains Descartes' famous defence of the existence of the thinking, judging self; indeed, his ontology is founded on it: for 'surely I must exist if I convinced myself something' (34–5). '[T]his proposition *I am, I exist*, is necessarily true whenever it is put forward by me or conceived in my mind' (35), he writes. But the Descartes gazing out of his window and exercising his judgement is also invoking another aspect of his sense of the relationship between mind and body. For elsewhere, he writes a materialist account of the body that seems more like the automaton that might whir away under a hat and coat than a person. The body becomes 'a statue or a machine made of earth' in which functions and movements are logically ordered to 'follow from the mere arrangement of the machine's organs every bit as naturally as the movements of a clock or other automaton from the arrangement of its counter-weights or wheels' (*Treatise*, 99, 108). In Descartes' terms, there is a soul, of course, that exercises will over the machine, but it 'is entirely distinct from the body ... and would not fail to be whatever it is, even if the body did not exist' (*Passions*, 127). It is this soul that subtends the idea of the human as a 'thinking thing .... a thing that doubts, affirms, denies, understands a few things, is ignorant of many things, is willing, is unwilling, and also which imagines and has sensory perceptions' (*Meditations*, 49); it is this soul, then, that is both within and somehow outside of the machine, that judgement uses, intuits, and meets when Descartes looks over the square.

For Henry Perowne, the neurosurgeon of Ian McEwan's *Saturday*, a suggestively similar scene produces meditations that at first glance seem to be both more monistic and more ontologically certain than Descartes':

Two figures in dark overcoats are crossing the square diagonally.... They cross towards the far corner of the square, and with his advantage of height and in his curious mood, he not only watches them, but watches over them, supervising their progress with the remote possessiveness of a god. In the lifeless cold, they pass through the night, hot little biological engines with bipedal skills suited to any terrain, endowed with innumerable branching neural networks sunk deep in a knob of bone casing, buried fibres, warm filaments with their invisible glow of consciousness – these engines devise their own tracks. (12–13)

An inheritor of the cognitive revolution and empirically subtended accounts of the relationship between brain matter and what have been understood as 'mental' experiences, Henry also stands at the end of a century of increasingly successful attempts to operate on the brain. He is someone who has scientifically observed the alterations to behaviour and sense of self that pathologies and surgical interventions can produce. Consequently, for him, consciousness cannot be separate from the body; rather, it is an epiphenomenon of these 'hot little biological engines'.

Via the literary modernist technique of free indirect style employed throughout the novel gently to transgress the barrier of the skull and allow the reader into Perowne's head, we hear much of the insistent certainty of his monistic materialism, underpinned by his role as someone who gets to peer at the brains of others: '[i]t isn't an article of faith with him, he knows it for a quotidian fact, the mind is what the brain, mere matter, performs' (67). Indeed, Perowne gets to exemplify what Michel Foucault, in *The Birth of the Clinic*, describes as the founding gesture of positivist modern clinical medicine: Bichat's breaking of the cranium at autopsy in the late eighteenth century. With the aim of extending the reach of the observation of physiological functions beneath the skin and uncovering to the medical gaze solid organs – shapes of corporeality and of pathology – that were previously below the threshold of the visible, the founder of modern pathology and histology cemented the link between seeing (autopsy: from the Greek *autoptes*, 'eye witness') and the production of empirical knowledge:

> The fruit is then opened up. From under the meticulously parted shell, a soft, greyish mass appears, wrapped in viscous, veined skins: a delicate dingy-looking pulp within which – freed at last and exposed at last to the light of day – shines the seat of knowledge. The artisanal skill of the brain-breaker ... the precise, but immeasurable gesture that opens up the plenitude of concrete things, combined with the delicate network of their properties to the gaze, has produced a more scientific objectivity for us than the instrumental arbitrations of quantity. (Foucault, xiii)

The clinical gaze produced samples, organs, and even individual bodies that assumed the solidity of discrete objects to be observed rather than encountered as ideal examples. For Foucault, the penetration of the cranium was thus the beginning of the labour of empirical observation and description in modern medicine.

And yet in McEwan's novel, although we observe Henry thinking of himself as a 'professional reductionist' (272) – a man who gets to see, with an atheist's God's eye view, into the heads of others – he cannot get inside these living 'engines' in the square, these machines of earth: 'You stare at a head, a lushness of hair, and can only guess' (205), he muses later. His position of height over the square does not enable a penetration that produces a kind of seeing that would lead to unmediated knowing; instead, his height makes explicit, through its impression of overseeing, of 'supervising their progress with the remote possessiveness of a god' (13), the fact that subjective representation and indeed a quasi-Cartesian form of judgement has inserted itself between object and seeing subject. But where, for Descartes, thinking and judgement anchors the thinking self to existence, for the contemporary Perowne, subjective judgement all too easily slides into 'guessing'. Here, in the theatre of personal life rather than on the operating table, the steady empiricism of his modern scientific gaze blurs and shades into the troublesome territory of representations – into the concerns of feeling, even of fantasy.

As I have noted elsewhere ('Narration and Neurology'), one of the reasons Perowne is a useful figure for McEwan is that the neurosurgeon and his activities act as a metaphor for both the possibilities and impossibilities of fiction. McEwan has said of the novel as a genre that the 'quality of penetration into other consciousnesses lies at the heart of its moral quest.... [W]hen it shows us intimately, from the inside, other people, it then does extend our sensibilities' ('Author Interview' n.p.). If one possibility of the novel linked to its purported moral purpose is its capacity to get inside people's heads, it is hardly surprising that McEwan's work might repeatedly turn to images of central nervous systems and their casings – spines and particularly skulls – transgressively opened up to the gaze of another. Of course, penetrating the skull without destroying the living brain is available to McEwan's imagination as a scientific possibility in a way that it barely was for, say, Virginia Woolf, when she was imagining herself into the mind of Mrs Dalloway for her one day in central London. While affirming the 'slowly diminishing but still vast ignorance of the brain, and the mind, and the relation between the two' (85–6), Perowne indeed notes that '[r]egularly penetrating the skull with some modest success is a relatively recent adventure' (86). But where Woolf swings and slips easily in and out of different consciousnesses – minds that seem weightless and permeable, as they form part of life as 'a luminous halo, a semi-transparent envelope' ('Modern Fiction' 189) – McEwan focuses on the excited possibility of seeing, even touching, the viscous material substrate inside the skull's box of bone that is taken to underpin the mind. This seems like a gesture that offers to take us beyond 'guessing'. Looking into a surgically opened cranium, Perowne notes that 'it's still not known how this well-protected one kilogram or so of cells encodes information, how it holds experiences, memories, dreams and intentions', but '[h]e doesn't doubt that in years to come, the coding mechanism will be known ... the brain's fundamental secret will be laid open one day' (254). At the same time, however, even Perowne goes on to think, or perhaps to feel as if 'the wonder will remain, that mere wet stuff can make this bright inward cinema of thought, of sight and sound and touch bound into a vivid illusion of an instantaneous present, with a self, another brightly wrought illusion, hovering like a ghost at its centre' (254–5). Despite Henry's belief that this secret will be 'laid open' to the scientific gaze – a faith from which the novel as a whole doesn't really demur – *Saturday* nevertheless implies that seeing is not yet, and perhaps cannot ever be, quite the same thing as truly knowing.

In *Saturday* we certainly become privy to Henry's paradoxical sense that although 'the mind is what the brain, mere matter, performs' (67), seeing inside the head doesn't offer much access to mental life. We hear that before he got to know the woman he will marry, before the intimate contacts of conversation, love, or sex, Henry had been witness to another kind of penetration. '[H]e knew more of her, or at least had *seen* more of her, than any prospective lover could expect' (25; my emphasis), because he had assisted on an operation to remove a tumour from Rosalind's brain. At this point it is the idea of the elegant simplicity of surgery, built on decades of work by others, that intrigues him. Rosalind's face, the stigmata of her identity, is peeled away as the head is entered through the nasal cavity and the tumour removed: 'the remedy was as simple as plumbing.... And yet the making of a safe route into this remote and buried place in the head was a feat of technical mastery and concentration' (44). Following this, her face, 'this particular, beautiful face, was reassembled without a single disfiguring mark' (45), as she is returned to herself with no discernible scar or cut either in her visage or her identity to mark the intrusion. This is a form of perfect surgery, then, where pathology is smoothly excised and an identity with a coherent past and continuous future is fully restored to itself – a future in which Henry can play the part of husband and gain a sense of Rosalind's mind in the humanist territory of a life lived together. But as the novel proceeds, the limits of surgery and indeed the limits of a cognitive neuroscience that takes the matter of the brain as its empirical object are also uncovered. For even when the bone of the skull is broken, a piece lifted away and the brain inspected, Henry knows there will be little to see of the mind. Pondering on the operation he is about to perform on the brain of the man who has threatened his family, Perowne wishes it were true 'that penetrating the skull brings into view not the brain but the mind. Then within the hour he, Perowne, might understand Baxter; and after a lifetime's routine procedures would be among the wisest men on earth' (243). Here, now, the elegant simplicity of knowing how the pipes join together is insufficient. By this point in his career, by this point in the novel, 'the limits of the art, of neurosurgery as it stands today, are plain enough: faced with these unknown codes, this dense and brilliant circuitry, he and his colleagues offer *only* brilliant plumbing' (255; my emphasis).

Penetrating the head and plumbing its material depths cannot explain Baxter to Perowne, nor even is the diagnosis of Huntington's Disease and the somatized, molecularized accounts of Baxter's neurobiology a sufficient explanation for his destructive desires for penetration. The novel does not linger on Baxter's psychology as it does on Henry's, however. Baxter's threats of raping Daisy and stabbing Rosalind are figured as both mindless and pointless penetrations; they are a kind of perverse surgery lacking in any capacity for repair, and are symbolized in the foot-long gash he tears in the skin of the family's leather sofa that dehisces like 'a wound, an ugly welt, swelling along its length as the ancient, yellowish-white stuffing oozes up like subcutaneous fat' (217). There is simply nothing significant to see here – just stuffing, meaningless matter. But novels, too, can fail to imagine. Henry is allowed a mind, while Baxter's inadequate motivations are denuded of hermeneutic depth; they are simply epiphenomena of his admittedly complex but nevertheless potentially graspable neurobiology. For Huntington's Disease is, by Henry's account, 'biological determinism in its purest form' (93); and although there is a narrative logic for keeping Baxter's motivations un-visible, unknowable, there is something troubling, upon which the novel only half reflects, about the working-class man serving as a neurobiologically, materially driven prompt – albeit a powerful and intrusive one – to the middle-class man's internal mentalized reflections.

Later, as Henry attempts to deflect himself from thinking about Daisy's archaeologist lover and her pregnancy, alongside the impending operation on Baxter's brain, his mind wanders back to a neurosurgery conference he attended in Rome and the glimpse the participants were offered of Nero's palace, the Domus Aurea. It is an underground space of dim, ivory chambers – clearly figured to seem as cranial as it is architectural – first penetrated by robbers and then Renaissance artists like Raphael and Michelangelo. Lowering themselves on ropes through the 'jagged hole in the immense domed ceiling' (242), the 'artists had drilled through this skull of brick to discover the mind of ancient Rome' (243), the mayor who is leading the tour tells the surgeons. 'If only the mayor was right', Henry thinks, 'that penetrating the skull brings into view not the brain but the mind' (243); but he knows the mind, at least at this historical moment, slips the empirical gaze of the scientist.

The archaeological metaphor does, however, bring Henry's neuroscientific world-view into contact with another discipline concerned with the shape of the mind – one that emerged precisely from the limitations of the empirical, neurological gaze. For in 1893 Sigmund Freud famously compared the discipline of psychoanalysis – what Eugen Bleuler called 'depth psychology' in 1914 – to archaeology. In his analysis of hysteria in Fräulein Elisabeth von R in *Studies in Hysteria*, he imagined the process of diagnosis and treatment as a 'clearing away of pathogenic material layer by layer', like 'the technique of excavating a buried city' (138). A short while later he noted a shared set of assumptions between archaeologist and analyst:

> the ruined walls are part of the ramparts of a palace or a treasure-house; the fragments of columns can be filled out into a temple; the numerous inscriptions, which, by good luck, may be bilingual, reveal an alphabet and a language, and, when they have been deciphered and translated, yield undreamed-of information about the events of the remote past, to commemorate which the monuments were built. *Saxa loquntuur!* [*Stones speak!*] (191)

Freud's metaphor articulates his conception of a mind composed of strata laid down in relation to experience and revealed through the patient's cryptic speech. The model is topographical, but here the broken columns, the detritus, the stones themselves speak. Neither archaeology, nor psychoanalysis, it turns out, is simply a question of drilling down through insignificant rubble to expose that which has been covered up; rather, both the structure of the mind and the meaning of the archeological site are to be found in the silted up layers of stone and debris – in what has been laid down over time. In *Civilization and its Discontents* (1930), Freud comes back to the archaeological metaphor, explicitly comparing the psyche to the city of Rome extended through history: a Rome 'in which nothing that has once come into existence will have passed away and all the earlier phases of development continue to exist alongside the latest one'; a Rome in which '[w]here the Coliseum now stands we could at the same time admire Nero's vanished Golden House [the *Domus Aurea*]' (70). Here, however, it is clear that everything that the city is and was cannot be contained in a static image. Though Freud remained committed to topographical accounts of the structure of mind, the Rome analogy allows him to show 'how far we are from mastering the characteristics of mental life by representing them in pictorial terms' (71). What Freud repeats in 1930, then, is the turn to the temporality of language that is the inception of his psychoanalytic method, as a mental architecture that can neither be seen nor pictured unwinds through the patient's mouth into the analyst's ear through processes of narration and translation. Although McEwan has the occasional dig at psychoanalysis,[4] the image of the Domus Aurea in *Saturday* seems to imply that even at this contemporary historical moment, getting into the mind, into what might still be experienced as the depths of the psychological, requires a different, perhaps a more linguistic kind of digging than a craniotomy can offer.

Henry Perowne can open the skull of a living patient for extended periods without them simply bleeding out; along with his colleagues in neuroscience, he is able to use new imaging techniques to infer mental correlates of what seems to be neurological activity; but the two neurologists who appear in Sebastian Faulks' *Human Traces* – Thomas Midwinter and Jacques Rebière – are placed at the inception of their discipline. Perowne's contemporary abilities are possibilities that inform Faulks' novel, although they remain tantalizingly out of reach for his characters. In *Human Traces*, the value of seeing inside the head is figured in a persistent fascination with the frisson of a taboo penetration, of boring into the skull and gasping at the apparent disconnect between this soft, unremarkable, grey matter – as Midwinter puts it, it is 'an organ, entirely comparable to the others' (101) – and the complexity of the sense of that transcendent immateriality of subjectivity that it somehow produces. Of course, Midwinter and Rebière's attempts to map mental functions on to areas of the brain and to understand the damage to the sense of psychological continuity wrought by the inferred brain lesions are circumscribed by history. Only gross brain lesions were visible at autopsy and the living mental function somehow produced by neuronal activity simply could not be seen, though Midwinter imagines that one day we will 'develop a magical apparatus for peering into the brain with such clarity that the function of each "neurone" ... is apparent to us' (493). Faulks puts into Sonia, Midwinter's sister and Rebière's wife, an early expression of the limits of the medical gaze of the nineteenth century:

> 'It is a shame you have to wait until they are dead,' said Sonia. 'I suppose there is no other way of inspecting someone's brain.'

'Not yet. Though one day we may be able to take a photograph through the bone of the skull.'

'Not with my Underwood,' said Thomas.

'But when the task of nosology is complete,' said Jacques, 'the majority of mental patients will become neurological.' (137)

Faulks goes on to dramatize, through his two protagonists, the fracturing of the neurology concerned with mental pathologies into the disciplines of psychiatry and psychoanalysis, as it splinters on the occlusions of the cranium. For without being able either safely to penetrate or see through the skull, Freud did swerve from his neurological training; he turned to those orifices into the head that required no technological enhancement – a mouth uttering language and an ear receiving it – to trace the complex psychological formations that were somehow produced by neurological workings but could not yet be subject to *in vivo* scientific observation. As Sander Gilman writes: 'Freud rejected the idea of seeing the patient, thus centring psychoanalysis on the process of listening'; and 'in rejecting the rigid representationalism of nineteenth-century theories of understanding mental processes, Freud also rejected their basis of empirical proof' (223). While the bio-psychiatry that maintained a sense of causative connections with neurobiology continued to prioritize the visual through static diagrams and images, psychoanalysis leaned on the temporally extended resources of language to diagnose patients, represent the twists and turns of their psychopathology within narrativized case studies, and to effect healing or repair.

Faulks thus has the alliance between the English Midwinter and French Rebière split along national lines; as Midwinter puts it: 'Yes. I suppose, for simplicity's sake, you might say that his guiding light is Charcot and mine is Darwin' (32). The continental Rebière, like the neurologist Charcot's historical student Freud, turns to psychoanalysis as a way of inferring the neural mechanism triggered by trauma that produces the symptom of hysteria. This mechanism effects a physical paralysis by an association with an idea and cannot be viewed either *in vivo* or post-mortem; nevertheless, it can seemingly be cured by bringing the repression of that idea back into consciousness through language. *Human Traces* is, however, clearly suspicious of psychoanalysis's notion of repair by words, of Freud's own admission that psychical treatment does not simply describe the 'pathological phenomena of mental life', it 'operate[s] in the first instance and immediately upon the human mind' ('Psychical (or Mental) Treatment' 282). Freud himself notes that:

> A layman will no doubt find it hard to understand how pathological disorders of the body and mind can be eliminated by 'mere' words. He will feel that he is being asked to believe in magic. And he will not be so very wrong, for the words which we use in our everyday speech are nothing other than watered-down magic. (282)

Faulks' pastiche of a Freudian case study does indeed mark the emergence of psychoanalysis as the moment when Rebière, like Freud, gives up on the idea of empirical proof as scientific method. *Human Traces* represents it as just too dependent on the vagaries of words, the slippery and paradoxical connections made by language. Rebière interprets a patient's physical manifestations – her inability to speak and abdominal pains – as hysteria brought on by a neurological trauma that cannot be seen, but this classical early Freudian interpretation of screen memories and unfulfilled wishes is revealed to be a misdiagnosis of organic disease. The young woman, Kitty, is taken to a doctor and her rheumatic fever is diagnosed and successfully treated. Faulks complicates the indictment of psychoanalysis by having Kitty, who marries the sceptical Midwinter, remain sympathetic to what is called 'the Viennese School', but it is Midwinter's view that is given textual authority. Talking may have important palliative effects, but it cannot be either a diagnostic instrument or what Anna O. claimed it to be – a cure. Midwinter, in the end, aligns himself with his mentor and predecessor at an asylum for the insane, Dr Faverill, who speaks both for pragmatism and for 'proof': 'The Viennese School. Ah yes. I found their stories equally entertaining. But when I read it was proposed to apply their techniques not to the comfort of high-strung Viennese girls but to the treatment of psychosis … I despaired' (481). Psychoanalysis is just stories – 'mere' words.

There is a sense that the turn to the neuroscientific in *Saturday* is part of a similar attempt to nail knowledge to the givenness, the solidity of matter, and to biological mechanisms freighted with the status of the real rather than linguistic representation's airy 'magic'. This is what Henry invokes when he invites Daisy, whose postmodern, poststructuralist Oxford education has suggested to her that 'madness was a social construct', for a 'tour of a closed psychiatric wing' (92). As I have argued elsewhere (Salisbury), here Henry becomes aligned with McEwan's own extratextual affirmations of the necessity of attending to the real, and the value he places on science's capacity to invoke curiosity in relation to evidence that is uncovered, empirically discovered, rather than faith in the putatively immaterial speculation of ideas – a faith that, because unfettered to the material, can so easily be hijacked.[5] So Henry is able to muse on his exasperation with the magical realist novels Daisy recommends to him that give up on the difficulties of the real all too easily. As we have seen above, for Henry 'the mind is what the brain, mere matter, performs.' This fact, however 'worthy of awe ... also deserves curiosity; the actual, not the magical, should be the challenge' (67).

In *Human Traces*, Midwinter also ventriloquizes a genetically subtended account of the evolved brain's relationship to the mind that determinedly retrofits contemporary evolutionary psychological and cognitive neuroscientific ideas to nineteenth- and early-twentieth century models. Indeed, precisely because he can be aligned with the aims of contemporary 'translational neuroscience' to reconceptualize disorders of the mind as disorders of the brain, the nineteenth-century neurologist John Hughlings Jackson, who worked to understand the brain and mind as products of evolutionary biology, is lauded; the anxious implication of neurology and psychiatry with eugenic concerns at that historical moment is brushed aside as a deflection from the real work of understanding. And Freud, imagined in the figure of Rebière, is represented as averting his gaze from the challenges of evidence-based medicine into the magical, into fantasy, as he hopes to find in spiritualism the traces and voices of the dead.

Human Traces' repeated invocation of the possibility that one day there will be 'a magical apparatus for peering into the brain' that might take us beyond Freud's suspect linguistic magic, seems animated by our contemporary cultural fascination with brain imaging technologies that offer to show, through that supposedly less distortive visual sense, the relationships between neuronal functioning, mental activity, and human behaviour that are the bedrock of cognitive neuroscience. In 1986, PET (positron emission tomography) researcher Henry Wagner suggested that in this brain-imaging technique 'we now have a new set of eyes that permits us to examine the chemistry of the human mind' (quoted in Dumit 168). By this account, PET offers neuroscience the instrument for which clinicians and scientists since Midwinter's time have been searching. But, as Joseph Dumit has shown in depth and detail, any sense that PET scans show an unmediated picture of mental events, or even of actual brain function, needs careful unpicking. Dumit assertively deconstructs the PET scan by demonstrating the relationships of interpretation – of reading and translation – that take place as sets of measurements taken over time of oxygen concentration in the blood are statistically evaluated, reworked into images of bloodflow in specific areas of the brain, and then translated as pictures from which cognitive, affective, and broadly 'mental' processes may be inferred. The tantalizingly coloured PET scans that supposedly show mental activity, so beloved of popular science, need then to be reconfigured as highly labile, constructed and knotty entanglements of complex scientific and more broadly socio-cultural activities and assumptions. That these images are translated further as they are disseminated to scientific and non-scientific audiences, speaks compellingly to the fact that such images are far from being transparent windows on to the mind.

Functional magnetic resonance imaging (fMRI) similarly registers bloodflow and, as Steven Rose puts it, bloodflow is only a 'surrogate measure for neural activity' (55), which, in turn, has only a relationship of correlation rather than causation to mental activity. FMRI may indeed 'magically' look into the brain; the mind, however, is still inferred through various acts of translation. In his reading of the fMRI image, Cornelius Borck suggests that in the contemporary fixation on brain imaging, a 'revived localizationism' (the diagram-making so beloved of mid- to late-nineteenth-century neurology) has 'replaced the mediation of metaphors and models with the immediacy of an artificial real brain image, allegedly revealing the functional activity of the psyche within the brain' (128). Of course, '[m]odels and metaphors may fail or betray' as much as images, Borck states, 'but they typically operate in the differentiality between the object and the concept, while images as objectifying representations always already tend to conflate the object with its representation' (129). Though one might take issue with the sense that pictures would always necessarily work in this way, it seems clear that images from fMRI and PET scanning tend to obscure rather than render visible the modes of translation, indeed the modes of reading, at work in their attempts to visualize the workings of both brain and mind. But if there is an as yet still poorly understood relationship of translation between neurological and mental processes (and indeed between the bloodflow we can measure and the neuronal), then perhaps theories of reading – of the complexity of modes of representation and of interpretation – might open up language and translation as sites that are not simply evasions of the 'real'. Language and translation might instead become forms that could render perceptible, and allow an analysis of, the complexity of how meaning and understanding make themselves known to consciousness. Perhaps, then, it is significant that a novel like *Saturday* holds its neuromaterialism alongside an insistent return, both thematically and formally, to questions of representation and to the judgements, beliefs, and feelings that emerge between the matter of things and our thought (and feeling) of the world. If this is so, neuronovels may be culturally significant not simply in their translation of new scientific models into narratives accessible for lay audiences; their significance might lie instead in their power to prise open a critical space and time for thinking through the modes of representation and translation that form in the gap between a perceiving mind (even a scientific mind) and world and, at an authentically unconscious level, between the neuronal and mental. For a culture in thrall to a neuro-turn obsessed with just looking, the emphasis on representation and translation that the neuronovel can foreground asks compelling critical questions of the limits of current neurobiological modes and models for understanding formations and experiences of mind.

Lost (and found) in translation

I want to suggest, then, that despite the use of Henry as a mouthpiece for the 'professional reductionist', the unbridged gap between the neuronal and the mental – the as yet untranslated account of how the neurological substrate of the brain feels lifted up and works towards telling the story of a particular conscious mind – becomes a chasm over which sparks of meaning arc in *Saturday*. Henry's certainty of the structuring relationship between brain and mind is not 'an article of faith ... he knows it for a quotidian fact' (67); and yet, McEwan repeatedly shows how knowledge combines with a frayed edge of belief that runs, like a pulled epistemological thread, throughout the novel: 'Could it ever be explained, how matter becomes conscious?', Henry asks:

> He can't begin to imagine a satisfactory account, but he knows it will come, the secret will be revealed – over decades, as long as the scientists and the institutions remain in place, the explanations will refine themselves into an irrefutable truth about consciousness. It's already happening, the work is being done in laboratories not far from this theatre. ... That's the only kind of faith he has. (255)

Of course, as with the penetration of Baxter's consciousness, this is for the future; here, on this Saturday in 2003, with thousands massing to demonstrate against the impending war in Iraq, questions of faith, belief, and judgement – where the limits of what can be known have always been most anxiously staged – stubbornly stagger on within the novel. And if *Saturday* is a novel of political uncertainty that asks searching questions of how liberal, autonomous, democratic individuals and societies understand themselves in a world characterized by seemingly irrational intrusions of violence, Henry's role as someone whose business is the brains of others gives McEwan the opportunity for an anxious exploration of precisely what can and cannot be known of our own and of other minds, and something of the processes of representation and judgement that both occlude and translate the world to and through our consciousness.

Over the last few decades, neuroscience has been intensely concerned with attempting to define, map, and understand what it calls the neural correlates of consciousness, or, as Vidal and Ortega have put it, 'the minimal set of neuronal events and mechanisms jointly sufficient for a specific conscious percept' (348). The neuroscientific community remains split, however, between those who suggest that the brain is sufficient in itself for consciousness, and those who argue that because the 'brain is an organism and an organism is always involved in a self-regulating relationship with the environment', consciousness is 'coupled with the world through sensorimotor and intersubjective interactions' (350) and therefore cannot usefully be reduced to brain activity. On the one hand, there is the hope that neural activity, viewed through an objective, third-person lens could be understood as having a causative rather than simply correlative relation to mental experience; on the other, if the individual brain supports but is not in itself sufficient to produce consciousness, for neurologically the brain does not and cannot function in isolation, the move from correlation to causation is, at the very least, severely complicated.

Andrew Gaedtke has noted that in neuronovels like *Saturday*, or David Lodge's *Thinks...*, this precise relationship between conscious experience and neurological processes is foregrounded, as if this 'hard problem' for neuroscience – technically, as Vidal and Ortega explain, 'a problem that persists after the relevant or causal mechanisms have been established' (351) – opens up territory in which the novel senses a possibility of intervention. If literary fiction is a genre that frequently dedicates itself to externalizing and reproducing subjective experience, while fashioning a seemingly objective world in which this consciousness can persuasively exist, then perhaps the neuronovel is sticking to and staking out its home ground by turning, in Gaedtke's terms, the '"hard problem" of qualia into a distinctively literary problem of narrative style' (187). By exploring the relationship between a '"third-person" materialist, neuroscientific account of mind' and 'qualia: the "first-person" feelings of phenomenal experience' (185), the neuronovel seems indeed to be asking what sort of literary form might be able to translate and contain a contemporary account of mind.

Saturday begins with Perowne moving to watch, through a clear pane of glass, a burning plane tearing through the early morning sky. In unusually precise detail, we get to see the exact contours of Henry's first-person impressions and sensations, some of which precede his individual reflective consciousness:

> [He] wakes to find himself already in motion, pushing back the covers from a sitting position, and then rising to his feet. It's not clear to him when exactly he became conscious, nor does it seem relevant. He's never done such a thing before,

but he isn't alarmed or even faintly surprised, for the movement is easy, and pleasurable in his limbs, and his back and legs feel unusually strong. (3)

Patricia Waugh has suggested that such a mode of narration might be described as 'neo-phenomenological' (25) in its attention to the shapes of subjective experience, to qualia, over a theoretical or more seemingly objective view of self and its position within the world. For phenomenology, in Edmund Husserl's terms, works to bracket off the existence objects might have in the exterior world by concentrating instead, with technical precision, upon the world's appearance to the self through mental experience. Perhaps we are meant to take it for granted that Henry, a scientist, would also be '[a]n habitual observer of his own moods', as he wonders why he feels euphoric: 'Perhaps down at the molecular level there's been a chemical accident ... prompting dopamine-like receptors to initiate a kindly cascade of intra-cellular events'; perhaps he is over-tired: 'It's true, he finished the week in a state of unusual depletion' (5). The scientific language reassures, perhaps – 'perhaps'? – that these are impressions to be trusted. But what is he seeing? Although, as Peter Boxall has noted (155), Perowne's vision is initially clear – 'his vision – always good – seems to have sharpened' (4) – Henry is soon left feeling 'disoriented and unsure of what he is looking at'. Possibilities rumble across his consciousness, and we follow each one: the 'trick[s] of vision' (16), swiftly pursued by the rational reorientation which allows him to flatten any 'excess of the subjective, the ordering of the world in line with your own needs' (17) into something on to which a mind searching for the real can settle.

As the above implies, a tension begins to emerge between a phenomenological narrative mode that borrows much from modernist free indirect style and its capacity to move seamlessly across the first and third-person divide, from those contours of inner experience into framing perspectives, and Henry's seeming certainties about how the world is. For we go on to hear his representations, ideas, his judgements, his feelings, as he imagines the narrative shape of the terrorist attack his obscured view of the aircarft might portend. Later, the reliability of our narrator appears affirmed by hearing that he 'knows he's subject to unexamined assumptions, and he tries to examine them now' (83); but stay in any mind long enough, even one of a 'coarse, unredeemable materialist' (134), as Henry supposedly is, and contradictions will emerge. As the novel progresses, *Saturday* becomes just as set on revealing Henry's liberal ambivalence, his wavering uncertainty: 'Did he, Henry Perowne, act unprofessionally, using his medical knowledge to undermine a man suffering from a neurogenerative disorder? Yes, no, not entirely' (111). A slightly implausible on the spot diagnosis of Huntington's

Disease in Baxter, who has run into Henry's car and threatened to assault him, leads to doubt in the surgeon who feels he should be able to assume an ethical, even a moral position. The penetration of Henry's borders – his Mercedes, his townhouse in Fitzrovia – finds an analogue, of course, with the imminent invasion of Iraq, and Henry is perceptive enough to sense the link, though subtle enough also to see that it is not exact. What matches more seamlessly are the contours of Henry's internal contradiction with broader political concerns, as he is pushed and pulled, like a puppet with its strings on the inside, by the judgements of others. Clearly, he is 'for the termination of an odious tyrant and his crime family … against the bombing of civilians, the inevitable refugees and famine, illegal international action. … His nerves, like tautened strings, vibrate obediently with each "news" release' (180–1); but he senses 'he's becoming dim with contradictory opinion, he isn't thinking clearly' (181).

See-sawing according to the pull of both internal neurological and external psychosocial elements over which his sense of self can have no full or conscious control, judgement is no longer the self's ballast that affirms existence in relation to thinking, as it was for Descartes; for here a mode of judgement inflected with feeling has already taken place in a pre-cognitive space. It was Maurice Merleau-Ponty who, in the 1940s, centred his account of phenomenological experience on a mind that could never be separated, in a Cartesian manner, from a perceiving, sensing body that is both the neurological ground of cerebration, and the medium through which any thinking becomes meaningful. For Merleau-Ponty, the experience of embodiment precisely gives the lie to the possibility that the subject might be able to exist in a world from which it has the structural capacity to separate itself, either in thought, or as an individual being discrete from its environment. Instead, the subject comes to a sense of itself through embodied experiences that emerge from the chiasmic intertwining of matter and idea, the natural and cultural, individual and social. As Merleau-Ponty puts it, the body is:

> rooted in nature at the very moment when it is transformed by cultural influences, never hermetically sealed and never left behind. Whether it is a question of another's body or my own, I have no means of knowing the human body other than that of living it, which means taking up on my own account the drama which is being played out, and losing myself in it. (198)

The story the neo-phenomenological narration of *Saturday* tells is also one where empirical knowledge and rational thought will always be pulled towards and by the embodiment, feelings, and porous relationships with an exterior world that Henry, at least at times, worries are murky undertows. *Saturday* frequently seems clear that as soon as things get turned into feelings, representations, judgements, a certain kind of empirical knowing is lost; nevertheless, its phenomenological narrative form works just as hard to articulate that without the translations of embodiment, there could be no knowledge at all.

Saturday thus finds itself poised between the hope for, and perhaps even the possibility of, a reliable account of rational knowing condensed into the promise of neuroscience, and the demands evoked by being held in a space of an embodied consciousness dominated by judgements, by representations, and by affects that feel as if they explode away from the ground of a material, neurological substrate sealed within a head. Peter Boxall has suggested that this tension forms part of the challenge of politics in the novel, with McEwan evoking the ways in which many Western, liberal subjects find themselves bound to a pragmatism freighted with a demand to be 'realistic' in the absence of irrefutable knowledge, while still feeling themselves, at least on occasion, capable of reaching for the possibility that things might be otherwise. Boxall lucidly describes how the novel loosens the bonds of realism of a post-ideological consensus by paradoxically yearning for those unbound feelings of utopianism that McEwan describes in 'The Day of Judgment' as a dangerous evacuation of the demands of the real. For Boxall, the novel's 'unbound poetics' (158) shimmer and shift into view intermittently: in Matthew Arnold's 'Dover Beach', which precipitates Baxter's mood swing and allows him, momentarily, to connect with Arnold's own idea of a 'best self'; they are present in Henry's mother's mind where the connections that make rational thinking sustainable are being destroyed by Alzheimer's disease. They also emerge in Henry's rare aesthetic experiences of music with his son, which nod back to Arnold by giving 'a glimpse of what we might be, of our best selves, and of an impossible world in which you give everything you have to others, but lose nothing of yourself' (171). This experience offers a glimpse of the potential transcendence of art, even as it remains anxiously linked to a feeling associated with the utopianism of 'all conflicts resolved, happiness for everyone, for ever – mirages for which people are prepared to die or kill' (171–2). Still, there is a feeling rather more than a thought of lightness, of transcendence, of a mind getting out of its individual head – unfettered, at least temporarily, from the putative givenness of matter. Boxall finds in *Saturday* an articulation of 'newly bound bodies that can bear moral responsibility, that can function as democratic, sovereign subjects under newly disarticulated global conditions, balanced against the opposite need to open bodies up, to loosen the bonds that construct us' (160). Unpeeling itself from the head (that synecdoche of the sovereign subject), this dispersed, open self radiates outwards and upwards in a mode that, as Boxall notes, remains linked to the body's vulnerability to deflagration – in this case to the terrorist explosion. Antithetical to the controlled drilling of a craniotomy and the millimetre precise cut of the scalpel – to the idea, or rather a fantasy of the conscious self as absolutely locatable within a localized map of neurological territory – this distributed self is shown feeling and finding itself elsewhere. In the personal and professional relationships with others in which Perowne has such faith, in aesthetic ecstasy, even in its potential vulnerability to the explosive where body and self may be horrifically morcellized, *Saturday* shows an opened-up self that finds itself formed and deformed in a world of intersubjective relations that exist beyond the autonomy of the individual that might have its seat inside the skull.

Despite the thread of biological reductionism, then, through its phenomenological attention to mind's complexity and drift, *Saturday* remains interested in a self that transcends the neurological by showing how brains, as they emerge into subjective selves, are enmeshed in history, in society, in culture. Indeed, it does this by prising open those in-between spaces and times of relationships with others and with the material world that allow brain matter to become meaningful, to become mind. For, as Steven Rose succinctly puts it: 'The meaning of any experience is not "in the brain" but in a mind which is an open system, depending to be sure on the brain, but not isolable within it' (63). Still, it seems to me that *Saturday* works in both thematic and formal terms to contain the unboundedness that Boxall links to utopian political possibilities; it persistently binds the affects that transgress the limits of the autonomous subject back to a shared world of commonality subtended by an idea of liberal consensus. For Henry muses on the transitory quality of aesthetic transcendence: 'only in music, only on rare occasions, does the curtain actually lift on this dream of community, and it's tantalisingly conjured, before fading away with the last notes' (172). The suggestion, of course, is that it is *conjured*, a magical feeling rather than an empirical fact on which one could ever really lean: 'Naturally, no one can ever agree when it's happening' (172), Henry mentally notes. Although the phenomenological mode of narration allows attention to drift between empirical consistency – a scientific mode of knowing *about* – and feelings of transcendence, *Saturday* remains, in the end, more concerned with inching intersubjective relations towards those containing forces of 'agreement' or consensus that might, at least pragmatically, hold and legitimize Henry's judgements, beliefs and faith *in* things.

Within the novel, it seems clear that Perowne's selfhood – both his empirical knowledge and his affective attachments – gains significance from its place in a richly textured world that exists beyond the confines of the skull. Perowne's knowing and feeling comes to itself via colleagues who can be trusted, through patients whose individual experiences render the abstractions of politics or syndromes concrete and meaningful, through a family held together by their instinct to love and defend one another. People are, in turn, bound into institutions where what is cracked or incomplete – whether it be Baxter's skull or scientific knowledge itself – can be pieced together, albeit imperfectly. There are also material containers, such as the car in which Perowne glides with the detached observation of a *flaneur* through the city, the generous townhouse in Fitzrovia, or the nursing home that holds and contains his mother. And although each is subject to intrusion, to violent penetration – from Baxter who wants to damage and disrupt, or from the Alzheimer's disease that turns over the mental furniture for Perowne's mother who was once able to keep everything so neatly in its place – these containers can, in the end, keep the violence in Perowne's immediate world within bearable limits. As the fourteen-page description of the squash match between Perowne and the American Jay Strauss suggests, aggression and conflict may emerge, but they can be played through and played out when relations and alliances are strong enough to maintain the rules of the game. These relations that hold things together in the given Western world of liberal, democratic consensus in which the novel, at least, imagines we live, thus become the translations by which, in *Saturday*, the biological, neurological self becomes meaningful; these relations of comity are the forms in which Henry can doubt, but through which he can also find himself.

At the end of *Human Traces*, while Rebière is left quasi-psychotically chasing the hope that all past experience is laid down in the brain and that it can therefore be accessed and be relived in some way, Midwinter is diagnosed with Alzheimer's disease. Despite the frailty of his brain matter, the loss of his connections, a certain contained transcendence is also offered in the bonds Midwinter has made with others and in the acts of kindness for which he will be remembered. And it is finally Rebière's wife Sonia's neurological matter, her maternal mind, that becomes the container for acts of remembrance in the novel.[6] She tells her husband: 'You did not need a brain surgeon or a medium. You did not need to chase the dead members of your family. All you needed was here' (602). Sonia is the mother of a son lost in the Great War, and yet, in her mind's eye and ear '[s]he heard Daniel's voice; she saw the flesh of his boy's arm creased by the weight of his wicker basket full of toys. The bones of his beautiful hands lived in the cells of her mind, preserved, and open to remembering' (608). The final image of *Human Traces* gestures back to the footprints Midwinter observes in the Rift Valley of a female and a child that predate *homo sapiens* but are nevertheless inferred to be holding hands in a bond of love; it sees Sonia walking on a beach, thinking of the traces of her son she retains in the fragile matter of her brain:

> The long trail of her footprints, stretching back towards the sea, became slowly indistinct as each one filled with water and edged in upon itself; and in a matter of minutes, as darkness began to fall, the shape of the foot was lost at every pace until the last vestiges of her presence were washed away, the earth closing over as if no one had passed by. (609)

In this last statement there seems to be an echo of Michel Foucault's final rhetorical gesture of *The Order of Things*, where he speaks of the idea of humanist Man as a 'recent invention', produced by particular historical and discursive conditions. Foucault writes:

> If those arrangements were to disappear as they appeared, if some event of which we can at the moment do no more than sense the possibility – without knowing either what its form will be or what it promises – were to cause them to crumble, as the ground of classical thought did, at the end of the eighteenth century, then one can certainly wager that man would be erased, like a face drawn in sand at the edge of the sea. (422)

The echo may be intended, for *Human Traces* does suggest that the human is subject to change, though of an evolutionary rather than a socio-historical kind. But there is also an irony, here, as it is clear that much of the contemporary neuroscience on which Faulks builds his nineteenth- and early twentieth-century narrative, has been keener to reinscribe than erase the historical conditions of 'Man'. As Jan Slaby and Suparna Choudhury have put it in their polemical 'Proposal for a Critical Neuroscience', 'scientific enquiry tends to mobilize specific values and often works in the service of interests that can easily shape construals of nature and naturalness' (29); and neuroscience has assumed a strong position in producing notions of 'normative facticity' that support the construction of liberal, yet finally responsible, autonomous individuals. Even as the 'deep space' of the psychological subject may be challenged by paradigms of the neurochemical self, both neuroscience and the neuronovel have found themselves discovering in the brain a set of needs, desires, and capacities that mirror a very particular formation of the social.

A significant element in the way *Saturday* and *Human Traces* both tend towards affirming existing Western, democratic models of autonomous selfhood by shaping transcendent, distributive, intersubjective affects into emotional containers of, say, nuclear familial love, is their forging of a link between this particular model of sociality and the formation and demands of the evolved human brain, represented as our common genetic inheritance. In his essay 'Literature, Science and Human Nature' (2005), McEwan is clear that it is precisely within literature's capacity to bind and connect humans to emotions that, *contra* Foucault, remain the same across cultures and across times. Against the authentic indifference of time's passage, McEwan indeed finds an emotional legacy, underpinned by evolutionary advantage, that connects people in a form of species commonality. 'Within the emotional and the expressive we remain what we are', he writes, and, significantly, it is this evolutionary legacy to which literature that has a particular containing shape bears witness: 'That which binds us, our common nature – is what literature has always, knowingly and helplessly, given voice to' (19), writes McEwan. In *Human Traces*, there is a similar foregrounding of the novel's own mode of binding, as Midwinter's evolutionarily subtended account of mind mirrors a form of narration that emphasizes the sensation of continuity rather than the gaps in consciousness: 'To think of ourselves as atoms in an infinite universe is in fact impossible', he states: 'it is just not how we experience life – which we feel as something linear and driven to an end' (511). *Saturday* also ends, perhaps it must end, not with a sense that things are scattered in a form of dissolution, with new formations, but with the sensation that they cannot be anything other than as and where they are. Even though Henry has no unmediated access to the world – his knowledge isn't enough to make sense of consciousness, to understand Baxter, to know what to do about Saddam Hussein – his affects are shaped by containers like the familial or the collegiate, and indeed by a particular kind of novel form, that enable imperfect judgements to seem good enough to keep things intact. His faith is thus held in people, in institutions and indeed in one of the dominant literary forms that Perowne's particular version of society has built to hold itself together – to explain itself to itself. And so this novel closes, with Henry returning to the containment of his bed, and to Rosalind, next to and within whom any falling might be held: 'There's always this, is one of his remaining thoughts. And then: there's only this. And at last, faintly, falling: this day's over' (279).

What remains

Both *Saturday* and *Human Traces* focus their imaginative resources on the experience of scientists. *Saturday* indeed offers a sustained technical account of neurological functioning as a counterpoint to its phenomenological attention to the felt depths of subjective experience. But Tom McCarthy's *Remainder* is not concerned with the neurological, nor with thickening its narrator's subjectivity by taking the reader through variegated modalities of experience and sustained relationships with past, future, or indeed with others. Instead, as Patricia Waugh has shown, the novel uses a phenomenological narrative mode to evoke and explore the emotional dissociation and disaffection that can be the result of brain damage. For the unnamed narrator, his 'loss of bodily and affective attunement to the world produces a hyper-reflexive disconnection after which everything has to be built from scratch and nothing feels real' (26). The world and the self that matches it are denuded of depth as they are transformed into distributions of elements on a flattened out surface.

The narrator aims to stem his free-fall by reproducing the sensation of the real he re-experiences in an aleatory fashion when gazing at a crack in a bathroom wall. The crack produces an echo of his head wound: it is '[f]leshy: grey-brown pinky. Sort of like flesh' (121), we hear. But where gazing into the cranium functions as an anchor to a material substrate that grounds the neurosurgeon, the narrator of *Remainder* cannot round on himself and see into his own head. He is speaking from within the experience of the crack, the gap, from inside the fissure in the subject the brain wound implies. Though he tries to reproduce the event, to remake and manage this crack in the wall into which he might peer, the sensation of a weighted reality and a freighted self cannot be recaptured in any sustained fashion. By repeatedly attempting to reenact the event, the narrator finds himself producing an excess of surface that, like tightly folded origami, might sometimes produce an illusion of volume or depth – something that can be penetrated. But it is only during the unplanned shootings that rupture the narrator's simulated event that there is an authentic, momentary intrusion of unmanageable, ungainsayable matter – the real. Though he hopes that merging his re-enactment with an event, that simulating a bank heist 'in an actual bank whose staff didn't know it was a re-enactment' (244), will enable him to 'penetrate and live inside the core, be seamless, perfect, real' (245), matter trips up his best-laid plans with an event, with death. Like a doubting Thomas penetrating the body of Christ, the narrator places his fingers within the gun-shot wound: 'the wound was raised, not sunk; parts of the flesh had broken through the skin and risen, like rising dough. The flesh was both firm and soft; it gave to the touch but kept its shape' (271). And this intrusion of the real through an event of wounding that allows the penetration of something felt to obtrude from the surrounding flatland, throbs with heavy, aesthetic sensation: '"Isn't it beautiful?"..."You could take everything away – vaporize, replicate, transubstantiate, whatever – and this would still be there"' (277). But matter is, of course, the narrator's disaster as much as it is his saviour: it is, simply, 'my undoing: matter' (17). He senses, early on in the novel, that his depthlessness, his weightlessness, could be tolerated if he might somehow become pure unconscious matter, like the murdered person he imagines transubstantiated, 'dying beside the bollards on the tarmac ... merged with the space around him ... merged in terms of having no more consciousness of them. He'd stopped being separate, removed, imperfect' (184–5). Equally, if he could volatilize himself into the ether, as in the fate he fantasizes for the vivid blue screenwash in his car that seems to disappear, he would be lifted from a consciousness figured here as excessively material, as the greatest weight. He imagines the screenwash 'vaporized, evaporated', '[a]nd do you know what? It felt wonderful. Don't ask me why. It was as though I'd just witnessed a miracle: matter – these two litres of liquid – becoming un-matter – not surplus matter, mess or clutter, but pure, bodiless blueness. Transubstantiated. I looked up at the sky: it was blue and endless' (159).

The novel finds its mood and its plot, of course, in what remains – in the remainder of matter than feels both excessive to and insufficient for the subject. For it is the fate of McCarthy's neurologically disturbed narrator to inherit the dissociation of Cartesian dualism with none of its attendant benefits. In each of the three novels considered in this chapter, there is a cognate exploration of how to bear witness to selves that continue to live on in a landscape where the deep spaces of psychology have been flattened intellectually, but not affectively. One could imagine novels in which this new neural subject might function as a figure of postmodernity, with the thickness and continuity of a self that feels as if it resides inside an autonomous body but does not believe that it is coterminous with it, reconfigured as a neurologically fabricated and sustained illusion. But the neuronovels that emerge in a period that recognizes itself to be post the postmodern are less interested in euphorically or anxiously unraveling the neurological constructedness of the human sense of reality than they are in exploring where the real may yet be felt to reside. A novel like *Remainder* evokes this from within its mood of loss. Affect may be alternately flattened or explosively distributed beyond the bounds of the self, but it persistently functions as a sign of a self unable to find its ballast. *Saturday* produces a much deeper, much more anchored sense of inner life, which, at one level, seems to belie Perowne's avowed neuromaterialism. For his is a self that understands and feels itself to exist within a thickened, sustaining social contract; it is a self formed according to modes of relationality and intersubjectivity, to modes of translation that might even imply an understanding of personhood that would disturb the ontological priority of the brain in the head – that metonym of the autonomous, sovereign subject. And yet, what affective bonds seem to offer both McEwan and Faulks is a reinscription of modes of sociality that are figured as having a graspable reality precisely because they are neurobiologically underpinned. The ways of being with others that might yet contain the violence of reality and the messy complexity of the material world are to be found in the neurological substrate of the human, in a shared genetic inheritance. And thus the brain assumes its position of authority once more. Still, by paying attention to the spaces of translation in operation between the neuronal and the mental, between theories of brain function and qualia, between the neurochemical self and the environment from which it can never be separated, the neuronovel does not simply duplicate those neurobiological accounts that seek to nail one to the other. The neuronovel may not erase the given conditions of 'Man', but in its attempts to explore and span these places of translation, it nevertheless offers a sense of how 'his' contours are being retraced.

Notes

1 See also Martin Amis' *Yellow Dog* (2003), which concerns a character suffering the effects of a head wound; Philip Hensher's *The Fit* (2004) that explores the position of a character taken to be on the autistic spectrum, and Samantha Harvey's *The Wilderness* (2009) that details the experience of a protagonist with Alzheimer's disease.
2 I have argued elsewhere (2010) that *Atonement* functions as a turning point in McEwan's work from a concentration on psychological splitting and damage to a concern with seeming 'reality' of neurological damage.
3 T.J. Lustig and James Peacock have noted a significant subgenre of both literary and more popular novels in this period that they neatly call 'syndrome fiction' (1). These fictions use the parallax effect of neurological atypicality to ask questions of the shape and meaning of the human in a post-cognitivist historical moment.
4 See, for example, his dismissal of Lacanian psychoanalysis in Pinker and McEwan (81).
5 In an article for the *Guardian* (2008) on apocalyptic thinking and the rise of religious fundamentalism, McEwan has suggested that faith, which has no recourse

to evidence and is suspicious of human inquiry, is the demonstration of a dangerous lack of curiosity about others and the world. For McEwan, this curiosity is, however, one of the fundamental motives behind scientific study. '[T]hat delightful human impulse – curiosity' is what has 'delivered us genuine, testable knowledge of the world and contributed to our under-standing of our place within it and our nature and condition' (n.p.), he writes.

6 See Salisbury for an account of McEwan's association of a material, neurological substrate with the maternal.

Works cited

Amis, Martin. *Yellow Dog*. London: Jonathan Cape, 2003.
Borck, Cornelius. 'Toys are Us: Models and Metaphors in Brain Research'. *Critical Neuroscience: A Handbook of the Social and Cultural Contexts of Neuroscience*. Eds Suparna Choudhury and Jan Slaby. Chichester: Wiley-Blackwell, 2012, 113–34.
Boxall, Peter. *Twenty-First-Century Fiction: A Critical Introduction*. Cambridge: Cambridge University Press, 2013.
Breuer, J. 'Fräulein Anna O'. In Freud, S. *The Standard Edition of the Complete Works of Sigmund Freud,* Vol. II (ed. J. Strachey). London: Hogarth Press, 1955.
Bush, George. 'Presidential Proclamation 6158'. July 17, 1990. Available online: http://www.loc.gov/loc/brain/proclaim.html (accessed 3 June 2015).
Cooter, Roger. 'Neural Veils and the Will to Historical Critique: Why Historians of Science Need to take the Neuro-turn Seriously'. *Isis* 105:1 (2014): 145–54.
Descartes, René. *The Passions of the Soul. The Philosophical Writings of Descartes*. Vol. I, trans. by John Cottingham, Robert Stoothoff and Dugald Murdoch. Cambridge: Cambridge University Press, 1985.
Descartes, René. *Treatise on Man. The Philosophical Writings of Descartes*. Vol. I, trans. by John Cottingham, Robert Stoothoff and Dugald Murdoch. Cambridge: Cambridge University Press, 1985.
Descartes, René. *Meditations on First Philosophy, with Selections from Objections and Replies: A Latin-English Edition*. Trans. and ed. by John Cottingham. Cambridge: Cambridge University Press, 2013.
Dumit, Joseph. *Picturing Personhood: Brain Scans and Biomedical Identity*. Princeton, NJ: Princeton University Press, 2004.
Faulks, Sebastian. *Birdsong*. London: Cornerstone, 1993.
Faulks, Sebastian. *Human Traces*. London: Hutchinson, 2005.
Foucault, Michel. *The Birth of the Clinic*. Trans. A.M. Sheridan. London: Tavistock Publications, 1976.
Foucault, Michel. *The Order of Things: An Archeology of the Human Sciences*. London: Routledge, 2002.

Freud, Sigmund. 'Psychical (or Mental) Treatment'. [1890] *The Standard Edition of the Complete Psychological Works of Sigmund Freud*. Vol. VII (1901–1905): 281–302. Trans. and ed. by James Strachey. London: Hogarth Press, 1953.

Freud, Sigmund. 'Fräulein Elisabeth von R, Case Histories from Studies in Hysteria'. [1893] *The Standard Edition of the Complete Psychological Works of Sigmund Freud*. Vol. II (1893–1895): 135–81. Trans. and ed. by James Strachey. London: Hogarth Press, 1955.

Freud, Sigmund. 'The Aetiology of Hysteria' [1896] *The Standard Edition of the Complete Psychological Works of Sigmund Freud*. Vol. III (1893–1899): 187–221. Trans. and ed. by James Strachey. London: Hogarth Press, 1962.

Freud, Sigmund. 'Remembering, Repeating and Working-Through (Further Recommendations on the Technique of Psycho-analysis)' [1914] *The Standard Edition of the Complete Psychological Works of Sigmund Freud*. Vol. XII (1911–1913): 145–56. Trans. and ed. by James Strachey. London: Hogarth Press, 1958.

Freud, Sigmund. 'Civilization and Its Discontents' [1930] *The Standard Edition of the Complete Psychological Works of Sigmund Freud*. Vol. XXI (1927–1931): 57–146. Trans. and ed. by James Strachey. London: Hogarth Press, 1957.

Gaedtke, Andrew. 'Cognitive Investigations: The Problems of Qualia and Style in the Contemporary Neuronovel'. *Novel* 45:2 (2012): 184–210.

Gilman, Sander. *Seeing the Insane*. New York: John Wiley, 1982.

Haddon, Mark. *The Curious Incident of the Dog in the Night-time*. London: Jonathan Cape, 2003.

Harvey, Samantha. *The Wilderness*. London: Jonathan Cape, 2009.

Hensher, Philip. *The Fit*. London: Fourth Estate, 2004.

Lodge, David. *Thinks . . . .* London: Secker and Warburg, 2001.

Luckhurst, Roger. *The Trauma Question*. London: Routledge, 2008.

Luckhurst, Roger. 'Beyond Trauma: Torturous Times'. *European Journal of English Studies* 14:1 (2010): 11–21.

Lustig, T.J. and James Peacock. 'Introduction'. *Diseases and Disorders in Contemporary Fiction: The Syndrome Syndrome*. London: Routledge, 2013, 1–16.

Malabou, Catherine. *The New Wounded: From Neurosis to Brain Damage*. Trans. by Steven Miller. New York: Fordham University Press, 2012.

McCarthy, Tom. *Remainder*. London: Alma Books, 2007.

McEwan, Ian. *Atonement*. London: Jonathan Cape, 2001.

McEwan, Ian. 'Author Interview'. Random House Readers' Group – Reading Guide. Available online: http://www.randomhouse.co.uk/readersgroup/readingguide.htm?command=Search&db=/catalog/main.txt&eqisbndata=0099429799 (accessed 3 June 2015), 2002.

McEwan, Ian. 'Literature, Science and Human Nature'. *The Literary Animal*. Ed. Jonathan Gottschall and David Sloan Wilson. Evanston, IL: Northwestern University Press, 2005, 5–19.

McEwan, Ian. *Saturday*. London: Jonathan Cape, 2005.

McEwan, Ian. *On Chesil Beach*. London: Jonathan Cape, 2007.
McEwan, Ian. 'The Day of Judgment'. *Guardian*. 31 May 2008.
Merleau-Ponty, Maurice. *Phenomenology of Perception*. Trans. Colin Smith. London: Routledge, 1962.
Nath, Michael. *La Rochelle*. London: Route, 2010.
Pinker, Steven, and Ian McEwan. 'Dating, Swearing, Sex and Language: A Conversation with Questions.' *Areté* 24 (2007): 81–100.
Rose, Nikolas. 'The Neurochemical Self and its Anomalies.' *Risk and Morality*. Eds Richard V. Ericson and Aaron Doyle. Toronto: Toronto University Press, 2003, 407–37.
Rose, Nikolas. *The Politics of Life Itself: Bio-medicine, Power and Subjectivity in the Twenty-First Century*. Princeton, NJ: Princeton University Press, 2007.
Rose, Steven. 'The Need for a Critical Neuroscience: From Neuroideology to Neurotechnology'. *Critical Neuroscience: A Handbook of the Social and Cultural Contexts of Neuroscience*. Eds Suparna Choudhury and Jan Slaby. Chichester: Wiley-Blackwell, 2012, 53–66.
Roth, Marko. 'The Rise of the Neuronovel'. *n+1* 8 (2009). Available online: https://nplusonemag.com/issue-8/essays/the-rise-of-the-neuronovel/ (accessed 3 June 2015).
Salisbury, Laura. 'Narration and Neurology: Ian McEwan's Mother Tongue'. *Textual Practice* 24: 5 (2010): 883–912.
Slaby, Jan, and Suparna Choudhury. 'Proposal for a Critical Neuroscience'. *Critical Neuroscience: A Handbook of the Social and Cultural Contexts of Neuroscience*. Eds Suparna Choudhury and Jan Slaby. Chichester: Wiley-Blackwell, 2012, 29–52.
Vidal, Fernando. 'Brainhood, Anthropological Figure of Modernity.' *History of the Human Sciences* 22:1 (2009): 5–36.
Vidal, Fernando, and Franciso Ortega. 'Are there Neural Correlates of Depression?' *Critical Neuroscience: A Handbook of the Social and Cultural Contexts of Neuroscience*. Eds Suparna Choudhury and Jan Slaby. Chichester: Wiley-Blackwell, 2012, 345–66.
Waugh, Patricia. 'The Naturalistic Turn, the Syndrome and the Rise of the Neo-Phenomenological Novel'. *Diseases and Disorders in Contemporary Fiction: The Syndrome Syndrome*. Eds T.J. Lustig and James Peacock. London: Routledge, 2013, 17–34.
Woolf, Virginia. 'Modern Fiction'. *The Common Reader*. London: Hogarth Press, 1925.

4

Postcolonial and Diasporic Voices
Contemporary British Fiction in an Age of Transnational Terror

Lucienne Loh

To speak about postcolonial literature in Britain as a collective body of work – whether in the 2000s or in the decades following the arrival of Empire Windrush in 1948 – risks falsely collapsing racial and ethnic categories while reducing the distinctness of various imperial contact zones and their legacies. Efforts to consider the category of postcolonial literature within the equally fluid boundaries of contemporary British literature are thus nebulous at best. Certainly reticence towards a term such as 'British Postcolonial Literature' reflects a hesitation over too facile an alignment and overlap between British Literature and postcolonial studies. Reflective of this reluctance, Graham MacPhee's 2011 study *Postwar British Literature and Postcolonial Studies* is one of the first books to analyse critically post-war British literature comprehensively through the reading strategies of postcolonial theory, 'rather than restricting the relevance of postcolonial studies to a particular body of writing by authors from British colonies and their descendants' (2). Similarly, this chapter, which focuses more specifically on British fiction of the 2000s, adopts MacPhee's assertion that 'all postwar British literature needs to be read with a consciousness of the continuing relevance of that imperial legacy' (2).

Historically, however, postcolonial literary studies have privileged regional and certainly national forms of identity as represented by national literature forged within the process of anti-colonial resistance movements and in the often fraught aftermath of decolonization and the continued effects of neocolonization. Thus, on the one hand, considering contemporary British literature within a postcolonial context involves foregrounding ways in which this literature engages with those imperial legacies that continue to complicate national identity, belonging and the cultural and linguistic stakes constitutive of nation formation and national transformation. These are complications frequently celebrated positively in terms of contemporary cosmopolitanism, a process that foregrounds transnational histories and subjectivities emerging from increased connectivity between communities and people across the globe which are not necessarily national in scope. Indeed, as Katharine Cockin and Jago Morrison argue, '[f]rom a critical point of view, moreover, a particularly thought-provoking dimension of postcolonial theory is the way it calls into question long-standing assumptions about the function of literary studies in relation to the idea of nation and the concept of the English, or British, National Literary Tradition' (7).

Indeed, since about the late 1970s, the confluence of the 'Thatcher revolution' and mass migration movements in tandem with circuits of globalization produced transnational narratives in British writing depicting personal and collective histories that lie beyond Britain's shores, but histories which are nonetheless interwoven with experiences that invoke Britain and British society. James F. English thus suggests that to consider the very nature of contemporary British fiction as a reflection of the 'worldiness' of late twentieth- and twenty-first century global literary culture and geography necessitated the inclusion of the quite distinct literary scene consisting of immigrant and postcolonial writers. Only then, he suggests, did British literature become fully contemporaneous and incorporated within the 'transnational scene and system in which British fiction was now being produced and received' (3). In her essay, 'Changes to the Canon: After Windrush', Ruvani Ranasinha argues that a number of twenty-first century contemporary British novels – Kamila Shamsie's *Salt and Saffron* (2000) and *Kartography* (2002), Monica Ali's *Brick Lane* (2003), Kiran Desai's Booker prize-winning novel *The Inheritance of Loss* (2006) and Roma Tearne's *Bone China* (2008) – represent 'constructions of identity and nation [which] are refigured within a transnational context' (190). These are novels, Ranasinha asserts, in which 'the integration of First and Third worlds' represents Britain's globalized fictions. Transnational literature also considered postcolonial British literature might reflect the process of this integration within contemporary Britain as specific colonial legacies. The extent to which the category of British fiction should necessarily include transnational and postcolonial fiction is further debated within critical anthologies published in the twenty-first century. James F. English's decision to privilege the global framework of British writing in his 2006 *A Concise Companion to Contemporary British Fiction* stands in marked contrast to Richard Bradford's 2007 *The Novel Now: Contemporary British Fiction*, which appears implicitly to emphasize and endorse the enduring, if shifting, nature of Englishness within contemporary British writing.

While these definitional anxieties surrounding British literary culture's incorporation into the transnational and postcolonial are not unique to the twenty-first century, since the 2000s, and particularly following 9/11, British literature that seeks to address the transnational threat of Islamist terror must necessarily be considered in a postcolonial light since this more recent form of terror reflects long standing colonial legacies and their attendant discourses. Indeed, writers of all ethnic hues – both British and those based in Britain – have sought to represent a range of ideological and political faultlines drawn in the wake of the 11 September attacks on the Twin Towers by Islamist terrorists, and later by the 7/7 London bombings. Postcolonial readings of these texts endeavour to represent interpretations that 'write back' against what Andrew Shyrock has identified as the international resurgence of Islamophobic sentiments within Europe and within British public culture (see Shyrock, 2010), sentiments embedded within neo-orientalist discourses derived from colonial orientalism. Other postcolonial writing written during the 2000s that does not directly address transnational terror aims to foreground persistent racism and the rights of minority cultures in contemporary Britain that remain as legacies of British imperialism and threaten national cohesion. Maggie Gee's *The White Family* (2008), for example, demonstrates both psychologically insidious and physically violent forms of racism and racial prejudice engendered by the lingering effects of the once deeply entrenched biological racism that structured British colonial discourse.

Residual effects of the colonial era are also evident in the deployment of British troops in 2003 and 2004 to support military attacks on Iraq by the United States in efforts to confront the threat of terror and the possible use of weapons of mass destruction by Saddam Hussein. The violent military tactics used by British personnel have even raised comparisons with Britain's brutal suppression of the anti-colonial Mau-Mau resistance movement in Kenya in the 1950s.[1] But Britain's collaboration with US military efforts in Iraq and Afghanistan also reflects a post-imperial British complex about a public and political recognition of a 'new colonialism [...] with its centre of gravity in the United States of America' (Sivanandan, 179). These extended foreign military involvements also suggest an attempt to discipline, control and intervene in a region that frequently maintains close cosmopolitan ties to immigrant and diasporic communities in Britain, even if only through the common thread of a globalized religious spirit. They furthermore express what Paul Gilroy terms a determined 'postimperial melancholia' present in post-war Britain, a pathology clearly attached to anti-immigrant hostility and paranoia (2004, 98). The new world order ushered in by the terrorist attacks on the Twin Towers in New York on 11 September 2001, and the various wars launched in the name of freedom and democracy, not only created heightened Islamophobia in much of Western Europe, including Britain, but inspired, in response, affective forms of political solidarity against oppression, discrimination and marginalization of immigrants in Britain. For Arjun Appadurai, young Muslims in Britain 'grow up as diasporic Britons in a multicultural world where they are by no means full citizens', plagued by everyday racism and exposed to Muslim clerics who assert that they 'truly belong not to a terrorized minority but to a terrifying majority, the Muslim world itself' (110–11). Yet, even while many Muslims in Britain feel a degree of religious and cultural persecution, other marginalized groups – especially those positioned outside the expectations and conventions of predominantly white, British, middle-class propriety and prosperity, or the codes of white working-class culture – may seek to identify with the renewed ideological power of the Muslim world.

In the name of securing the nation against terror, then, a range of geographical loci, ideological spheres and ethnic loyalties that constitute individual and communal hybrid identities in Britain are subjected to intensified monitoring through institutional networks of discipline, surveillance and punishment overseen by the state. Thus, hybridity in this charged political context is not simply, as Philip Tew argues in *The Contemporary British Novel* (2004), a fundamental condition of contemporary British identity, and one that posits false centres of unchanging traditions and white ethnic essentialism against which postcolonial critics have a tendency to define equally false peripheral postcolonial identities. Tew further suggests that hybridity in contemporary British culture and its fiction functions in ways more akin to creolization, of acculturation and reciprocity (153). Yet, forms of hybridity which now involve elements of Muslim fundamentalism that Zadie Smith lampoons through the character, Millat Zulfikar Iqbal in *White Teeth* (2000), who joins KEVIN (the Keepers of the Eternal and Victorious Islamic Nation) are cast in a more politicized light since 2001. The ironic portrait of Millat contrasts with the more laconic stance adopted by a Brixton teenager, Dennis Huggins, in Alex Wheatle's *The Dirty South* (2008), who proclaims: '[i]f you're a wannabe rebel you wanna do something that really fucks off your parents, your grandparents, the Feds and those Tory voters who listen to the *Today* programme on Radio 4. You become a Muslim. Simple as' (104). Against the backdrop of 9/11, hybrid identities that include identifying as Muslim now constitute a form of social rebellion against the status quo, resistance against the inherent prejudices perceived within institutional authority and a rejection of middle-class aspirations. But these very terms of hybridity, fuelled by misperceptions about the Muslim community, have also engendered renewed debates about the position, roles and responsibilities of immigrants, their relationship to patriotism, nationalism and their social and economic contribution to the nation. Indeed, they raise questions about the degree to which immigrants more broadly are integrated and assimilated into British society and culture. More particularly, forms of hybrid identity coterminous with cultural practices that contravene the law, such as the Muslim honour killings, which serve as the focus for the plot of Nadeem Aslam's novel, *Maps for Lost Lovers* (2004), also become acute sites of social tension and ethnic scrutiny. This kind of hybridity constitutes a very different set of politics from 'the plural cultural identities' and 'fragmented notion of "Britishness"' invoked in the Scottish novels of James Kelman and Irvine Welsh, which Richard J. Lane and Philip Tew also view as hybrid (143). Nick Bentley similarly extends the 'postcolonial' position to writers from Scotland, Wales and Northern Ireland through their use of demotic forms to resist and subvert the imposition of standard English (19). Instead, as Andrew Smith cautions, 'it is worth remembering that hybridity is a quality of narratives or discourses in specific circumstances, rather than a quality that is radical in its own right' (252). The specific political circumstances in an age of transnational terror imply some forms of postcolonial hybridity aligned with being Muslim are now intensely politicized.

While being cognisant of colonial legacies in any consideration of postcolonial studies' relevance to British literature of the twenty-first century is crucial, the scope of postcolonial studies in Britain can also expand to include immigrants from Eastern Europe, for whom the colonial encounter is less pertinent. Nick Bentley has argued in *Contemporary British Fiction* (2008), that '[o]ne of the aims of postcolonial literature has been to readdress the way in which ethnic minorities have been constructed in British literature' (18). Postcolonial British literature, however, can also readdress ways in which other minority groups – those less frequently aligned with the term 'ethnic' in Britain – have been negatively constructed. Marina Lewycka's depiction, in *Two Caravans* (2007), of rural migrant workers in the Kent countryside whose illegal status thrusts them, frequently unwillingly, into a shadowy underworld economy, depicts sympathetically the marginalization and ostracization of more recent immigrants from Eastern Europe. Indeed, the growing interest in considering Eastern Europe within a postcolonial framework, within a burgeoning area of 'postcommunist postcolonial' scholarship suggests that representations of Eastern Europeans within British literature could also be read through the lens of postcolonial studies (see Lazarus, 2002).

The task, then, of postcolonial criticism within contemporary British literature of the twenty-first century may be to suggest on-going but different modes of resistance seeking to overcome forms of prejudice faced by minority groups within Britain. These struggles over representation need to be located within the cultural and political specificities of minority groups both in national and transnational contexts and in this sense, some groups have been affected more than others by the repercussions of 9/11. The rest of this chapter broadly explores recent Black British writing and Black Asian writing, before turning, in the second half, to a more considered reflection on new lines of postcolonial inquiry by considering conflicting forms of cosmopolitanism within a Britain transformed by the global war on terror. As with Edward Said's earlier theories around orientalism, contemporary representations of the other within the cultural production of Europe determine much of the current neo-orientalist politics of race, ethnicity and religion. To situate this particular condition of postcoloniality in the twenty-first century through the lens of literature, this second section will focus on recent work by Nadeem Aslam, David Dabydeen and Leila Aboulela *alongside* fiction by Ian McEwan, Martin Amis and Chris Cleave.

Black British writing in the 2000s

Discussing the idea of a 'Black British Canon', John McCleod argues that the term 'British is deeply problematic', since collectively approaching the works of 'black' writers 'in terms of a national paradigm ultimately fails to address the transnational cultural influences and affiliations which impact upon their attempts to render the experience of black peoples in Britain' (59). James Procter, on the other hand, explicitly invokes the term 'Black British' in his study, *Dwelling Places: Postwar Black British Writing* (2003), as does Mark Stein in *Black British Literature: Novels of Transformation* (2004). The editors of the *Oxford Companion to Black British History* (2007), David Dabydeen, John Gilmore and Cecily Jones, similarly use the term. However, an aversion to representing a collective black literary experience mapped onto national space is reflected in the title of the publication *IC3: The Penguin Book of New Black Writing in Britain* (2001), an anthology of fiction and non-fiction edited by Courttia Newland and Kadija Sesay. Unlike the academic publications that employ the term 'Black British', the decision to decouple 'Black' from 'Britain' in the title of a commercial publication by Penguin Books bears some significance. Newland's and Sesay's individual introductions are emotionally charged with the momentousness of the occasion as a triumph over the fact that 'Black writing has been stifled in many ways' (x). Newland argues: '[t]he fact that IC3, the police identity code for Black, is the only collective term that relates to our situation here as residents ('Black British' is political and refers to Africans, Asians, West Indians, Americans and sometimes even Chinese) is a sad fact of life I could not ignore' (x). Sesay further asserts that 'this landmark anthology' represents not only a textual site that resists racism but underscores 'the advances that Black people in England have made and the positive impact [they] have made on British society' (xiii). While any generalization about movements within Black British writing during the first decade of the twenty-first century would be difficult, a number of notable publications with significant public impact on perceptions of 'Black culture' within British society should be highlighted. Whether these necessarily present the 'positive impact [...] on British society' by black people that Sesay hopes for nonetheless remains debatable. Without doubt, Zadie Smith's *White Teeth* introduced the language of black urban youth in an aesthetically palatable form to the largely white, middle-class novel-reading public and the patrons of literary culture. Yet, *White Teeth* can be distinguished from fiction by other black writers such as the gritty urban novels, *East of Acre Lane* (2001) and *The Dirty South* (2008) by Alex Wheatle, as well as *Society Within* (1999) by Courttia Newland. Committed to the social realism of black youths growing up rough on council estates faced with daily struggles to overcome drugs, organized crime, poverty, violence, police brutality and an education system in which they feel marginalized, Newland's and Wheatle's fiction contrasts with what James Wood has now infamously termed Smith's 'hysterical realism', where an exhausted style trumps ethics and literary realism evades social commitment. Newland's and Wheatle's social realism embraces the troubled elements of inner city life that Smith's hyperreal novel eludes. Newland asserts that he wrote with accuracy in mind as a form of social and artistic responsibility: 'I was actually trying to get away from the "everything is fine and alright in the community attitude". Most people I know felt they were not seeing themselves represented. There is a lot of pressure on you to be literary, not to talk about the crime and stuff. How many people talk about the youth right now' (cf. Roberts, 5).

Writers such as Smith, Newland and Wheatle seek to privilege the experiences of those born and raised in Britain over those who are newly arrived in the country as adults. Other black writers focus on the latter. Caryl Phillips' *A Distant*

Shore (2003) centres around the story of a refugee from an unnamed African nation rent by civil war who initially manages to escape illegally to England. But just as he believed he would find a home there, he is murdered in a racist attack by white youths in a northern village. Philips acknowledges the violent hostility directed against black African asylum seekers and represents an effort by writers to depict the tenuous plight of refugees in Britain. Similarly, Abdulrazak Gurnah's *By the Sea* (2001) concerns an elderly man seeking asylum from Zanzibar.

Even though some black writers in the twenty-first century continue to confront contemporary forms of social and political marginalization experienced by black people in Britain, others turn to a longer genealogy of four centuries of recorded black experience in Britain in an attempt to establish a black British heritage within the nation's cultural sphere. Based on Hogarth's painting of 1732, David Dabydeen's *A Harlot's Progress* (2000) returns to the origins of black fiction in the eighteenth-century slave narrative. His novel depicts the personal history of Mungo, an elderly slave who dictates the main events of his life to a white abolitionist, Mr Pringle. Andrea Levy's much lauded *Small Island*, the 2004 winner for the Orange Prize for Fiction, Whitbread Book of the Year and the Commonwealth Writers' Prize, depicts the elided experiences and personal histories of post-war black immigrants in London. Levy places her characters into specific historical and social contexts that resist not only any homogenization of the black experience in Britain, but also any singular account of Caribbean migration to Britain. Like David Dabydeen and Caryl Phillips, Levy stresses the inherently transnational nature of black identity in Britain. Part of these writers' efforts involves resurrecting forgotten histories of black slavery both in Britain and through the transatlantic slave trade. In Dabydeen's novel and in Levy's later novel *The Long Song* (2010), both writers strive to assert the importance of observing and commending historical contributions by black people to the British economy and its culture, contributions that might otherwise mitigate the often negative images of contemporary urban black youth culture.

Black writers in Britain attempt to create historical and contemporary accounts of their experiences that are not only transnational, cosmopolitan and cross-cultural, but frequently intertwine different historical time periods and geographic locales. Even though there may well be a substantial enough body of work by black writers for Gail Low and Marion Wynne-Davies to claim tentatively the existence of 'a Black British canon' (2006), it is also crucial to consider, as Paul Gilroy suggests, the way in which British and global literary culture and the country's cultural industry more generally, can commodify black experiences to the extent that blackness yields 'a user-friendly, house-trained, and marketable "reading" or translation of the stubborn vernacular that can no longer be called a counterculture' (Gilroy, 2000, 242).

Asian British writing in the 2000s

Many difficulties also accompany the category of Asian British writing, not least because of the transnational nature of the British empire and therefore its legacies. David Dabydeen, for example, identifies himself as a West Indian writer of Indian descent, as does V.S. Naipaul, who was awarded the Nobel Prize for literature in 2001. While it is easy to construct such writers within a transnational framework, Susheila Nasta, however, chooses to include Naipaul as a South Asian diasporic writer in her 2002 collection *Home Truths: Fictions of the South Asian Diaspora in Britain*. Nasta's study positions Naipaul, Salman Rushdie and Hanif Kureishi alongside other less well known writers such as Ravinder Randhawa, Romesh Gunesekera, Sunetra Gupta and Aamer Hussein – all of whom continue to publish novels in the early twenty-first century. These writers are all considered within a specifically South Asian diasporic framework attentive to the particularities of these writers' South Asian descent and their South Asian origins. In doing this, Nasta hopes to recuperate these writers not only from the excessive 'celebratory elements of exile and displacement, the *heroic* potential of migrancy as a metaphor for a "new" form of aesthetic freedom' (4), but also from the tendency for these writers 'to be incorporated by a Western readership as "exoticized" representatives of "otherness" [...] readily assimilated into the "mainstream"' (6). Similarly, in Neil Murphy and Wai-chew Sim's *British Asian Fiction: Framing the Contemporary* (2010), the editors are wary of an over inflated celebration of transnationalism inattentive to particular South Asian genealogies, even as they are aware that 'divided national/ethnic loyalties or [...] problematisations of Britishness' implies that 'British literature can no longer be discussed in monocultural terms' (2).

In the 2000s, two of the most established diasporic Indian writers in Britain who contributed to the expansion of British postcolonial literature in the 1980s – V.S. Naipaul and Salman Rushdie – continue to publish in the later stages of their literary careers. Despite being increasingly committed to non-fiction, Naipaul published two significant, interrelated novels, *Half a Life* (2001) and *Magic Seeds* (2004) in the first half of the decade. These novels return again to the consistent themes of Naipaul's earlier portraits of Britain. Through the peripatetic Willy Chandra, the protagonist of both novels, Naipaul underscores the disillusionment, dislocation and deferred hopes of the immigrant experience in Britain. Willy is uncertain about his place within the oppressive codes of the British class system, seen to be both opaque and omnipresent. Against the backdrop of the tawdriness and apathy forged from the over-indulgent post-war socialist ideals that created post-imperial Britain, Naipaul uses Chandra as a foil to keenly observe the performance and pomp of the upper classes at the same time as he scrutinizes the drab material aspirations of the London suburbs peopled by immigrants. These multicultural urban landscapes of the late twentieth and early twenty-first century are a far cry from the 'central casting' (2004: 214) – the idealized, romantic, naive stage of Dickensian, imperial London – Naipaul himself felt had eluded him so cruelly. Indeed, Richard Bradford cynically suggests that 'Naipaul leaves the reader with an impression that half a century after the British Empire began to disintegrate all that remains is a past and present comingled as dismal burlesque' (203).

In contrast to Naipaul, Salman Rushdie retreats from depicting immigrant life in Britain and turns instead to the Indian diasporic experience with *Fury* (2001). He returns to his native India to explore its rich historical store in several novels published during this decade, focusing on the impact of partition in Kashmir through *Shalimar the Clown* (2005) and the history of the Mughal empire in *The Enchantress of Florence* (2008). If Naipaul and Rushdie were writing with a nostalgic lens to a past bordered by national identity – whether English or Pakistani – then in Hari Kunzru's fiction, the transnational, the global and the cosmopolitan define the present and anticipate the future. Kunzru's first novel, *The Impressionist* (2003) was swiftly followed by *Transmission* in 2004 and a third novel, *My Revolutions* (2007). All three novels emphasize the fact that to exist in the contemporary world, especially as a bourgeois character, is to simultaneously live in a heady world of cosmopolitan cultural circuits, international political currents and a globalized economy. Similar cosmopolitan and transnational narratives abound in the novels by Kamila Shamsie, whose prolific output in this decade forms part of the growing body of work by English-language writers of Pakistani origin. Granta recently celebrated this phenomenal rise by dedicating its Autumn 2010 issue specially to Pakistani writing. Yet, alongside this outpouring of creative energy, as Muneeza Shamsie argues in a recent special issue of the *Journal of Postcolonial Writing* on 'Literature, Politics and Violence in Pakistan', '[t]oday, Pakistan is at the centre of geopolitical conflict and has been overtaken by increasing violence and religious extremism' (119).

If South Asian writers, many of whom are based in the UK, are increasingly defining themselves more narrowly by the specificities of regional affiliations,

Monica Ali's detailed portrait of an isolated Bangladeshi immigrant woman in *Brick Lane* (2003) counters the image of the privileged cosmopolitan figures in much of Naipaul's, Rushdie's and Kunzru's work and brings to light the experiences of a traditionally insular Bangladeshi community in London. Responses to Ali's novel were highly divisive: it received accusations of depicting negative ethnic stereotypes of Bangladeshi immigrants alongside praise for portraying the highly gendered experiences within the harsh realities of immigrant life set against a deprived inner city London estate. Yet, if Ali's South Asian immigrant characters are defined by their working-class status, their dislocation from mainstream British life and their linguistic insecurities, then Gautam Malkani's *Londonstani* depicts the confidently aggressive youth subculture of second generation South Asian immigrants supported by the economic successes and growing affluence of their parents' generation, even as they are equally dismissive of their parents' struggles to assimilate into British culture. Malkani captures the largely oral culture of suburban *desi* boys within a novel littered with text speak, slang, acronyms and swear words as well as countless references to the brands, commodities and material signifiers that define individual status and the different facets of each character. The novel's twist comes with the revelation that the central narrator, Jas, a white working-class character whose real name proves to be Jason, has convincingly posed as an Indian rudeboy throughout. This literary turn highlights not only that the performative aspects of urban youth identity are frequently racialized, but that the performance itself holds its own allure and sense of social empowerment. Postcolonial studies in Britain, however, has yet to analyse fully literary representations of British youth and its ever shifting modalities of cultural resistance.

Another area of recent British Asian writing that has developed through diasporic connections includes English writing by South East Asian diasporic writers who have links not only with Britain but also the British ex-colonies of Malaysia and Singapore. Malaysian-born Tash Aw's *The Harmony Silk Factory* received the Whitbread First Novel Award in 2005, while Tan Twan Eng's *The Gift of Rain* was longlisted for the Man Booker Prize in 2007. Both novels are set in Malaysia during the start of the Second World War against the tense backdrop of competing Japanese and British imperial interests in South East Asia. While conscious of the negative historical impact of British colonization on Malaysian communities, both Aw and Tan, however, also draw heavily on an orientalist discourse, couching landscapes, characters and settings within an exoticness that also inspires and supports an element of colonial nostalgia.

Conflicting cosmopolitanisms in twenty-first-century British fiction

Colonial legacies loom large in our post 9/11 world. In the months immediately following the attacks on the Twin Towers on 11 September 2001, prominent British writers publically declared not only their vehemence against the terror and violence witnessed by the world, a desire to combat the spectre of fear and paranoia lodged by the terrorists within British public consciousness, but chariness, as well, towards the retributive cycle of violence inevitably to ensue. Ian McEwan declared a day after the attacks, 'that the world would never be the same. [...] it would be worse' (2001, n.p.). Martin Amis, a week later, in an article entitled 'The Second Plane', an image that itself would drive Amis' persistent fascination and horror with the 11 September attacks, predicted that '[v]iolence must come; America must have catharsis. [...] the American retaliation is almost sure to become elephantine. Then terror from above will replenish the source of all terror from below: unhealed wounds' (9). Amis presciently observed an enduring global conflict between the strong and the weak, the terrifying will of ineffably powerful forces unleashed upon the poor and ineffectual that we can now observe in the systematic targeting and policing of Muslims in many European countries in waves of Islamophobic sentiment, as well as in the on-going wars in Iraq and Afghanistan waged in the name of democracy.

Salman Rushdie, writing with a little more distance a month after the attacks, in October 2001, couched the 11 September events in terms insinuating class conflict within a globalized capitalist economy: to New York, 'this bright capital of the visible, the forces of invisibility have dealt a dreadful blow'; but Rushdie also asserts that 'we must ensure [...] that the world of what is seen triumphs over what is cloaked' (2001, n.p.). In the midst of the endlessly proliferating terms of assessment, arraignments and accusations engendered by the attacks and later by the London bombings of 7 July 2005, the fiction produced by British writers of the twenty-first century appears eager to depict those who might represent Amis' 'terror from below' or Rushdie's invisible and cloaked social forces. In more theoretical terms, these writers construct a more material basis for an understanding of contemporary Britain's economic disparities ineluctably but not exclusively linked to the legacies of empire and to Britain's post-imperial insecurities harboured in the overwhelming shadow of American might. Yet, these writers succeed to very different degrees in articulating and addressing the repressed resentment of the disenfranchised. This chapter's second half explores these efforts through a range of writers – both white and non-white – who both explicitly and implicitly engage with the politics of 11 September. Indeed, not only are these politics connected to the discourses of neo-orientalism, the state of multiculturalism in Britain and the implementation of immigration policy that form important analytical lenses of postcolonial studies in contemporary Britain, but they also crucially impact on everyday lives.

This section focuses, in particular, on a cluster of fiction published in the middle of the decade by a range of writers, beginning by writing from arguably two of Britain's most celebrated living writers: Amis' short story, 'The Last Days of Mohammad Atta' (2006) and Ian McEwan's *Saturday* (2005). I argue that Amis and McEwan reflect white middle-class (and particularly male) anxieties about the threat posed by terrorism to the loss of bourgeois prosperity, the self-entitled privileges of material comfort and the long-term demise of British imperial pride. Conversely, Chris Cleave's epistolary novel *Incendiary* (2005) radically suggests that the spectre of terror in the mid-2000s offers an opportunity to foreground the exploitative nature of the British middle classes. While McEwan and Amis simplify the threat they demonize, two novels published around the same time as *Saturday* give voice and complexity to the perspective of Muslim identities within a populist culture of trepidation and anti-Muslim paranoia. Nadeem Aslam's 2004 *Maps for Lost Lovers* and Leila Aboulela's *Minaret*, published a year later, both focus on Muslim immigrant women in Britain for whom the global Muslim community and the social rules and norms that regulate women's behaviour offer security and a comforting bulwark against their own fear of racist hostility. Concentrated on the women's private and domestic spheres, these novels quietly resist the Islamaphomic sentiments that claim the purported repression of Muslim women. This section ends with a brief analysis of David Dabydeen's magical realist novel *Molly and the Muslim Stick* (2008), which offers an important alternative to the social realism of Aslam and Abdoulela.

Postcolonial readings of these writers' works suggest that crude terms which set up false dichotomies such as the 'clash of civilizations' obfuscate, in reality, the new global configurations of class, race and ethnicity spawned in the wake of the 11 September attacks. These readings also point to a more subtle national and cultural self-analysis about the role Britain plays in the vitiating effects of late capitalism and its longer participation in the history of capitalist imperialism upon which the promulgation of western ideologies throughout the world depends.[2] I would further suggest that these new lines of global affiliations – some affective, some political – are cosmopolitan by nature, operating beyond the bounds of the nation state, and that exploring conflicting forms of cosmopolitanism in British society may at the same time address new forms of transnational conflict mediated through Britain. One has to look no further for the terms of these conflicting cosmopolitanisms than to a recent 'mini-manifesto' by Carlos Cortiglia, the British National Party candidate for the 2012 London Mayoral elections. 'Dear Londoners' he asserts, 'I am of Italian descent which, I guess, makes me the most "cosmopolitan" candidate standing for London Mayor in 2012. I was outraged to find some immigrant communities refusing to respect the British people and their way of life' (8–9).

Cortiglia's claims to a cosmopolitan immigrant identity seem unwarranted while his party rallies around cries that the BNP defends Britain's 'traditional Christian faith', which should 'protect our national identity from the threat of Islam'. Yet Cortiglia's assertions also underscore forms of conflicting cosmopolitan identities in contemporary British fiction written in response to 9/11 and its global repercussions. While Cortiglia promotes an image of the ideal cosmopolitan immigrant as a 'cosmopolitan patriot' – a term K. Anthony Appiah (1997) uses to assert that patriotism and cosmopolitanism can complement each other – British writers have also been keen both to critique and celebrate the cosmopolitan immigrant whom Cortiglia constructs as the source of his outrage. This particular imagining of the immigrant figure is one who holds personal and national affiliations that are nebulous, unstable and potentially threatening to the British people Cortiglia has in mind. Yet, this debate equally obscures the cosmopolitan immigrant's relationship to what Marx has termed a 'global bourgeoisie [which] has through its exploitation of the world-market given a cosmopolitan character to production and consumption in every country' (cf. Tucker, 476). In Britain's post 9/11 world, turning to global Islam as a means of articulating resistance or resentment to the exploitative processes and the asymmetrical benefits of the world-market, linked historically to the spread of capitalism and racism through colonial technologies, becomes frequently confused and wrongly conflated with support for Islamism and acts of terror, just as these same sentiments also come into conflict with the interests of a global bourgeoisie and market ideology.

Since the 1990s, contemporary theories of cosmopolitanism in such forms as 'cosmopolitanism from below', 'minority cosmopolitanism', and 'discrepant cosmopolitanism' attempt to address Marx's argument about the victims of the cosmopolitan nature of global capital, yet how British fiction articulates, and participates in, these theories within the context of the twenty-first century has yet to be fully discussed.[3] I suggest that the work by writers discussed here can be positioned relative to an argument by one of cosmopolitanism's most astute theorists, Pheng Cheah, who argues that we now contend with a new world order where 'new radical cosmopolitanisms from below can regulate the excesses of capitalist economic globalization' (19–20). In Amis' short story 'The Last Days of Muhammad Atta', this 'new radical cosmopolitanism' forms the unconscious irony of the text. Amis unconsciously concedes his shared disgust with Atta for the very 'excesses of capitalist economic globalisation' Atta despises and whose suicide forms a violent statement of protest against those same excesses. In McEwan's novel *Saturday*, the conflict between the two central characters – ostensibly ciphers for various forms of terror on the one hand, and middle-class Britain, on the other – suggests the lingering racial and economic legacies of British colonialism present in contemporary Britain, at the heart of which lies a longer genealogy of capitalist expansion and exploitation on a global scale.

How the other half dies: Martin Amis' 'The Last Days of Muhammad Atta' (2006)

Amis' short story 'The Last Days of Muhammad Atta', first published in *The New Yorker* in April 2006, re-imagines the last 28 hours of Muhammad Atta's life before he flies American Airlines flight 11 into the North Tower of the World Trade Center in New York on the morning of 11 September 2001. The story itself was inspired by the 9/11 Commission report that curiously stated a lack of explanation for why Muhammad Atta drove to Portland in Maine from Boston on the morning of September 10, only to return to Boston on another flight, which would then connect Atta onto American Airlines flight 11. In a review of the story for *The Observer*, Peter Conrad suggests Amis undertakes his own form of jihad 'against the brawling squalor of obese humanity' (n.p.), but it is notably the image here of sordid excess and decay underpinning Amis' personal jihad that also insinuates what might be viewed as the short story's 'political unconscious'.[4]

While Amis' 1984 novel *Money: A Suicide Note* self-consciously reflects Amis' thinly veiled disdain for the British working-class making its way in the globalized economy of the 1980s, through the character of Mohammad Atta, Amis' antipathy is seemingly directed against a nebulously constructed image of racially disenfranchised cultures angered by the global economic power wielded by American neoimperialism. Atta's radical cosmopolitanism broadly represents such cultures. While Atta has lived in many countries, is fluent in Arabic, German and English, boasts skills such as being a trained architect, and frequently flies on American commercial airlines, his outrage at American power, which he terms monstrous, perverse and cruel, and his disgust for 'Americans and American purpose and automatic self-belief' (Amis, 117) are all unequivocal. Indeed, Atta echoes the voice of what Arjun Appadurai calls, in the British context, a new self-constructed minority forged from the rubble of 9/11 and one very different from that imagined by the British state. For Appadurai, this minority is 'born out of the shreds and patches of British multiculturalism, the new minorities [form] the rogue voice of an injured global majority [...] one of the myriad ways in which a deep colonial history joins the dynamics of global minority politics' (111).

Amis' loathing of this new minority draws on prejudices stemming from colonial history that continue to run deep within contemporary British society. Much like the crudest biological basis for colonial racism, Amis depicts Atta as bilious, grotesque and decrepit, while being sexually rapacious, repulsive and repressed: he suffers severe constipation, possesses a 'frank animus of the underbite' (97) set within a face 'growing more gangrenous by the day' (98), exudes rancid breath and endures constant waves of nausea and splitting headaches. Yet the detailed minutiae of Amis' warped version of the pathological make-up of a terrorist overshadows the short story's 'political unconscious', which traces Amis' own distaste for the very excesses of a globalized economy against which Atta directs his hatred, an unconscious in which Amis' privileged cosmopolitanism mingles with Atta's radical cosmopolitanism from below.

Indeed, the budget hotel where the story opens captures a landscape littered with Amis' keen perception of the detritus within postmodern life and all the trappings of bland commercial hopes, entrenched apathy and tedious routine. The Repose Inn, where we first encounter Atta, signifies Amis' view of the iterative nightmare of late capitalism with its indistinguishable rooms lined with cheap TVs, dented white fridges and vapid music piping away in the lobby while the whole insipid building is wrapped around by a soulless carpark in which Atta has parked his 'brand-new, factory-fresh Nissan Altima', the car that will ferry his fellow terrorists around (106). Amis portrays Atta as alienated and frustrated by an atomized life eviscerated of human connections where Atta futilely struggles to locate meaning in 'citations, pilgrimages, conspiracy theories [...] as other people collected autographs or beermats' (101). Religious fervour seems to represent a response to postmodern ennui. Amis coins the term 'pan-anathema' (121) for Atta's hatred of this life, personified ironically by airports in which Atta derides the risible rigmarole of fatuous security questions and inane and ultimately irrelevant displays of technological advancement such as CAPPS (the Computer Assisted Passenger Prescreening System) (108). But Atta's contempt may as well reflect Amis' distaste for America's excessive displays of its own power and superior technology. The excess and decay that Atta sees infused in American life is also unconsciously shared by Amis through the repulsive image of the 'fat blonde with a scalp disease' (109) whom Atta sits next to on the first leg of his plane journey between Portland and Boston.

The short story's structure itself betrays its submerged political unconscious. Amis eventually reveals that the reason for Atta travelling to Portland in Maine was to visit an imam in a Portland hospital downtown, which Amis describes as a slew of indistinguishable businesses. Atta meets the imam for a quick 'quid pro quo' where the imam gives Atta an 8-ounce Volvic bottle purportedly containing holy water from Mecca in exchange for Atta swapping the story of his induction by a Sheikh in Kandahar. Amis focuses not on the political narrative of Taliban operatives training in Afghanistan, but on the ironic image of holy water commodified and packaged in a Volvic bottle, the water's supposed sanctity sullied by cheap plastic and a packaging label attesting to levels of purity. Amis appears to despise the absurdity of global marketing and brand consciousness as much as he detests the fetishization of holy water.

Atta, and by implication Amis, then, steep themselves in shared scorn for what Atta identifies as the perpetual 'condition of unbounded boredom' (113) at the heart of Western mass culture. The endless act of repetition and 'the themes of recurrence and prolongation' (99), and what he sees as 'the misery of recurrence' (113) drives Atta to suicidal despair. However, this is the point where the two clearly part ways. Atta declares a point about radical cosmopolitanism during his last moments of life: 'Who's going to do it, if we don't? If we don't, who else is going to risk death to save the lives of strangers?' (117). In 'The Last Days of Muhammad Atta', Amis' ineluctable satire of one of the 9/11 terrorists reveals the author's own repressed desire to confront the banality of lives produced out of the excesses of a global economy dominated by the United States. In Amis' story, radical cosmopolitanism and privileged cosmopolitanism commingle through Amis' barely repressed abhorrence for the shallow materialism underpinning postmodern life.

How the other half lives: Ian McEwan's *Saturday* (2005)

In Ian McEwan's *Saturday*, the enemy is clearly quashed. Termed McEwan's creative response to 9/11, the novel is set on Saturday 15 February 2003, the day of the anti-Iraq war demonstrations held in central London. On this particular Saturday, the novel's protagonist, Henry Perowne attempts to enjoy a leisurely day off from being a highly regarded and overworked neurosurgeon. Not only is Perowne highly successful professionally, but he is sexually attractive and able, a deft squash player and a seafood connoisseur who also summers in a French chateau that his wife, a lawyer, will someday inherit. Situated somewhere between personification and caricature, Perowne, whose name reflects a degree of self-preoccupation, stands as a clear cipher for bourgeois privilege as well as the material excesses of global capital. Contemporary radical cosmopolitanism from below, signified by the thuggish working-class character of Baxter and his cronies, however, defines itself against the kind of privileged cosmopolitanism Perowne exemplifies. Yet, these broader politics elude Perowne, even if McEwan is only too aware of them. Perowne's own material security – while undermined during the course of the day in a car accident involving Baxter and a later attack led by Baxter on his family at home – is eventually secured and reaffirmed by the novel's awkward end when Perowne performs life-saving surgery on Baxter's brain.

Perowne and his nemesis Baxter represent political values in an age of transnational terror. McEwan suggests that the ostensible political excuse for the Anglo-American alliance's declaration of war against Iraq is, in many ways, in defence of the values that Perowne holds dear. Perowne serves as a contemporary manifestation of the modern cosmopolitan consciousness of eighteenth-century European Enlightenment, itself the source of colonial discourse that elevated the enlightened, rational human subject over the purported irrational barbaric native other. Perowne, endowed with the powers of reason, science, material wealth and culture, possesses, above all, a profound conviction in the rational and a suspicion of what he repeatedly terms 'the supernatural' (17, 68, 74), upon which he assumes religious fundamentalism depends.

Indeed, Perowne fears that acts of terror by extremist groups, whom he refers to several times in the novel as 'radical Islamists' (34, 151, 167, 191) or Al-Qaeda (73, 100, 181, 186, 191), threaten what his musician son, Theo, calls, rather vaguely, 'our whole way of life' (35). However, Perowne singularly fails to see his own role within the reasons driving the forces of jihad that terrify him. For much of the novel, he neglects to realize that his unease about the overhanging spectre of terror and his sense that his days are 'baffled and fearful' (4) are intricately linked to a threatened sense of the relative material ease of his own life. McEwan metaphorically represents this image of conflict by the minor collision of Perowne's and Baxter's cars.

This encounter, which disrupts Perowne's Saturday, leads a humiliated and chagrined Baxter to seek revenge by infiltrating Perowne's house and threatening to both kill his wife and rape his daughter. Needless to say, it is not a typical Saturday for Perowne, who is used to enjoying his Saturdays 'thoughtlessly content' (124–5). At the scene of the car accident, Perowne studies his mildly dented 'silver Mercedes S500 with cream upholstery', and angrily notes that '[h]is car will never be the same again. It's ruinously altered, and so is his Saturday' (75). This confrontation serves as a cipher for the 9/11 attacks as the accident wrecks the comfortable domestic routines and material security to which Perowne and his family are accustomed.

Thus, if Perowne stands broadly for western civilization as well as its financial might, then as Robert Eaglestone points out, Baxter serves as a problematic and awkward metonym for its enemies: degeneracy, Saddam Hussein, Osama bin Laden, terrorism, the 'War on Terrorism' (22). Baxter, I would suggest, stands also as the figure of the cosmopolitan from below, resentful of the smug accumulation of capital wealth and the material excess Perowne represents. Indeed, McEwan frequently alerts us more overtly to Perowne's own detached presumptuousness as well as his hankering for control and power. Perowne is depicted as possessing the 'remote possessiveness of a god' (13), and likens himself to a 'god' in the operating theatre where he performs nothing short of medical miracles.

Michael L. Ross, Lynn Wells and Elizabeth Kowaleski Wallace, amongst other critics, have pointed out that Perowne fails to see his own class position within a system of oppression. Despite Perowne's concern for the 'state of the world' – which he says repeatedly is what 'in fact troubles him the most' (McEwan, 81) – he fails to understand his own stake in that state. Perowne neglects his own material conditions which implicate him in the system of global capital that the jihadists he so fears aim to resist. Indeed, his inability to see past his own class position reaches a parodic pitch in the novel's climactic scene when Baxter returns to threaten his family and Perowne tries to see his living room from Baxter's point of view:

> Before Baxter speaks, Perowne tries to see the room through his eyes, as if that might help predict the degree of trouble ahead: the two bottles of champagne, the gin and the bowls of lemon and ice, the belittlingly high ceiling and its mouldings, the Bridget Riley prints flanking the Hodgkin, the muted lamps, the cherry wood floor beneath the Persian rugs, the careless piles of serious books, the decades of polish in the thakat table. The scale of retribution could be large. (207)

The carefully weighted phrases evoke the richly layered details of Perowne's wealth and comfort – embodied by the Riley prints, the Hodgkin, Persian rugs, thakat table – all of which are rendered farcical by the persistent pride and self-gratifying satisfaction he takes in his accumulated possessions, drawn out and visually showcased over a lengthy series of clauses. The simple economy of the pronoun 'the' in reference to a Howard Hodgkin painting, the personification of a condescending ceiling, the reflection of time in the sheen of the table all signify the aestheticization of a discourse of English class distinction and of material privilege that remains ironically unabated, from Perowne's point of view, even in this evidently life threatening situation. In offering the reader the carefully crafted details of the room, McEwan calibrates a disjunct between Perowne's view, which Perowne assumes is sympathetic, and Baxter's point of view, whose own perspective may be quickly summarized by one of Baxter's side-kicks, Nige, who, while pausing 'self-consciously in the doorway', utters the following piercing observation: 'Fucking size of this place' (208). Simultaneously politicized, then, is the aesthetic distance between Perowne's blindness to his cosmopolitan privilege and the insight suddenly gained by Nige's realization of Perowne's self-indulgent excesses.

Perowne's own economic and social privilege, and indeed, his worldview can be placed within a longer genealogy of British colonial history and colonial discourse. His patronizing and degrading attitude to Baxter draws on racist terms reminiscent of orientalist ideology as Baxter consistently recollects, for Perowne, simian images. He has 'a bulbous mouth' creating 'the effect of a muzzle', and a 'general simian air' (88). Indeed, the link between Baxter and bestial features, especially ape-like attributes, clearly relates to nineteenth-century colonial discourse in which the colonized and the colonized working class, in particular, were described in animalistic terms, frequently belittled as child-like, and therefore requiring the education, discipline and beneficence of England's civilizing mission, all of which Perowne symbolizes. If Baxter stands in for terrorist, Islamist terror, or the cosmopolitan from below who objects to global bourgeois entitlement, then the inherently biological prejudices Perowne holds towards Baxter exemplify the forms of racism inspiring Islamist fervour. Thus McEwan subtly demonstrates the motivations for radical Islam positioned more narrowly within a broader spectrum of radical cosmopolitanism, which aims to realign the disproportionate degree of power, and readdress the prejudices, held by those who believe in the innate superiority of western civilization. Yet, Baxter's subjugation by Perowne at the end of the novel crucially reinstates the power structures of global class hierarchies and suggests that western civilization will prevail in any enduring confrontation with Islam.

The resoundingly awkward ending to *Saturday* fundamentally structures the novel's underlying ideology. Arthur Bradley and Andrew Tate argue in *The New Atheist Novel* that both Amis and McEwan represent 'New Atheist' writers who not only use fiction to promote 'a cluster of beliefs – militant atheism, evolutionary biology, neuroscience and even political Neo-Conservatism', but also 'the ideological war against religion, religious fundamentalism and, after 9/11, religious terror' (11). Certainly contemporary British writers such as Amis and McEwan are now participants within the political discourses surrounding transnational terror, but literature written in the wake of the horror of 9/11 must continue to be read with a multitude of interpretations if it is to defeat the very dogmatism that fundamentalism seeks to defend. As Robert Spencer argues, '[i]t is time for postcolonial critics to obey the hermeneutic imperative to analyse contemporary fiction in such a way as to reveal its frequent capacity to be *radically* democratic: to combat all forms of fundamentalism, the obvious dangers of religious militancy and colonial arrogance (403). To read contemporary British fiction through conflicting and, at times, elusive forms of radical cosmopolitanisms contributes to this democratic discourse and places the production and consumption of British literature itself within the politics of the twenty-first century's new world order.

It's all kicking off: Chris Cleave's *Incendiary* (2005)

In delineating the class inequalities that exist within contemporary British society, Chris Cleave's *Incendiary* complicates the false terms of global conflict – pitting the multitudes of globally oppressed against the privileged, exploitative and imperialist West – which the terrorists of 11 September sought to galvanize.[5] Slavoj Žižek has suggested that the 'ideological antagonism' between a 'Western consumerist way of life and Muslim radicalism' is misplaced (40), and instead what is at stake is not the notion of the 'clash of civilizations' but 'clashes *within* each civilisation' (41; emphasis in original) and 'the clash of *economic* interests' (42; emphasis in original). Written in the tone and style of a white working-class woman, whose son and husband die in a violent terrorist bomb attack at the Emirates Arsenal football stadium, Cleave's epistolary novel unfolds over a series of letters written by the grieving woman to Osama bin Laden. The unnamed female character who functions as a cosmopolitan figure from below, suggests multiple ways in which Britain's middle classes oppress, exploit and demean the working classes, frequently for their own voyeuristic pleasure. The novel both dismisses and discredits the political message of 11 September's terrorists who indiscriminatingly posit the West as a homogeneous bloc of economic advantage constituted of national spaces populated wholly by privileged cosmopolitans. Conversely, *Incendiary* also further suggests that the rigid political and ideological fault lines imposed by British and American government rhetoric and institutional discourses following 11 September necessarily excludes, denies and precludes any possibility of 11 September affording a political and social statement about class inequalities within Britain.

Cleave rejects any claims made by Osama bin Laden and Al-Qaeda to represent a collective voice of oppression through acts of terrorism and violence. The narrator reminds Osama: 'I'm what you'd call an infidel and my husband called working class. There is a difference you know' (3). The narrator underscores the fallacy in Al-Qaeda's mutually exclusive groupings of white Westerners, or infidels, regardless of class, and a non-Western, non-white underclass of economically disenfranchised people whom Al-Qaeda purportedly seeks to defend as victims of global capitalism.

Cleave articulates the institutional prejudices and economic marginalization faced by Britain's white working class who are exploited by forces of globalization and particularly by a white managerial, financial, professional and creative class personified in the novel by the bourgeois journalist Jasper Black and his lavish, self-possessed girlfriend, Petra Sutherland. Jasper and Petra both regard the narrator's working-class status with sadistic voyeurism and later exploit and betray her trust in them for their own personal and financial gain, leaving her economically destitute and socially vulnerable. At the end of the novel, mentally fragile and at the risk of losing her home, the narrator takes up a job stacking shelves at her local Tesco Metro in Bethnal Green. She imagines filling in her application form with the following reason for desiring to work at Tesco:

> BECAUSE MY HUSBAND AND MY BOY WERE RECENTLY BLOWN UP BY ISLAMIC TERRORISTS AND THIS HAS CAUSED A NUMBER OF PROBLEMS FOR ME BUT THE MOST URGENT NOW IS MONEY AND THAT IS WHY I WANT TO WORK AT TESCO'S ALSO BECAUSE IT IS CLOSE TO MY FLAT AND I WOULD MUCH RATHER STACK YOUR SHELVES FOR MONEY THAN GO ON THE GAME.

Instead, she writes, 'BECAUSE I AM A TEAM PLAYER AND I BELIEVE TESCO'S IS AN EXCELLENT COMPANY THAT RESPECTS TEAM WORK' (324–5). Cleave's novel radically repositions the political and economic alliances crudely drawn by Islamic terrorism in a post 9/11 world and, by doing so, creates new forms of cosmopolitanism from below in Britain's white working-class population. Having been driven into a desperate situation not only by the tragedy of the death of her husband and son by a bomb set off by Islamic terrorists, but as much by Jasper's and Petra's cruel machinations, the narrator draws parallels between these two causes for her financial woes and deprivation. In the novel's closing pages, the narrator's sympathies seem tenuously to lie with Osama, to whom she says: '[s]ome people are cruel and selfish and the world would be better off without them. You were absolutely right the whole time some people only deserve to burn' (330). *Incendiary* subtly intimates that the war against terror in the twenty-first century has also lent blind justification and forced allegiance to the righteousness of neoliberal economics whose victims the world over also often include the white working class in Britain.

Against 9/11 exceptionalism: Nadeem Aslam's *Maps for Lost Lovers* (2004) and Leila Aboulela's *Minaret* (2005)

Several British novels published in the 2000s concerning Muslims in Britain attempt to domesticate the politics of Islam and fundamentalism by focusing on the everyday, the private and the affective. The Muslims in these novels can also be considered cosmopolitans from below because of their working class status and their transnational familial and religious ties. Even though Nadeem Aslam's 2004 novel, *Maps for Lost Lovers*, does not explicitly engage with 9/11, the closeted Muslim world he depicts lie at the heart of much of the controversy around supposedly inassimilable Muslim immigrants in Britain. The focalized perspective of Kaukab, the insular, disillusioned immigrant protagonist in *Maps for Lost Lovers*, suggests a Pakistani Muslim woman's deeply conservative and dogmatic approach to Islam, sadly one that not only contributes to her failing and uncompromising relationships with her immediate family, but also a sense of isolation and dislocation from British life. The novel, however, also depicts the lives of a closely knit transnational, cosmopolitan Pakistani community based in Britain, for whom traditional values transposed from Pakistan shore up frequently brutally misogynistic cultural practices. The novel's plot is driven around the ramifications of a set of revenge killings for an illicit affair between the characters Jugnu and Chanda, but it also depicts several instances of Islamic exorcists hired in rituals to banish spirits from purportedly wayward daughters and women in order to discipline and confine them within the strict gender and ethnic roles prescribed for Muslim women. Aslam castigates such fundamentalist interpretations of Islam. He argues that '[i]n a way, the book is about September 11, I asked myself whether in my personal life and as a writer I had been rigorous enough to condemn the small scale September 11s that go on every day. Jugnu and Chanda are the September 11 of this book' (Aslam, 2004). Depictions of both Kaukab's religious fundamentalism and the violence against women practised within her Muslim community may contribute to the negative stereotypes of Muslims in Britain that represent sources for Islamophobic sentiments intensified in the wake of 9/11 and following the 2005 London bombings. However, Aslam's novel also suggests that these fundamentalist cultural practices are supported by global religious networks that extend well beyond Britain and, like the terror attacks, are organized on a transnational scale.

Islam also plays a crucial role for the lonely female narrator, Najwa, of Leila Aboulela's 2005 novel *Minaret*. Like Kaukab, Najwa also represents the experiences of a cosmopolitan from below living in Britain and, similar to Kaukab, Najwa views the local Islamic community as an intrinsic part of a wider global, indeed, cosmopolitan spiritual community that offers her a life-giving source of comfort, security and belonging. When her privileged life in Khartoum ends abruptly following a political coup, Najwa seeks refuge in London as an asylum seeker in London. Her precarious new life in London as a maid to a wealthy Egyptian-Sudanese family places her on a constant precipice of fear and insecurity. While parts of the novel are set in 2002 and 2003, the impact of 9/11 on perceptions of Muslims plays no explicit part in Aboulela's novel, even though the racist aggression and abuse on a London bus Najwa suffers hints at this context. Resisting what Graham Macphee calls 'the paradigm of post 9/11 exceptionalism' (116), Aboulela appears to underscore other local and global political concerns beyond the politics of Islamic terror that overwhelmingly affect Muslim immigrants' everyday lives in Britain. Instead, she focuses on the repercussions of the Gulf War of 1991–2, political insecurity, failed states, civil war and violent religious divisions in their home nations.

Magical Realism in an age of terror: David Dabydeen's *Molly and the Muslim Stick* (2008)

Set both against the backdrop of the political and social discourses that have dominated the debate over the 'clash of civilizations' purportedly sealed by 9/11 as well as the dissolution of the British empire in the decades following the end of World War II, David Dabydeen's strange, magical realist novel, *Molly and the Muslim Stick* self-consciously exceeds the divisive racial, ethnic and religious ideologies that surround the supposed incompatibility of Christianity and Islam that also defines twenty-first-century geopolitics. Molly, the novel's white, working-class female narrator from a mining town in Lancashire, recounts her childhood memories of her father repeatedly subjecting her to violent and brutal sexual abuse. Broken, dispirited and isolated from society around her as an adult, her walking stick becomes her comforting companion with whom she forms both an antagonistic and loving relationship. The stick, who begins to converse with Molly, explains his pride in both his English and Muslim forebears since he is forged from wood that Christian crusaders brought back to England from the East and cross fertilized with local English trees. His 'sap is the splendour of merged continents, at once Muslim and Christian' (72) and, indeed, Molly acknowledges Stick's hybrid 'distinguished and ancient pedigree'. Through the extended metaphor of the Muslim stick and his inherently cosmopolitan nature, consisting of 'different climes, across cultures, in different forms' (118), Dabydeen resists blinkered attitudes to any essentialized construction of either Muslim or Christian civilizations as fundamentally antithetical or mutually incompatible with each other, or indeed, of one as necessarily inferior to the other.

Yet having largely been produced from English stock, the memory of Stick's Muslim heritage has subsided. It takes Molly's and the Stick's encounter with a lost Amerindian asylum seeker from the jungles of British Guiana to fully reawaken Stick's Islamic heritage, even though Molly and the Stick initially both treat the black stranger with hostility and the combined contempt of English propriety and racism. They both call him a savage (90; 102), with Stick even labelling the new arrival 'a nigger' (90). Through the fantastical narrative of Molly's enduring friendship with the Muslim stick, Dabydeen suggests not only cosmopolitanism's peaceful utopian vision for all Muslims in Britain, and the possibility of nurturing relationships with white Britons, but in creating a magical stick as a central Muslim character, he inserts an element of humour and farce that satirizes claims about the triumphant nature of Islamic civilizations.

In a postmodern era in which grand narratives are supposedly dead, we witness a dangerous resurrection of national and religious teleologies that reflect a global clash of ideologies in the twenty-first century. Whether in the name of democracy, peace or capitalism defined by the United States, or in the name of the global oppressed poor, self-determination or Islamist justice, Britain and its immigrant communities today partake in an ever more heated environment of paranoia, racially and ethnically circumscribed recriminations as well as more virulent forms of nationalism that are themselves legacies of Britain's vast erstwhile empire. Contemporary British fiction engages with this global landscape in a multitude of ways, even if the writers considered within the category of 'British fiction' of the twenty-first century often sit uncomfortably with being yoked to any national literary paradigm.

Notes

1 See Curtis, 'The colonial precedent'. Paul Gilroy makes a similar argument about parallels between British brutality in Iraq in 2003–4 and Britain's treatment of Mau-Mau insurgents. See Gilroy 2004: 101.
2 For the argument that the wars in Iraq and Afghanistan as well as the War on Terror are part of a longer history of capitalist imperialism, see Lazarus 2011: 15–18.
3 See for example, Bruce Robbins 1998, 1–2. Fuyuki Kurasawa's 'cosmopolitanism from below' has proved enduring and influential (2004). See also Susan Koshy's term 'minority cosmopolitanism' (2011) and James Clifford's term 'discrepant cosmopolitanism' (1997, 36).
4 This term is taken from Jameson (1981), while also acknowledging the important recent work by Neil Lazarus, *The Postcolonial Unconscious*.
5 It could be argued that Cleave contributes to a limited body of work that could be considered British working-class literature written within a new post 9/11 era of globalization in which America operates as the pinnacle of global capitalism. What is distinct about Cleave's novel is his choice of a white, working-class female narrator. Nicholas Coles and Janet Zandy have published a range of working-class portraits in the post 9/11 American context, highlighting particularly working-class people who died in 9/11 'at the pinnacle of American global capitalism' (669–70).

Works cited

Aboulela, Leila. *Minaret*. London: Bloomsbury, 2006.
Ali, Monica. *Brick Lane*. London: Doubleday, 2003.
Amis, Martin. *Money: A Suicide Note*. London: Jonathan Cape, 1984.
Amis, Martin. 'The Last Days of Muhammad Atta'. *The Second Plane*. London: Jonathan Cape, 2008, 95–124.
Amis, Martin. 'The Second Plane'. *The Second Plane*. London: Jonathan Cape, 2008, 3–10.
Appadurai, Arjun. *Fear of Small Numbers: An Essay on the Geography of Anger*. Durham and London: Duke University Press, 2006.

Appiah, Kwame Anthony. 'Cosmopolitan Patriots'. *Critical Inquiry* 23:3 (1997): 617–39.
Aslam, Nadeem. 'A Question of Honour'. *The Independent* 11 June 2004. Available online: http://www.independent.co.uk/artsentertainment/books/features/nadeem-aslam-a-question-of-honour-6167858.html (accessed 15 January, 2015).
Aslam, Nadeem. *Maps for Lost Lovers*. London: Faber and Faber, 2005 [2004].
Aw, Tash. *The Harmony Silk Factory*. New York: Harper Perennial, 2005.
Bentley, Nick. *Contemporary British Fiction*. Edinburgh: Edinburgh University Press, 2008.
Bradford, Richard. *The Novel Now: Contemporary British Fiction*. London: Blackwell Publishing, 2007.
Bradley, Arthur, and Andrew Tate. *The New Atheist Novel: Fiction, Philosophy and Polemic After 9/11*. London: Continuum, 2010.
Cheah, Pheng. *Inhuman Conditions: On Cosmopolitanism and Human Rights*. Cambridge: Harvard University Press, 2006.
Cleave, Chris. *Incendiary*. London: Sceptre, 2005.
Clifford, James. *Routes: Travel and Translation in the Late Twentieth Century*. Cambridge: Harvard University Press, 1997.
Cockin, Katharine, and Jago Morrison, Eds. *The Post-War British Literature Handbook*. London: Continuum, 2010.
Coles, Nicholas, and Janet Zandy. 'The New World Order and Its Consequences: 1980s to 2005'. *American Working-Class Literature: An Anthology*. Eds Nicholas Coles and Janet Zandy. Oxford: Oxford University Press, 2006.
Conrad, Peter. 'You're facing the unthinkable . . .'. *The Observer*, 28 May 2006. Available online: http://www.guardian.co.uk/film/2006/may/28/martinamis (accessed 15 January, 2015).
Cortiglia, Carlos. 'BNP Manifesto'. 'Mayor of London & London Assembly Elections'. London 2012. London: Greater London Returning Officer London Elects, City Hall, The Queen's Walk, London SE1 2AA, 8–9.
Curtis, Mark. 'The colonial precedent'. *Guardian* 26 October 2004. Available online:http://www.guardian.co.uk/world/2004/oct/26/iraq.military (accessed 15 January, 2015).
Dabydeen, David. *A Harlot's Progress*. London: Vintage, 2000.
Dabydeen, David. *Molly and the Muslim Stick*. London: Macmillan Publishers, 2008.
Dabydeen, David, John Gilmore and Cecily Jones, Eds. *Oxford Companion to Black British History*. Oxford: Oxford University Press, 2007.
Desai, Kiran. *The Inheritance of Loss*. London: Hamish Hamilton, 2006.
Eaglestone, Robert. 'The Age of Reason is Over . . . An Age of Fury was Dawning'. *Wasafiri* 22:2 (2007): 19–22.
Eng, Tan Twan. *The Gift of Rain*. Newcastle: Myrmidon, 2007.
English, James F. 'Introduction: British Fiction in a Global Frame'. *A Concise Companion to Contemporary British Fiction*. Ed. James F. English. London: Blackwell Publishing, 2006.

Gee, Maggie. *The White Family.* London: Saqi Books, 2008.
Gilroy, Paul. *Between Camps: Race, Identity and Nationalism at the End of the Colour Line.* London: Allen Lane, 2000.
Gilroy, Paul. *After Empire: Melancholia or Convivial Culture?* London and New York: Routledge, 2004.
Granta 112: Pakistan. London: Granta Books, Autumn 2010.
Gurnah, Abdulrazak. *By the Sea.* London: Bloomsbury, 2001.
Jameson, Fredric. *The Political Unconscious: Narrative as a Socially Symbolic Act.* Ithaca: Cornell University Press, 1981.
Koshy, Susan. 'Minority Cosmopolitanism'. *PMLA* 126:3 (2011): 592–609.
Kunzru, Hari. *The Impressionist.* London: Penguin, 2003.
Kunzru, Hari. *Transmission.* London: Penguin, 2004.
Kunzru, Hari. *My Revolutions.* London: Penguin, 2007.
Kurasawa, Fuyuki. 'A Cosmopolitanism from Below: Alternative Globalization and the Creation of a Solidarity without Bounds'. *Journal of Intercultural Studies* 29:4 (2004): 347–61.
Lane, Richard J., Rod Mengham and Philip Tew, Eds. *Contemporary British Fiction.* Cambridge: Polity Press, 2003.
Lazarus, Neil. 'Spectres haunting: Postcommunism and postcolonialism'. *Journal of Postcolonial Writing* 48:2 (2002): 117–30.
Lazarus, Neil. *The Postcolonial Unconscious.* Cambridge: Cambridge University Press, 2011.
Levy, Andrea. *Small Island.* London: Hodder Headline, 2004.
Levy, Andrea. *The Long Song.* London: Hodder Headline, 2010.
Lewycka, Marina. *Two Caravans.* London: Penguin, 2007.
Low, Gail, and Marion Wynne-Davies, Eds. *A Black British Canon?* Basingstoke: Palgrave Macmillan, 2006.
MacPhee, Graham. *Postwar British Literature and Postcolonial Studies.* Edinburgh: Edinburgh University Press, 2011.
Malkani, Gautam. *Londonstani.* London: Fourth Estate, 2006.
McCleod, John. 'Some Problems with "British" in "a Black British Canon"'. *Wasafiri* 17:36 (2002): 59.
McEwan, Ian. 'Beyond Belief'. *Guardian* 12 September 2001. Available online: http://www.guardian.co.uk/world/2001/sep/12/september11.politicsphilosophyandsociety (accessed 15 January, 2015).
McEwan, Ian. *Saturday.* London: Vintage, 2006.
Murphy, Neil, and Wai-chew Sim, Eds. *British Asian Fiction: Framing the Contemporary.* New York: Cambria Press, 2008.
Naipaul, V.S. *Half a Life.* New York: Knopf, 2001.
Naipaul, V.S. *Magic Seeds.* London: Picador, 2004.
Nasta, Susheila. *Home Truths: Fictions of the South Asian Diaspora in Britain.* Basingstoke: Palgrave, 2002.
Newland, Courttia. *Society Within.* London: Abacus, 1999.

Newland, Courttia, and Kadija Sesay, Eds. *IC3: The Penguin Book of New Black Writing in Britain*. London: Penguin, 2001.
Procter, James. *Dwelling Places: Postwar Black British Writing*. Manchester: Manchester University Press, 2003.
Ranasinha, Ruvani. 'Changes in the Canon: After Windrush'. *The Post-War British Literature Handbook*. Eds. Katharine Cockin and Jago Morrison. London: Continuum, 2011, 177–93.
Roberts, Maureen. 'Does the Writer Have a Responsibility to Their Community? Courttia Newland and Jacob Ross'. *Wasafiri* 19:4 (2004): 3–7.
Robbins, Bruce. 'Actually Existing Cosmopolitanism'. *Cosmopolitics: Thinking and Feeling Beyond the Nation*. Eds Pheng Cheah and Bruce Robbins. Minneapolis: University of Minnesota Press, 1998, 1–2.
Ross, Michael L. 'On a Darkling Planet: Ian McEwan's *Saturday* and the Condition of England'. *Twentieth-Century Literature* 54:1 (2008): 75–96.
Rushdie, Salman. *Fury*. London: Jonathan Cape, 2001.
Rushdie, Salman. 'Let's Get Back To Life'. *Guardian* 6 October 2001. Available online: http://www.guardian.co.uk/books/2001/oct/06/fiction.afghanistan (accessed 12 July, 2012).
Rushdie, Salman. *Shalimar the Clown*. London: Jonathan Cape, 2005.
Rushdie, Salman. *The Enchantress of Florence*. London: Jonathan Cape, 2008.
Shamsie, Kamila. *Salt and Saffron*. London: Bloomsbury, 2000.
Shamsie, Kamila. *Kartography*. London: Bloomsbury, 2002.
Shamsie, Muneeza. 'Introduction: Duality and Diversity in Pakistani English Literature'. *Journal of Postcolonial Writing* 47:2 (2011): 119.
Shyrock, Andrew. *Islamophobia/Islamophilia: Beyond the Politics of Enemy and Friend*. Bloomington: Indiana University Press, 2010.
Sivanandan, Ambalavaner. *Catching History on the Wing: Race, Culture, and Globalization*. London: Pluto Press, 2008.
Smith, Andrew. 'Migrancy, Hybridity and Postcolonial Literary Studies'. *Cambridge Companion to Postcolonial Literary Studies*. Ed. Neil Lazarus. Cambridge: Cambridge University Press, 2004, 241–61.
Smith, Zadie. *White Teeth*. London: Penguin, 2000.
Spencer, Robert. 'Reading *Lolita* in Tel Aviv: Terrorism, Fundamentalism and the Novel'. *Textual Practice*. Special issue 'Postcolonial Literature and Challenges for the New Millennium'. Eds Lucienne Loh and Malcolm Sen. 27:3 (2013), 399–417.
Stein, Mark. *Black British Literature: Novels of Transformation*. Columbus, Ohio: Ohio State University Press, 2004.
Tearne, Roma. *Bone China*. New York: Harper Collins, 2008.
Tew, Philip. *The Contemporary British Novel*. London: Continuum, 2004.
Tucker, Robert C. *The Marx-Engels Reader*. New York: Norton, 1978.
Wallace, Elizabeth Kowaleski. 'Postcolonial Melancholia in Ian McEwan's *Saturday*'. *Studies in the Novel* 39:4 (2007): 465–80.
Wells, Lynn. 'The Ethical Otherworld: Ian McEwan's Fiction.' *British Fiction Today*:

Critical Essays. Eds Philip Tew and Rod Mengham. London: Continuum, 2006, 117–27.
Wheatle, Alex. *East of Acre Lane*. London: Fourth Estate, 2001.
Wheatle, Alex. *The Dirty South*. London: Serpent's Tale, 2008.
Wood, James. 'Human, All Too Inhuman'. *The New Republic Online*. 30 August 2001. Available online: http://www.powells.com/review/2001_08_30.html. (accessed 15 January, 2015).
Žižek, Slavoj. *Welcome to the Desert of the Real*. London: Verso, 2002.

5

Historical Representations
Reality Effects: The Historical Novel and the Crisis of Fictionality in the First Decade of the Twenty-first Century

Leigh Wilson

That the fortunes of the historical novel changed rapidly at the end of the twentieth century has been widely noted and commented on by many critics. From the ghettos of the middle-brow genre novel in which it resided for most of the century – eschewed by most of the modernists and, when practised, always parodied – it has come to dominate contemporary literary culture in Britain. The serious historical novel wins literary prizes, is the primary choice of book clubs, dominates bestseller lists and is snapped up for film and TV adaptations. The origins of this move from periphery to centre has been linked to the resurgence of the English-language novel powered by the epistemological scepticism, political challenges and formal experiment that came to be grouped under the name 'postmodernism'. From John Fowles' *The French Lieutenant's Woman* (1969) to Salman Rushdie's *Midnight's Children* (1981), the 'English' novel displayed its renewed force and confidence by watching itself looking back. While the political significance of this historical turn has been the subject of intense debate, what seems incontestable is the extent to which the historical per se has been at the heart of this resurgence. More recently, it has been argued that this historical turn has spread from its 'experimental' beginnings to colonize the mainstream novel. De Groot has referred to this as the 're-bourgeoising' of the historical novel (de Groot 98) and Suzanne Keen has argued that this kind of novel has the appearance of postmodernism without having its underlying philosophical positions or political challenge (Keen 171). If, before the 1990s, the historical novel belonged either to genre or to the experimental, from the early 1990s and into the twenty-first century, it has not been so much that the historical novel infiltrated the world of mainstream literary fiction; more that the mainstream literary novel per se became historical.

If the historical novel of the 2000s has seen a move away from the 'postmodern' celebration of story over history, a number of things may account for this. The engagement with history by those writers of the 1980s called 'postmodernist' drew on elements that had been eschewed by the literary novel in Britain since the experiment of the modernists. As Jerome de Groot has noted, after the First World War the historical novel moved from the mainstream and became genre fiction, marketed mainly to women and not taken seriously (45). Its strengths and justification were presumed to exist in its closeness to history, rather than in those elements that constitute fictionality. Its power was its ability to outdo the discipline of history by making the past live again. De Groot quotes Ernest Baker's claim in 1908 that the historical novel 'will probably succeed in making a period live in the imagination when textbooks merely give us dry bones' (47). Of course, as de Groot stresses, such claims implicitly reveal the techniques of fiction, but this implicitness is precisely their difference from 'historiographic metafiction'. This has been noted by Jim Collins in his *Bring On the Books For Everybody* (2010), who goes on to see in this an aspect not fully taken on by those critics more focused on the *historical* than the fictional. For him, what distinguishes the novel of the early twenty-first century is, not the extent to which the mainstream novel has taken on the techniques of postmodernism, but the extent to which the literary novel has become popular. Collins argues that the novels of what he calls 'Lit-lit' – contemporary literary fiction that has become a genre – are obsessed by reading and by those who read. In these novels 'you can't throw a rock without hitting a novelist, professor, or a graduate student of literature' (250), and these novels are always, at least partly, historical, as they return to periods when writing and reading seem to have been taken seriously. What they are not, though, is experimental: 'These self-consciously literary novels about the writing and reading of literary texts, however, do not "show their workings" ... in the Lit-lit novels, which endlessly celebrate the joys of the literary experience ... there is simply no room for ambivalence in a world that imagines literary reading to be so imperilled' (251–2).

Collins is suggesting that the Lit-lit novel cannot risk experiment in its defence of reading fiction; I want to suggest that the formal timidity of contemporary fiction is caused rather by its loss of faith in fiction. The thinning of the boundaries between the literary and genre was used by the postmodernist novel of the 1980s to challenge assumptions about the relation between the fictional and the real in a way that privileged the fictional; the thinning of the boundaries in the contemporary historical novel reasserts the ability of the novel to represent the real and asserts a disguised referentiality because of its loss of faith in the fictional.

This situation has been noted by one of the most vocal critics of the major trends in the contemporary British novel, Gabriel Josipovici. In his work *What Ever Happened to Modernism?* (2010), he argues that contemporary British fiction is a poor and thin successor to modernism. This is because, for him, what distinguishes modernist literary work is, in Roland Barthes' words, 'to know that which is not possible any more' (139). And for Josipovici, what is no longer possible is realism and the most critically acclaimed contemporary British writers fail because they do not know this, or know it but write as if they don't. Like the modernists, they want to connect their work with that which is alive and real, but unlike the modernists they believe that realism is the way to make this connection. Josipovici sums up the assertion of the British novelist Adam Thirlwell in his *Miss Herbert* (2007) that the modern novel has at its heart a connection to the real by arguing that the 'touchstone of this new form ... is the telling detail' (171). For Josipovici, the significance given to the telling detail is mistaken because '[t]he notion that the new reality inhering in novels depends on their attention to detail fails to distinguish between "reality" and what theoreticians call "the reality-effect"' (172). Josipovici's argument is a powerful one and, as I will show in this chapter, contemporary British novelists and the novels they write demonstrate much in the way of evidence for it. However, this chapter will argue that the incongruity between the adherence to realism in the contemporary British novel and the simultaneous knowledge that such an adherence is problematic is most clearly demonstrated in the historical novel because it is in the historical novel that this incongruity is most powerfully denied.[1] Historical novels have returned with a vengeance in an attempt to smuggle realism in by the back door, even though it is a realism that strains against itself, and reveals in its techniques a profound discomfort.

The term 'reality effect' comes from Roland Barthes' influential essay, 'The Reality Effect' (1968), and via his argument we can see both why these effects are so closely linked to the historical turn, but also suggest why, in the historical novel of the 2000s, the 'reality effect' of choice is not quite the one that either Barthes or Josipovici have in mind. Roland Barthes begins his essay with a moment from the story, 'A Simple Heart', by Gustav Flaubert where the room occupied by the employer of the protagonist is described. Quoting Flaubert, Barthes notes that he 'tells us that "an old piano supported, under a barometer, a pyramidal heap of boxes and cartons"' (141). The barometer is Barthes' starting point, for the barometer, along with other such 'useless details' in the texture of a fictional narrative, is 'apparently detached from the narrative's semiotic structure' (142). The barometer is 'an object neither incongruous nor significant' and it does not therefore 'at first glance' participate in the 'order of the *notable*' (142; emphasis in original). The question Barthes asks, prompted by the existence of such details in narratives, is 'what is ultimately ... the significance of this insignificance?' (143). Barthes answers that the function of such 'useless details' is precisely to challenge the meaning given through representation. These 'useless details', in their very uselessness and lack of significance, denote the real as opposed to signification:

> The pure and simple 'representation' of the 'real', the naked relation of 'what is' (or has been) thus appears as a resistance to meaning: this resistance confirms the great mythic opposition of the *true-to-life* (the lifelike) and the *intelligible*; it suffices to recall that, in the ideology of our time, obsessive reference to the 'concrete' (in what is rhetorically demanded of the human sciences, of literature, of behaviour) is always brandished like a weapon against meaning, as if, by some statutory exclusion, what is alive cannot signify – and vice versa. (146)

The realism of the realist text lives, then, in the useless detail. However, of course, the reality of the reality effect is an illusion: 'The truth of this illusion is this: eliminated from the realist speech-act as a signified of denotation, the "real" returns to it as a signified of connotation: for just when these details are reputed to *denote* the real directly, all that they do – without saying so – is *signify* it' (148; emphasis in original).

However, in Barthes' terms via Josipovici, what distinguishes the contemporary novelist from the nineteenth-century realist novelist is that in between the two came novelists who knew 'that which is not possible any more'. Flaubert's barometer, then, cannot work in the same way for the contemporary novelist. To use it, the contemporary novelist has to know and not know at the same time.

So for Josipovici, the novelist Adam Thirlwell uses the two terms 'reality' and 'reality effect' 'indiscriminately' (172), and Josipovici sees in the bulk of contemporary writing this lack of discrimination. For him, then, the contemporary British novel is made weak by its continued use of Barthes' 'reality effect', and its dogged determination not to let modernism stand in the way of this. However, I want to argue that the contemporary British novel, far from blithely and happily continuing to reproduce the reality effects of nineteenth-century realism, in fact is riven with anxiety about the use of realism – for the very reasons used by Josipovici to argue that it is no longer possible – but that its response to this crisis has not been, as Josipovici would wish, to take on the challenge of modernism, but rather to turn to history. The novel of the first decade of the twenty-first century has become historical because realism is no longer possible and yet realism appears to offer the only guarantee for fiction's continuing relevance. The turn to history appears to solve this contradiction because it asserts a connection with the 'real' of history at the same time as asserting fiction's privileged role in accessing that 'real'.

This relation between an anxiety about the role and function of fiction and its apparent assuaging via the historical can be seen in an article in the *Guardian* by Ian McEwan at the beginning of 2013. McEwan is arguably the most successful and critically acclaimed novelist in Britain. He has been nominated for the Booker Prize six times and has won it once, in 1998. Nevertheless, sometimes, McEwan admits in the article, he has moments when his 'faith in fiction falters and then comes to the edge of collapse'. When the disbelief begins, the first to go, without much of a fight, is experimental writing – 'Ach well . . .' is his response, making it clear at the outset that his faith in fiction is dependent on its referentiality rather than its fictionality. Next to go, as may be expected, then, is magical realism. McEwan knows that trouble is really ahead, however, when belief in realism is threatened: 'It's when the icy waters of scepticism start to rise around the skirts of realism herself that I know my long night has begun'. In the full sway of his disbelief, McEwan writes, he feels it is a waste to spend the reading time he has left on the novel:

> Teach me about the world! Bring me the cosmologists on the creation of time, the annalists of the Holocaust, the philosopher who has married into neuroscience, the mathematician who can describe the beauty of numbers to the numbskull, the scholar of empires' rise and fall, the adepts of the English civil war. A few widely spaced pleasures apart, what will I have or know at the end of yet another novel . . . ? Will a novelist please tell me why the Industrial Revolution began, or how the Higgs boson confers mass on fundamental particles, or how morality evolved or what Salieri thought of the young Schubert in his choir. ('When Faith in Fiction Falters' n.p.)

Those books that McEwan could read while not reading novels will tell him about two broad categories of things – about the past and about apparently transhistorical scientific laws. These are the real for McEwan, the real with which, during his moments of crisis, novels – especially those that revel in their fictionality – fail to connect.

McEwan's confession is, according to him, that of a recovered sceptic. However, his recovery of belief attests as much to his disbelief in the fictional as did his loss of it, and demonstrates even more clearly the role of historical fiction in this crisis. His last bout of disbelief began to end, he tells us, when he read two short stories, one by Vladimir Nabokov and one by John Updike. In each, a mundane detail brought the world of the stories to life and reminded McEwan what it is that fiction is for: 'In the act of recognition, the tight boundaries of selfhood give way a little. This doesn't happen when you learn what a Higgs boson does'. McEwan's recovery of faith seems, at this point, to justify Josipovici's assertion that contemporary realism relies centrally on a version (in bad faith, because it should know better) of Barthes' 'reality effect'. However, McEwan supplements the place given to Nabokov and Updike in his renewal of faith with an account of an epiphanic moment from childhood, the memory of which also works to restore his faith in fiction, again a moment of 'caressing the detail', which showed him 'how the worlds of fact and fiction can interpenetrate', but that also demonstrates how central the historical is in this renewal. Reading L.P. Hartley's historical novel *The Go-Between* (1953) in his school library, the young McEwan came to the moment where the protagonist, a young boy called Leo, is obsessed, during the sweltering summer of 1900, with the greenhouse thermometer and checks it again and again to see if it has reached a hundred degrees. Leo then sees in the most recent copy of *Punch* a drawing showing 'Mr Punch under an umbrella, mopping his brow, while Dog Toby, with his tongue hanging out, wilted behind him'. The schoolboy McEwan, in what the adult McEwan calls an 'inspired move', crossed the library to find the volumes of *Punch*, and picked out the number from July 1900. He found the drawing: 'It was true. I was captivated, elated by the power of something both imagined and real. And briefly, I felt an unfamiliar sadness, nostalgia for a world I was excluded from'. McEwan now reads that moment as a realization that 'realism may be bolstered by the actual'. The absorption of the real by the fictional returned McEwan to the 'one true faith'. What we can see here too, however, is the extent to which McEwan's faith in (realist) fiction is dependent on history as a necessary advocate. Hartley, writing in the 1950s, must have done his research, as the young McEwan does his, for historical evidence in the form of the *Punch* cartoon proves that the July of 1900 was indeed a hot one. It is the contact with the 'actual' that excites the young McEwan and demonstrates why the adult one can return to the fold of fiction, but in order for this to work the contact with the 'actual' must not be possible empirically. It is the 'actual' of a world that is in every other way lost that is necessary; it is contact with history that validates realism.

The necessity of history to justify realism is part of Barthes' argument in 'The Reality Effect'. For him all reality effects in realist fiction are grounded in the discourse of objective history because both realism and history assert that they are describing the real rather than constructing meaning:

> 'reality' becomes the essential reference in historical narrative, which is supposed to report 'what really happened': what does the non-functionality of a detail matter then, once it denotes 'what took place'; 'concrete reality' becomes the sufficient justification for speaking. History (historical discourse: *historia rerum gestarum*) is in fact the model of those narratives which consent to fill in the interstices of their functions by structurally superfluous notations, and it is logical that literary realism should have been – give or take a few decades – contemporary with the regnum of 'objective' history, to which must be added the contemporary development of techniques, of works, and institutions based on the necessant need to authenticate the 'real'. (146)

For McEwan and other contemporary novelists, this 'objective' version of history is too problematic for the contemporary, and if realism set in the contemporary leads to a loss of faith in fiction, the historical novel is an attempt to recuperate this loss, but problematically is also an indication of how, in this attempt, the novel (and novelist) must pretend not to know what is in fact known. The photograph used to accompany McEwan's article on his loss of faith on the *Guardian* website is a still from the film adaptation of *The Go-Between* (dir. Joseph Losey, 1970, UK). It shows Leo, portrayed by Dominic Guard, and the novel's female protagonist, Marian, portrayed by Julie Christie. McEwan's account of the ecstatic moment from his childhood when he realized that novels could be directly linked to the real through his reading of an historical novel, *The Go-Between*, written in the early 1950s about the turn of the nineteenth and twentieth century, and his confirmation of its truth by reading *Punch*, is represented for the reader of his article by a different temporal moment, 1970, in order to assert the 'actual' of history as it is secured in the novel. But McEwan's memory in the present of a moment, in the late 1950s or early 1960s, when he read a novel published in 1953 set in 1900 is illustrated by a moment in 1970 of actors pretending to be in 1900. The layers of mediation here undermine precisely that securing of the 'real'. However, it is also the case that in McEwan the reality effect as described by Barthes is no longer easily usable. The difference between McEwan's *Punch* cartoon (or Hartley's cartoon as interpreted by McEwan) and Flaubert's barometer is that in post-war historical writing the moment of the 'reality effect' as described by Barthes is not enough. In McEwan, the significance of the cartoon in the end is not in the reality effect so much as it is in the extent to which it demonstrates the mediated nature of the supposed reconnection with the 'actual'. McEwan as a young boy had to go to the issue of *Punch* from 1900 in order to secure his perception that fiction could connect with the real (to know that the thermometer watched so closely by Leo would indeed have shown very high temperatures). Hartley's 'useless details' did not have this effect alone, yet the young McEwan's trip to the library shelf to find the issue of *Punch* shows exactly the gap between the novel and the actual. If the contemporary novel seems to be invested in the historical in order to sustain its belief in fiction, but the 'reality effects' as outlined by Barthes are no longer enough, what has taken its place? In looking at one of the most successful and critically acclaimed historical novels of the decade, Hilary Mantel's *Wolf Hall* (2009), and its successor *Bring Up The Bodies* (2012), I want to suggest that the serious historical novel, which knows indeed what is no longer possible, has turned instead to another kind of reality effect.

'He, Cromwell . . .': New reality effects

For Josipovici, what makes the lack of discrimination between 'reality' and 'reality effects' unforgivable in contemporary writing is modernism. Modernism is what contemporary writers know that Flaubert did not. For contemporary writers who 'know' modernism, who are strongly aware of modernism as a privileged and critically valued predecessor, writing as if Flaubert's barometer still works as a reality effect should be impossible. Josipovici's criticism of contemporary British novelists is that they still write as if they don't know, but I want to argue rather that this isn't the whole story. Literary writers know that relying on the barometer as their strongest reality effect is problematic so instead their reality effects have become precisely what Josipovici claims they have forgotten, modernism. The difference between Flaubert's barometer and McEwan's cartoon via Hartley is that the cartoon is a new reality effect in that it both establishes the 'concrete reality' of the past *and* makes clear the dependence of the effect on an organizing consciousness – the novelist who has done his research.

The serious contemporary novelist who 'knows' what modernism has done does not, then, jettison the reality effect, but rather folds modernism into their anxious desire to connect the novel with the real. Modernist techniques, re-used, have become their reality effect. Jesse Matz has noted this in his work on the contemporary uses of modernist Impressionism, the technique developed by a number of modernist writers through which to represent the complexity of human perception and its imbrication in the very act of representation. Matz has recently argued that the mimicking of impressionism in Colm Tóibín's *The Master* (2004), which, although in the third person, is entirely focalized through the consciousness of its protagonist, the novelist Henry James, and Michael Cunningham's *The Hours* (1998), which is both a rewriting of Woolf's *Mrs Dalloway* and a fictional biography of Woolf herself, at least in part seriously misunderstands the daring nature of modernist experiment and reproduces impressionism as banal, indeed as a 'pseudo-impressionism'. Matz argues that:

> Tóibín's Jamesian Impressionism is only vague and elusive – without the immediate intensity that came along with James' ambiguous intuitions. Cunningham's Woolfian Impressionism is only sensuously receptive – without the philosophical wonderment Woolf's characters found in the appearance of things. Seeing these Impressionists impressionistically, Tóibín and Cunningham betray the legacy they would claim. Moreover, they trivialise their subjects, even as they try to enrich our understanding of them. Impressionism's legacy could have been James's feelings about sex and Woolf's last transcendence; instead, a cheapened neo-Impressionsism gives us caricatures. (116)

In accounting for the use and mis-use of the modernist legacy in these novels, Matz argues that:

> In other words, fiction that lays claim to the legacy of Impressionsism has not inherited the full wealth of its critical process. What was once a more comprehensive programme has narrowed into one part only, on account of a kind of cynical disregard for the motives of the original Impressionism. The original Impressionists took real risks, pitching themselves into the crux of modernity by trying for a new way to encompass its perceptual effects. Impressionism today settles for appearances and gestures, mainly to claim the cultural distinction that has now accrued to their predecessors, and the result is a kind of sell-out to the very forces those predecessors (albeit ambiguously) opposed. (120)

Matz does argue that, in the end, each novel is recuperated by making itself into a 'postmodern Impressionism, juxtaposing different perceptual worlds and reflecting critically on their differences rather than trying for transparent realism' (125), but I want to focus rather on why, in their early sections, each novel should wish to reproduce impressionism in the way they do. While Matz does not comment on this aspect of either novel, they are both (in part in the case of *The Hours*) *historical* novels that aim to reproduce a sense of the period of their setting. In this, their reproduction of impressionism can be seen, not just as an attempt to skim off some of the cultural distinction of the modernists, but rather to establish a new kind of reality effect. Here, the real is established not through the 'useless detail' of barometers, but through the fixing of the limits of the narrative in the interior world and perceptual processes of the protagonists. Both *The Master* and *The Hours*, although in the third person, use free indirect discourse to suggest unmediated access to the thoughts of their characters. Tóibín's novel begins, not by establishing the real of the world, but by establishing the real as the mind of Henry James. As we enter the novel we enter his most fleeting and ephemeral mental experiences, his dreams: 'Sometimes in the night he dreamed about the dead – familiar faces and the others, half-forgotten ones, fleetingly summoned up. Now as he woke, it was, he imagined, an hour or more before the dawn' (1). The opening of Cunningham's novel, its prologue, is an account of Virginia Woolf's suicide in 1941 in the present tense. We remain inside Woolf's consciousness until the moment of death: 'For a moment, still, it seems like nothing; it seems like another failure; just chill water she can easily swim back out of; but then the current wraps itself around her and takes her with such sudden, muscular force it feels as if a strong man has risen from the bottom, grabbed her legs and held them to his chest' (5).

What is true of both of these pieces of writing is that the states described – dreams and death – are among the least articulable experiences a human being can have, but they are communicated in these novels – despite the smokescreen of impressionism – as complete, orderly, familiar and knowable. James' disturbing dreams are communicated in full and perfect sentences; Woolf's death, despite the present tense, is communicated via a sentence of orderly and balanced rhythm that has the time and leisure to construct a simile. On the following page Cunningham reproduces the actual note Woolf left for her husband, Leonard Woolf, before she committed suicide, in which she says: 'You see I cant even write this properly. I cant read' (6). The agony of reality here transforms language, rather than language securing the real as the known. Where the modernists privileged the representation of interiority in order to question and destabilize the question of reality, to make the familiar unfamiliar, and to thin the boundaries between real and representation, the contemporary writer of the historical novel uses them to *secure* the real.

This use of interiority as reality effect can be seen in Hilary Mantel's *Wolf Hall*. The novel is the first of Mantel's projected trilogy on the life of the Tudor lawyer, statesman and 1st Earl of Essex, Thomas Cromwell. Both *Wolf Hall* and the second in the trilogy, *Bring Up The Bodies* (2012), won the Booker Prize, among numerous other awards. Mantel has said that her aim in these novels was 'to reproduce a life from the inside' ('Taking Command Over Memory' 6). To do this, her novel is a first person narration disguised as a third person. As Mantel has admitted in an article in the *Guardian* from 2012, her narrative technique in *Wolf Hall* was not to everyone's taste. The entire narrative is focalized through the consciousness of Thomas Cromwell; as Mantel explained 'the person on the ground was Cromwell and the camera was behind his eyes':

> The events were happening now, in the present tense, unfolding as I watched, and what followed would be filtered through the main character's sensibility. He seemed to be occupying the same physical space as me, with a slight ghostly overlap. It didn't make sense to call him 'Cromwell', as if he were somewhere across the room. I called him 'he'.

This narrative position, as Mantel dryly notes, was for many readers a stumbling block, blocking, specifically, a clear view of the world of the novel, and a clear sense of who is who and what is what: 'This device, though hardly of Joycean complexity, was not universally popular. Most readers caught on quickly. Those who didn't, complained.' In addition, because Mantel wishes to show the world via Cromwell, she says, the narrative needed to be in the present tense. In *Writing Degree Zero*, Barthes argues that it is narration in the *passé simple* or preterite, the tense of the complete action in the past, which creates in fictional narration the claim (and the illusion) of objective description, of the world as ordered, stable and complete. For Barthes it 'presupposes a world which is constructed, elaborated, self-sufficient, reduced to significant lines, not one which has been sent sprawling before us, for us to take or leave' (Barthes 30). It also inherently suggests third person omniscient narration: 'Behind the preterite there always lurks a demiurge, a God or reciter ... he who tells the story has the power to do away with the opacity and the solitude of the existences which made it up, since he can in all sentences bear witness to a communication and to a hierarchy of actions' (30–1). The two novels then eschew all those things that are for Barthes central to the realist attempt to ground writing in 'concrete reality': the third person narrator, the preterite and the reality effect. Mantel's narration is utterly uninterested in describing the physical world of Cromwell. While the physical characteristics of significant characters are sometimes described, objects never are. This can be seen when Cromwell enters for the first time in the novel the presence of his employer, Cardinal Wolsey. Cromwell registers impressions that *both* appear to give us unmediated access to his mind *and* tell us what we need to know about the Cardinal and Cromwell's relation to him:

> Then the whole room is in motion: food, wine, fire built up. A man takes his wet outer garments with a solicitous murmur. All the cardinal's household servants are like this: comfortable, soft-footed, and kept permanently apologetic and teased. And all the cardinal's visitors are treated in the same way. If you had interrupted him every night for ten years, and sat sulking and scowling at him on each occasion, you would still be his honoured guest.
>
> The servants efface themselves, melting away towards the door. 'What else would you like?' the cardinal says. (18–19)

The crucial element of Mantel's narration in terms of focalization via Cromwell is her breaking of the rule in English grammar that says that a pronoun refers to the last named noun. In both *Wolf Hall* and *Bring Up The Bodies*, Mantel uses an unprecursed pronoun when referring to Cromwell. Early in the novel, during the scene quoted above in which we are first introduced to the adult Cromwell, visiting his boss and patron, Cardinal Wolsey, for example, a passage during which Cromwell considers one aspect of Wolsey's character threatens to take the narrative out of Cromwell's mind and towards a focalization via Wolsey. Mantel's flouting of the rule of antecedent pronouns brings it firmly back to Cromwell's consciousness:

> The cardinal, a Bachelor of Arts at fifteen, a Bachelor of Theology by his mid-twenties, is learned in the law but does not like its delays; he cannot quite accept that real property cannot be changed into money, with the same speed and ease with which he changes a wafer into the body of Christ. When he once, as a test, explained to the cardinal just a minor point of the land law concerning – well, never mind, it was a minor point – he saw the cardinal break into a sweat and say.... (20–1)

The 'he' of 'he once, as a test' is Cromwell, even though the previous noun refers to Wolsey. This non-precursed pronoun acts as the way back into Cromwell's mind from Wolsey's.

Mantel's only concession is the fairly frequent use of the construction, 'He, Cromwell'. Here she does not revert to using the rule – the anaphor precedes rather than follows the noun – but helps the reader out. Significantly, though, this is risked most often when actions, rather than thoughts, are described. Following Wolsey's fall from favour with the king, we read the following: 'They told the cardinal he was dismissed as Lord Chancellor, and demanded he hand over the Great Seal of England. He, Cromwell, touched the cardinal's arm' (47).

What Mantel's novels use to persuade us to suspend our disbelief, to invest in the world of the novel as real, is, then, the mind of Thomas Cromwell himself, but this is a mind whose subjectivity is not the issue (as it is in Woolf, say, or Joyce), rather it is a mind that we trust utterly (at least in the first two novels of the trilogy) and Cromwell's mind is trustworthy, is a channel to the real, because he is made familiar to the reader. Cromwell's relation to the contemporary reader is made very clear in a moment in *Bring Up The Bodies* during which a mention of Cromwell's legal reforms shades into the suggestion that he imagined, five hundred years before its founding, the idea of the welfare state and a notion of social constructivism.

> He is preparing a bill for Parliament to give employment to men without work, to get them waged and out mending the roads, making the harbours, building walls against the Emperor or any other opportunist. We could pay them, he calculated, if we levied an income tax on the rich; we could provide shelter, doctors if they needed them, their subsistence; we would all have the fruits of their work, and their employment would keep them from becoming bawds or pickpockets or highway robbers, all of which men will do if they see no other way to eat. What if their fathers before them were bawds, pickpockets or highway robbers? That signifies nothing. Look at him. Is he Walter Cromwell [his father]? In a generation everything can change. (43)

What a reviewer has called Cromwell's 'Whiggish modernity of consciousness' (Burrow 20) binds the 'real' that Cromwell perceives to the reader's sense of the real. In Mantel, then, the historical novel is used to reassert the ability of realism to connect the reader with the real not via the completed actions of the past tense nor the barometers of the reality effect, but through the 'reality effect' of the familiar mind. But in the end, the fact that the limit of the narration is the limit of Cromwell's consciousness serves not, as in modernism, to question the relation between perception and the real, and to align perception itself with representation, but to assert that the individual mind and its perceptions, as the truest thing there is, is the best connection to the real.

Atonement: Multiple reality effects

As we have seen, the desire to connect fiction to the real, and anxiety about how to do this, is clear in the work of Ian McEwan. His article in the *Guardian* discussed above reveals a tortuous attempt to connect Barthes' reality effects, the past and a prevailing consciousness. His novels from the 2000s could be read, unlike Mantel's, as explicit about these issues – about the legacy of modernism and the problematic status of realism – but in them too, I will argue, the historical is used to secure the relation between fiction and the real through reality effects that, in the end, rely most heavily on the use of a controlling consciousness outside the story to connect it with the past.

In her recent work on McEwan's novel *Saturday* (2005), which is set in London on 15 February 2003, the day of the largest demonstration against the plan to invade Iraq, Patricia Waugh sees the novel as struggling to balance the tension between the desire to connect with the real and its necessary fictionalization:

> The problem of how to *represent* an experiencing mind is the problem of preserving a sense of the tacit flow of feeling and consciousness that anchors the individual in an environment, while accepting that in order to build such a picture in a verbal medium, what is normally tacit must of necessity be explicitly constructed and selected and therefore carries the potential to disturb the 'flow' by intruding the act of representation and an ontological awareness of the condition of fictionality, the status of 'as if'. (92–3; emphasis in original)

As Waugh notes, McEwan acknowledges the terms of this debate in *Saturday* by intertextual allusions to some of the central prose works of modernist fiction in English. Like *Mrs Dalloway* (1925) and *Ulysses* (1922), the novel is set in one day; like *Mrs Dalloway*, it begins with its protagonist looking out onto a London street, and follows their movements through London during the day. The novel ends with an almost direct quotation of the final words of James Joyce's short story 'The Dead', the final story of *Dubliners* (1914) (*Saturday* 279). However, Waugh argues, unlike either Woolf or Joyce, McEwan is unable to use the limits of individual consciousness as the frame of his narration because he will not put at risk the supposed ability of fiction to directly connect with the real. Because of this, his focalization through his protagonist, Henry Perowne, is not about the problematic relation to the real of both fiction and consciousness, but instead it shows, as in Mantel, but even more so, that 'it is easier by far to effect an "inward turn" and to depict the self-communing or introspecting or internally dialogic mind' (Waugh 93). And the ultimate effect of this, Waugh argues, is precisely to raise rather than secure, as McEwan wishes, the question of the relation between the real and the fictional.

> Ironically, of course – and McEwan knows it – in bringing into such explicit focus what is normally tacit and lived, the novel's *hyper-realism* produces

something of the very hyper-reflexivity that he is attempting to avoid. The effort to be more 'truthful' about how the mind works seems to produce instead the kind of effect of those neo-realist paintings that look so much more real than photographs that our ontological certainties concerning the distinction between artifice and reality are uncannily and profoundly disturbed. (93; emphasis in original)

Many of these same questions are raised in *Atonement*, but I want to argue that this novel's status as *historical* fiction, while ostensibly part of the problem of the relation between the fictional and real that McEwan is exploring, in the end allows McEwan to secure (in a way he cannot in *Saturday* as a novel of the contemporary) the novel's direct relation to the real. The reality effect of *Atonement* is in the end neither just the barometer nor the consciousness of a familiar character; it is, in the end, the controlling and ordering effected by the author that Barthes sees as central to realist narrative and as crucial in its relation to the historical, but it is a controlling and ordering that is disguised.

If Mantel's novel, in its creation of the real, relies on the reality effect of the familiar and trustworthy mind – modernism made into a reality effect – in *Atonement* McEwan goes beyond Mantel in that he acknowledges that the representation of the mind of the individual is per se problematic, because it is necessarily representation and indeed fabrication. McEwan's main (and indeed only, as we eventually learn) focalizing consciousness is not, like Cromwell's, familiar and like 'us' as we would prefer to think of ourselves. She is self-serving, a liar and in bad faith. The novel consists of four parts; the first an account in the third person of a day in 1935 in the country house of the Tallis family. At the climax of this, Briony Tallis, the 13-year-old youngest daughter of the family, accuses Robbie, the son of the family's cleaner and the nascent lover of her older sister, Cecilia, of raping her cousin Lola. The second and third parts of the novel chart the consequences of Briony's accusation. Part two is an account in the third person, but from Robbie's perspective, of the retreat to Dunkirk. He has joined the army as a way of truncating the prison term he received for being found guilty of rape. Part three of the novel returns to London, where Briony is nursing injured soldiers, and where she eventually meets up with her sister and Robbie, safely back from France, in their flat in Balham, and promises to retract her original accusations. These parts of the novel are straight historical fiction whose reality effects are based on the real of individual consciousness as the primary connection to reality. While parts one, two and three are in the third person, part one asserts thematically the importance of consciousness as the connection with the real, and the place of fiction in this, and parts two and three are entirely focalized through Robbie's and Briony's consciousness respectively. The strongest line through the narrative of the first part of the novel is the creation of the 13-year-old Briony as a writer. What she experiences during that day in the summer of 1935 is a revelation about the way that fiction connects with the real. She abandons her melodramatic plays, and embraces instead the fiction of consciousness. What effects this revelation is watching through an upper window a scene in the garden between her sister and Robbie. Following this, she realizes that:

> She could write the scene three times over, from three points of view.... None of these three was bad, nor were they particularly good. She need not judge. There did not have to be a moral. She need only show separate minds, as alive as her own, struggling with the idea that other minds were equally alive. It wasn't only wickedness and scheming that made people unhappy, it was confusion and misunderstanding; above all, it was the failure to grasp the simple truth that other people are as real as you. And only in a story could you enter these different minds and show how they had an equal value. That was the only moral a story need have. (40)

What we learn by the end of the novel, however, is that Briony has precisely failed to do this. The final part of McEwan's novel is in the first person, narrated by Briony in old age, and reveals that the three preceding parts were all written by her, and that some of the crucial details were not a true representation of what actually happened, but were made up: 'Robbie Turner died of septicaemia at Bray Dunes on 1 June 1940', 'Cecilia was killed in September of the same year by the bomb that destroyed Balham Underground' and Briony 'never saw them in that year' (370). Numerous critics have noted the extent to which the novel makes problematic the fictional per se, and historical fiction in particular. Lynn Wells, for example, points out that Briony's central error – her belief that she has seen Robbie assaulting Lola – is in large part because she 'trusts her literary instincts more than sensory data' (Wells 102). De Groot argues that the final section of *Atonement* draws attention to the innate dishonesty of historical fiction (106). Peter Boxall sees the novel as one that has 'most closely' investigated the relation between history and narrative, and *Atonement* is his primary example of how novels in the twenty-first century 'struggle towards a historical realism that remains beyond the grasp of a narrative that is alive to its own limitations' (64). But of course, McEwan himself is a novelist who asks the reader to believe in what is essentially a deception. Wells suggests that McEwan's revelation of what Briony would conceal – that she has made up the ending – assures his good faith:

'McEwan thus places the onus on the reader to see beyond the elaborate literary deception of his novel to the ethical position of genuine compassion for the other only apparently represented by his narcissistic main character' (100). This appears to be validated by McEwan's response to Wells' questions during an interview in her book:

> What fiction does better than any other art form is represent consciousness, the flow of thought, to give an interior narrative, a subjective history of an individual through time, through every conceivable event, through love, crises or moral dilemmas. This inner quality is what I now value.... In other words, it is a basic human quality, to have a sense of what someone else is like, a sense that they're fundamentally like you.... And I believe this is the moral basis of the novel, in that ability, in the 'reading' of character, and in the invention of character. (126–7)

In *Atonement*, then, McEwan acknowledges the problem of this view of consciousness – what happens when it is the consciousness of someone in bad faith? – but gets out of it at the same time by effectively presenting the reader with three novels, and allowing the experience of reading these to be quite distinct. The novel *Atonement* contains an historical novel and its pleasures of direct referentiality, an historical novel framed by epilogue, where questions of referentiality – the relation of the novel to the real – are made problematic, and the novel of McEwan in which the relation back and forth between the historical novel and the epilogue is more than the sum of the parts of the two of them, and enables the reader to retain the power of the historical to connect with the real while at the same time castigating Briony (but not McEwan) for her bad faith. So while Briony's novel tells lies, McEwan's tells the truth. Briony as author/narrator cannot see the true link between her 'novel' and her epilogue, but the author of the novel (that is, of the novel that is Briony's novel plus the epilogue as a whole) can, and so, therefore, can the reader.

Despite McEwan's engagement with modernism in the content of the novel, in its form it denies the epistemological scepticism of modernism. Briony's Woolfian version of the scene by the fountain is one of 'pure geometry' and 'defining uncertainty', which acknowledges the fact that the 'age of clear answers is over' (281), but McEwan's novel acknowledges nothing of the sort. While the knowledge gained through the epilogue can be disappointing to the reader (who has been emotionally invested in something that is not true), the reader is compensated precisely by the gaining of a full knowledge – the full knowledge that comes through a realist assumption of the possibilities of historical retrospectivity. While the novel appears to question such assumptions, then, in the end it relies on them.

It is Briony who is in bad faith; to spare her readers, or more likely to spare herself, she has written a novel that is a deception. McEwan, a novelist in good faith, reveals this in his fourth part, where Briony would conceal it. McEwan's revelation at the end does not impugn the fiction writer's position per se. The final part of the novel does not, as in the famous chapter 13 of Fowles' *The French Lieutenant's Woman*, break down the realist façade by speaking to us in the voice of the fabulator, he who has made it up. Rather than directly linking the world of the novel to the real, the final part of *Atonement* increases the world of the novel in the sense that the 'novel' now is the novel we have just read plus the frame of its writing, but a frame that is equally fictional, unlike Fowles', but equally silent about its fictionality, again unlike Fowles'. Fowles exchanged reality effect for reality. The voice of the novelist intrudes into the novel precisely in answer to a question about what a character is thinking, about the supposed ability of the novel to enter the minds of others. Chapter 12 of *The French Lieutenant's Woman* ends with the third person narrator asking of his protagonist 'Who is Sarah? Out of what shadows does she come?' (96). The next chapter begins:

> I do not know. This story I am telling is all imagination. These characters I create never existed outside my own mind. If I have pretended until now to know my characters' minds and innermost thoughts, it is because I am writing in (just as I have assumed some of the vocabulary and 'voice' of) a convention universally accepted at the time of my story: that the novelist stands next to God. He may not know all, yet he tries to pretend that he does. But I live in the age of Alain Robbe-Grillet and Roland Barthes; if this is a novel, it cannot be a novel in the modern sense of the word. (97)

As we have seen, McEwan's anxiety about fiction – his sense that what makes fiction valuable also makes it weak – returns again and again to assert the link between fiction and the empirically verifiable. As he explains in his interview with Wells:

> The recursive, or self-referential or intertexual in literature has to be embedded in the warmth of the real, the warmly living. Otherwise, it's dull and dry. In fact, all these elements that postmodern critics like to discuss only arise with any interest if they grow out of the effect, the sweat of passionate commitment to creating the humanly real.... In *Atonement*, the moment I decided to include a young girl in love with writing, everything else, the

intertextuality, the lifetime of successive drafts, just followed, rather in the service of realism. (134)

While critics, then, have read *Atonement* as a masterly display of the possibilities of fiction that engages with some of the most important philosophical questions of the postwar period, for McEwan it is, in the end, a defence of realism as the only possibility for contact with the real. Lynn Wells, in her interview with McEwan, tells him that she finds the theoretical work of Emmanuel Levinas very useful in reading his fiction. McEwan responds: 'I don't know Lévinas's [sic] work. Perhaps he belongs to the tradition of non-evidential literary theorizing' (128).

The Red Riding Quartet: Fictionality as the real

Hilary Mantel's use of the consciousness of Cromwell to secure the reality effect, I have argued, relies on Cromwell's mind being familiar and sympathetic to the reader. As has been noted by Burrow in his review of *Bring Up The Bodies*:

> The novel's present-tense mode of narrative, focalised through a single principal character, has an intrinsic problem. It would be almost impossible to write this kind of fiction and make the central character a brute, since so much depends on what he or she notices and feels, on sensitivity. If a fiction represents the sensorium of one character's feelings, then an inert or insensitive sensorium would probably generate inert fiction. (20)

But Cromwell is a brute. A portrait of him done by Holbein makes Cromwell see what everyone else already knows – that he looks like a murderer (527) – and he looks like a murderer because he is one. Indeed the question of whether Cromwell is a murderer or not haunts both *Wolf Hall* and *Bring Up The Bodies*. The question raised by this is: what is the reason for the absence of his villainous acts from the consciousness that constructs Mantel's narrative? These 'forgotten' acts do not, as in Leopold Bloom's interior monologue in *Ulysses*, intrude themselves when he least expects, they are not the surprising and disturbing end points of a seemingly safe meandering of thought. They are, in terms of the novels, entirely external to Cromwell's consciousness so that it can function as a reality effect. It will be interesting to see what Mantel will do in the third novel of the trilogy, as Cromwell slides towards his fate, and his implication in the brutality, oppression and deception of Henry's court is necessarily revealed, but Burrow's suggestion that focalization through a 'brute' would lead to inert fiction assumes that the vitality of fiction is entirely referential, is indeed limited entirely to its reality effects. This raises the question of whether a contemporary historical fiction is possible which neither relies on reality effects that can only be used in bad faith nor denies the fictional in its anxious desire to connect the narrative (and the reader) with Barthes' 'concrete reality'. In the rest of this chapter, I will look at David Peace's four novels in the Red Riding Quartet to suggest that in them we can see an engagement with history not in order to eschew fictionality, but rather to assert fictionality as enabling a powerful, disturbing contact with history. What is 'real' in these novels is not the supposedly recreated past but the effect that fiction has on the reader, which could not be achieved in any other way. It is through this effect – the fictional effect rather than the reality effect – that the reader experiences the real of history. If Mantel asserts the real of her novels by suggesting that Cromwell is like us, Peace asserts that we are like his murderous narrators in a way that produces not a sense of 'concrete reality' that can be experienced through the senses, but a sense that we are *part* of the horror of history that has been previously hidden from us.

Superficially, if the contemporary British historical novel continues to confuse 'reality effects' of various kinds with reality, the novels that make up the Red Riding Quartet – *1974* (1999), *1977* (2000), *1980* (2001) and *1983* (2002) – seem to make the same mistake. The novels are, as the titles indicate, obsessed with precise locations in time and in space. The early chapters of *1974*, for example, all begin as follows – 'Friday 13 December 1974' (Peace 3), '7.55am. Saturday 14 December 1974. I was sitting in the Millgarth office of Detective Chief Superintendent George Oldman, feeling like dogshit' (23), and 'Just gone midnight, Sunday 15 December 1974. The Hunslet and Beeston exit of the M1' (45). The narratives tell us time, date and place again and again. The novels are also, like Mantel's, intensely focalized but through a variety of characters rather than just one. However, despite these elements, they eschew the reality effects that would appear to ground them in the 'concrete reality' of the past, and instead use a flagrant fictionality to transfer the real from the page to the reader.

The novels are set in Yorkshire in the 1970s and 1980s and present the conventional subjects of crime fiction. Through the quartet Peace's protagonists – morally aware but deeply flawed journalists, cops and lawyers – investigate a series of child abductions and murders, the crimes of the Yorkshire Ripper, police corruption, and the tortuous, murky connections between the three. But while Peace's novels are obsessed with dates, while they do use the conventional content of crime fiction and they do of course use actual events, rather than eschewing the practice of fictionality in the representation of the real, Peace *practices* fictionality in such a way as to assert its problematic, compromised but necessary power. In Peace, as I shall go on to show, fictionality is not opposed to but intimately related to the real, and it is only through the practice of fictionality that the real can be properly, ethically experienced and interrogated.

Peace's novels have so far been read most often through the metaphor of haunting. Certainly it is the case that the gothic asserts a relation to the past more troubling than the supposed unmediated and full knowledge that realism implies. Jerome de Groot has suggested that gothic novels: 'see history not as a source of information or something to understand but as a place of horror and savagery. The historical place, in Gothic ... is not a repository of pastness but a site where history might attack the visitor, a charnel house of remains that still have the power to harm' (16).

However, the more recent critical incarnations of this gothic frame that consider Peace's work, while acknowledging de Groot's point, seem to continue to insist in the end on realism's 'concrete reality'. The ideas of 'hauntology' dominate readings of Peace in a recent collection of essays on him (Shaw 2011) and in an essay that compares the work of Peace with that of J.G. Ballard, Dean Lockwood invokes the hauntological to suggest the past as precisely not ordered, knowable or fully recoverable, yet still wants his fictions to be finally in touch with 'concrete reality': 'Peace, unlike Ballard, clearly takes a moral stance, derived from the fact that his fabulation is concretely anchored by means of the restless ghosts of the time under interrogation' (44).

However, Peace is not wedded to what is as a writer, to reproducing the surface of a 'concrete reality', despite the repeated use of dates and pop songs. Peace has described his work as an attempt to speak of a 'hidden history' (Hart 558), and this is an historical reality that cannot be made via the reality effect because it does not exist within the terms of existence assumed by reality effects. Its non-existence is precisely the point. In taking away both reality and reality effect from readers through an assertion of fictionality, Peace's novels, for all their horror, create a place of possibility: the world is not all there is; making things up changes the world. It is fictionality that makes the difference for Peace, not history.

At the centre of Peace's four novels are at least two serial killers – the Yorkshire Ripper and an abductor and murderer of at least three young girls. At the same time, the Moors murderers and their crimes and victims haunt the characters as they criss-cross the countryside between Leeds and Manchester, and murder and other acts of violence are committed with nauseating repetition by the police. As with so many kinds of crime narrative over the last few decades – true crime, films, crime fiction – the serial killer is central. But the serial killer is at the heart of Peace's quartet precisely because he is attempting to show how the real is linked with fiction in difficult ways but yet can still be ethically interrogated via fictionality. Barthes argues that Flaubert's reality effect is based on the assumption that the real does not signify. This ideological assumption can be seen as the basis of the construction of the bogeyman of late modernity, the serial killer. The serial killer's actions are repeated because he wants to but never can secure finally the relationship between the real and signification (see Seltzer especially 17–18, 163–4, 169; Warwick). For the serial killer, for Peace's novels and for their readers, then, the relation between the 'real' and the fictional is neither straightforward nor securable, but rather is one that precisely undoes the assumption that, in Barthes' terms, the 'concrete' and 'meaning' are in opposition.

This link between the serial killer and the production of that which is beyond the facts of events is crucial, but of course for Peace and his readers the 'real events' surrounding his central serial killer – the Yorkshire Ripper – are well established and known. So here, it is not that the 'unknowability' around the crimes of the serial killer are being used to produce fictionality (as argued by Alexandra Warwick of narratives of Jack the Ripper), but rather that the figure and work of the serial killer is being linked *to* fictionality. In the 'work' of the serial killer as imagined in the narratives of crime, whether 'real' or 'fictional', the real, in all its visceral horror and abject corporeality, is absolutely entwined with signification, with, indeed, fictionality. As Mark Seltzer has argued, with the serial killer, '[t[he distinctions between fact and fiction and between bodies and information vanish' (16).

The crimes carried out by the serial killer can be seen as an attempt to *unify* the real and fictionality, to unify what is in the world with the patterns and new meanings and made up elements that constitute fictionality; these crimes are an attempt to make matter signify. And it is for this reason, I think, that Peace's novels obsessively, uncomfortably and painfully mine the crime genre, and more particularly the narratives of serial murder – they are the terrible, twisted Mr Hyde to the Dr Jekyll of the contemporary British historical novel. Here fictionality is crime, not redemption. Crucially, in making this clear, Peace's novels *practise* fictionality, rather than just thematizing it, as in McEwan. This practice opens up the dangers of fictionality and links it to crime and violence, but it is only by doing this that fiction's power to effect something in the world is unlocked.

One of the ways history – the real in the past – and fictionality are linked over and over in the quartet, both within single novels and across the series, is by repeating the representation of past events via several different modes of writing, contrasting those that claim to be direct, literal repetitions of events with those that are insistent on powerfully displaying their fictionality. The middle two novels of the quartet, *1977* and *1980*, have as one of their central plotlines the hunt for the Yorkshire Ripper by the deeply corrupt West Yorkshire police force. The chapters of *1977* alternate between being narrated by Jack Whitehead, a disturbed, drunken and cynical crime correspondent for the *Yorkshire Evening Post*, who nevertheless retains a remnant of desire for the truth, and chapters narrated by Bob Fraser, a police officer who also retains a sense of truth and morality, despite his own compromised relation to the corruption, exploitation and violence that link the various plot strands of the quartet. A third of the way through the novel another women is attacked in a way that suggests she is a victim of the Yorkshire Ripper. Two accounts of this are given, one is a reasonably straight account, narrated by Whitehead but dominated by the direct speech of the police officer in charge, of the police press conference called after the attack, and the other is Whitehead's description of this press conference in a newspaper article. The first is dominated by information – dates, names, locations – which asserts the account as grounded in the real:

> 'Gentlemen, as you are aware, at approximately three a.m. on Saturday morning, the 4th, Mrs Linda Clark, aged thirty-six, of Bierley, was subjected to a violent assault on wasteland behind the Sikh temple on Bowling Back Lane, Bradford. In the course of the attack, Mrs Clark sustained a fractured skull and stab wounds to her back and abdomen. On Saturday Mrs Clark underwent surgery and will have to undergo another operation later this week. However, despite the seriousness of her injuries, Mrs Clark has been able to provide us with a detailed account of the time leading up to her attack.' (130)

A few pages later, Whitehead's narration includes his writing of his newspaper article on the press conference and the article itself:

> *Police yesterday stepped up the hunt for the so-called Yorkshire Ripper, the man police believe could be responsible for the murders of four prostitutes and assaults upon three other women, following a fourth attack on Saturday morning.*
>
> *Mrs Linda Clark, aged thirty-six of Bierley, Bradford, was attacked on wasteland off Bowling Back Lane, Bradford, following a night out at the city's Mecca Ballroom.*

> Mrs Clark suffered a fractured skull and stab wounds to her stomach and back, after accepting a lift from a driver on the Wakefield Road. Mrs Clark will undergo a second operation later this week. (134; emphasis in original)

The next novel in the quartet, *1980*, is narrated by a 'good' cop, Peter Hunter, who has been brought over from Manchester to investigate the West Yorkshire police for its own investigation of the Ripper murders. Preceding each of his chapters, but not linked to them in any way in terms of plot, narrative or voice, are densely written pages, without pagination, each of which details the experiences of each of the women thought to have been attacked or murdered by the Yorkshire Ripper. However, while the pages stick to the events outlined, for example, in the police press conference and newspaper report from *1977*, they are written in a style the opposite of these. They are staccato, elliptical, dreamlike. Each page begins in a sort of third person, then transforms into the victim's own voice. This may seem at first a demonstration of the ability of the fictional to allow us to occupy the consciousness of those – the exploited, the marginal and the silenced – who are excluded by other narratives – the ability, in other words, to 'think ourselves into the minds of others', the absence of which, according to McEwan in an article published just after the 9/11 attacks, allowed the perpetrators to carry out their acts (McEwan 'Only Love Then Oblivion' n.p.). But in each of these pages the woman's voice merges with, is textually and typographically indistinguishable from, the voice of her attacker. What follows is from the page on the attack on Linda Clark, who was the subject of the police press conference and newspaper report quoted above.

> but e am drunk from dancing and e keep nodding off and we are bumping up and down across some wasteland and e know what he wants but e am too drunk from dancing to care and e hate my husband who is a spoilsport does not like my drinking and dancing not that he has ever bothered to watch me dance and e ask the driver if he fancies me and he say he does so e tell him to drive to wasteland over yonder behind where pakis go nodding off bumping up and down across some wasteland e know what she wants and she says stop here because e have to have a pee and she gets out and is squatting down in the dark the sound of her urine on the wasteland under the starless endless black summer air of this here hell e hit her with the hammer and e rip her black velvet dress to the waist and stab her repeatedly in the chest in the stomach and in the back. (146)

Here the voice of the attacker is heard, not just the voice of his victim, indeed they merge into one another. This resonates with many points in the novels where the supposed 'goodies' are uncomfortably linked with violence and corruption. Even more disturbingly than this, though, for us as readers, *our* pleasure in fictionality, in the *way* the books are written is linked to the aesthetic aspect of serial killing. The unpunctuated pages that precede every chapter in *1980* make visible in their difficulty, in the attention it needs to read them, in their insistent textuality, in their blatantly invented subject position, fictionality per se. In this they are in extreme contrast to the deadened and tendentious police and newspaper accounts of the attack on Linda Clark quoted above. Here we have the 'real thing', the thoughts as they cross the mind, the experience of those involved as they experience it, but this exercise in fictionality implicates our readerly pleasure in the voice and experience of the criminal too. Like the actions of the serial killer, this work of fictionality takes the real and makes it something else, something that is meaningful, something that, in its meaningfulness, gives, horrifically, pleasure.

However, crucially, this is not where Peace leaves it. What rescues the reader and the novels from finishing in this place of identity with the serial killer is the refusal of the novels themselves to unify the real event and its representation. Even at the end of *1983* the actual events of the whole quartet are never fully recoverable by the reader, at least not by any reader who resists the temptation of the obsessive, paranoid will to signification of both Peace's deeply flawed heroes and of the serial killer himself. Alec Charles has suggested that Peace's novels can be seen in Barthesian terms as 'writerly' in that they demand an active reader and open themselves up to 'active interpretability' (63) (although he does acknowledge too that this invitation masks an imprisonment, 'once you're in, you can't get out' (67)). However, what is really powerful about these novels is that it is impossible for the reader to 'fill in the gaps, to cobble together coherence from inherently impossible narratives' (63). We read the Quartet neither to learn about the past as we would a realist text nor to actively complete the texts, but to *experience* the way that fiction both deadens the past and imposes order on it – like a serial killer – but also to experience the truth that fiction is the only place for imagining the world other than it is. The Quartet does not assert, unlike contemporary novels criticized by Josipovici, 'this is true' through the use of reality effects, but rather the novels of the Quartet make us consider the use of lies, some of them deathly, some not. What remains at the end of the Quartet is fictionality, but not in the sense that Peace denies the existence of the real events represented by the novels in some supposedly postmodern exercise in all-encompassing textuality. It is not that the fictionality is privileged over the real, it is rather that in Peace fictionality makes the events real by implicating the reader in them. Peace's novels suggest that it is only in fictionality that the real event can be truly real as, horrifically, the work of the serial killer shows, but the novels refuse the finality of the serial killer, that is, they refuse to finally unite the events and their representation. While novels and serial killers are the same in that they attempt to bring together the real and fictionality, the ethical position of the novel is guarded not by finally denying fictionality but by asserting it.

Note

1   Fredric Jameson's recent *The Antinomies of Realism* (2013) came out as I finished this chapter. In it, Jameson argues too for the impossibility of realism as the 'compact between chronology and the present' (46) on which its existence is based dissolves. Jameson's reading of nineteenth-century realism is more nuanced than Josipovici's, seeing from the beginning this compact as a struggle that produces the effects of realism, rather than a monolith whose continued naivety is made impossible by modernism.

Works cited

Barthes, Roland. 'The Reality Effect'. In *The Rustle of Language*, translated by Richard Howard. Berkeley and LA: University of California Press, [1968]1989.
Barthes, Roland. *Writing Degree Zero*, translated by Annette Lavers and Colin Smith. New York: Hill and Wang, 1997.
Boxall, Peter. *Twenty-First-Century Fiction: A Critical Introduction*. Cambridge: Cambridge University Press, 2013.
Burrow, Colin. 'On Your Way, Phantom'. *London Review of Books*, 7 June 2012: 19–20.
Charles, Alec. '"Pictures At An Atrocity Exhibition": Modernism and Dystopian Realism in David Peace's Red Riding Quartet'. In *Analysing David Peace*. Ed. Katy Shaw. Newcastle: Cambridge Scholars Publishing, 2011.
Collins, Jim. *Bring Up The Books For Everyone: How Literary Culture Became Popular Culture*. Durham: Duke University Press, 2010.
Cunningham, Michael. *The Hours*. London: Fourth Estate, 1999.
De Groot, Jerome. *The Historical Novel*. London and New York: Routledge, 2010.
Fowles, John. *The French Lieutenant's Woman*. London: Vintage, [1969]1996.
Hart, Matthew. 'An Interview With David Peace'. *Contemporary Literature* 47:4 (2006): 546–69.
Jameson, Fredric. *The Antinomies of Realism*. London: Verso, 2013.
Josipovici, Gabriel. *What Ever Happened to Modernism?* New Haven: Yale University Press, 2010.

Joyce, James. *Ulysses* London: Penguin, [1922]2000.
Keen, Suzanne. 'The Historical Turn in British Fiction'. In *A Concise Companion to Contemporary British Fiction*. Ed. James English. Oxford: Blackwell, 2006.
Lockwood, Dean. 'The Great Yorkshire Fugue: Bare Life in the Red Riding Quartet'. In *Analysing David Peace*. Ed. Katy Shaw. Newcastle: Cambridge Scholars Publishing, 2011.
Mantel, Hilary. *Wolf Hall*. London: Fourth Estate, 2010.
Mantel, Hilary. 'Taking Command Over Memory: Hilary Mantel Talks To Sarah O'Reilly'. In Hilary Mantel. *Giving Up The Ghost*. London: Fourth Estate, 2010.
Mantel, Hilary. *Bring Up The Bodies*. London: Fourth Estate, 2012.
Mantel, Hilary. 'Hilary Mantel: How I Came to Write *Wolf Hall*'. *Guardian*, 7 December 2012. Available online: http://www.theguardian.com/books/2012/dec/07/bookclub-hilary-mantel-wolf-hall (accessed 21 May 2015).
Matz, Jesse. 'Pseudo-Impressionism?'. In *The Legacies of Modernism: Historicising Postwar and Contemporary Fiction*. Ed. David James. Cambridge: Cambridge University Press, 2012.
McEwan, Ian. *Atonement*. London: Jonathan Cape, 2001.
McEwan, Ian. 'Only Love and Then Oblivion. Love Was All They Had to Set Against Their Murderers'. *Guardian*, 15 September 2001. Available online: http://www.theguardian.com/world/2001/sep/15/september11.politicsphilosophyandsociety2 (accessed 30 May 2015).
McEwan, Ian. *Saturday*. London: Jonathan Cape, 2005.
McEwan, Ian. 'When Faith in Fiction Falters – and How It Is Restored'. *Guardian*, 16 February 2013. Available online: http://www.theguardian.com/books/2013/feb/16/ian-mcewan-faith-fiction-falters (accessed 30 May 2015).
Peace, David. *1974*. London: Serpent's Tail, 1999.
Peace, David. *1977*. London: Serpent's Tail, 2000.
Peace, David. *1980*. London: Serpent's Tail, 2001.
Peace, David. *1983*. London: Serpent's Tail, 2002.
Rushdie, Salman. *Midnight's Children*. London: Jonathan Cape, 1981.
Seltzer, Mark. *Serial Killers: Death and Life in America's Wound Culture*. New York and London: Routledge, 1998.
Shaw, Katy, Ed. *Analysing David Peace*. Newcastle: Cambridge Scholars Press, 2011.
Tóibín, Colm. *The Master*. London: Picador, 2004.
Warwick, Alexandra. 'Blood and Ink: Narrating the Whitechapel Murders'. In *Jack the Ripper: Media, Culture, History*. Eds Alexandra Warwick and Martin Willis. Manchester and New York: Manchester University Press, 71–87, 2007.
Waugh, Patricia. 'Thinking in Literature: Modernism and Contemporary Neuroscience'. In *The Legacies of Modernism: Historicising Postwar and Contemporary Fiction*. Ed. David James. Cambridge: Cambridge University Press, 2012.
Wells, Lynne. *Ian McEwan*. Basingstoke: Palgrave, 2010.

6

Generic Discontinuities and Variations

Daniel Weston

Discontinuities and variations within a genre and around its borders are the effects of artistic experimentation and innovation. To assess those features across a decade is to begin to sketch a periodization and build a literary history of directions taken. This critical task has not been the sole preserve of academics: authors often contribute to this process alongside their creative output in the form of journalism and essays. In 'Two Paths for the Novel', a 2008 article for *The New York Review of Books*, Zadie Smith undertook an assessment of the contemporaneous state of the novel. As a piece with this ambition, written by a prominent British author and published towards the end of the decade that this volume addresses, it is taken here as a point of departure for a discussion of generic discontinuities and variations in the noughties. Reviewing a pair of recently published texts – Joseph O'Neill's *Netherland* (2008) and Tom McCarthy's *Remainder* (2005) – Smith finds that 'a story emerges about the future of the Anglophone novel' ('Two Paths' n.p.).

In this story, the 'two paths' that Smith maps out (employing a metaphor recycled from David Lodge, as will be seen) are not just a fork in the road, but lead in opposite directions: 'the two novels are antipodal – indeed one is a strong refusal of the other'. If at one pole *Netherland* is hailed as the apotheosis of a certain familiar type, what Smith calls 'lyrical realism', then *Remainder* is at the other, experimental end of a spectrum of novelistic variation. The former might be more or less self-conscious in its construction of a fictional world and its deployment of familiar novelistic techniques, but it does not allow this content such prominence as to call into doubt the worth of the project; the latter goes further in questioning conventions, asking what kinds of meaning they foreclose as well as what they permit or imply. While *Netherland* represents a kind of sensibility, *Remainder* constitutes a commitment to style. As Smith's essay moves towards its final assessment, shifting gears from critical evaluation towards manifesto and call-to-arms, it focuses increasingly on the way these two traditions might productively come together. However, at its outset, the prognostication is gloomier. The extreme divergence that Smith perceives in the current field is 'a function of our ailing literary culture' wherein the dominance of realism leads inexorably to increasingly extreme forms of rejection in experimental writing: 'a breed of lyrical Realism has had the freedom of the highway for some time now, with most other exits blocked'. The spatial metaphors here – paths and highways – are helpful in characterizing the stylistic routes that novels in the noughties have taken, but divergence need not be the only trend that is identified as a result.

Smith's essay is an important and helpful evaluation of the poles around which experimentation has been oriented, but even if these two particular novels might be 'antipodal' many of the important texts of the noughties have attempted to reconcile experimentation and realism. If the 1980s and the 1990s represented the high-water mark of postmodern, hyperconscious metafiction and formal deviation, then the 2000s have been a decade in which writers have sought to digest these trends and move beyond them. This has meant that some critics have not noticed the experimental work of many novelists in the 2000s. Peter Childs has noted the way in which a generational shift has been formulated critically through comparisons of the Granta Best Young British Novelists lists of 1983, 1993 and 2003. Whilst those on the first list have 'gone on to become the celebrated stalwarts of contemporary fiction' (2), the 2003 grouping 'has generally been considered inferior to the two previous generations' (3). Indeed, 'inasmuch as it is useful to talk of literary decades', Childs writes, the 1980s has 'generally been seen as the foremost period for British fiction since the war', and associates this period with a trend for 'novelists returning to the postmodernist styles of the 1960s' (10–11). Introducing the 2003 list, the then editor of *Granta* Ian Jack suggested that comparisons to the 1983 list 'do no good at all', but then goes on to note that 'that was a special generation' and, far more equivocally, 'this *may* be one as well' (14, my emphasis). Such judgements, open or veiled, arise out of a certain way of conceiving of innovation and citing it in a particular period. In this chapter, I will look to other models of novelistic variation to establish a vocabulary for thinking through the relations between realism and experimentation, and for noticing dialogues as well as divisions, before spotlighting key interventions that offer an overview of the 2000s. In place of Smith's divergent paths, I will revisit David Lodge's idea of 'the novelist at the crossroads' and Andrzej Gąsiorek's notion, set out in his *Post-war British Fiction* (1995), of post-war writers attempting to transcend the dichotomy between realism and experimentalism. I will assess the ways in which the 2000s witnessed an accommodation of postmodern trends that it inherited, and suggest that precisely what it means to be narratologically and formally inventive has shifted significantly for the post-millennial novel.

'Two Paths for the Novel' is an essay of a kind that returns perennially. Zadie Smith's modulation from considering the contemporaneous state of the novel towards predicting (and influencing) its future direction conforms to a well established pattern for such writing. When David Lodge – like Smith, a novelist reflecting in a critical mode on novelists' practices – wrote his 1969 essay 'The Novelist at the Crossroads', the 'the old guessing game of "Whither the novel?"' was already a familiar remit (3). Returning to this earlier construction of the same set of issues that Smith is addressing in 2008 will throw into relief both the investments being made in orienting novelistic variety around the poles of realism and experimentalism, and the different possible ways of conceiving of variation in the genre. Discontinuity, I suggest, is not the only marker of innovation in the noughties. If Lodge and Smith are working to a similar brief, the historical moments in which they are writing are very different, with important implications for the relationship between tradition and innovation as they see it.

In 2008 Smith begins with a lament for the paucity of variety in the contemporary scene: 'All novels attempt to cut neural routes through the brain, to convince us that down this road the true future of the novel lies. In healthy times, we cut multiple roads', but alas, 'these aren't particularly healthy times'. *Netherland* – the paradigm of lyrical realism around which Smith's argument is initially based – is disappointing in part because it is familiar: 'our receptive pathways are so solidly established that to read this novel is to feel a powerful, somewhat dispiriting sense of recognition.... It's so precisely the image of what we have been taught to value in fiction that it throws that image into a kind of existential crisis'. As the apotheosis of a certain style and mode, O'Neill's novel is also a statement of the limitations of that style and mode. Smith finds in the noughties the dominance of one kind of novel above others and a marginalization of the rest (though a chapter such as this ought to go some way to arguing otherwise, or at least modifying her terms). For Lodge writing in 1969, the opposite was true: 'We seem, indeed, to be living through a period of unprecedented cultural pluralism which allows, in all the arts, astonishing variety of styles to flourish simultaneously. Though they are in many cases radically opposed on aesthetic and epistemological grounds, no one style has managed to become dominant' (18). Though consensus has not been reached, diversity is healthy. The situation that Lodge identifies, or perhaps attempts to argue into being, is one in which the novel manages to contain divergence and allow for co-existing difference. I suggest here that this accommodation comes fully to the fore only several decades later in the noughties, when the assimilation of variant traditions occurs.

For Lodge, plurality presents an opportunity. In the essay's famous central image, the novelist stands at a crossroads: 'There are formidable discouragements to continuing serenely along the road of fictional realism. The novelist who has any kind of self-awareness must at least hesitate at the crossroads; and the solution many novelists have chosen in their dilemma is to *build their hesitation into the novel itself*' (22).

Hesitation, then, is a valuable textual manifestation of the uncertainty that the novelist experiences. The same model might still be the best available to provide purchase for a survey of more recent modal variety in the novel form. From this perspective, what Smith perceives to be a lack of diversity might be reconceptualized as a thorough going absorption of divergent trends. If novelists do not perform their experimentalism and their doubt over the continuing viability of realism on the surface of their texts, an awareness of these issues underlies their writing in submerged and subtle ways. In the wake of postmodernism, now thought of by many as a spent force that has been surpassed, the terms in which innovation is conceived have shifted. The decade in question is that in which this view has gathered momentum: as early as 1994, Malcolm Bradbury pondered whether 'we have reached the end of postmodern times, and are entering an age that has no clear shape, no clear prospects, and no clear name' (458), but it was not until the early 2000s that a paradigm shift began to be declared with more certainty by literary critics such as Valentine Cunningham (2001) and Terry Eagleton (2003), as well as more broadly across the arts, humanities and social sciences (for example, by José López and Gary Potter in 2001). Discontinuity is now to be balanced against a certain kind of continuity wherein the trends that Lodge identified several decades ago are still being digested across the 2000s.

This decade has been characterized by a convergence of the traditions that were occurring in parallel at the time Lodge wrote his essay. There is not a simple opposition between the plurality that he saw then and the self-sameness that Smith has identified more recently. The latter might be thought of as a later stage of the broader process whereby innovation is assimilated into tradition. In short, I do not suggest that Smith is incorrect in asserting that the noughties did not produce the same range of fictions as previous decades, but this is not to say that innovation and testing of the genre did not take place. 'Creative literary movements', Dominic Head writes, 'have not necessarily depended upon extravagant or iconoclastic innovations for their productive energy. A more gradual process of evolution, as is certainly the case with post-war British fiction, can be equally significant' (224). If Head cites this model in the post-war period, it is one that is also applicable, perhaps more so, after the millennium. The texts considered here might be thought of as existing within a tradition that Andrzej Gąsiorek, in *Post-war British Fiction*, has identified as a broad tendency in the post-war novel. Gąsiorek argues that 'the dichotomy between realism and experimentalism is misleading in the post-war context because numerous novelists have sought to transcend it in their writing. Their work is marked by the tension between a wish to represent various aspects of post-war reality and the recognition of the artistic difficulties thereby entailed' (17). The survey to follow exhibits the fuller gestation that this tension comes to in the noughties.

While *Netherland*, by an Irish writer, is outside of the purview of a volume addressing British fiction, dwelling briefly on Zadie Smith's reading of the text will frame the discussion of other texts to follow. O'Neill's *Netherland* was well received on publication in 2008 and was subsequently Booker long-listed, making it unsurprising that for Smith it is a text representing the status quo. The text was 'the post-September 11 novel we hoped for', approaching issues of personal and national identity, immigration, terrorism, and the American dream, through the narrative of Hans van den Broek, a Dutch stock analyst working in New York after 9/11, his marital difficulties, and his relationships with other foreign newcomers to the city, oriented around their shared interest in cricket. It is a first-person retrospective narrative that exploits patterns and symbols, loaded descriptions, metaphors and analogies to make coherence and meaning – a life story reflects and engages wider social concerns. However, Smith finds that the novel is concerned with formal as much as thematic problems: the text 'certainly is about anxiety, but its worries are formal and revolve obsessively around the question of authenticity. *Netherland* sits at an anxiety crossroads where a community in recent crisis – the Anglo-American liberal middle class – meets a literary form in long-term crisis, the nineteenth-century lyrical Realism of Balzac and Flaubert'. *Netherland* sits squarely within this tradition but, in the wake of numerous waves of postmodern attacks on its commonplaces, 'unlike much lyrical Realism, has some consciousness of these arguments, and so it is an anxious novel, unusually so. It is absolutely a post-catastrophe novel but the catastrophe isn't terror, it's Realism'. Lodge's 'hesitation' (22) is reconceived less positively here as Smith's 'anxiety'.

The text is given some credit by Smith for 'plant[ing] inside itself its own partial critique' in the form of an acknowledgement of the narrative techniques that it deploys: it is aware of, and states, the possible inauthenticity of its effects, the mechanisms by which realism imbues the world of the text with meaning. For example, from the outset Hans makes clear that he would 'like to believe that my own retrospection is in some way more important than [another's]', but he cannot be certain of this (2). The occasional opinions of his wife, who often 'had reason on her side' (23), act as a counterpoint undermining his narrative voice: 'Then again, as Rachel pointed out, I'm liable to misplace my sensitivities' (19). Thus, according to Smith, 'by stating its fears *Netherland* intends to neutralize them'. It is around this point that Smith's judgement turns. This signifies, for her, the novel's failure to follow through on the implications of its own reckoning: 'In the end what is impressive about *Netherland* is how precisely it knows the fears and weaknesses of its readers. What is disappointing is how much it indulges them. Out of a familiar love, like a lapsed High Anglican, *Netherland* hangs on to the rituals and garments of transcendence, though it well knows they are empty'.

Out of these observations, Smith builds a call-to-arms for writers in a lyrical realist tradition (and she counts herself among these). The project she envisages is different in scope rather than in kind from that which O'Neill undertakes: if lyrical realism is to survive, its practitioners 'will have to push a little harder on their subject'. The hesitation that Lodge praised and the anxiety that Smith is ambivalent about are not dissimilar. Rather, the measure against which this kind of novelistic variety might be tested is the balance of realist story-telling and self-reflexive examination within a given text. If the heyday of the latter is over, it has not simply been forgotten. Rather, novels and recent critical articulations inflect it in different, more modest ways. Hence, for example, Liam McIlvanney and Ray Ryan, in their introduction to *The Good of the Novel* (2011), find that across the 2000s, 'we are emerging from a period of heavily theoretical criticism' and that, as a result, what might be called 'the novelness of novels is coming back into focus' (vii/viii). Accordingly, critical accounts are returning to a focus on 'technique' (vii) and judging value based on a sense of subtlety: 'A good novel's truths are never portentously explicit or categorical. In forwarding its own truths, the novel will rely on the implicit – on patterns of imagery, on parallel episodes whose significance is nowhere made explicit but remains unstated, open-ended' (xiii). The remainder of this chapter will be taken up with assessing the balance, the degree and the range of generic discontinuity to be found across a number of key texts of the noughties. Focus will shift across a continuum of variety, from mild to more radical examples of experimentation, over the course of the survey.

The writers considered might be roughly divided into two groups: those who were already writing during the era of theory and postmodernism – through the 1980s and 1990s – and those who have made their breakthrough during the 2000s. I begin with the first group and, in particular, with Ian McEwan. There are a number of factors tying McEwan to several strands of the foregoing discussion. In summing up his survey of post-war realist/experimentalist accommodations, Gąsiorek cites a statement McEwan made in 1978. McEwan's comments seem incredibly prescient when looking back from after the noughties:

> [After the] formal experimentation of the late Sixties and early Seventies, there can surely be no more mileage to be had from demonstrating yet again through self-enclosed 'fictions' that reality is words and words are lies. There is no need to be strangled by that particular loop – the artifice of fiction can be taken for granted. Experimentation in its broadest and most viable sense should have less to do with formal factors like busting up your syntax and scrambling your page order, and more to do with content – the representation of states of mind and the society that forms them. ('The State of Fiction' 51)

McEwan is not dismissing postmodernism, but he is suggesting that there are more and less 'viable' manifestations of it. If self-enclosed fictions are one dead end, then blithe innocence is another. Rather, two traditions need to be made to speak to one another. Developing these thoughts much more recently in interview, McEwan has spoken of 'the dream' that is 'to write this beautiful paragraph that actually is describing something but at the same time in another voice is writing a commentary on its own creation, without having to be a story about a writer' (in Smith, 'Zadie Smith talks with Ian McEwan' n.p.). If McEwan has been aware of these problems in some form for a long period – as long as he has been writing fiction – then his novels of the noughties signify a new kind of synthesis not reached in his earlier writing.

Atonement (2001) signals a new departure from novels McEwan had written previously. It does so in a pattern that plays out as a major trend across a number of the texts considered in this chapter, by a return to and a reconsideration of tradition. Legacies – often modernist legacies – play a significant role in novelistic variety in the noughties. *Atonement* opens in the 'big house' genre, and as such it is a historical novel, but it is also a species of literary history and a historiography of twentieth-century writing. The novel shares with postmodern historiography a desire to rewrite the past but goes about it by different means. The plot concerns thirteen-year-old Briony Tallis' misunderstanding of her older sister Cecelia's relationship with Robbie Turner, son of the charwoman living on the family estate, and the repercussions of Briony's subsequent action. In 1935, on the day of a dinner party, Briony misreads an altercation between the two in the gardens and later, after interrupting and not understanding their love-making in the library, accuses Robbie of the rape of a cousin that is actually perpetrated by another guest. Subsequent sections detail the three central characters' war experiences: after arrest and imprisonment, Robbie signs up and finds himself amidst the horrors of Dunkirk; Cecelia and Briony, though estranged, both become nurses. The text describes how Robbie and Cecelia come back together and are visited by Briony, who leaves the encounter feeling that rapprochement for her wrongdoing might come about in time. Throughout the text attention has been focused on Briony's writing, both as a child and as an adult, but it is only in a coda that this mild or covert self-reflexivity becomes explicit. In this final section, told first-person by an elderly Briony, the reader learns that in fact both Robbie and Cecelia died during the war without reunion and that the happy ending is imaginary, that the text thus far has been written by Briony, and that it signifies her attempt to atone.

In summation of this kind, *Atonement* would appear to be engaged in the same kind of deferred revelation that is typical of an earlier generation of postmodern novelists, *pace* B.S. Johnson's *Albert Angelo* (1964) or John Fowles' *The French Lieutenant's Woman* (1969). In these works, as Lodge noted, the disclosure of the frame around the text serves to 'expose and destroy the fictiveness of the narrative' (13); but in *Atonement*, to deploy Lodge's terminology again, hesitation is built into the narrative by less violent means. For McEwan's contemporaries in the 1980s, the issues of authorship and the artificiality of narrative coherence often manifested themselves in the appearance of the author him/herself or his/her cypher in the world of the novel – for example, characters called Martin Amis in *Money* (1984) and Julian Barnes in *A History of the World in 10½ Chapters* (1989). For McEwan, the same issues are inflected through an invented character who is a writer (a technique with a long history of its own) in a text that, for the most part, is written in a broadly realist vein, though infused with some modernist style in the matter of perspective and point of view. In the coda, McEwan has Briony explicit in her concern for realist worldmaking – arguing for the 'pointillist approach to verisimilitude, the correction of detail that cumulatively gives such satisfaction' (359) – but also drawing attention to fictional artificiality – 'convenient distortion' (356) – and defending the novel's autonomy: 'No one will care what events and which individuals were misrepresented to make a novel.... As long as there is a single copy, a solitary typescript of my final draft, then my spontaneous, fortuitous sister and her medical prince survive to love' (371). Despite this assertion of fiction's autonomy, the doubt in to which a reading of the text is thrown by the revelation itself must infect the argument here. The reader cannot share Briony's certainty – McEwan is more equivocal than this. The interruption of the narrative that characterizes earlier phases of novelistic experimentation is thus inflected differently in this text: McEwan's self-reflexivity does not intervene in the sense of halting narrative progression; rather, it is folded into the textual world of dramatic events and emerges out of the narrative.

Assimilation of the concerns and techniques habitually located within the purview of postmodernism is not limited to the coda of *Atonement*. Part one of the text is underscored with more or less obvious commentaries on writing through discussion of Briony's practices, but it is also replete with furtive yet loaded descriptions that pertain to the same issues. As James Wood expresses it, 'in addition to explicit ruminations', this part of the text is 'carefully mined with signifiers of fictionality' (6). If precision and tight control of narrative have always been hallmarks of McEwan's writing, in *Atonement* the balance between creating a reality and noticing the artificiality of its order turns those characteristics to a new end. Thus, Briony's yearning for order is explicitly signalled in her writing: 'Her passion for tidiness was ... satisfied, for an unruly world could be made just so' (7). There is no rupture between the realism and metafiction here. Yet even this subtler form of self-reflexivity is not McEwan's final position. The middle sections of the text, concerned with Robbie's war experiences and then with Briony's nursing, are flatter and less freighted, less consciously 'literary'. The novel thus ranges over and inflects a variety of historical experiments with style whilst maintaining a realist through-narrative. Description and commentary on that description occur simultaneously. As such, *Atonement* is not only a postmodern text, but one that looks to move beyond critical self-scrutiny. Wood's pithy summation of the novel's balance – that it 'pampers our old-fashioned readerly expectations then dashes them' (16) – facilitates a comparison with the fault that Zadie Smith finds with *Netherland*. McEwan does not indulge expectations as O'Neill does. Rather, the experimentalism of *Atonement* goes some way towards undermining novelistic consolation.

McEwan's 2005 novel *Saturday* also engages in the same debates, though by different means. It records the events of a single day in the life of neurosurgeon Henry Perowne. This single day focus and its recording of the peregrinations around London of a protagonist whose every thought the reader is constantly privy to recall prevalent features of modernist texts. Indeed, the novel's opening scene with Perowne ruminating at a window alludes to the similar opening of Woolf's *Mrs Dalloway* (1925). *Saturday* is concerned, Patricia Waugh notes, with problems that preoccupied modernist writers, chiefly 'how to represent an experiencing mind' (92). The novel is simultaneously very much of the present: Perowne's movements (told, significantly, in the present tense) intersect the huge Iraq war protests of 15 February 2003, the date of the novel's events. Its concern with interiority is brought to focus in Perowne's profession – neurosurgery – and plays out as a relentlessly detailed appraisal of everything that normally remains tacit in fiction writing, both the minutiae of the situation and the elaborate thought processes behind every small decision. The acknowledgement that Perowne is 'an habitual observer of his own moods' is something of an understatement (5). Here, then, McEwan's solution to modernist problems is a kind of extreme form of realism and realist detail. The same tension between description and metafiction that operates in *Atonement* is present. Waugh's summation finds that 'in bringing into such explicit focus what is normally tacit and lived, the novel's *hyper-realism* produces something of the very hyper-reflexivity that he is attempting to avoid' (93). In the context of the overarching argument of this chapter, this appears more like careful accommodation of competing fiction-writing paradigms than overcompensation.

McEwan's novels of the noughties exemplify a much wider return to literature of the past, in particular to modernism, as a springboard for innovation in the present. Furthermore, they demonstrate that this engagement is formal and modal rather than simply thematic (though it has often been that too). Another clear example might be found in several writers returning to Henry James' aesthetics and commitment to form: Colm Tóibín's *The Master* and David Lodge's *Author, Author*, both featuring James as a character, and Alan Hollinghurst's *The Line of Beauty*, featuring a character writing a thesis on James and often read as a homage to him, were all published in 2004. Commenting on the broad trends that these dialogues exemplify, David James has argued for the importance of 'exploring the coexistence of tradition and invention in fiction today', and of an engagement with 'the stylistic, thematic and political afterlives of the formal and intellectual ambitions of modernism' (1). Similarly, Marjorie Perloff has compared poetics 'at the beginning of the twentieth century and at the millennium, so as to discover how [they] converge and cross', finding that is it the 'particular legacy of early modernism that the new poetics has sought to recover' (6).

For this chapter, there is a methodological implication to this dimension of innovation in the 2000s. James goes on to note that 'by charting myriad continuities across the phases of twentieth- and twenty-first-century writing we can alter the axis of debates not only about the way we pinpoint transitions in fiction's development from mid-century to the present day, but also about how the very nature of those transitions can only be fully understood *as* dialogues with, rather than departures from, their modernist past' (6). There is, of course, also a modernist precedent for this model: T.S. Eliot's 'Tradition and the Individual Talent' (1919) aligns innovation and assimilation rather than setting them as opposites. As I have argued, experimentation in fiction of the noughties does not necessarily involve a departure from the past. Rather, an ongoing negotiation between seemingly traditional modes and experimental forms – in the guise of modernism and/or postmodernism – defines the variety of novelistic discourse. The return to modernism, the digesting of its meanings and procedures, is one form of this accommodation.

McEwan is also paradigmatic in a second sense: he is one of a generation of writers, first coming to critical attention in the 1980s, who were associated with postmodernism earlier in their careers and have since appeared to refocus and inflect those concerns in subtler aesthetic forms. To compare recent texts by writers of this generation with their early novels is often to draw such a distinction. The interest in the artificiality of narrative and the suspicion of historical metanarrative that characterized a text such as Julian Barnes' *A History of the World in 10½ Chapters* (1989) is not absent from his 2011 Booker winner *The Sense of an Ending*, but these features are no longer so much on the surface of the text as they are contained within and held in check by realist narrative. The multiple registers of the later text's title – making reference both to the narrative that it tells and to narratological arguments that it implicitly engages in – sum up the balance between realism and experimentalism. Self-reflexivity and narrative are not allowed to become divorced from each other: the uncertainty of memory and the falsity of narratives of self *are* the novel's subject matter and central to its plot. The transition between early and late Barnes could be traced in intervening texts such *Arthur and George* (2005). The same kind of comparison could be made between Graham Swift's hyper-reflexive *Waterland* (1983) and his *Wish You Were Here* (2011), where disordered chronology is less obstructive; or between Jonathan Coe's *What a Carve Up!* (1994) and *The Rain Before It Falls* (2007). Coe's *Like a Fiery Elephant: The Story of B.S. Johnson* (2004), a biography of one of the chief figures in the development of the British postmodern novel, is testament to the fact that these transitions are not *away* from that movement but perhaps *beyond* it. The noughties is the decade in which this older generation of writers have switched to composite models for what the novel can be if it encompasses and accommodates realist *and* experimental impulses.

To turn towards a younger generation of writers is not to shift to a completely new set of characteristics, but to note an overlapping set of pervading concerns even where these are weighted differently. I opened with a discussion of Zadie Smith's critical intervention in debates surrounding realism and experimentalism, and now turn to the ways these two priorities register in her fiction. *White Teeth* (2000), Smith's acclaimed first novel, won several prizes and quickly became canonical. The text's mode, as Nick Bentley notes, is 'predominantly realist' (62) and it performs 'a gentle social satire' (55). Philip Tew finds that 'its density and sentimental commitment to characters make it quasi-Dickensian in mood' (xii). The omniscient narration of *White Teeth*, shuttling between and joining together numerous narrative threads and London lives, certainly recalls the narrative strategies of Dickens' metropolitan novels, but it is also invested in distinctly contemporary issues, multiculturalism chief amongst them. This tactic of bringing historically grounded forms to bear on current themes is one that plays out in more complex and nuanced ways in *On Beauty* (2005). Of Smith's novels, this is also the one that answers most clearly to her critical position in 'Two Paths for the Novel'.

On Beauty is written in dialogue with E.M. Forster's *Howards End* (1910) in plot and theme, as well as in voice – Smith is interested in investigating the continued suitability of Forster's omniscient third-person narrator as the means by which to address contemporary issues. Like Forster's text, *On Beauty* concerns two feuding families representative of broader social tensions. The web of social and sexual relationships between the Belseys and Kippses and their circles does not map those of the Schlegels and Wilcoxes in *Howards End* precisely: the system of equivalence is one of increased complication. An ambivalent set of priorities emerges from this novel in the setting up of patterns (the whole idea of the Forster intertext can be viewed in this way) and the simultaneous fascination with showing the places where those patterns break down. Contradictory impulses hold each other in check. If, as Tew argues, *White Teeth* should be thought of as 'very much a pre-9/11 narrative' because it balances 'contending forces optimistically' (195), *On Beauty* displays a discernible shift: the multiculturalism of the former novel is under pressure in the latter, as is the formal means by which it is managed. Here, 'the flight from the rational, which was everywhere in evidence in the new century' (*On Beauty* 38) is a central concern that figures most prominently in *On Beauty* in the form of the challenge Monty Kipps' conservatism poses to the liberalism of the Belseys. While 9/11 is only mentioned in passing, the threat of fundamentalism and liberal responses are issues that shadow the narrative and the world of the text. The unresolved plotlines of the novel's conclusion testify to a new recognition of the elusive nature of balance and tolerance. The text registers but does not fall down before Kipps' attack on 'liberal fairytales' (326). Indeed, it brings to focus the need, in the contemporary milieu, for liberalism to admit and answer to other perspectives. Thematic commitments thus register formally and structurally.

These issues play out in the debt to Forster. As Gąsiorek notes, '*On Beauty* pays homage to Forster's *Howards End* less by following its plot and more by trying to imagine how its dilemmas could play out in an early twenty-first-century context' ('A renewed sense of difficulty' 175); thus, 'in this text the various issues explored by Forster aren't just brought up to date but are heightened' (178). Smith is concerned with interpreting and interpolating modernism in a broadly liberal and lyrical realism. The occasional pronouncements of the narrating voice jar strongly in Smith's text (by design), and undermine the coherence-making force of a single point of view, instead conveying the chaotic in life. Often, occurrences are not tidied up. Instead chance is allowed to register in what is merely stated rather than explained: 'They did not mean it to be like this. But it *was* like this. Both had other intentions' (296). In this way, Smith's fiction might be aligned with McEwan's. Here, as there, the legacies of modernism for contemporary novelistic discourse are played out but are also brought into dialogue with the contingency associated with realism. The desire to overcome the deformations of crystalline form is present here too. *On Beauty* broadly endorses a liberal realist mode of novel writing, whilst drawing attention to the flaws in its premises and attempting to remain open to the critiques levelled against it. Smith has written that McEwan's prose is 'controlled, careful, and powerfully concise', whilst admitting in the same paragraph that he 'is a writer as unlike me as it is possible to be' ('Zadie Smith talks with Ian McEwan'). The aesthetic of messiness in *On Beauty* – wrought rather than accidental – signifies both its experimentation in incorporating a greater degree of contingency, and its attempt to press against realism's subject as Smith prescribes in 'Two Paths for the Novel'.

Jon McGregor's novels lie slightly further along the continuum of variety than Smith's. If her formal innovation for accommodating more of everyday life and contingency is a loosening of style, then the opposite is true of McGregor. The everyday – quotidian and mundane – is subjected to heightened attention and an elaborate poetics across his first three novels: *If Nobody Speaks of Remarkable Things* (2002), *So Many Ways to Begin* (2006) and *Even the Dogs* (2010). In an interview with Caroline Edwards, McGregor has seemed to endorse realistic depiction – 'I think it's pretty essential for a work of fiction to be a story about some people to whom some things happen, and as soon as you start trying to put an agenda onto that you kill the story' (224) – but reluctance to have characters speak ideas is not to be interpreted as reluctance to include self-reflexivity in texts. There is significant evidence to the contrary. Rather, McGregor works to a formal aesthetic that allows for the presence of this kind of material in the text but that does not allow it to become separated from narrative. Commentary or explanation does not appear as such, peripheral to the action, but occurs *through* narrative. This mode is itself Jamesian: resisting an excess of analysis, the 'sense of observing' that McGregor has drawn attention to in his aesthetic (in Edwards 220), recalls Henry James' famous declaration in 'The Art of Fiction' that 'the air of reality (solidity of specification)' is 'the supreme virtue of the novel' (53). Other critics have noted similar legacies in McGregor's work – for example, Berthold Schoene calls him a 'neo-modernist' (169).

If Nobody Speaks of Remarkable Things focuses on the ordinary lives of the residents of an inner city street on a single summer day culminating in a car accident, and interweaves this narrative with the recollections of this day from the first-person perspective of a former resident three years hence. The text is documentary but also stylistically adventurous. The coalescence of these two elements is the crux of McGregor's experimental strain of realism – that is, the deployment of experimental prose styles in the service of aims that could broadly be considered realist. Third-person narration employs free indirect discourse to drop into characters' perspectives whilst simultaneously withholding names, relying instead on identifying details – 'the man with the carefully trimmed moustache' (61) – or linking people to house numbers – 'the young girl from number nineteen' (57). The cinematic register of the text supplements this hovering perspective to create a highly wrought prose style deployed on mundane subject matter. This extended attentiveness is itself framed by an opening panorama that approximates the song of the city (1–6) – the poetics of the passage imitate the rhythms of nocturnal city sound that it describes.

If the title of this novel alludes to its theme, then explicit self-referentiality is limited therein. In *So Many Ways to Begin*, the prose style is flatter, but this type of content is more apparent. The text concerns the attempts made by David Carter, a museum curator, to trace his life and his true identity after he discovers that he is adopted. For the bulk of the text, each chapter is developed out of a significant object from David's life, described at its opening in archival style. In this, *So Many Ways to Begin* is indebted to Peter Carey's influential 2001 Booker-winning *True History of the Kelly Gang* (2000), which opens each section with a precise account of the material condition of the manuscript documents that the novel purports to reproduce. In McGregor's text, narrative organization is linked to the act of curation, a link that is cemented by the oblique metafictional commentaries embedded in descriptions of David's museum work and his childhood fascination with 'piecing together stories around the objects he found' (38). While David finds comfort in 'making a story … to fit' (100), the text balances this desire against contingency and uncertainty that registers thematically but also formally. As in *If Nobody Speaks*, the chance event again has a role to play: David considers 'the people we would have been if these things had been otherwise' (66) and finds (echoing the text's title) that 'there were so many ways it could have been different' (67). As the narrative progresses, it increasingly incorporates an uncertain stance with regard to the events on which it reports, describing how a character did this 'or' did the other (148), 'could have' said one thing or another (152), 'might have' taken one course of action or another (304). This 'or' logic competes with the archiving and creation of narrative order that the novel elsewhere embodies, instead emphasizing contingency.

The text also holds individual lives and 'historical importance' in tension with one another (210) – David's personal trauma of adoption stands in metonymically for the public trauma of war, an alignment that is bolstered by the location of much of the novel in Coventry, an apparently ordinary city that, as Edwards notes, McGregor presents as a microcosm of England's twentieth-century history (218). Further common ground shared with Carey's *True History of the Kelly Gang* might be established here. That text's title emphasizes an assertion of authenticity ('true' history), but the lack of definite or indefinite article neither endorses a claim to definitiveness nor admits relativity, thus signalling an uncertain relationship to the discourse of history. Both Carey and McGregor are concerned to think through the traffic between literature and history, but they are not merely restating a postmodern question established decades before. They are exploring connections between personal and national histories rather than delineating ruptures between official and alternative versions. McGregor's title foregrounds the numerous 'ways' of telling, the narrative by which history is formulated in an attempt to move forward from the problems an earlier generation of novelists had established and very clearly stated. Like its predecessor, the novel's formal mechanics emphasize the significance of the everyday as a crucible for fictional investigations of what David in *So Many Ways to Begin* calls 'things that were usually left unspoken' (199). The same issues carry over into *Even the Dogs*, where stylistic experimentation – time shifts, formal replication of fractured consciousness and a spectral plural narratorial voice – is again matched with prosaic subject matter.

Other texts of the noughties have taken up equally innovative approaches to fiction's relation to history. Hilary Mantel's *Wolf Hall* (2009) is written in the historical present tense to recover the contingency of sequential events from the set patterns of the historical record, and takes up the perspective of the supposed villain rather than that of the victor or the victim. The text is not told first-person by its protagonist Thomas Cromwell, but adopts a third-person perspective looking over his shoulder. Simon Mawer's *The Glass Room* (2009) refocuses twentieth-century history by tracing the multiple lives that are focused in a particular building, and the resulting fractured narrative reflects the modernist architecture of the Czech house at its centre. David Mitchell's *Cloud Atlas* (2004) draws together spatially and temporally disparate narratives into a revealing synthesis of connections. Adam Thorpe's *Hodd* (2009) concerns the myth-making and distortion that have gone into the Robin Hood folk legend. These examples indicate the complexity of fiction/history dialogues taking place over the decade.

If these writers are paradigmatic of a concern for the interaction of fiction and history, then David Peace has taken this interest to another level in his relentless incorporation of historical events and processes into his novels. The Red Riding Quartet, with which Peace came to public attention, is loosely based on the Yorkshire Ripper murder investigations of the 1970s and early 1980s. Each novel in the sequence focuses on a particular year – *Nineteen Seventy-Four* (1999), *Nineteen Seventy-Seven* (2000), *Nineteen Eighty* (2001) and *Nineteen Eighty-Three* (2002) – explicitly linking plotlines and historical discourse. *GB84* (2004) continues the precise temporal and spatial location of these earlier novels. It constitutes a week-by-week account of the 1984/5 miners' strike (fifty-three chapters, one for each week) told through the intersecting narratives of various figures involved in the dispute on both sides (some fictional, some real). Peace's prose style is highly wrought. As Matthew Hart notes, his writing 'sometimes reads like prose poetry or modernist montage' ('The Third English Civil War' 578). The novel's imbrication of historical events situates it as a kind of 'documentary realism', but it is 'far from straightforwardly realist' and 'irreducible to any one literary mode' (577). There is a tension here: 'for all its disjunctive prophecies, *GB84* can't be described as antirealistic. As historical fictions, Peace's novels operate on multiple social and diegetic levels' (580). Like McGregor, Peace is concerned to turn an experimental style towards realist ends.

The narratives that *GB84* weaves together focus on union officials, government ministers and aides, and secret service functionaries whose interrelations, loyalties and dealings are unclear, just as their identities often are through the shuttling between names and aliases that the text performs without explication. These machinations are interspersed with the diary-style accounts of two striking miners, Peter and Martin, and the increasingly desperate circumstances they find themselves in. The presentation of these sections in very small print in two columns – newspaper-style – is the most explicit example of Peace's pervasive typographical experimentation to denote the different voices of a composite narrative. As Randall Stevenson describes, each voice is 'more or less continuous, but fragmented in its presentation by repeated interruptions from the others' (21). This is one of the ways that, as Hart expresses it, 'the political vision of *GB84* informs its generic and formal qualities' ('The Third English Civil War' 573). As Peace has himself set out in interview, 'the central theme of the book ... is the division and almost state of civil war that existed not only between the government and the unions but within the government and the unions themselves' (in Hart 'An Interview with David Peace' 566). This registers stylistically in the fractured form of the text. Formal decisions do not deflect from its documentary drive but strengthen it. These techniques build towards a defamiliarizing aesthetic paradoxically in the service of documentary realism. Peace's subsequent texts also play out this lengthening of attention, particularly in *The Damned Utd* (2006), a fictionalized account of the forty-four days in 1974 (one chapter for each day) during which Brian Clough managed Leeds United Football Club.

Ali Smith is another novelist who has written innovative fiction in the noughties and shares with Peace a proclivity for fracturing perspective into a number of characters. She has been most prolific as a short story writer, but the opportunities for establishing patterns and interrelations between narratives that the short story collection offers have also carried over into her novel writing. *Hotel World* (2001) narrates the overlapping experiences of five women – the different narratives might stand alone but the events they describe are also intricately interwoven. *The Accidental* (2005), which won the Whitbread Novel Award and was Booker shortlisted, tells of the Smart family's holiday in Norfolk in sections focusing on husband, wife and each of the two children in turn. Against a backdrop of the Iraq War, the associated political manoeuvrings and the anxieties of public life (a very present context frequently alluded to in passing), the family's private concerns play out: Michael is an academic with a penchant for seducing female students; Eve is an author blighted by writer's block; her daughter Astrid, troubled by her parents' divorce and her mother's remarriage, is obsessed with recording the minutiae of life on her video camera;

and son Magnus is filled with remorse for his part in teasing a girl at school who subsequently committed suicide. Though these narratives overlap, they often contradict one another and are characterized by gaps in knowledge and misunderstandings that suggest a fractured family. Smith's novel employs a complex rendering of free indirect discourse to focalize events through characters and to include highly wrought idiosyncratic forms of speech and thinking for each narrator. Thus, the scientifically minded Magnus often thinks in the form of equations, which Smith's writing emulates; passages told from the perspective of Michael, the pedantic academic, break into verse form; and Eve's chapters drop into an author interview Q&A style. The similarities between Ali Smith and David Peace are thus not only structural: the two writers also share a formal inventiveness at the level of the sentence and a keen awareness of linguistic formations and deformations.

In *The Accidental*, the family holiday is disrupted by the arrival of the mysterious Amber, a youngish woman who may be the same person as the similarly named Alhambra, the narrator of short sections between the main narrative. Amber insinuates herself into the family and irreverently deconstructs each of their self-delusions, often through conduct showing contempt for social mores. She is an extremely equivocal figure who re-establishes sorely lacking dialogue between characters but is also a disruptive force without clear motivation. Furthermore, the text is also replete with other forms of disruption within its own narrative procedures. It employs a multitude of techniques for drawing attention to the mechanics of fiction, though they all emanate from within the world of the text. Michael's academic musings consider 'who in the world gave a damn ... about what things were called, about devices and conceits and rules and the boundaries of genres, the learned chronologies, the sorted and given definition of things' (76), while Eve's anxieties around her writing emphasize similar concerns. In addition, the formal and linguistic playfulness of the narrative is supplemented by the division of the text into sections explicitly titled 'The beginning', 'The middle' and 'The end'. In all of these ways, Smith's novel presses hard against the premises of novelistic discourse, harder than the other texts considered thus far, but this can still be said to serve recognizably novelistic ends. The eruption of strangeness in the ordinary, here in the form of Amber, the 'accidental' of the text's title, is a step towards reassessing that ordinary reality afresh. Likewise, the metafictional assessment of novels' workings is in the service of a kind of verisimilitude.

In the character of Amber, if she can be called a character in the usual sense, Smith's novel goes some way towards questioning the psychological realism and coherence that is at the centre of much novelistic discourse. Amber's motivations and backstory are left pointedly unclear. The same questioning of selfhood is taken much further in Tom McCarthy's *Remainder* (2005) and is one of the reasons that Zadie Smith, in 'Two Paths for the Novel', found it to be such a 'strong refusal' of lyrical realism. She finds that this text 'empties out interiority entirely'. If I have argued thus far that experimentalism in the noughties has not necessitated a complete break with more traditional forms, McCarthy's writing signifies a more serious threat to this thesis. The extent to which his fiction works towards undermining the novel form is open to debate.

A radical philosophical position underpins McCarthy's fiction writing. He is the General Secretary of a semi-fictitious organization called the International Necronautical Society, along with Chief Philosopher Simon Critchley. Their 2007 'Joint Statement on Inauthenticity' declared that 'being is not full transcendence, the plenitude of the one or cosmic abundance, but rather an ellipsis, an absence, an incomprehensibly vast lack scattered with debris and detritus' (n.p.). Out of this position, *Remainder* looks to offer a novelistic critique of novels based – implicitly or explicitly – in ideas of self, agency and authenticity. The unnamed narrator of the text has been injured in a mysterious accident involving 'something falling from the sky' (1). Following physiotherapy he is restored to physical health but is left mentally damaged, feeling that after the 'rerouting' – the relearning of every movement of the body – all of his actions and thoughts are inauthentic (19). Without a psychologically rounded protagonist, the novel offers a parody of all the procedures that usually accompany that format. When he learns that the compensation pay-out for his accident will be eight and a half million pounds, the narrator only wonders if eight million would have been a neater sum. From here, the text's flatness refutes the habitual symbolic and psychological charge attached to places and things in much contemporary fiction: 'Other than that, I felt neutral.... I looked around me at the sky: it was neutral too – a neutral spring day, sunny but not bright, neither cold nor warm' (10). As Zadie Smith describes it, the novel refutes the 'adjectival mania' that is 'still our dominant mode': 'In place of the rich adjective we have an imagined world in which logistical details and logical consequences are pursued with care and precision.... Every detail is attended to except the one we've come to think of as the only one that matters in the novel: how it *feels*'. In the process of relearning movements following the accident, the narrator of *Remainder* becomes convinced that acts are not genuine but 'a performance for [those] watching me, to make my movements come across as more authentic' (15), and 'set[s] about wondering when in my life I'd been the least artificial, the least second-hand' (24).

The novel's direction shifts after the narrator has an epiphany when he recalls a mundane moment in which he felt authentic. He remembers looking at a crack in a bathroom wall of a particular flat, in which he can hear a piano playing and smell a neighbour cooking liver. He uses his post-accident fortune to employ an agency to reconstruct this scenario from scratch in extreme detail and restages the moment in order to feel authentic. Other increasingly elaborate scenarios – a visit to have a car tyre changed at a garage, a shooting in the local area, a bank robbery – are subsequently re-enacted for the same purpose. Under these recreated circumstances, objects are no longer neutral but, aping novelistic procedures, are 'silently zinging with significance' (133). This is in sharp contrast to the 'real' world: 'one day I had an urge to go and check up on the outside world myself. Nothing much to report' (155). The rationale for all this is embedded in the text. The re-enactments all have the same goal: 'to allow me to be fluent, natural, to merge with actions and with objects until there was nothing separating us – and nothing separating me from the experience that I was having: no understanding, no learning first and emulating second-hand, no self-reflection, nothing: no detour. I'd gone to these extraordinary lengths in order to be real' (222–3).

In McCarthy's text, the paradoxical complete artificiality of recreations of the real is the game that fiction plays. Realism, and the idea of the self on which it is predicated, is deconstructed from within; that is, in a fictional narrative that is stylistically normative (at least superficially) even if what it describes is radical. The mechanics of the novel form, usually supressed, are here exposed.

McCarthy's iconoclasm need not be situated in direct opposition to more traditional forms though. In 'Two Paths for the Novel', Smith begins by setting up a clear antithetical relationship between this text and O'Neill's *Netherland*, but as the essay progresses this initial premise is revised. Smith comes to find that the 'constructive deconstruction' of *Remainder* offers a complex corrective rather than a simple negation: 'In its brutal excision of psychology it is easy to feel that *Remainder* comes to literature as an assassin, to kill the novel stone dead. I think it means rather to shake the novel out of its present complacency. It clears away a little of the dead wood, offering a glimpse of an alternative road down which the novel might, with difficulty, travel forward'.

Smith's essay may have begun to facilitate this kind of assimilation. Though McCarthy's relationship to the mainstream has continued to be a combative one, his 2010 novel *C* was well received and shortlisted for the Booker prize. This novel is invested in familiar themes for McCarthy – technology and transmission, war and death – but is not as openly confrontational in its procedures as

Remainder had been. For all its self-conscious radicalism, the trajectory of McCarthy's fiction might be paradigmatic of a wider process that can be described as one of accommodating the energies of dissent within novelistic discourse. The extent to which this accommodation shades into assimilation, or even neutralization, is a moot point. It might be argued that the cultural institution that is the novel operates in a similar manner to hegemony here, managing local reforms as necessary but always deflecting the possibility of any genuine revolution in style or content. Though this interpretive option ought to be registered, it cannot be reasonably verified at this short historical remove. The trends identified here play out over the end of the arbitrary decade endpoint and the fullest account of their import requires a longer perspective and, to some extent, exceeds the scope of this chapter anyway.

If dissent from within can be handled as progressive and rejuvenating, a transition to and beyond the borders of the literary mode might signify another method by which some authors have opted to navigate twenty-first century writing. During the noughties, a number of writers previously associated primarily with fiction have opted to step outside the realm of the novel, but not to abandon fictional treatments of apparently non-fictional material. The tensions that are balanced in the fiction writing that I have dwelt on in this chapter (broadly, between realism and experimentalism) are also articulated in texts that cannot be called novels in any uncomplicated way. John Burnside has been regarded as a poet first and a novelist second, but during the noughties has also begun to write memoirs. The first volume of these, *A Lie About My Father* (2006), in its very title brings into focus the tendency to treat non-fictional material to fictional rendering, subjecting it to rhetorical strategies that reveal themselves as artifice rather than making straightforward claims to truth-telling. Burnside's novels often incorporate autobiographical material in variously processed forms – perhaps most strongly in *Living Nowhere* (2003) – but memoir has not been a clean break with this activity. From the very opening of *A Lie About My Father*, it is made clear that 'this book is best treated as a work of fiction' (n.p.). Indeed, the narrative is frequently punctuated with asides drawing attention to simulation rather than simple recording, reports on conversations and events that could not have been witnessed but are described in terms that undoubtedly embellish, and includes scenarios and things that were not said or done but might have been if characters had acted or spoken otherwise. Burnside is keen to close the supposed distance between non-fiction and fiction in autobiography, stating explicitly that 'Every life is more or less a secret narrative' (10). On occasion, he is aware of the limitations that this sets – 'I knew, *of course*

I knew, that life is always more complicated than our narratives' (12) – but more often exploits the increased range of possibilities that it opens up. Here, as elsewhere in this chapter, there is a modernist precedent for innovation in the noughties: the fictionality of biography explored in Woolf's *Orlando* (1928) and in numerous of her essays opens up new opportunities for that mode of writing which have been picked up again in the 2000s.

The same is the case for 'non-fiction' texts by Iain Sinclair and Will Self, both of whom might have been thought of primarily as novelists in previous decades. Sinclair's trajectory has been from early poetry, through a phase dominated by novel writing, towards a more recent run of non-fiction texts during the noughties. However, Sinclair has not abandoned the techniques of fiction; rather, he foregrounds their continuing presence in his work. *Hackney, That Rose-Red Empire* (2009), blending autobiography with what might be called place-writing, is 'a documentary fiction; where it needs to be true, it is. . . . This is a story of fallible memory, inaccurate or inventive transcriptions, hard-earned prejudices, false starts and accidental epiphanies' (579). In *Ghost Milk* (2011), Sinclair reflects that he has 'never been that good at recognizing the division between fiction and reality' (138). Sinclair's writings at the edges of fiction undoubtedly bear the traces of W.G. Sebald's legacy – merging novelistic discourse with autobiography and an idiosyncratic form of history – and the same influence can also be felt in the generic uncertainty of Will Self's writing. In particular, *Walking to Hollywood* (2010) follows Sebald's lead in the inclusion of photographic materials documenting the narrative (but also disrupting it), and is prefaced with a subtly opaque send-up of the novelist's formulaic disclaimer: 'While the names of some real persons are used for characters in this text, these characters appear in fictionalized settings that are manifestly a product of the narrator's delusions' (n.p.). For these three writers as for numerous others, the destabilizing of the boundary that surrounds the novel allows for the benefits of that mode to infiltrate the procedures of others.

In a timely intervention, David Shields' *Reality Hunger: A Manifesto* (2010) crystallizes the trend that I am identifying here as one that has gathered momentum across the 2000s. Shields argues that 'fiction' need not designate imagined content, but rather that 'any verbal account is a fashioning and shaping of events' (10). Writers are now returning 'to the roots of the novel as an essentially Creole form, in which "nonfiction" material is ordered, shaped, and imagined as "fiction"' (14). Shields makes a case for the lyric essay as the capacious form most suited to the present moment at the expense of the novel: 'Increasingly, the novel goes hand in hand with a straitjacketing of the material's potential. One gets so weary watching writers' sensations and thoughts get set into the concrete of fiction that perhaps it's best to avoid the form as a medium of expression' (23). Shields' argument has produced counter-claims for the continued pre-eminence of the novel. McIlvanney and Ryan's edited volume *The Good of the Novel* can be conceived in this way, and their introduction certainly frames the collection as a celebration of 'what is distinctive and indigenous to the novel form' (viii). The trajectory that Shields correctly identifies need not, I argue, be interpreted as he does. Instead, the step outside of novel writing is not an implicit critique of limitations of novelistic discourse but an endorsement of its continued potentials through the noughties. Indeed, this move signifies an expansion of the novel's techniques beyond its generic boundaries as they have been conceived to date.

Challenges to novelistic form, whether they emanate from inside or outside its parameters, can thus be conceived as a sign of health rather than of sickness. In this nexus, the texts on which this chapter has dwelt demonstrate that experimentalism and realism do not always exist as polar opposites, but that they cohabit in particular texts and, increasingly over the course of the decade under discussion here, that the accommodation of one to another is perhaps a defining feature of novelistic variation. In this context, experimentation is not best described as discontinuity, but as rejuvenation of the novel as a viable mode. This is particularly the case where novelists have returned to literary history – to modernism and to other more traditional inheritances – in order to establish new paths. Rod Mengham and Philip Tew's assessment of the contemporary field in 2006 drew attention to 'a need to contend with referentiality in a period obsessed with obstructions to mimesis' (xv). From beyond the end of the decade, the state of plays looks less like obsession. Rather, writers have developed new ways to negotiate the obstructions: obstacles in the path have not, in any straightforward sense, been overcome, but they have been navigated in various ways. During the noughties, authors have sidestepped what is often presented as a choice between two options, and instead incorporated both imperatives in their fiction writing. The calibration of realism and experimentalism has not been resolved but this is perhaps the point: novelistic variation is now dependent on the accommodation of discontinuities.

Works cited

Amis, Martin. *Money*. London: Jonathan Cape, 1984.
Barnes, Julian. *The History of the World in 10½ Chapters*. London: Jonathan Cape, 1989.

Barnes, Julian. *Arthur and George*. London: Jonathan Cape, 2005.
Barnes, Julian. *The Sense of an Ending*. London: Jonathan Cape, 2011.
Bentley, Nick. *Contemporary British Fiction*. Edinburgh: Edinburgh University Press, 2008.
Bradbury, Malcolm. *The Modern British Novel*. London: Penguin, 1994.
Burnside, John. *Living Nowhere*. London: Jonathan Cape, 2003.
Burnside, John. *A Lie About My Father*. London: Vintage, 2007. First published 2006.
Carey, Peter. *True History of the Kelly Gang*. London: Faber, 2001.
Childs, Peter. *Contemporary Novelists: British Fiction Since 1970*. Basingstoke: Palgrave Macmillan, 2005.
Coe, Jonathan. *What a Carve Up!* London: Viking, 1994.
Coe, Jonathan. *Like a Fiery Elephant: The Story of B.S. Johnson*. London: Picador, 2004.
Coe, Jonathan. *The Rain Before it Falls*. London: Viking, 2007.
Cunningham, Valentine. *Reading After Theory*. Oxford: Blackwell, 2001.
Eagleton, Terry. *After Theory*. London: Allen Lane, 2003.
Edwards, Caroline. 'An Interview with Jon McGregor'. *Contemporary Literature* 51 (2010): 217–45.
Eliot, T.S. 'Tradition and the Individual Talent' [1919] In *Selected Prose*. Ed. John Hayward. London: Penguin, 1953.
Forster, E.M. *Howards End*. London: Edward Arnold, 1910.
Fowles, John. *The French Lieutenant's Woman*. London: Jonathan Cape, 1969.
Gąsiorek, Andrzej. *Post-War British Fiction: Realism and After*. London: Edward Arnold, 1995.
Gąsiorek, Andrzej. '"A renewed sense of difficulty": E.M. Forster, Iris Murdoch and Zadie Smith on ethics and form'. In *The Legacies of Modernism: Historicising Postwar and Contemporary Fiction*. Ed. David James. Cambridge: Cambridge University Press, 2012, 170–86.
Hart, Matthew. 'An Interview with David Peace'. *Contemporary Literature* 47(4) (2006): 546–69.
Hart, Matthew. 'The Third English Civil War: David Peace's "Occult History" of Thatcherism'. *Contemporary Literature* 49(4) (2008): 573–96.
Head, Dominic. *The Cambridge Introduction to Modern British Fiction, 1950–2000*. Cambridge: Cambridge University Press, 2003.
Hollinghurst, Alan. *The Line of Beauty*. London: Picador, 2004.
Jack, Ian. Ed. 'Best of Young British Novelists 2003'. Spec. issue of *Granta* 81 (2003).
James, David. Ed. *The Legacies of Modernism: Historicising Postwar and Contemporary Fiction*. Cambridge: Cambridge University Press, 2012.
James, Henry. 'The Art of Fiction'. In *Literary Criticism: Essays on Literature, American Writers, English Writers*. New York: Library of America, 1984.
Johnson, B.S. *Albert Angelo*. London: Constable, 1964.
Lodge, David. *The Novelist at the Crossroads, and other Essays on Fiction and Criticism*. London: Routledge and Kegan Paul, 1971.

Lodge, David. *Author, Author*. London: Secker & Warburg, 2004.
López, José, and Gary Potter. Eds. *After Postmodernism: An Introduction to Critical Realism*. London: Athlone Press, 2001.
Mantel, Hilary. *Wolf Hall*. London: Fourth Estate, 2009.
Mawer, Simon. *The Glass Room*. London: Little Brown, 2009.
McCarthy, Tom. *Remainder*. Richmond: Alma Books, 2006.
McCarthy, Tom. *C*. London: Vintage, 2010.
McCarthy, Tom, and Simon Critchley. 'International Necronautical Society Joint Statement on Inauthenticity'. Statement given at the Drawing Center, New York, 25 September 2007. Available online: http://www.listen.to/necronauts (accessed 2 July, 2012).
McEwan, Ian. 'The State of Fiction: A Symposium'. *The New Review* 5(1) (1978): 14–76.
McEwan, Ian. *Atonement*. London: Vintage, 2005.
McEwan, Ian. *Saturday*. London: Vintage, 2006.
McGregor, Jon. *If Nobody Speaks of Remarkable Things*. London: Bloomsbury, 2003.
McGregor, Jon. *So Many Ways to Begin*. London: Bloomsbury, 2007.
McGregor, Jon. *Even the Dogs*. London: Bloomsbury, 2010.
McIlvanney, Liam, and Ray Ryan. Eds. *The Good of the Novel*. London: Faber, 2011.
Mengham, Rod, and Philip Tew. Eds. *British Fiction Today*. London: Continuum, 2006.
Mitchell, David. *Cloud Atlas*, London: Sceptre, 2004.
O'Neill, Joseph. *Netherland*. London: Fourth Estate, 2008.
Peace, David. *Nineteen Seventy-Four*. London: Serpent's Tail, 1999.
Peace, David. *Nineteen Seventy-Seven*. London: Serpent's Tail, 2000.
Peace, David. *Nineteen Eighty*. London: Serpent's Tail, 2001.
Peace, David. *Nineteen Eighty-Three*. London: Serpent's Tail, 2003.
Peace, David. *GB84*. London: Faber, 2005.
Peace, David. *The Damned Utd*. London: Faber, 2006.
Perloff, Marjorie. *21st-Century Modernism: The 'New' Poetics*. London: Blackwell, 2001.
Schoene, Berthold. *The Cosmopolitan Novel*. Edinburgh: Edinburgh University Press, 2009.
Self, Will. *Walking to Hollywood*. London: Bloomsbury, 2010.
Shields, David. *Reality Hunger; A Manifesto*. London: Hamish Hamilton, 2010.
Sinclair, Iain. *Hackney, That Rose-Red Empire*. London: Penguin, 2010. First published 2009.
Sinclair, Iain. *Ghost Milk: Calling Time on the Grand Project*. London: Hamish Hamilton, 2011.
Smith, Ali. *Hotel World*. London: Hamish Hamilton, 2001.
Smith, Ali. *The Accidental*. London: Penguin, 2006.
Smith, Zadie. *White Teeth*. London: Hamish Hamilton, 2000.
Smith, Zadie. 'Zadie Smith talks with Ian McEwan'. *The Believer* 26 August 2005. Available online: http://www.believermag.com/issues/200508/?read=interview_mcewan (accessed 8 June, 2012).
Smith, Zadie. *On Beauty*. London: Penguin, 2006.

Smith, Zadie. 'Two Paths for the Novel'. *The New York Review of Books* 55 (20 November 2008). Available online: http://www.nybooks.com/articles/archives/2008/nov/20/two-paths-for-the-novel/ (accessed 13 April, 2012).

Stevenson, Randall. 'Big Sister.' *TLS* 19 March 2004: 21.

Swift, Graham. *Waterland*. London: Heinemann, 1983.

Swift, Graham. *Wish You Were Here*. London: Picador, 2011.

Tew, Philip. *The Contemporary British Novel*. London: Continuum, 2007.

Thorpe, Adam. *Hodd*. London: Jonathan Cape, 2009.

Tóibín, Colm. *The Master*. London: Picador, 2004.

Waugh, Patricia. 'Thinking in literature: modernism and contemporary neuroscience'. *The Legacies of Modernism: Historicising Postwar and Contemporary Fiction*. Ed. David James. Cambridge: Cambridge University Press, 2012, 75–95.

Wood, James. 'Ian McEwan, *Atonement*'. *The Good of the Novel*. Ed. Liam McIlvaney and Ray Ryan. London: Faber, 2011, 1–20.

Woolf, Virginia. *Mrs Dalloway*. London: Hogarth Press, 1925.

Woolf, Virginia. *Orlando: A Biography*. London: Hogarth Press, 1928.

7

International Contexts 1
The American Reception of British Fiction in the 2000s

Ann Marie Adams

One may as well begin a study of the reception of twenty-first-century British fiction in America with a brief discussion of the most celebrated British novelist of the new millennium, Zadie Smith, as reviews of her Orange Prize-winning novel, *On Beauty* (2005), illustrate an important national distinction. When Smith published *White Teeth* in 2000, her debut novel was met with wide acclaim on both sides of the Atlantic. Critics were less pleased with her second work, *The Autograph Man* (2002), an inventive homodiegetic tale that promised more than it was able to deliver, yet British and American critics continued to aver that she was a writer of great promise. Shortly after her appointment as a Radcliffe fellow at Harvard University for the 2002–3 academic year, Smith produced an homage to E.M. Forster's *Howards End* that returned to the omniscient (if not fully comedic) narrative mode of her debut novel. While *On Beauty* was generally praised in the American press, it was not lauded for its metafictive efforts. In fact, extended reviews by Robert Alter, William Deresiewicz, J.A. Gray and Wyatt Mason explicitly faulted the award-winning novel for its muddled invocation of its Edwardian predecessor. What is so interesting about the reviewers' frustration is that the American critics appeared to be as troubled by Smith's decision to conjoin the English literary past with the (postcolonial) present as they were with the limitations of her characterization and plotting. Even though Smith was revisiting an Edwardian masterpiece that was itself rife with nostalgia, she did not offer a careful recreation of the English past that could sate a hunger for heritage, and she refrained from thematizing the 'Break-up of Britain' in her racially and culturally sensitive text. As a result, she elided the two most common frames through which contemporary evocations of Englishness are understood in America, and this elision may explain why so many American reviewers critiqued her nod to Forster's Edwardian fiction while a number of

British critics, from Stephanie Merritt to John Sutherland, Colin McCabe and Frank Kermode (who was admittedly more equivocal in his assessment), were able to praise it.

As Smith's subsequent 2010 appointment to the tenured faculty of New York University's Creative Writing programme demonstrates, celebrated British writers of the noughties are recognized within the American academy and literary establishment. They just do not tend to be rendered as part of a viable national tradition in the twenty-first century. A few careful reviews, like Ruth Franklin's reading of Smith's most recent fiction, *NW* (2012), may place the author in the fluxes and flows of twentieth- and twenty-first-century British fiction (and in productive dialogue with the work of David Foster Wallace and Franz Kafka), but many commentaries tend to treat Smith as a breakout star who largely transcends national considerations. (She is, after all, one of a select number of authors Paul Jay discusses in *Global Matters: The Transnational Turn in Literary Studies* [2010].) Smith's interest in fellow British novelist Ian McEwan, whom she has interviewed and written about, would seem to invite a critical comparison, yet the only significant study of an authorial connection to come out of North America, Kathleen Wall's 'Ethics, Knowledge, and the Need for Beauty: Zadie Smith's *On Beauty* and Ian McEwan's *Saturday*', was written by a professor at the University of Regina in Saskatchewan. Given the obvious disparity between Smith's and McEwan's narrative styles, this specific point may seem somewhat trifling, as the paucity of American scholarship could reflect the fact that there is not much to fruitfully compare; still, the omission can be said to gesture towards the general absence of a critical conversation regarding contemporary British literature in the United States.

For many American critics and scholars, 'the novel now' means something very different from what it does for Richard Bradford, not in the least because American commentators are more likely to ponder Michael Bérubé's questions regarding the very existence of postmodern fiction, and his emphasis on the 'worlding' of literature, than they are to analyse fictive trends in the context of the British Isles. Max Watman, in 'The Ever-Present Human Hint of Yellow' (2006), for example, may notice a certain 'trade deficit' when he ponders the fact that most 'interesting novels today seem to have been for sale in the U.K. first', but his focus on a novel's availability, as opposed to its author's origin, shows how uncomfortable he is with 'generalizations based on national stereotypes' (58). After asserting that Smith's *On Beauty* 'grants us remarkable insight into the current state of British fiction', he adds a parenthetical aside ('if such a thing, etc., etc.') that actually calls into question the possibility of 'British fiction' itself (58).

Coy references to textual commonalities at the end of the piece gesture towards recurrent themes, yet the ironic conclusion offers no summation of a 'state' (national or otherwise), just a way to sum up a laundry list of disparate readings. While few reviewers share Watman's concern with a 'trade deficit', many appear loath to ascribe British fiction to a national tradition.

This rarity is somewhat understandable in reviews. Reviews are supposed to focus on the particularities of a given work, and the relatively limited space they are allotted in periodicals ensures that whatever context they provide will be brief. Furthermore, the majority of fiction reviewed in the American press is American works of art, so the critical conversation crafted in and through this discourse is unlikely to uncover peculiarly British moods or trends. Additionally, because non-American fictions tend to be 'sold' to American audiences via articulations of their 'universality', many critics wisely avoid references to 'foreign' traditions in their reviews, even if those reviews offer substantive criticisms of non-American texts. As the literary triumphs of Zadie Smith and the popular success of J.K. Rowling demonstrate, authorial accomplishments can and do 'cross the pond', but the passage itself necessarily converts 'British' into 'international'.

What needs more explanation is why American literary scholarship rarely discusses contemporary British fiction as part of an extant national (British) tradition. Contemporary works that self-consciously engage with British literature and/or history, such as Ian McEwan's *Atonement* (2001), will invariably be located in the contexts that they themselves so cleverly provide, but even this dutiful contextualization does not ensure that a celebrated novel like McEwan's will be analysed for the ways in which it, in Geoff Dyer's words, 'creatively extend[s] and haul[s] a defining part of the British literary tradition up to and into the 21st century'. Brian Finney's 'Briony's Stand Against Oblivion', one of the best articles written on the novel to date, manages to seamlessly integrate a discussion of *Atonement*'s uncanny recreation of the mid-century country house novel into an exploration of the fiction's foregrounding of narrative ethics. Other American studies, though, tend to shift the focus from McEwan's utilization of literary tradition to the traditional elements themselves. Both Juliette Wells' 'Shades of Austen in Ian McEwan's *Atonement*' and Mary Berhman's 'The Waiting Game: Medieval Allusions and the Lethal Nature of Passivity in Ian McEwan's *Atonement*' extract McEwan's novel from the 'Great Tradition' it lovingly recreates in order to fix the narrative to a particular author or era. Earl G. Ingersoll's 'Intertextuality in L.P. Hartley's *The Go-Between* and Ian McEwan's *Atonement*' openly engages with the modern fiction McEwan evokes (particularly in Part I of the novel), but his carefully focused argument of modern influence tends to pale in comparison with British studies that explore McEwan's complex invocation of the varieties of modernism, such as Richard Robinson's 'The Modernism of Ian McEwan's *Atonement*' and Laura Marcus' 'Ian McEwan's Modernist Time: *Atonement* and *Saturday*'. Critics who wish to study the ways in which McEwan's individual talent interacts with the tradition *Atonement* inscribes are better off reading the various book chapters authored outside of the United States.

As James Phelan's discussion of *Atonement*'s 'narrative judgment' and Kathleen D'Angelo's exploration of the novel's 'critical readership' attest, substantive American scholarship on contemporary British fiction need not concern itself with the classification of 'British literature' to offer an original and important contribution. These studies provide useful ways to understand McEwan's complex use of metafiction and, in the case of Phelan's work, may even augment *Atonement*'s literary status by locating it as an exemplar of narrative technique. The problem here is not that Phelan brings his narratological expertise to McEwan's fiction without discussing what is peculiarly British about the tale or, in the case of less impressive scholarship, that a critic like Wells is more concerned with Austen than with she is with McEwan. The real issue is the absence of a critical conversation that allows works designated as British works to be placed at the forefront of literary trends. As the reception of two of the most celebrated British writers in twenty-first-century America (McEwan and Smith) attests, the critical and commercial success of individual British authors has done little to raise the status of British fiction in general because the authors and their texts tend to be treated in isolation.

This, of course, is not to say that all American commentary atomizes British fiction. There are a number of American scholars who are working diligently to facilitate a larger critical conversation. In the first decade of the twenty-first century alone, Susan Keen published *Romances of the Archive in Contemporary British Fiction* (2001), Brian Finney authored *English Literature Since 1984* (2005) and *Martin Amis* (2008), James F. English compiled *A Concise Companion to Contemporary British Fiction* (2005), M. Hunter Hayes produced *Understanding Will Self* (2007) and Brian W. Shaffer edited *Conversations with Kazuo Ishiguro* (2008) – co-edited with Cynthia F. Wong – and *A Companion to the British and Irish Novel* (2005). Unfortunately, these works tend to be the exceptions, not the rule. Most book-length studies of contemporary British fiction are produced outside of the United States (as the press of Keen's study would suggest), and many edited collections (such as English's) are populated with the work of non-

American scholars. If the current Macmillan *Contemporary British Novelists* series is any indication, the sustained study of contemporary British fiction appears to be the purview of critics outside of the United States who are able to recognize that there is still such a thing as the British novel.

It would be somewhat comforting to attribute this absence to the blurring (and dissolution) of national distinctions in literary studies. The beginning of the twentieth century, after all, was dominated by an aesthetic movement that prized transnational connections, such as those that facilitated the synchronization of British and American literature into Anglo-American modernism, and the later part of the century witnessed an intensified interest in cosmopolitanism in postmodern (and postcolonial) discourse, as well as the 'global turn' in literature that radically questioned the usefulness of national designations altogether. Placed in this context, the atomization of British fiction could be seen as the logical outcome of international movements that have effected what Tom Nairn has so memorably termed 'the Break-up of Britain'. This tidy summarization, though, does not account for the fact that the literary synchronicity of Anglo-American modernism was short-lived and that subsequent modern recalibrations have rendered American fiction the standard against which all others are judged in this 'global' age (a point acknowledged in John Sutherland's review of *On Beauty*, which contends that Smith's 'transatlantic pilgrimage' to America 'serv[es] the higher purposes of her art' [51]). If contemporary fiction studies were truly global in the American academy, there would be a great deal more coverage of works outside of the United States, and more analyses that integrate recent works of contemporary British literature into studies of global trends, like Rebecca Walkowitz's *Cosmopolitan Style: Modernism Beyond the Nation* (2006) and John Su's *Ethics and Nostalgia in the Contemporary Novel* (2005). At the very least, there would be more scholarship that interprets contemporary British fiction alongside American works of art.

The absence of a critical conversation regarding British fiction in the American age is actually attributable to another, albeit related, factor – contemporary British literature's uneasy relation to modernism, the movement that continues to dominate discussions of contemporary literature in general. As even the staunchest advocates of the innovations of postmodernism would contend, this 'cultural logic' exists on a continuum with the aesthetic movement that preceded it, so even late twentieth-century fictions can be said to be influenced by modernist precedent. The somewhat clunky attempt to move past the late twentieth-century 'posting' in twenty-first-century conceptions of (an unfortunately named) post-postmodernism or (a more felicitously conceived) metamodernism necessarily privileges the defining movement, as everything produced from the start of the twentieth century on is still understood in continuous relation to modernism itself. This continuous relation is not evident in twentieth-century British literature. During and immediately after the Second World War, a number of British writers (and influential critics) cast modernism itself as a foreign influence that needed to be rejected in order for more traditional forms to be resuscitated and flourish. These intellectuals turned away from internationally dominant trends and effected what C. Hugh Holman and William Harmon, in their influential *A Handbook to Literature*, term the 'Diminishing Age of English Literature', a 'time of literary effort and respectable activity [that] lacked the dominating literary voices needed to make it a superlative age' (142). While Holman and Harmon do offer an end date for this less than stellar era (1965), neither they, nor any other scholar, have articulated a succeeding age (or periodized argument) that fully counters the diminishing thesis. Amy J. Elias' intriguing 1994 analysis of 'postmodern realism' is noteworthy for its attempt to define what is uniquely innovative about contemporary British fiction, but even this articulation demonstrates that British literature is at odds with dominant trends, as the postmodernity it expresses is on a continuum with realism, not early twentieth-century narrative experimentation. In consequence, the study implicitly affirms contemporary British literature's diminished status.

Contemporary American literature, on the other hand, blossomed in the wake of a modern renaissance. As the cultural landscape in postwar Britain was shifting to fit a more curtailed national mood, modernism, as Alan Sinfield argues in *Literature, Culture and Politics in Postwar Britain*, 'was being reinvigorated and recentered just where Englishness was most distressed: in the United States, the former colony to which world power had passed' (185). Even more significantly, this reinvigoration was coupled with a renewed cultural nationalism that used modern innovation and experimentation to 'free the [contemporary] US artist or writer from the authority of traditions (it was felt) he or she only partially shared' (186). This shift not only helped to revalue the 'individualism' (and erstwhile idiosyncrasy) of American literature in general, but it also created a special status for contemporary American writers, who were assumed to be at the vanguard of literary trends. What is so interesting about this modern shift is not that it realizes John Sutherland's pithy 1978 contention – 'In the nineteenth century, according to the famous insult, there was no American literature – only English literature published in America. [In the late twentieth century] it seemed there might be no English literature, only American literature published in England' (47) – but that this mid-twentieth century reversal remains stubbornly in place in America, even though the innovative work of recent British writers (such as Jim Crace, Jeanette Winterson and Tom McCarthy) and twenty-first century critical recalibrations should have destabilized (or displaced) it.

In this regard, Michael Bérubé's 2000 opinion piece in *The Chronicle of Higher Education*, 'Teaching Postmodern Fiction Without Being Sure That the Genre Exists', is instructive. The brief essay not only calls into question the usefulness of distinguishing postmodern and modern forms of experimentation and self-reflexivity at the start of the twenty-first century; it also highlights the fact that many celebrated contemporary writers do not display the modern techniques that are said to be the hallmark of the age. Bérubé concludes that:

> The crucial difference between the major English literature of the first half of the 20th century and the major English literature of the second half is not that one was modern and the other postmodern. The crucial difference is that one was produced largely in the United States, Britain, and Ireland, whereas the other was written in the United States, Britain, Ireland, and South Africa (J. M. Coetzee, Nadine Gordimer, Bessie Head), India (Salman Rushdie), Nigeria (Chinua Achebe, Wole Soyinka), Guyana (Wilson Harris), Kenya (Ngugi wa Thiong'o), Canada (Margaret Atwood, Michael Ondaatje), and Trinidad (V. S. Naipaul). (B4)

This all but asserts a new playing field where merit is divorced from narratives of national exceptionalism and Western conceptions of aesthetic experimentation. Still, even this opening salvo in new millennial literary debates implicitly rehearses the diminishing thesis. Bérubé's admitted point of departure is a course he teaches in Postmodernism and American fiction, which, he contends, could just as easily be titled 'Recent Intellectual Debates in the Humanities, Along With a Bunch of Novels Written Since 1965'. The slippage between 'American fiction' and 'a Bunch of Novels Written Since 1965' is particularly telling, not in the least because the 'Intellectual Debates' Bérubé covers are far from localized to American sources. The only British work mentioned in an essay designed to rethink the current classification of literature – an essay, it must be noted, that carefully decouples the writings of James Joyce and Salman Rushdie from the designation of British – is the eighteenth-century, proto-postmodernist *Tristram Shandy* by Laurence Sterne.

The growing body of scholarship on Smith's *White Teeth* demonstrates that critics are more than willing to engage in the twenty-first-century debate Bérubé wishes to begin (over what is 'postmodern' and what is 'global'): Paul Jay's chapter on *White Teeth* in *Global Matters* even shows how productive and inventive such analyses can be. This 'global' discussion, though, has not displaced the critical importance of modernism in the first decades of the twenty-first century, as the reception of Smith's most recent work illustrates. Alexandra Schwartz's review of *NW* in *The Nation* explicitly lauds the narrative's stylistic difficulty in terms of modernist precedent. Particular passages are said to reach 'for the quicksilver rhythm invented by James Joyce and Virginia Woolf, attempting, through words, to press as close as possible to all forms of sensory and cerebral experience', while the 'cacophonous jumble of character, voice and thought that builds as the sentences accrete' conjures T.S. Eliot's *The Waste Land* (42). When Schwartz offers an almost obligatory overview of Smith's previous fiction, she makes a point of praising the 'lush realism' of *On Beauty* for its admirable focus on 'form', a focus, she avers, that should not be read as abandonment of 'an experimental sensibility for a more traditional vein' (40). Kathryn Shultz is much more equivocal about Smith's stylistic pyrotechnics (playing on James Woods' criticism of Smith and others as 'hysterical realists', the critic terms *NW* a species of 'hysterical formalism'), yet modern style remains paramount in her more measured review. The fault Shultz finds is not with Smith's narrative innovation in and of itself but with the text's unevenness. In her view only one section of the novel is fully realized. Darin Strauss, who reads the very London-specific novel in relation to two American texts also published in 2012, Ben Fountain's *Billy Lynn's Long Halftime Walk* and Michael Chabon's *Telegraph Avenue*, finds reasons to 'Re-Joyce' in *NW* because Smith's new work, like that of her American counterparts, revives James Joyce's (high modern) legacy. In such reviews, references to modern writers affiliated with British literature, such as Woolf and Joyce, do not denote the vitality of a national tradition Smith is carrying on. Rather, they secure the modernist credentials that allow her (international) work to stand alongside innovative American fiction.

Admittedly, not every reader displays the same interest in experiment or modernist innovation. Many contemporary works of British fiction have been well received by American audiences precisely because they offer more traditional narrative pleasures. Hilary Mantel's careful historical recreation of sixteenth-century England, *Wolf Hall* (2009), was a critical and commercial success. The Man Booker prize-winning novel earned the National Book Critic's Circle award for fiction during its long stay on the New York Times bestseller's list (a feat that McEwan's *Atonement* had accomplished seven years before). Like Philippa Gregory's romanticized Tudor series (also published in the noughties), Mantel's celebrated fiction provides its readers with a compelling narrative set in a highly detailed historical milieu. Terry Pratchett's ever-expanding Discworld, Neil Gaiman's mythic landscapes, Jasper Fjorde's parallel republic of England and, most especially, J.K. Rowling's Hogwarts continue to enthrall readers precisely because the twenty-first-century tales efface their own textuality in and through the development of immersive new realities. (The blurred lines between literature and life in the Thursday Next novels are actually safely contained within the alternate world Fjord creates. The joke of the series is that the textual transgressions in his republic of England only end up replicating the canonical versions of literature his readers already know.) Mark Haddon's charming debut, *The Curious Incident of the Dog in Night-Time* (2003), reconceives the detective novel in the twenty-first century, just as Kazuo Ishiguro's *When We Were Orphans* (2000) and Graham Swift's *Light of Day* (2003) do, but Haddon's fiction focuses on the external details and objective observations that are anathema to the contemplative interiority of Ishiguro's and Swift's narratively complex fictions. Interestingly enough, Haddon's more 'traditional' tale has garnered greater praise, and sold more copies, than either novel from the Man Booker prize-winners. As the occasional complaints lodged against the postmodern trickery of *Atonement*'s conclusion suggest, a number of readers would have preferred McEwan's metafictive masterpiece to remain, as Tom Shone observes in his complimentary review of McEwan's clever pastiche, 'the sort of English novel that English novelists stopped writing more than 30 years ago'. This 'simple' desire, though, remains a mainstay of commercial, not critical, success.

Readers' abiding interest in 'traditional' narrative pleasures, and critical affirmations of the simplicity (and non-innovative nature) of these pleasures, is perhaps most obvious in the reception of bestselling neo-Victorian tales, like Susanna Clarke's *Jonathan Strange & Mr. Norrell* (2004), which are frequently lauded for their 'readability'. *Fingersmith* (2002), Sarah Waters' intriguing tale of crime, women and madness, follows in the wake of *Tipping the Velvet* (1998) and *Affinity* (1999) by conjuring a richly realized Victorian past. The reader's guide provided by Waters' US publishers (Penguin USA) describe the novel as 'Dickensian' while various reviews note its debt to another Victorian master, Wilkie Collins. Waters' most recent novels, *The Night Watch* (2006) and *The Little Stranger* (2009), have shifted forward in time, focusing on the 1940s in Britain, but neither the chronological experiments in *The Night Watch* nor the tonal effects in the gothic *Little Stranger* have troubled Waters' categorization as a captivating storyteller. Julian Barnes, a writer whose early work was often included as an exemplar of form in studies of postmodern fiction, earned arguably his greatest commercial success with *Arthur & George* (2005), a novel that reimagines Sir Arthur Conan Doyle's investigation of the Great Wyrley Outrages. The novel, clearly set at the turn of the last century, was read as an homage to the Victorian triple decker. André Bernard, in a piece for the *Kenyon Review* significantly titled 'The Casual Reader', argues that Barnes' 'addictive' text is 'reminiscent of the better English novels of the nineteenth century' (2), while Vince Passaro's review for *The Oprah Magazine* declares that Barnes' neo-Victorian tale has finally returned to the 'shapes and approaches' that suit the novel form. After 'fooling around in complex, intelligent ways with 19th-century figures' in early works such as *Flaubert's Parrot* (1984), Barnes is now able to provide 'an utterly absorbing, beautifully crafted old-fashioned novel based on the true story of Sir Arthur Conan Doyle's taking up a miscarriage of justice at the turn of the last century' (88). 'Traditional' modes remain popular with readers: they just do not rate highly in critical conversations that implicitly privilege 'innovation' and 'change'.

As the phenomenal success of A.S. Byatt's *Possession* (1990) in the last decade of the twentieth century demonstrates, even the literary accolades offered popular neo-Victorian novels do little to change the way in which contemporary fiction is received in America. The apparent returns to previous forms in Byatt's most famous metafiction are read as either pre-modern nostalgia or (as is most often the case) postmodern pastiche; either way, the novel's relation to modernism still determines its status as an exemplar of contemporary fiction. This relation remains in place for all British fictions produced in the noughties. Seemingly despite the fact that a number of celebrated American novels, as Bérubé himself concedes, appear to be reaching back to the older fictive forms that many British texts employ, the weight of tradition appears only to hamper serious British fictions. Alice Walker's Pulitzer Prize- and National Book Award-winning *The Color Purple* (1982) can resurrect the epistolary novel in an historicized account of African-American experience and still be considered a masterpiece of contemporary fiction, while Sarah Waters' scholarly re-creation of the nineteenth-century (English) gothic renders her fiction a species of neo-Victorianism that necessarily (and perhaps nostalgically) traffics with the literary dead. Even largely realist works of contemporary American fiction, such as Richard Russo's *Empire Falls* (2001), can be lauded as the next 'Great American Novel'. Contemporary British fictions that work in the realist mode, on the other hand, are assumed to be relics of the past, looking back to a tradition that ended at the start of the last century.

The assumption of antiquation is particularly evident in the reception of A.S. Byatt's most recent novel, *The Children's Book* (2009). Like all of the fiction Byatt has published in the noughties, the novel is set largely in the twentieth century and includes a number of artisans and intellectuals who self-consciously explore a range of scientific and artistic issues throughout the narrative. The encyclopedic recording of economic, educational, sociological and political detail in *The Children's Book*, as well as the long passages devoted to outlining the finer points of pottery production, do not obscure the novel's predominant focus on the golden age of children's literature, a focus that allows Byatt to combine her longstanding interests in fairytales, children's literacy and the latent dangers in literary production into one cautionary tale. The mixed reviews invariably mention *Possession*, Byatt's most famous novel, and touch upon at least one of the author's stylistic tics – her tendency to layer physical description, overpopulate her fictive worlds, and arrest the flow of the narrative to lay out a philosophical argument or critical treatise – as a way to either praise or criticize the novel's density. American critics, though, also work from the assumption that this historical novel, which labours so diligently to record the major intellectual currents from 1885 to 1919, is a neo-Victorian tale. Jennifer Schuessler, who makes an almost obligatory comparison to *Middlemarch*, contends: 'there's something bracingly old-fashioned in [Byatt's] insistence that encounters with works of art can transform experience as powerfully as the making of them can deform the lives of their creators' (n.p.), while Elaine Showalter, who also mentions Eliot's masterwork in her review, refers to the text as a 'virtuoso Victorian novel' (1667).

To be fair, Byatt herself seems to beg for such comparisons. She has made no secret of her admiration for nineteenth-century literature, and she repeatedly notes that the seeds for her post-war tetralogy were planted when a student asked why contemporary authors did not write novels like *Middlemarch* anymore. *Possession*, the novel that secured her literary fame, renders Victorian verse more alive than the contemporary criticism that would explain it, and the twinned novellas in *Angels and Insects* (1992) conjure *In Memoriam* in order to revisit Tennyson's still relevant materialist debates. Furthermore, *The Children's Book* does begin at the end of the Victorian era, so it makes sense that Diana Maltz's study of the novel's invocation of E. Nesbit would be published in *The Journal of Victorian Culture*. Byatt's most recent fiction, though, as even Showalter's review notes, actually returns to the apparent 'innocence' of the Edwardian period in order to outline modern concerns that will haunt the twentieth century. Thus, when Showalter argues '*The Children's Book* is a dazzling performance but inside this virtuoso Victorian novel, there is a slim modernist masterpiece trying to get out' (1668), she is not just faulting Byatt's tendency to overstuff; she is also indicting the novelist's failure to marry content and form. The narrative method, the review intimates, should fit with the times if it wishes to render what is 'modern'. Like many of the critics of *On Beauty*, then, Showalter suggests that more contemporaneous forms of social change cannot be adequately rendered in pre-modern modes.

At issue here is not Byatt's (understandable) placement within a neo-Victorian canon, or even the paucity of scholarship that mines the modernist subtexts in her fiction (although it would be nice to see someone really explore how *The Biographer's Tale* [2000] engages with Bloomsbury's debates regarding biography); the problem is that Byatt's 'old fashioned' approach is either explained away as ironic knowingness (and hence proof of her postmodernity, as many studies of *Possession* attest) or cited as evidence of her literary nostalgia (as it tends to be in reviews of *The Children's Book*). It is never once addressed in terms of a 'New Sincerity' or identified as a possible instance of post-postmodernism or metamodernism, even though such a categorization could explain the relation between *The Children's Book* and Byatt's seemingly anomalous *The Biographer's Tale*, and help to draw useful lines of connection between Byatt's rendering of the early twentieth century and Barnes' recent treatment of the Edwardian era in *Arthur & George*. Such designations, in the American academy, are reserved for the American writers who can make modernism, or movements past it, 'new' again.

In a 1993 essay originally published in *Review of Contemporary Literature*, 'E Unibus Pluram: Television and U.S. Fiction', American essayist and novelist David Foster Wallace argued that the 'next real literary "rebels"' might actually be 'anti-rebels . . . who dare somehow to back away from ironic watching, who have the childish gall actually to endorse and instantiate single-entendre principles' (192–3). Wallace prophesied that such 'anti-rebels would be outdated, of course, before they even started. Dead on the page. Too sincere. Clearly repressed. Backward, quaint, naive, anachronistic' (193). As the wide distribution of the essay, and the reception of Wallace's *Infinite Jest* (1996) attest, a number of critics agree that this 'quaint' trend is a new vanguard. Unfortunately, this approbation, and the subsequent studies of 'New Sincerity' it fostered, only extends to the group Wallace specifically identifies in his article, American fiction writers. Byatt's complex use of metafiction, particularly in her delineation of what she terms, in *Possession*, as 'good and greedy reading,' could also be said to renegotiate the contract between the reader and the writer, but obligatory references to her as a 'postmodern Victorian' somewhat ironically render her 'outdated . . . before [she] even start[s]' (Wallace 193). Byatt's choice to treat 'untrendy human troubles and emotions' in the Edwardian age 'with reverence and conviction' (Wallace 193) thus sates a hunger for heritage, not unlike the surprise public television hit that followed a year later, *Downton Abbey*. A movement way from 'ironic watching' can make American fiction 'new'. An apparently analogous return to 'sincerity' in British fiction is 'bracingly old-fashioned'.

The critical interest in a return to sincerity, and a possible focus on what may be 'clearly repressed', is particularly germane to the work of the author who won the Booker prize a year before Byatt, Kazuo Ishiguro. All of Ishiguro's fictions focus on unreliable narrators whose oblique explorations of moral dilemmas necessarily raise ethical concerns. The most celebrated of these are *The Remains of the Day* (1989), the international sensation than won the Booker Prize, and *Never Let Me Go* (2005), the *New York Times* bestseller that was declared one of the top books of the 2000s by *Time* magazine. Even though Ishiguro began the decade by publishing a novel that he admits is not his best work (*When We Were Orphans*), and closed it with a short story collection (*Nocturnes*) that received comparatively little notice, his reputation continues to rise because his melancholic fiction can be said to participate in global literary trends. Rebecca L. Walkowitz's 2006 study, *Cosmopolitan Style: Modernism Beyond the Nation*, rather surprisingly does not include any of Ishiguro's works from the noughties, but there is no doubt that *When We Were Orphans* is as 'treasonous' as Ishiguro's earlier fiction, not in the least because it renders 'global comparison . . . a formal as well as a thematic preoccupation' ('Location of Literature' 536). Likewise, the transnational cast of the interlocking stories in *Nocturnes* could be said to literalize Ishiguro's frequent claim that he strives for an 'international audience' by dealing with 'moveable' themes. While there is much to be gleaned from studying how Ishiguro, in Walkowitz's terms, moves 'modernism beyond the nation', there is also something to be said for analysing why British literary traditions figure so heavily in fiction Walkowitz herself could classify as 'comparison literature'. It is quite significant that the 'international' or 'postnational' author is best known for his mythic constructions of England, and that he fashions this fabular England (and, in the case of *When We Were Orphans*, early twentieth-century cosmopolitan Shanghai) by invoking peculiarly British fictive forms. (*The Remains of the Day* relies upon the same country house tradition McEwan explores in *Atonement*; *When We Were Orphans* ironically recasts British detective fiction; and *Never Let Me Go* draws upon English boarding school tales as well as famous mid-twentieth century dystopias, most notably Aldous Huxley's *Brave New World* (1932). *The Buried Giant* (2015), his most recent novel, reimagines the dark ages of Britain in a fantasy world as immersive, if not as richly realized, as J.R.R. Tolkein's or J.K. Rowling's. The strategic redeployment itself could be said, in the language of Geoff Dyer's review of *Atonement*, to 'creatively extend ... and haul ... a defining part of the British literary tradition up to and into the 21st century'.

John Su's chapter on *The Remains of the Day* in *Ethics and Nostalgia in the Contemporary Novel* is one of the few American studies of Ishiguro's fiction to seriously discuss the author in relation to an extant national tradition. Like so many critics before him, Su highlights the way in which the performative novel thematizes the enigma of Englishness, yet his discussion of the 'end' of what he terms the 'British estate novel' does not renounce tradition or eschew previous literary forms in favour of a postnational designations; rather, it offers a complex revaluation of narrative praxis in the light of new realities. When Su places Ishiguro in dialogue with Evelyn Waugh, and shows readers how Ishiguro reconceives the country house novel to account for the American age, he effectively renders a still vital British literary tradition (carried on by Ishiguro) that is responsive to innovation and change. In many ways, Su's scholarly interests aid in this flexible reconceptualization. As a theorist of nostalgia, he recognizes that not all invocations of the past are necessarily painted in artful sepia hues, and he is more than cognizant of the fact that nostalgia itself comes in more than one (politicized) form. Such understandings could aid in the analysis of other contemporary British authors who also offer contemplative takes on the past, such as Julian Barnes. The fictive pleasures the Victorian triple decker *Arthur & George* provides are no more uncritical replications of previous (narrative) praxis than Stevens' outline of professional standards is in *The Remains of the Day*. The compelling plot regarding the formation of the Court of Appeals is complemented by critical musings on the limitations of the very empiricism that undergirds realist masterpieces, just as the self-conscious nostalgia of *The Sense of an Ending* (2011) is complicated by numerous discussions of what is knowable (and what the narrator Tony Webster himself is able to know). Put in terms of Barnes' recent Man Booker Prize-winning fiction, Su's study underscores the fact that the 'ending' that characters like Stevens (and Sir Arthur Conan Doyle and Tony Webster) attempt to 'make sense of' in and through the exploration of the 'beginning' is not just the final element of the fabula but also the possible start of a new and more productive syuzhet. These nostalgic re-creations may not bring about immediate change or effect the liberation some readers may wish for, but they offer future paths for ethically informed iterations that are undeniably 'new'.

This 'future path' is particularly evident in Ishiguro's most celebrated novel of the noughties, *Never Let Me Go*. The speculative exploration of clones could have been set anywhere at virtually any time, yet Ishiguro chose to place his 'brave new world' in an alternative England of the 1990s. This England, a number of reviewers have noted, conforms a great deal to contemporary reality. The only significant difference is the oft hidden, and rarely addressed, presence of the clones themselves – a cunning occlusion that, for some readers, spoils the possibility of a truly 'new' world. If such a tale were objectively narrated in a straightforward fashion, critics would indeed have reason to question the speculative nature of this fiction. The surreal tale, though, achieves its hallucinatory effect through subtle temporal distortions that purposefully disorient the reader and undermine the 'reality' of the tale. Kathy H.'s 'college' years, ostensibly set in the early 1980s, evoke the sexual liberation of the 1960s, while her 'school days', which span the 1970s, are self-consciously rendered as a time of Edwardian splendour. (In this regard, it is not insignificant that the jacket design for the American hardcover reworks a 1913 autochrome, 'Christina', by Lieutenant-Colonel Mervyn O'Gorman. The early photograph, which uses an additive colour process, requires a much longer exposure in order to produce a subtly stylized, and dark, picture of its subject, not unlike Ishiguro's fiction.) This temporal blurring, in Michiko Kakutani's estimation, gives the novel a timeless aura that allows it to present the chilling tale as 'an oblique and elegiac meditation on mortality and lost innocence: a portrait of adolescence as that hinge moment in life when self-knowledge brings intimations of one's destiny' (n.p.). Ishiguro would surely approve of *The New York Time*'s critic's 'universal' reading, but he would also likely have to admit that this 'elegiac meditation', like his Booker prize-winning masterpiece, self-consciously relies upon British literary precedents (boarding school narratives and post-war dystopias) that have taken on mythic status internationally. Just as in *The Remains of the Day* and *When We Were Orphans*, Ishiguro renders a particularly contemporary sense of loss in *Never Let Me Go* through an experimental reappropriation of mid-twentieth-century British works that have been deemed part of a 'diminished' age.

While no critic has explored how or why Ishiguro keeps on returning to the apparent end of high modernism, and earning accolades by reworking popular fictive forms that flourished in the middle of the last century (the British country house, detective and dystopia novels), the growing body of criticism on *Never Let Me Go* demonstrates that American critics are comfortable placing Ishiguro's novel in a British speculative tradition. One of the most intriguing interpretations, Shameem Black's articulation of the novel's 'inhuman aesthetic', even illustrates how Ishiguro's future vision builds on literary and intellectual precedent from the past. Like Su's reading of *The Remains of the Day*, Black's article begins by placing

Ishiguro's novel in relation to the mid-twentieth-century British fiction it evokes (in this case, Huxley's *A Brave New World* and Orwell's *Nineteen Eighty-Four*) and draws lines of relation that trace a much longer literary lineage. While Black's references to Ishiguro's other works implicitly show how 'moveable' his themes are, her invocation of British literary and historical figures, such as (the admittedly Scottish) Adam Smith, also highlights how deeply Ishiguro's dystopia is marked by what can be considered a 'British' tradition. Given Black's obvious interest in the relationship between empathy and commodification, it makes sense that she would work her way from Smith's moral sentiment to the empathy endorsed by British Romantic writers such as William Wordsworth and Percy Shelley and from thence on to George Eliot and Ishiguro's clones, but her astute analysis could have been made even stronger had she articulated a connection other critics have noted – the novel's relation to *Frankenstein* (1818). Almost two centuries before Ishiguro published *Never Let Me Go*, Mary Shelley fashioned a potent myth for the future that also narrated an 'inhuman' creation in the recent past. Following in Shelley's fictive footsteps, Ishiguro's equally unreliable novel even recreates the aporia of the infamous 'workshop of filthy creation' by purposefully eschewing the scientific explanation of its originary event in its own posthuman narrative. Using Black's careful articulation of the (British) tradition Ishiguro relies upon, a critic could argue that the novelist's formulation of a future that is lodged securely in the past is itself an acknowledgement of the fact that previous works of British genre fiction pose relevant questions that continue to haunt us well into the twenty-first century.

Although there is no easy or singular way to redress the 'diminishing' thesis in an era of rapid globalization that is still dominated by American hegemony, the reception of Ishiguro hints at one method for subversion – a focus on productive movements back to the future in contemporary British writing. (Walkowitz, Su and Black implicitly cast Ishiguro's innovation as re-creation by highlighting how his invocations of the past speak to current concerns.) Ishiguro may be rightly canonized as a 'postnational' writer whose immigrant status fashions him a 'citizen of the world', but careful attention to his specific narrative choices can still help to show that the contemporary author, like so many of his British colleagues, is reformulating and reconceiving a British tradition for the twenty-first century. Like McEwan, Ishiguro has reformulated the country house novel for the present age, while his updated dystopia, like Neil Gaiman's *Neverwhere* (1996) and China Miéville's *Un Lun Dun* (2007), demonstrates that 'future' problems are already part of the present. In this regard, it is important to note that Ishiguro's invocations of *Nineteen Eighty-Four* and *A Brave New World* in *Never Let Me Go* do not just return the narrative to the mid-twentieth-century forms he favours: they also position his work in an evolving canon of speculative fiction that necessarily includes a number of well regarded twentieth- and twenty-first-century British fictions (Orwell's and Huxley's dystopias, J.R.R. Tolkien's *Lord of the Rings* trilogy, C.S. Lewis' *Chronicles of Narnia*, Neil Gaiman's dark dreamscapes, J.K. Rowling's *Harry Potter* series and the New Weird fictions of Steph Swainston and China Miéville). Perhaps even more intriguingly, his specific movements back to the future create interesting parallels with perhaps the most celebrated graphic novelist of the age, Alan Moore.

As a practitioner of a fictive form that has only quite recently been elevated to critical analysis (graphic narrative), Moore has never been subject to the diminishing thesis. According to many critics, the British author is second only in his field to Will Eisner, and he has been consistently lauded for his narrative innovation: he reworked the anarchic potential of the dystopia in *V for Vendetta* (1982–5), reconceived monster stories in *Saga of the Swamp Thing* (1984–7) and revolutionized the superhero tale in *Watchmen* (1986–7). What is so interesting about Moore's variegated output, though, is that his narrative innovation has increasingly been coupled with investigations of British historical and literary pasts. *From Hell* (1989–96) reoriented the crime novel in order to explore the perennial question 'Who is Jack the Ripper?', while *Lost Girls* (1991–2) melded the female bildungsroman with erotica in order to reframe the 'woman question' in twentieth-century thought. Late in 1999, Moore united his twinned interests in British literature and history in *The League of Extraordinary Gentlemen*, a series that culled a number of famous characters from widely read works of genre fiction and cunningly combined them in an alternative universe wherein they are called upon to protect the British state (which itself is overseen by the Blazing World). Just as he had done with the Swamp Thing, Moore freed his preexisting characters from extant narrative arcs (such as Mina Harker's marriage to Jonathan Harker in *Dracula*) by removing them from the moral logic of their tales, hence placing them in new circumstances where previous pieties or seeming absolutes no longer hold sway. Set in a steampunk world where western 'peace keeping' missions are shown to be naked acts of aggression and medical advances lead more immediately to biological warfare than healing, Moore's admittedly flawed nineteenth-century heroes have to grapple with difficult questions that were never posed in their host texts. Quite significantly, Moore 'ends' Volume III with a literal staging of the culture wars that demonstrates the resiliency of British narrative traditions. Orlando (an ancient vestige from a previous League) and Mina are almost undone by the media-saturated horrors of the late twentieth century, yet they are ultimately saved by a deity whose command of imaginative works allows her to demonstrate how insubstantial the seemingly monstrous Antichrist is. The death of the Apocalyptic Moonchild in *Century 2009* is thus not an end but a new beginning, wherein the seemingly interminable life of a literary figure like Mina Harker (who wears her immortality more heavily than Orlando) can be revitalized by the vicissitudes of (alternative) history.

Much like F.R. Leavis' 'Great Tradition', Moore's comic series manages to construct an English-oriented canon that is not exclusively English (as Captain Nemo fights alongside his British colleagues and Brecht's *Three Penny Opera* serves as an important subtext in Volume III) while it displays a decided distaste for contemporary popular culture. Without one jot of irony, Moore indicts the degradation of late-twentieth-century literary and artistic culture while he recrafts Margaret Cavendish's seventeenth-century utopia and appropriates some of Shakespeare's most memorable characters in his rendering of an alternative Blazing World. His unstable Antichrist may be able to kill Allan Quatermain, but the admittedly powerful figure is unable to effect a new future because he does not have a past that he can productively draw upon. Provided only with an imagistic understanding of what things should look like, not a firm understanding of possible realities, the paper tiger is ultimately incapable of bringing the end times because he himself has been unmoored from history and redeployed without purpose or vision. When Orlando and Mina visit the magical school that the Antichrist destroyed, they not only discover that the 'Moonchild might actually be a child', but also that the 'whole environment seems artificial, as if it's been constructed out of reassuring imagery from the 1940s. . . . A storybook place gone horribly *wrong*' (Moore and O'Neill; emphasis in original). Dreamtime, in Moore's speculative universe, can only produce lasting effects if it is anchored in history. Nostalgia alone makes things go 'horribly *wrong*'. In contrast, the recontextualized Mina and Orlando are granted a chance to live and potentially thrive again. Reaching back to the future in a speculative work of fiction that plays with alternate realities, Moore graphically demonstrates that there is no productive move forward in literature that is not also attended by a critical (and ethical) look back. Like Ishiguro (and, one could argue, Barnes, Smith and McEwan), Moore displays the narrative regeneration that can be achieved by never letting go of the British literary traditions that can help to define present and future realities.

While it is more than possible, and perhaps even desirable, that global trends in Anglophone literary study in the twenty-first century will eventually render literature from Britain as but one category among others, currently global movements in the American academy have only tended to diminish the classification of British literature without displacing the primacy of an American literature that was newly reborn with a modern renaissance in the latter half of the twentieth century. This has led to the implicit understanding that celebrated writers from contemporary Britain are necessarily removed from a literary tradition that has not kept pace with the times. Until more American critics begin to recognize that British literary traditions have survived into the twenty-first century, and can help to define present and future realities, it will remain increasingly difficult to assess the reception of contemporary British fiction in America because that fiction will be selected and atomized as the work of singular postmodern stars or exemplary 'writers from elsewhere'.

Works cited

Alter, Robert. 'Howards End'. Rev. of *On Beauty* by Zadie Smith. *The New Republic* 3 October 2005: 29–32.

Barnes, Julian. *Arthur & George*. New York: Vintage International, 2005.

Barnes, Julian. *The Sense of an Ending*. New York: Vintage International, 2012.

Berhman, Mary. 'The Waiting Game: Medieval Allusions and the Lethal Nature of Passivity in Ian McEwan's *Atonement*'. *Studies in the Novel* 42(4) (2010): 453–70.

Bernard, André. 'The Casual Reader'. *Kenyon Review* 29(2) (2007): 2–3. Available online: http://www.kenyonreview.org/journal/spring-2007/selections/the-casual-reader/ (accessed 2 July, 2013).

Bérubé, Michael. 'Teaching Postmodern Fiction Without Being Sure That the Genre Exists'. *The Chronicle of Higher Education* 46(37) (2000): B4.

Black, Shameem. 'Ishiguro's Inhuman Aesthetics'. *Modern Fiction Studies* 55(4) (2009): 785–807.

Bradford, Richard. *The Novel Now: Contemporary British Fiction*. Malden, MA: Blackwell, 2007.

Byatt, A.S. *Possession*. New York: Vintage, 1991[1990].

Byatt, A.S. *Angels and Insects*. New York: Vintage, 1994.

Byatt, A.S. *The Biographer's Tale*. New York: Knopf, 2001.

Byatt, A.S. *The Children's Book*. New York: Vintage, 2010.

Clarke, Susanna. *Jonathan Strange & Mr Norrell*. New York: Bloomsbury, 2004.

D'Angelo, Kathleen. ' "To Make a Novel": The Construction of Critical Readership in Ian McEwan's *Atonement*'. *Studies in the Novel* 41(1) (2009): 88–105.

Deresiewicz, William. 'On Everything'. Rev. of *On Beauty* by Zadie Smith. *The Nation*. 3 October 2005: 25–8.

Dyer, Geoff. 'Who's afraid of influence?' Rev. of *Atonement* by Ian McEwan. *Guardian*. 22 September 2001. Available online: http://www.theguardian.com/books/2001/sep/22/fiction.ianmcewan (accessed 10 March, 2009).

Elias, Amy J. '*Meta-mimesis*? The Problem of British Postmodern Realism'. *British Postmodern Fiction*. Eds. Theo D'haen and Hans Bertens. Atlanta, GA: Rodopi, 1993, 9–31.

English, James F. Ed. *A Concise Companion to Contemporary British Fiction*. Malden, MA: Blackwell, 2005.

Finney, Brian. 'Briony's Stand Against Oblivion: The Making of Fiction in Ian McEwan's *Atonement*'. *Journal of Modern Literature* 27(3) (2004): 68–82.

Finney, Brian. *English Fiction Since 1984: Narrating a Nation*. New York: Palgrave MacMillan, 2005.

Finney, Brian. *Martin Amis*. New York: Routledge, 2008.

Franklin, Ruth. 'Reader: Keep Up!' Rev. of *NW* by Zadie Smith. *New Republic*. 4 October 2012: 52–6.

Gaiman, Neil. *Neverwhere*. 1996. New York: Harper Collins, 2003.

Gray, J.A. 'Beauty is as Beauty Does'. Rev. of *On Beauty* by Zadie Smith. *First Things*. November 2006: 48–53.

Grossman, Lev. 'Top 10 Novels of the 2000s'. *Time*. 18 December, 2009. Available online: http://www.entertainment.time.com/2009/12/29/the-10-best-books-of-the-decade/ (accessed 1 July, 2012).

Haddon, Mark. *The Curious Incident of the Dog in Night-Time*. New York: Vintage, 2004.

Hayes, M. Hunter. *Understanding Will Self*. Columbia, SC: University of South Carolina Press, 2007.

Holman, C. Hugh and William Harmon. 'Diminishing Age in English Literature, 1940–1965'. *A Handbook to Literature*. 6th edn. New York: Macmillan, 1992, 141–2.

Huxley, Aldous. *A Brave New World*. 1932. New York: Perennial Classics, 1998.

Ingersoll, Earl G. 'Intertextuality in L.P. Hartley's *The Go-Between* and Ian McEwan's *Atonement*'. *Forum for Modern Language Studies* 40(3) (2004): 241–58.

Ishiguro, Kazuo. *The Remains of the Day*. New York: Vintage International, 1993.

Ishiguro, Kazuo. *When We Were Orphans*. New York: Knopf, 2000.

Ishiguro, Kazuo. *Never Let Me Go*. New York: Knopf, 2005.

Ishiguro, Kazuo. *Nocturnes*. New York: Knopf, 2009.

Ishiguro, Kazuo. *The Buried Giant*. New York: Random House, 2015.

Jay, Paul. *Global Matters: The Transnational Turn in Literary Studies*. Ithaca, NY: Cornell University Press, 2010.

Kakutani, Michiko. 'Sealed in a World that is Not as It Seems'. Rev. of Ishiguro's *Never Let Me Go*. *The New York Times*. 4 April 2005. Available online: http://www.nytimes.com/2005/04/04/books/04kaku.html?_r=0 (accessed 19 May, 2015).

Keen, Susan. *Romances of the Archive in Contemporary British Fiction*. Buffalo: University of Toronto Press, 2001.

Kermode, Frank. 'Here She Is'. Rev. of *On Beauty* by Zadie Smith. *London Review of Books* 27(19) (2005): 13–14.

MacCabe, Colin. 'Zadie Smith and Salman Rushdie: Writing for a New World'. Rev. of *On Beauty* by Zadie Smith and *Shalimar the Clown* by Salman Rushdie.

openDemocracy, 10 October 2005. Available online: http://www.opendemocracy.net/arts-Literature/rushdie_2907.jsp (accessed 3 March, 2008).

Maltz, Diana. 'The Newer New Life: A.S. Byatt, E. Nesbit and Socialist Subculture'. *The Journal of Victorian Studies* 17(1) (2012): 79–84.

Mantel, Hilary. *Wolf Hall*. New York: Henry Holt, 2009.

Marcus, Laura. 'Ian McEwan's Modernist Time: *Atonement* and *Saturday*'. *Ian McEwan: Contemporary Critical Perspectives*. Ed. Sebastian Groes. New York: Continuum, 2009, 83–98.

Mason, Wyatt. 'White Knees: Zadie Smith's Novel Problems'. Rev. of *On Beauty* by Zadie Smith. *Harper's Magazine*. October 2005: 83–8.

McEwan, Ian. *Atonement*. New York: Anchor, 2001.

Merritt, Stephanie. 'A Thing of Beauty: Zadie Smith's Homage to E.M. Forster, On Beauty, Confirms Her as a Writer of Remarkable Wit and Originality'. Rev. of *On Beauty* by Zadie Smith. *The Observer*, 4 September 2005. Available online: http://www.theguardian.com/books/2005/sep/04/fiction.zadiesmith (accessed 19 May, 2015).

Miéville, China. *Un Lun Dun*. 2007. New York: Del Rey, 2008.

Moore, Alan and Eddie Campbell. *From Hell*. Marietta, GA: Top Shelf Productions, 1999.

Moore, Alan and Melinda Gebbie. *Lost Girls*. Marietta, GA: Top Shelf Productions, 2009.

Moore, Alan and Dave Gibbons. *The Watchmen*. New York: DC Comics, 1995.

Moore, Alan and David Lloyd. *V for Vendetta*. New York: Vertigo, 2008.

Moore, Alan and Kevin O'Neill. *The League of Extraordinary Gentlemen: Volume I*. La Jolla, CA: America's Best Comic, 2000.

Moore, Alan and Kevin O'Neill. *The League of Extraordinary Gentlemen: Volume II*. La Jolla, CA: America's Best Comic, 2004.

Moore, Alan and Kevin O'Neill. *The League of Extraordinary Gentlemen: Volume III: Century: 1910*. Marietta, GA: Top Shelf Productions, 2009.

Moore, Alan and Kevin O'Neill. *The League of Extraordinary Gentlemen: Volume III: Century: 1969*. Marietta, GA: Top Shelf Productions, 2011.

Moore, Alan and Kevin O'Neill. *The League of Extraordinary Gentlemen: Volume III: Century: 2009*. Marietta, GA: Top Shelf Productions, 2012.

Moore, Alan, Stephen Bissette and John Totleben. *Saga of the Swamp Thing: Book One*. New York: DC Comics, 2012.

Nairn, Tom. *The Break-Up of Britain: Crisis and Neonationalism*, London: New Left Books, 1977.

Passaro, Vince. 'Riveting, My Dear Watson'. Rev. of Julian Barnes' *Arthur & George*. O, The Oprah Magazine. Jan. 2006, 7(1), 88. Available online: http://www.oprah.com/omagazine/Arthur-and-George-by-Julian-Barnes–Book-Review (accessed 2 May, 2012).

Phelan, James. 'Narrative Judgments and the Rhetorical Theory of Narrative: Ian McEwan's *Atonement*'. Eds James Phelan and Peter J. Rabinowitz. *A Companion to Narrative Theory*. Malden, MA: Blackwell, 2005, 322–36.

Robinson, Richard. 'The Modernism of Ian McEwan's *Atonement*'. *Modern Fiction Studies* 56(3) (2010): 473–95.

Russo, Richard. *Empire Falls*. 2001. New York: Vintage, 2002.

Schuessler, Jennifer. 'Dangerous Fictions'. Rev. of *The Children's Book* by A.S. Byatt. *The New York Times*. Sunday Review of Books. 8 October 2009.

Schwartz, Alexandra. 'I'm Nobody, Who Are You? On Zadie Smith's "NW"' Rev. of *NW* by Zadie Smith. *Nation*. 12 October 2012: 36–45. Available online: http://www.thenation.com/article/171387/im-nobody-who-are-you-zadie-smith-nw# (accessed 5 July, 2013).

Shaffer, Brian. Ed. *A Companion to the British and Irish Novel 1945–2000*. Malden, MA: Blackwell, 2005.

Shaffer, Brian and Cynthia Wong. Eds. *Conversations with Kazuo Ishiguro*. Jackson, MS: University Press of Mississippi, 2008.

Shelley, Mary. *Frankenstein*. Norton Critical Edition. Ed. J. Paul Hunter. 2nd edn. New York: Norton, 2012.

Shone, Tom. 'White Lies'. Rev. of *Atonement* by Ian McEwan. *The New York Times*. 10 March 2002. Available online: http://www.nytimes.com/2002/03/10/books/white-lies.html (accessed 2 July, 2013).

Showalter, Elaine. 'A Virtuoso Victorian Novel'. Rev. of *The Children's Book* by A.S Byatt. *The Lancet*, 374 (9702), 1667–8. 14 November 2009. Available online: http://www.download.thelancet.com/journals/lancet/article/PIIS0140-6736(09)61977-2/fulltext (accessed 15 July, 2015).

Shultz, Kathryn. 'Hysterical Formalism'. Rev. of *On Beauty* by Zadie Smith. *New York* 42(28) (2012): 76–7.

Sinfield, Alan. *Literature, Culture and Politics in Postwar Britain*. London: Athlone Press, 1997.

Smith, Zadie. *White Teeth*. New York: Vintage, 2001.

Smith, Zadie. *The Autograph Man*. 2002. New York: Vintage International, 2003.

Smith, Zadie. *On Beauty*. New York: Penguin, 2005.

Smith, Zadie. *NW*. New York: Penguin, 2012.

Strauss, Darin. 'Reasons to Re-Joyce'. Rev. of *NW* by Zadie Smith, *Billy Lynn's Long Halftime Walk* by Ben Fountain, and *Telegraph Avenue* by Michael Chabon. *The New York Times*. 7 December 2012. Available online: http://www.nytimes.com/2012/12/09/books/review/reasons-to-re-joyce.html (accessed 19 May, 2015).

Su, John. *Ethics and Nostalgia in the Contemporary Novel*. New York: Cambridge University Press, 2005.

Sutherland. J.A. *Fiction and the Fiction Industry*. London: Athlone Press, 1978.

Sutherland. J.A. 'A Touch of Forster'. Rev. of *On Beauty* by Zadie Smith. *New Statesman*. 12 September 2005: 50–1.

Swift, Graham. *The Light of Day*. New York: Vintage International, 2004.

Walker, Alice. *The Color Purple*. 1982. New York: Houghton Mifflin, 1992.

Walkowitz, Rebecca L. *Cosmopolitan Style: Modernism Beyond the Nation*. New York: Columbia UP, 2006.

Walkowitz, Rebecca L. 'The Location of Literature: The Transnational Book and the Migrant Writer'. *Contemporary Literature* 47(4) (2006): 527–45.

Wall, Kathleen. 'Ethics, Knowledge, and the Need for Beauty: Zadie Smith's *On Beauty* and Ian McEwan's *Saturday*'. *University of Toronto Quarterly* 77(2) (2008): 757–88.

Wallace, David Foster. 'E Unibus Pluram: Television and U.S. Fiction'. *Review of Contemporary Fiction* 13(2) (1993): 151–94.

Wallace, David Foster. *Infinite Jest*. New York: Little, Brown, 1996.

Waters, Sarah. *Tipping the Velvet*. New York: Riverhead, 1999.

Waters, Sarah. *Affinity*. New York: Riverhead, 2000.

Waters, Sarah. *Fingersmith*. New York: Riverhead, 2002.

Waters, Sarah. *The Night Watch*. New York: Riverhead, 2006.

Waters, Sarah. *The Little Stranger*. New York: Riverhead, 2009.

Watman, Max. 'The Ever-Present Human Hint of Yellow'. *New Criterion* 24(6) (2006): 58–65.

Wells, Juliette. 'Shades of Austen in Ian McEwan's *Atonement*'. *Persuasions: The Jane Austen Journal* 30 (2008): 101–12. Available online: http://www.jasna.org/persuasions/printed/number30/wells.pdf (accessed 15 July, 2015).

8

International Contexts 2

From Multicultural Enthusiasm to the 'Failure of Multiculturalism': British Multi-ethnic Fiction in an International Frame

Ulrike Tancke

The end of the first decade of the new millennium saw some remarkably similar statements by leading European politicians about the state of the multicultural reality in their countries. On 16 October 2010, at a rally of the youth organization of her party, German Chancellor Angela Merkel claimed, with uncharacteristic vehemence, that multiculturalism 'has failed, utterly failed' ('Merkel: "Multikulti ist absolut gescheitert"' n.p.).[1] With remarkably similar wording, British Prime Minister David Cameron pronounced a scathing indictment of multiculturalism in a speech at the Munich Security Conference on 5 February 2011: 'Under the doctrine of state multiculturalism, we have encouraged different cultures to live separate lives, apart from each other and apart from the mainstream. We've failed to provide a vision of society to which they feel they want to belong. We've even tolerated these segregated communities behaving in ways that run completely counter to our values' (n.p.).

These pronouncements are symptomatic of an increasing disaffection with multiculturalism as a political imperative in Britain and across Europe that has become discernible in the past ten years or so. This is, of course, at odds with the demographic fact of multicultural diversity. As Katya Vasileva has shown, in 2011, all major European countries (the UK, France, Germany, the Netherlands, Spain) boasted a population of which around 11 per cent could be classified as 'foreign born'. To these 'foreign born' citizens can be added those sections of the population whose families migrated to Europe a few generations back. According to the census of 2011, about 13 per cent of the UK population is composed of 'non-white' ethnicities, with similar figures for the whole of Western Europe. In spite of this evidence of multiculturalism, looking at the political climate, at public opinion and at, in some cases, violent acts in Britain and beyond, in various European countries, it is obvious that the 2000s have been marked by an increasing emphasis on difference, incommensurability and potential danger in the popular perception and political discourse about multicultural coexistence. For instance, in the early 2000s German politicians debated the need for a German *Leitkultur* ('leading' or 'dominant' culture) that immigrants should be obliged to adopt (see Manz 481–9; Pautz). Several European countries, such as France and Belgium, banned the Islamic headscarf from public institutions such as schools and, along with Spain, they have now introduced outright prohibition of the full veil in all public places. The Netherlands witnessed increasing politicized violence, for instance with the assassination of right-wing populist politician Pim Fortuyn in 2002, who had openly proposed a 'cold war on Islam' (see Buruma), and of controversial filmmaker Theo van Gogh in 2004 for comments critical of Islam. In the summer of 2001, Britain saw the most violent race riots in decades when young South Asians in Oldham, Bradford and other northern cities took to the streets in a climate of increasingly perceived racial segregation and growing Islamophobia, which was only exacerbated by the 9/11 attacks, the subsequent discovery of 'home-grown' terror cells and the like.

These rather disconcerting scenarios mark the violent end of a diverse spectrum of responses to the multicultural realities of Western European countries. In particular, these actions contrast sharply with the optimistic celebration of multiculturalism that was a political imperative especially in Britain in the early years of Tony Blair's first New Labour government. The so-called 'Chicken Tikka Masala Speech', given to the Social Market Foundation in London in April 2001 by Robin Cook, the Foreign Secretary, is exemplary of the then-common celebratory stance, which stands in harsh contrast to the violent conflicts that erupted only a few months later. Cook's speech ended with the following 'passage: 'We should celebrate the enormous contribution of the many communities in Britain to strengthening our economy, to supporting our public services, and to enriching our culture and cuisine. And we should recognise that its diversity is part of the reason why Britain is a great place to live' (n.p.).

Cook's speech captured the enthusiastic approach of the Labour government of the late 1990s and early 2000s to Britain's ethnic and cultural diversity. In a similar vein, the government-contracted 'Parekh Report' issued by the Commission on the Future of Multi-Ethnic Britain' in 2000, *The Future of Multi-Ethnic Britain*, promoted the Blairite commitment to creating 'a society in which all citizens and communities feel valued, enjoy equal opportunities to develop their respective talents, lead fulfilling lives, accept their fair share of collective responsibility and help create a communal life in which the spirit of civic friendship, shared identity and common sense of belonging goes hand in hand with love of diversity' (x).

This is clearly a far cry from the current political climate as outlined at the start of this chapter. Of course, these obvious differences in rhetoric are also related to shifts in political and governmental power – after all, the celebration of multiculturalism as a social ideal is closely tied up with the New Labour philosophy, while the critical statements quoted at the beginning of this chapter hail from conservative quarters. Beyond these obvious political inclinations, however, I would argue that government policies and political rhetoric have undergone a shift during the last fifteen years or so, in relation to which the literary works I am analysing function as a kind of avant-garde. In order to understand the recent sea change in political attitudes and to grasp its implications, it is necessary to consider the political history of the concept of multiculturalism and to examine the ideological assumptions attendant to it. While in its oft-encountered, everyday usage, the term simply denotes the coexistence, peaceful or otherwise, of different ethnic communities, it has in fact been charged with an array of associative components that situate it in a particular ideological context. As Rajeev Balasubramanyam argues, '[t]he word multiculturalism describes a form of propaganda used to define the corporate identity of Great Britain.... [It] is disseminated by both [private corporations and the state] via the advertising and entertainment industries, the news-media, and the mass-produced, or at least mass-advertised, works of art' (33). As Balasubramanyam's terminology implies, to invoke multiculturalism is to communicate a particular national self-image. There exists 'an entire propaganda industry' (33) to promote the idea that '[m]ulticulturalism is fashionable.... To re-brand Britain as Multicultural Britain, is to re-brand it as modern, fun, sexy, and Cool, as in [the Blair government's slogan] "Cool Britannia"' (34). As Balasubramanyam's wording suggests, the ideas behind this multiculturalist ideology are far removed from the reality of multi-ethnic coexistence in contemporary Britain. Moreover, the 'chicken tikka multiculturalism', as Amir Ali calls it, propagated by the Blair government, fell short of adequately accounting for the social realities because of its exclusive attention to the visible and superficial aspects of multicultural coexistence at the expense of denying the material inequalities that blight British society:

> [W]here British multiculturalism has miserably failed has been its inability to address the economic marginalisation of black and Asian ethnic minorities....

> [T]his 'chicken tikka' variety of multiculturalism ... is content to showcase Britain as a happy blend of so many diverse cultures and ethnic backgrounds. Significantly it stresses only the more cosmopolitan and sophisticated aspects of British life that are highly visible, like cuisine. (2821)

This ties in with Anne-Marie Fortier's observation that 'multiculturalism is not so much a policy and governing *response* to the "realities" of cultural and ethno-racial pluralism, as it is an *ideal* aimed at the achievement of well-managed diversity' (3; emphasis in original). As Fortier further argues, while multiculturalism post-2000 is a coercive strategy of political think-tanks aimed at covering over a much more complex social reality and oppressive hierarchies, the concept itself may no longer be an apt strategy to approach the status quo: 'Today, the discourse about multiculturalism is in turmoil in several Western countries and it appears that its days as a state-sponsored strategy are numbered' (1). According to Fortier, this 'anti-multiculturalist backlash' (4) has resulted in:

> a vision of a post-multicultural British future that retrieves and aggrandizes past glories of Empire and of the Great British Union [and] replace[s] ... multiculturalism with a fiercer and more adamant assertion of the Nation Thing and of the possibility of full national representation, which clears a space for more, rather than less, inequality, resentment, and hostility against those whose 'cultural identity' and 'cultural ways' are marked as hindering national unity and disturbing national comfort. (105)

In a related vein, Hartwig Pautz situates the German *Leitkultur* debate in the context of what he calls 'neo-racist' tendencies (10) aimed at propagating the conflictual nature of multicultural living-together.

The key question for my purposes is whether a similar shift in attitudes about multiculturalism can be discerned in literary production and, if this is the case, how literature and literary criticism position themselves vis-à-vis this shift. Moreover, I will investigate also to what extent British literature can be regarded as making significant contributions of these debates in an international, European context. As will become clear from my readings of a number of post-millennial works of fiction, fictional representations of multicultural scenarios confront us with a strikingly similar unease about the multicultural ideal. They do not, however, express a fear of a return to nationalist particularism and discrimination, but position their critique of multiculturalism within a new, universalist agenda that takes the constants of human nature as its point of reference and as the most crucial reality to be inevitably reckoned with.

Obviously, I am aware of the fraught nature of the term 'universalism', especially in the postcolonial context, since it has all too often been used as a smokescreen for Western bias. However, I use the term in opposition to the belief that all human behaviours are dependent on social, cultural or political factors and posit the notion of an evolutionary human nature as an underlying level determining human actions and attitudes (see Pinker).

As regards literary engagements with multiculturalism, I will argue that literary criticism, surprisingly, has been slow to pick up on the increasing awareness of the shortcomings of the multicultural ideal as expressed in the literature. Informed by the parameters of postcolonial theory and identity politics, critics have, with almost ritualistic predictability, emphasized the ways in which the victim status of postcolonial subjects can be turned to an advantage in view of the alleged emancipatory potentials of multi-faceted identities and ethnic diversity (and this is a trajectory that can be observed in literary criticism from all European contexts; see Cheesman, Kongslien, Adelson). For instance, recent publications on the current state of postcolonial criticism, such as that of Wilson, Şandru and Lawson Welsh, argue that postcolonial identities are of a 'rhizomatic' quality and move in an 'imaginative space ... which gives them a choice of subjective identification and political gesture' (10). Their 'polycentric' identities (10), so the argument goes, mean that they can explore 'multiple routes of action and subjectivity' (10). This emphasis on potentiality, fluidity and openness dovetails with the recent critical parameters of cosmopolitanism and transnationalism which have been introduced into postcolonial studies in order to take account of the changing geopolitical landscapes in the wake of the diverse economic, political and cultural changes commonly captured as 'globalisation'. In spite of critics' avowed awareness of the political and economic power imbalances at the heart of the globalized world, as in Wilson et al. (4–5) and in the work of Robert Spencer (38–9), these paradigms are attended by a curiously optimistic vision of globalized living-together and the transformative function of literature within it. As Wilson et al. argue, '[t]he "literary transnation" ... is not only unbound by nationalism, but has the capacity to embody potentiality: its transformative impetus is linked to the utopian function of literature which embodies imagination's power to envisage a better world' (5). In a similar vein, Berthold Schoene argues that there is a 'world-creative consciousness beginning to stir within the imaginative realm' of contemporary fiction which is indicative of 'the novel's power not only to react to the world, but to recast it' (186).

The recent approaches of the cosmopolitan and transnational bent mark a certain shift of focus vis-à-vis the postcolonial, yet they still propose an overwhelmingly positive response to cultural hybridity and heterogeneity. While in some cases this reading may at first glance be warranted by contemporary literary texts that represent cultural diversity, migration and the like, in the great majority of cases the textual evidence is much more complex than this critical categorization appears to suggest. The notion that literature envisages a 'better world' characterized by mutuality and a positive vision of difference jars with the literary representation of the global multicultural reality, which is often at odds with this affirmative perception. My readings of three British novels suggest that the texts develop an alternative approach to the political agenda of multiculturalism, which reveals its central flaw to be an all too optimistic appreciation of human potentials and inclinations. My argument is based on an understanding of the evolutionary nature of the human according to which violence is an integral part of the human condition. As Müller-Wood and Carter Wood have argued, 'the potential for physical aggression is a normal part of our species-typical psychology rather than a psychological aberration' (n.p.). This is not to say, of course, that human living-together is always and in all cases marred by violence, conflict and the like, but these negative capacities are a potential to be reckoned with, and their existence stands in direct contrast to the assumption that there may be a progressive development towards greater understanding, tolerance and mutuality, which is at the core of multicultural rhetoric.

Probably the most obvious case in point that demonstrates the critical short circuit by which texts are read as evidence of an affirmative multicultural vision is Zadie Smith's *White Teeth*, published in 2000, that is, at the very start of the period in question. On publication, the novel garnered rave reviews, and Stephanie Merrit in *The Observer* hailed the author – then only 24 years old – as 'the first publishing sensation of the millennium' (n.p.). This enthusiasm was, to some extent, due to Smith's age, ethnicity and background. If Zadie Smith herself quickly developed into a publishing phenomenon, her novel seemed to tie in with the prevailing, cheerfully positive vision of multicultural Britain in the early Blair years. For Merrit the novel boasts '[an] imaginative element ... [that] extends to the way in which race relations are portrayed in the book. Smith offers a very optimistic vision: prejudice exists, but tolerance appears in equal measure, and racist violence is only mentioned briefly and at second hand' (n.p.). In a similar vein, Black British writer Caryl Phillips reviewed *White Teeth* for *The Observer* and stated that the book 'recognises and celebrates' the 'helpless heterogeneity' of multicultural Britain. Greeted with such an enthusiastic reception, *White Teeth* almost instantly became canonical, as an epochal novel celebrating the heterogeneity of British urban society around the millennium, and this positive response was widely mirrored by commentators beyond Britain such as Daniel Kehlmann and Gunnar Luetzow. It even seems to be representative of a literary format that has been drawn upon by writers outside the UK. To give just one example, Turkish-German writer Yadé Kara's 2004 novel *Selam Berlin* focuses on the tragic-comic fates of a set of Turkish and German characters. Set at the same historical moment as *White Teeth*, around the fall of the Berlin Wall, the novel depicts the German capital as a multicultural space peopled by quirky bohemian characters who lack direction, but are thoroughly endearing at that. Tellingly, the sequel to the novel, *Café Cyprus* (2010), sees the protagonist make a fresh start in a different locale – 1990s' London.

At first glance, novels such as *White Teeth* and its international equivalents do indeed seem to tie in with the 'feel-good politics' of Blairite multiculturalism. To return to *White Teeth*, the novel is replete with irony, quirky characters and caricatured yet recognizable titbits of multicultural interaction. And yet, on a closer look, its memorably comical side glosses over a deeply disturbing underbelly: fundamentally, *White Teeth* explores the dark sides of migration, the violence of history, the painful and poignantly irresolvable search for roots that determines individual lives and the hurt they inevitably inflict on each other. I would even go so far as to argue that the initial critical response to the novel constitutes a fundamental misreading that is informed largely by the critics' own agenda and is not supported by the text itself.

The novel chronicles the lives of a set of London families of Caribbean, Bengali, English and Jewish-British origins, with the main strand of the action being set in the 1980s. It centres on the friendship between Archie Jones, a white British man whose second marriage is to Clara, a Black Caribbean woman, and Samad Iqbal, originally from Bangladesh, who met as soldiers during the Second World War. Undeniably, the novel's complex relationships and tightly interwoven connections between a set of London families of various ethnic and geographical origins takes cultural heterogeneity to its extreme. Superficially, the novel seems to be about a trouble-free intermingling of races and cultures that often creates rather funny but ultimately unproblematic situations. However, it consistently pokes fun at the ideology of multiculturalism that invites such a reading. One example of the flippantly mocking style in which the novel approaches multiculturalist discourse is the following passage in which a teacher at the primary school attended by Irie Jones and Magid and Millat Iqbal justifies the school's multicultural practices:

> [T]he school already recognizes a great variety of religious and secular events: amongst them, Christmas, Ramadan, Chinese New Year, Diwali, Yom Kippur, Hanukkah, the birthday of Haile Selassie, and the death of Martin Luther King. The Harvest Festival is part of the school's ongoing commitment to religious diversity. (129)

The familiar liberal platitudes implicit in this list are stereotyped variants of the politically correct discourse on multiculturalism that pervaded public and political debates on immigration in the late 1990s. It is implemented in the classroom, too, as what might be called normal children's behaviour is subjected to rigorous judgement. For instance, during a rehearsal of the school orchestra, the children amuse themselves by imitating Indian music, or what they think it sounds like. The teacher quickly reprimands them:

> 'I don't think it is very nice to make fun of *somebody else's culture*.'
> The orchestra, unaware that this is what they had been doing, but aware that this was the most heinous crime in the Manor School book, looked at their collective feet....
> 'Sometimes we find other people's music strange because their culture is different from *ours*,' said Miss Burt-Jones solemnly. 'But that doesn't mean it isn't equally good, now does it?'
> 'NO, MISS.'
> 'And we can learn about each other through each other's culture, can't we?'
> 'YES, MISS.' (155–6; emphasis in original)

Expected to blindly regurgitate platitudinous banalities about interactions between cultures and its effects, the children are brainwashed into subscribing to a watered-down, formulaic and thus ultimately irrelevant form of multiculturalist belief. After all, the teacher's plea not to devalue 'somebody else's culture' implies a clear dichotomy of 'them' and 'us', thus masking a continued monoculturalism. Obviously, the scene is rendered in a comically exaggerated and thus highly ironic fashion (and in fact, the reality of the school's everyday functioning reveals that this is mere lip-service to an unlikely ideal). With this ridicule – which, in fact, pervades the novel's portrayal of race relations and multicultural coexistence – the text distracts from the very disturbing dimensions of this social reality.

What is most striking about *White Teeth*, however, and what this surface impression occludes, is the characters' almost obsessive preoccupation with the search for roots that is the result of the experience of migration. Of course, searching for one's roots is not a problem in itself – far from it; it may be very positive, interesting and even necessary. It is the fact that their roots lie 'elsewhere' that creates problems and tensions for the characters. Hence I take issue with those readings of the novel that regard it as an innovatively carefree and affirmative take on the multicultural situation. The novel's ubiquitously ironic and comical tone appears to be at odds with its poignant commentary on the multicultural reality. While the reader is inevitably taken in by the text's surface humour, underneath this comedic layer *White Teeth* presents uncomfortable truths not just about British multicultural society, but also about the human condition at large. For what the characters' experiences reveal, above all, is that the struggle to uncover one's roots entails pain and frustration.

This is most poignantly apparent in the passage where Irie, the fifteen-year-old daughter of Black Caribbean Clara Bowden and white British Archie Jones, is examining herself in the mirror, only to find that her voluptuous figure does not conform to Western ideals of beauty: 'The European proportions of Clara's figure had skipped a generation, and she [Irie] was landed instead with Hortense's [her grandmother's] substantial Jamaican frame, loaded with pineapples, mangoes and guavas; ... ledges genetically designed with another country in mind, another climate' (265–6).

It is interesting that the narrator's comment focuses on the fact that these features are inherited; that is, they cannot be changed at will. Obviously, this observation belies the cherished postmodern assumption that identity is unstable and shifting and can be shaped according to our own desires. As Irie painfully realizes, a significant part of who she is – her body – is something she was born with. Her attempts to change her appearance – having her hair straightened and trying out various diets – fail miserably and only highlight the futility of her endeavour. By extension, Irie's Caribbean roots, which her shape points to, are equally irremovable, beyond the scope of individual self-fashioning. As a result, Irie feels disconnected from her English home country. It is almost as if her difference has prevented her individuation and thwarted her sense of self: 'There was England, a gigantic mirror, and there was Irie, without reflection. A stranger in a stranger land' (266).

Irie's profound alienation from the culture in which she has grown up is heightened when she is confronted at school with William Shakespeare, the quintessentially English writer. For a moment, Shakespeare's 'Sonnet 130' ('My mistress' eyes are nothing like the sun') seems to provide a parallel – a mirror – for Irie, the mistress' imperfection reflecting her disenchantment with the unattainable ideal of the 'English Rose'. Yet when Irie dares to voice in class her observation that the 'dark lady' might have been a black woman, her teacher is quick to correct her ('[She is] not black in the modern sense' (271)). The latter's authoritative reading of Shakespeare establishes a monolithic view of Englishness and silences Irie's struggle to find a space for herself: Irie 'had thought, just then, that she had seen something like a reflection, but it was receding' (272). Again, her mirror provides a perversion of identity formation.

Like Irie, the other characters, too, have suffered the 'original trauma' (161), as the novel calls it, of not belonging, of being torn between conflicting origins and their respective demands and impulses. An oft-quoted passage from the novel explains this condition:

> This has been the century of strangers, brown, yellow and white. This has been the century of the great immigrant experiment. It is only this late in the day that you can walk into a playground and find Isaac Leung by the fish pond, Danny Rahman in the football cage, Quang O'Rourke bouncing a basketball, and Irie Jones humming a tune. Children with first and last names on a direct collision course. Names that secrete within them mass exodus, cramped boats and planes, cold arrivals, medical checks. (326)

The passage juxtaposes two fundamentally distinct worlds: The seemingly carefree atmosphere of a London school playground, and the harshness that makes up the typical immigrant fate. The reader is all too easily deluded by the initial sense of playfulness and made to believe that this is all somehow 'fun', the result of a large-scale 'experiment'. It is this turn of phrase that sets the tone for the remainder of the passage, somewhat mellowing the harsh reality evoked in the following sentences. What is more, the narrative voice goes on to state an even more brutal truth: 'Yet despite all the mixing up, despite the fact that we have finally slipped into each other's lives with reasonable comfort ... [t]here are still young white men who are *angry* about that; who will roll out at closing time into the poorly lit streets with a kitchen knife wrapped in a tight fist' (327; emphasis in original).

This explicit allusion to racist violence suggests that to read *White Teeth* as a novel about multiculturalism as simply a fact of life falls short of honestly accounting for its dark underbelly: underneath its comic veneer, it is primarily a book about the pains and anxieties of the multicultural experience. While the novel self-consciously mocks the idea of 'Happy Multicultural Land' (465), the character cast and their biographies epitomize the futile search for a coherent identity and acceptance by mainstream British society, and their fates exemplify the tangible implications of heterogeneity.

On the one hand, the result of the 'immigrant experiment' is the disappearance of 'Englishness' as a distinct, clearly definable category – the very concept of Englishness has become a mere 'fairy-tale' (236), as one of the characters observes. Yet on the other hand, 'Englishness' is still taken as the standard, the internalized yardstick by which identities are measured. It is not simply a set of norms and values imposed by the outside world, but it continues to feature prominently in the characters' own perceptions of self – even if they constantly battle with it, and even though nobody is able to pin it down to any fixed categories. In the case of Millat, one of the twin sons of Samad and Alsana Iqbal, who are originally from Bangladesh, the sense of uprootedness has obviously destructive implications, as he co-funds a radical Islamic organization. Admittedly, the group is pictured as a silly project of bored and disillusioned adolescents of less than dogmatic Muslim faith and it lacks a proper ideological back-up, yet it does imitate fundamentalist ideas of violently upholding cultural difference. It is a helpless counter-reaction, fuelled by a diffuse 'anger' (232), to the sense of alienation he experiences in a society that responds to ethnic difference with blunt and discriminatory categorizations:

> He knew that he, Millat, was a Paki no matter where he came from; that he smelt of curry; had no sexual identity; took other people's jobs; or had no job and bummed off the state; or gave all the jobs to his relatives; that he could be a dentist or a shop-owner or a curry-shifter, but not a footballer or a film-maker; that he should go back to his own country; or stay here and earn his bloody keep; that he worshipped elephants and wore turbans; that no one who looked like Millat, or spoke like Millat, or felt like Millat, was ever on the news unless they had recently been murdered. In short, he knew he had no face in this country, no voice in the country. (233–4)

This collection of stereotypical racist accusations aptly demonstrates that Millat, indeed, has 'no voice': all he can do to express his sense of self negatively is cite populist formulae that ostracize him.

The racist attitudes that exist alongside the reality of ethnic diversity and that Millat counters with fundamentalist ideas are brought to a head in a different way towards the end of the novel, when the sense of indeterminacy that is at the root of these developments reaches its most extreme climax. Irie has sex with both of the twins, Magid and Millat, on the same day and falls pregnant with a child whose father is forever unknown. While all this is told in a comical, nonchalant and often ironic tone, there is an existential fear of 'dissolution, disappearance' (327) running through the novel. It casts doubt on readings of the novel that understand it, as Stefanie Schäfer has argued, as 'offer[ing] a surprisingly affirmative approach to the complicated multiplicity of postcolonial subjectivity' (109). Elaine Childs rightly observes that 'hybridity itself is less a utopia than a source of anxiety for many of *White Teeth*'s characters' (8), and it is this experience of anxiety that counteracts the seemingly emancipatory potential of hybridity that the novel's light-hearted comic mode seems to promote. This stance renders Irie's vision of a neutral place a mere charade: 'In a vision, Irie has seen a time, a time not far from now, when roots won't matter any more because they can't because they mustn't because they're too long and they're too tortuous and they're just buried too damn deep. She looks forward to it' (527). While this may be a reassuring fantasy, the novel proves wrong the hope that history can be erased and confines the idea that roots can be dispensed with to the realm of the imaginary. The disappearance of firm categories does not simply imply freedom from restricting definitions. Instead, its disturbing flip side, which the narrator envisages for Irie's child – and which her vision conveniently covers up – is an all-out loss of identity: 'Irie's child can never be mapped exactly nor spoken of with any certainty' (527). That this should be something to look forward to is an attitude that is belied by the very insistence on roots and origins that the novel's characters are continually preoccupied with. Even though they repeatedly endeavour to move beyond the oppressive pull of their histories (in the sense of individual and group identity), there is a sense that the impact of history – of roots – will always be more powerful than any human attempts to transcend it, as a number of characters – most prominently Samad and Irie – are preoccupied with their families' past. Read in this light, Irie's curiously fatherless child is set to repeat the very quest that its parents' generation have been caught in. Rather than promising a new form of identity that is not tied to the categories of ethnicity and origin, the child is proof of an earlier statement about the particularity of the immigrant experience:

> [I]mmigrants have always been particularly prone to repetition – it's something to do with that experience of moving from West to East or East to West or from island to island. Even when you arrive, you're still going back and forth; your children are going round and round. There's no proper term for it – *original sin* seems too harsh; maybe *original trauma* would be better. (161)

The phrase 'original trauma' captures the key dimension of the novel: cultural fusion and ethnic mixing inevitably entail a disturbing underbelly of violence, pain and loss of identity. Difference necessarily involves power struggles and painful if often futile processes of self-definition.

What the designation of the experience as traumatic suggests is that it is so fundamental as to cause a shattering of self; it is so momentous that it cannot be grasped or made sense of. Apart from the obvious poignancy that accrues to this observation, it is just as important to stress, I believe, that the novel does far more than simply present immigrants and mixed-race individuals as mere victims of colonial oppression and its postcolonial repercussions. Rather, the immigrants themselves have a share in perpetuating the 'original trauma' that has been inflicted on them. Irie's child is an obvious case in point, as is Samad's decision to wrench apart his twin sons to have them brought up in separate countries and at different corners of the globe. In a more subtle fashion, the novel also suggests that the migrant's search for roots has in itself the potential to entail violence and follows the same instincts and inclinations as did the colonial project from which it results. Irie, for instance, at the height of her confusion about her roots and her family's Jamaican past, fiercely clings to any scrap of information on her origin that she can lay her hands on. When she is staying with her grandmother during a brief stint of adolescent rebellion, she is obsessed with 'the secrets [about the Jamaican branch of her family] that had been hoarded for so long' (399) and dedicates herself to unearthing the hidden recesses of the past:

> She laid claim to the past – her version of the past – aggressively, as if retrieving misdirected mail. So *this* was where she came from. This all *belonged* to her, her birthright, like a pair of pearl earrings or a post office bond. X marks the spot, and Irie put an X on everything she found, collecting bits and bobs (birth certificates, maps, army reports, news articles) and storing them under the sofa, so that as if by osmosis the richness of them would pass through the fabric while she was sleeping and seep right into her. (400; emphasis in original)

Clearly, Irie is not the stereotypical postcolonial subject here, condemned to marginalization and victim status. Rather, her gestures of 'la[ying] claim to the past' are suffused with images of mastery: it is 'her version of the past' that her research conjures up, and her marking of texts and objects smacks of a positively 'colonialist' act of taking possession. These implications are even made explicit in the text itself: two pages onwards, the narrator comments that 'Jamaica appeared to Irie as if it were newly made. Like Columbus himself, just by discovering it she had brought it into existence' (402). What this historical analogy suggests is that underneath both the colonialist violent acquisition of new territories and also the migrant's quest for roots is a fundamental self-interest and, ultimately, the desire for power and dominance.

The reason why *White Teeth* deserves the prominent position in the critical reception of post-millennial migrant fiction is, thus, because it forcefully acknowledges that migration, uprootedness and the upheavals of history are all inherently painful. Violence is inherent in the human condition, and self-interest, the desire for power and dominance are human constants. This is not to deny counter-examples in the novel – for instance the valuation of Archie's deliberately non-violent behaviour in World War II – but the fact that such behaviours repeatedly appear seems to contradict the idea of multiculturalism as progressively geared towards understanding and tolerance. With this emphasis, the novel questions the postmodernist credentials that view experiences of violence and conflict as socially, politically, culturally or economically constructed and dependent. In so doing, *White Teeth* exemplifies in a comprehensive fashion the ways in which recent British multi-ethnic fiction obviously complicates the well-rehearsed parameters of postcolonial or migrant fiction. In so doing, the novel can be understood as being in the vanguard of a nuanced and critically self-aware contemporary understanding of the complexities of the European multicultural reality, which literary criticism is only slowly beginning to catch up with. In other words, these literary texts expose the fault lines of the multicultural ideal and thereby show up the idealistic myopias that both political discourse and literary criticism have too long subscribed to. In the remainder of this chapter I will discuss two less well-known novels that further develop the points made by *White Teeth*, especially its emphasis on the painful underbelly of the experience of migration and its critical interrogation of the multicultural reality.

One discernible tendency in recent British multicultural literature clearly is an increasing focus on violent manifestations of cultural conflict. Where in *White Teeth* we are presented with disaffected would-be jihadist Millat, Monica Ali's *Brick Lane* (2003) presents us with a young Islamist who counters his sense of alienation in Britain with a nostalgic quest to recapture Bengali culture in his affair with the protagonist, whom he sees as a 'real' Bangladeshi woman, and Leila Aboulela's *Minaret* (2005) tells the story of a budding love affair between a Sudanese maid and her Arab employer's brother, whose worldview revolves around strict adherence to Muslim culture and values. A more recent novel puts the figure of the Islamist terrorist centre stage: Sunjeev Sahota's *Ours Are the Streets*, published in January 2011, retrospectively narrates an Islamist suicide bomber's gradual radicalization, from a first-person point of view. The narrator-protagonist, second generation British Pakistani, Imtiaz Raina, in his early twenties, has grown up in Sheffield, but feels increasingly disenfranchised in Britain and joins an Islamist training camp in Afghanistan, where he eventually plots to blow himself up in a Sheffield shopping centre. This subject matter is a far cry from the increasingly fashionable notion of cosmopolitan identity as the result of cultural and ethnic diversity and its transformative potentials in a globalized world. The term's connotations of enlightened liberalism certainly sit uneasily with the myopic fanaticism we encounter in *Ours Are the Streets*.

In purely plot-related terms, the novel may seem to present a rather clichéd scenario that taps in to a media-propagated standard perception of 'home-grown' terrorism. Indeed, the novel boasts all the commonplace elements of a terrorist's conversion story: as noted in a review by Robin Yassin-Kassab, Imtiaz displays the 'anguished inbetweenness suffered by so many second-generation immigrants' (n.p.) when he declares: 'I wanted to talk about why I felt fine rooting for Liverpool, in a quiet way, but not England. I wanted to talk about why I found myself defending Muslims against whites and whites against Muslims' (137–8). Commenting on his pre-conversion lifestyle, he admits to a sense of purposelessness and futility: 'I used to hang out with my mates and wear their clothes and be part of their drift towards nothing' (3). When he spends an extended period in Pakistan after his father's funeral in his family village, Imtiaz's quest for roots seems to have come to an end: 'standing there [at his father's funeral] as the final prayers were being said, with all these people behind me, I felt really solid, rooted to my earth. I felt magnificent' (98). He revels in his new-found origins and experiences a hitherto unknown sense of belonging: 'I were always so and so's grandson or such and such's nephew or whatever. I were never just me, on my own.... And I loved that. It were like for the first time I had an actual real past, with people who'd lived real lives' (115).

So far, the novel boasts a somewhat predictable scenario of generalized alienation and juvenile fantasies of completeness and meaning. However, precisely *how* Imtiaz moves from a vague sense of alienation to passive support for the worldwide Muslim cause to actively planning an attack on civilians in his British hometown does not become sufficiently clear to the reader (as noted in reviews by Yassin-Kassab, Tom Sutcliffe and Jake Wallis Simons). We do get some hints at his political motivation, for instance when he observes about the population of Sheffield: 'Everyone sleeping contentedly. So indifferent to the crimes of their land' (29) – a comment that obviously relates to Britain's alliance with the US and its resulting entanglement in the US-led War on Terror. The overwhelming impression that the novel conveys, however, is one of what Arifa Akbar calls 'psychopathology and emotional meltdown' (n.p.) rather than an intellectually convincing account of increasing fanaticism.

While one may criticize the novel for this apparent disavowal of its political dimension or lack of psychological credibility, I would argue that this is of secondary importance as its underlying rationale lies elsewhere. The author, Sunjeev Sahota, himself has argued that he intended his novel as an attempt to fictionally explore the way in which Islamist terrorism can only partly be approached with the help of neat explanatory patterns. In an interview with Jill McGivering from 2011 in which he talks about the genesis of *Ours Are the Streets* in the wake of the 2005 London suicide bombings, he observes that '[t]here was a sense at the time that either it [Islamic fundamentalism] was completely explainable in terms of geo-politics or these people were incomprehensible, just crazy fanatics. I wanted the novel to look at some of the grey area in between' (n.p.). In order to make sense of this murky scenario, which eschews any black-and-white categorizations, the novel's confessional/epistolary form is the key. This narrative position is invoked on the very first pages, when the narrator-protagonist declares: 'I want to leave something behind for you all ... I guess knowing that you're going to die makes you want to talk' (1). This narratorial stance carries the problem, of course, as noted by Sutcliffe, of the extent to which 'a suicide bomber [can] be a sympathetic character for a general readership' (n.p.). And yet, what the novel does, in effect, is to create a multi-layered set of connections between the narrator-protagonist and the reader that goes beyond the moral implications of this question. These connections are established at the level of narrative mode and perspective (rather than ideological correspondence). Imtiaz's informal speech and abundant colloquialisms play one part in creating this form of unwitting identification, as the reader is drawn in to his adolescent world of relationship trouble, insecurity and general unease (and, I would argue, easily ignores his frequent insertions of Arabic religious phrases, which are supposed to mark Imtiaz as a devout Muslim). This is also the rationale behind the – at first glance almost kitschy – clichés that Imtiaz repeatedly voices as the basis for his discontent, such as his enthusiasm about 'real lives' (115) quoted above or his sense of being 'connected to the world' (203) that he feels once in Pakistan. Although they are indicative of Imtiaz's growing identification with Islam and with (his idea of) his parents' country of origin, such notions are familiar to the reader as stock phrases of adolescent idealism.

On the other hand, we also witness Imtiaz indulge in fantasies of power and destruction. For instance, during a shooting practice in his Islamist training camp in Afghanistan, he is struck by the degree of power that he now holds: 'I felt how commanding my position were. It were like I were ripping free, like my skin were tearing apart to reveal a new and stronger man. The thought flashed into my mind that if I wanted to I could just suddenly turn round and shoot them [his fellow combatants] all dead' (217). Passages of this kind are doubly significant with respect to the novel's overall purpose. For one thing, focusing on the revulsion that readers are likely to feel in view of Imtiaz's growing radicalization and his violent intentions – Imtiaz's narrative exposes the uncomfortable truth that we may *not* always understand another's mindset. In other words, the confessional mode of the narrative is brought to its limits. However, while Imtiaz's violent desire for power may evoke revulsion in the reader, it also combines with the identificatory narrative strategies of the text to a disturbing effect: even if we do not sympathize with his attitudes and decisions, this narrative perspective inevitably draws us in to the protagonist's mindset. We are thereby forced to share his point of view and, in the process, to acknowledge our common humanity and the uncomfortable realities it implies: our capacity to behave irrationally, be misled by fanatical worldviews and potentially exert violence that follows no rationale except the sheer desire for power.

A similar point – though somewhat differently inflected – is being made in the second novel I would like to discuss, Zahid Hussain's *The Curry Mile* (2006). The novel centres on middle-aged first generation British Pakistani Ajmal Butt, who has built up a veritable empire of Indian restaurants in Manchester and the north of England, and his daughter Soraya, estranged from her family because of her modern lifestyle, who returns to Manchester from London to escape a disastrous love affair. Rather than allowing her father to turn her into his ideal of a dutiful daughter, Soraya soon plays her father at his own game, joining rank with his fiercest business rival and opening her own restaurant.

Yet *The Curry Mile* is more than a novel about intergenerational conflict exacerbated by the inevitable culture clash (see 'Zahid Hussain on The Curry Mile' n.p.). It marks a move away from 'traditional' topics in migrant literature, such as the emphasis on victimhood, the inevitable inbetweenness of second-generation immigrants and the gradual emancipatory struggle. With its thematic and contextual setting, the novel departs from the oft-encountered representations of immigrant communities as oppressed, discriminated against and powerless. The British Pakistani characters we meet, most prominently restaurant magnate Ajmal Butt, are fully integrated in the economic structures of their new country, with Butt incessantly emphasizing his capitalist 'Killer Instinct' that has made him the 'Curry King' of Manchester and the entire region. His daily prayer is indicative of his drive to succeed and his willingness to do so at any cost: 'My Lord, keep my heart strong and make my enemies wither. And make me more successful today than yesterday. Ameen' (23). Butt's self-image as the local curry magnate is epitomized by his self-designation as an autocratic ruler: 'He was the proud owner of a dozen restaurants, six on Manchester's Curry Mile, and with his fingers in other businesses around the north-west and Yorkshire; he had a growing kingdom to govern' (28).

Together with the fact that white British characters are strikingly absent from the novel (which signals a turn away from the oft-rehearsed black versus white conflict that has long characterized migrant fiction and its reception), Butt's economic clout in the area also means that he has left behind the usual markers of powerless immigrant status. Importantly, this is not a niche trade disconnected from the British mainstream, but his restaurant empire means that Butt holds influence even among the political and cultural establishment. His connections with Greater Manchester Police allow him to occasionally circumvent the law or to make sure his competitors are exposed to biased health-and-safety checks, and his acquaintance with the local papers (31) means that his restaurants are guaranteed positive reviews and cheap advertising space. His is a story of assimilation that does not stop at the mere adoption of customs and thought patterns – Butt remains a conservative patriarch in his dealings with his family and his mistress – but that culminates in his ability to see through and adapt the fashionable discourses that shape the self-understanding of his new country:

> England was a total shock to him when he first arrived in 1967. The early days were hard, but he worked day and night, using his considerable guile to amass enough money to hire a stall in Longsight Market.... He'd earned the title of 'Curry King' by working tirelessly, a name he intended to keep no matter what the cost.
>
> At the height of his fame, he owned twenty restaurants in northern England.... He appeared on countless documentaries and loved to talk about how curry was 'allowing everyone to come closer'. *That's total bakwaas, but the goray love to hear it.* His apna food fed the masses and cost mere pennies to make. (54–5, emphasis in original; see also 102–3, 104)

Butt combines lip-service to multicultural parlance with shrewd business sense, and it is this capitalist impulse, combined with his adherence to patriarchal tradition, which determines the novel's plot development. In other words, in *The Curry Mile* the emphasis on victimhood has been supplemented with a nuanced recognition of power structures, self-interest and economic difference *within* immigrant communities. Beyond its local colour, geographical and cultural context and political implications, this novel, too, points to a kind of shared humanity, but again not in the facile sense promoted by liberal advocates of multiculturalism. Rather, it highlights common human traits that often go unacknowledged, such as our propensity for self-interest, self-advancement and the desire to succeed and make a name for ourselves. It suggests that, as John Gray puts it, 'the human animal will stay the same: a highly inventive species that is also one of the most predatory and destructive' (4).

With the shifting thematic concerns I have traced in recent novels, British multicultural fiction marks a turn away from any form of multicultural hype, but highlights the misguided idealism behind the paradigm that fails to take account of basic human needs and desires. The texts reveal the faultlines of the multicultural ideal and its recent critical permutations: surface enthusiasm about diversity is irrelevant, mutual understanding is a myth. In other words, the purpose of these texts is not to imagine a better world, but to instil a form of humility in us as readers. We are asked to acknowledge that, if there is one significant impediment to harmonious coexistence of different cultures, it is not to be sought in societal structures and the like, but it fundamentally resides in human nature and is therefore much harder to eradicate. With this decidedly realistic stance, British migrant fiction has moved away from representing the specifics of the postcolonial situation, to appreciating internationally relevant developments and concerns – concerns that are rooted in unsettling constants of the human condition. These preoccupations are also relevant in a meta-critical sense, asking us to reconsider our own critical paradigms with which we approach texts – and this is the second site of these texts' internationally relevant potential.

Note

1 My translation. Merkel's full sentence reads: 'Der Multikulti-Ansatz – wir leben so nebeneinander her und freuen uns aneinander – ist gescheitert, absolut gescheitert' ('The idea of multiculturalism [the German "Multikulti" is somewhat informal and has slightly satirical connotations] – we live alongside each other and are blissfully happy about each other – has failed, utterly failed' [my translation]).

Works cited

2011 Census: KS201UK Ethnic group, local authorities in the United Kingdom. Available online: https://www.ons.gov.uk/ons/rel/census/2011-census/key-statistics-and-quick-statistics-for-local-authorities-in-the-united-kingdom—part-1/ (accessed 13 May 2014).

Aboulela, Leila. *Minaret.* London: Bloomsbury, 2005.

Adelson, Leslie A. *The Turkish Turn in Contemporary German Literature: Toward a New Critical Grammar of Migration.* New York and Houndmills: Palgrave Macmillan, 2005.

Akbar, Arifa. '*Ours Are the Streets*, by Sunjeev Sahota.' *The Independent*, 7 January 2011. Available online: http://www.independent.co.uk/arts-entertainment/books/reviews/ours-are-the-streets-by-sunjeev-sahota-2177730.html (accessed 4 March 2011).

Ali, Amir. 'Chicken Tikka Multiculturalism.' *Economic and Political Weekly* 36:30 (2001): 2821–2.

Ali, Monica. *Brick Lane* (2003). London: Black Swan, 2004.

Balasubramanyam, Rajeev. 'The Rhetoric of Multiculturalism'. In *Multi-Ethnic Britain 2000+: New Perspectives in Literature, Film and the Arts.* Eds Lars Eckstein, Barbara Korte, Eva Ulrike Pirker and Christoph Reinfandt. Amsterdam and New York: Rodopi, 2008, 33–42.

Bhabha, Homi. *The Location of Culture.* London and New York: Routledge, 1994.

Buruma, Ian. 'The Strange Death of Multiculturalism'. *Project Syndicate*, 10 April 2007. Available online: http://www.project-syndicate.org/commentary/buruma2/English (accessed 23 February 2012).

Cameron, David. Speech at Munich Security Conference, 5 February 2011. Available online: http://www.number10.gov.uk/news/speeches-and-transcripts/2011/02/pms-speech-at-munich-security-conference-60293 (accessed 2 March 2011).

Cheesman, Tom. 'Talking "Kanak": Zaimoğlu contra *Leitkultur*.' *New German Critique* 92 (2004): 82–99.

Cheesman, Tom. *Novels of Turkish German Settlement: Cosmopolite Fictions.* New York: Camden House, 2007.

Childs, Elaine. 'Insular Utopias and Religious Neuroses: Hybridity Anxiety in Zadie Smith's *White Teeth*'. *Proteus* 23 (2006): 7–12.

Commission on the Future of Multi-Ethnic Britain (CFMEB), *The Future of Multi-Ethnic Britain: The Parekh Report.* London: Profile Books, 2000.

Cook, Robin. 'Chicken Tikka Masala Speech' (extracts). 19 April 2001. Available online: http://www.guardian.co.uk/world/2001/apr/19/race.britishidentity (accessed 3 March 2011).

Fortier, Anne-Marie. *Multicultural Horizons: Diversity and the Limits of the Civil Nation.* London and New York: Routledge, 2008.

Gikandi, Simon. 'Between Roots and Routes: Cosmopolitanism and the claims of Locality'. In *Rerouting the Postcolonial: New Directions for the New Millennium.* Eds. Janet Wilson, Cristina Şandru and Sarah Lawson Welsh. London and New York: Routledge, 2010, 22–35.

Gray, John. *Straw Dogs: Thoughts on Humans and Other Animals.* London: Granta, 2002.

Hussain, Zahid. *The Curry Mile.* London: Suitcase Books, 2006.

Kara, Yadé. *Selam Berlin*. Zürich: Diogenes, 2004.
Kara, Yadé. *Café Cyprus*. Zürich: Diogenes, 2010.
Kehlmann, Daniel. Ein Klassiker von morgen. *Die Zeit*, 28 September 2006. Available online: http://www.zeit.de/2006/40/L-ZadieSmith (accessed 29 January 2011).
Kongslien, Ingeborg. 'New Voices, New Themes, New Perspectives: Contemporary Scandinavian Multicultural Literature'. *Scandinavian Studies* 79:2 (2007): 197–226.
Luetzow, Gunnar. 'Die Versuchungen der Großstadt.' *Der Spiegel*, 15 January 2001. Available online: http://www.spiegel.de/kultur/literatur/0,1518,112377,00.html (accessed 29 January 2011).
Manz, Stefan. 'Constructing a Normative National Identity: The *Leitkultur* Debate in Germany, 2000/2001'. *Journal of Multilingual and Multicultural Development* 25:5 (2004): 481–96.
McGivering, Jill. 'Dual Identity: An Interview with Sunjeev Sahota.' *Writers' Hub*, 7 March 2011. Available online: http://www.writershub.co.uk/features-piece.php?pc=870 (accessed 19 February 2012).
McGowan, Murray. 'Turkish-German Fiction since the Mid 1990s'. In *Contemporary German Fiction: Writing in the Berlin Republic*. Ed. Stuart Taberner. Cambridge: Cambridge University Press, 2007, 196–214.
'Merkel: "Multikulti ist absolut gescheitert"'. *Süddeutsche Zeitung*, 16 October 2010. Available online: http://www.sueddeutsche.de/politik/integration-seehofer-sieben-punkte-plan-gegen-zuwanderung-1.1012736 (accessed 2 March 2011).
Merrit, Stephanie. 'She's young, black, British – and the first publishing sensation of the millennium'. *The Observer*, 16 January 2000. Available online: http://www.guardian.co.uk/books/ 2000/jan/16/fiction.zadiesmith (accessed 29 September 2009).
Müller-Wood, Anja and John Carter Wood. 'How is Culture Biological? Violence: Real and Imagined'. *Politics and Culture: Symposium on the Question 'How Is Culture Biological?' – Six Essays and Discussions*, 29 April, 2010. Available online: http://www.politicsandculture.org/2010/04/29/symposium-on-the-question-how-is-culture-biological-six-essays-with-discussions-essay-2-by-anja-mueller-wood-and-john-carter-wood-how-is-culture-biological-violence-real-and-imagined/ (accessed 23 April 2014).
Pautz, Hartwig. *Die deutsche Leitkultur: Eine Identitätsdebatte. Neue Rechte, Neorassismus und Normalisierungsbemühungen*. Stuttgart: ibidem, 2005.
Phillips, Caryl. 'Mixed and Matched.' *The Observer*, 9 January 2000.
Pinker, Steven. *The Blank Slate: The Modern Denial of Human Nature*. London: Allen Lane, 2002.
Sahota, Sunjeev. *Ours Are the Streets*. London: Picador, 2011.
Schäfer, Stefanie. '"Looking back, you do not find what you left behind": Postcolonial Subjectivity and the Role of Memory in White Teeth and The Inheritance of Loss'. In *'Hello, I Say, It's Me': Contemporary Reconstructions of Self and Subjectivity*. Eds Jan D. Kucharzewski, Stefanie Schäfer and Lutz Schowalter. Trier: Wissenschaftlicher Verlag Trier, 2009, 107–27.

Schoene, Berthold. *The Cosmopolitan Novel*. Edinburgh: Edinburgh University Press, 2009.
Simons, Jake Wallis. 'Book Review: *Ours Are the Streets* by Sunjeev Sahota'. *The New Humanist* 126:2 (2011). Available online: http://newhumanist.org.uk/2531/book-review-ours-are-the-streets-by-sunjeev-sahota (accessed 26 February 2012).
Smith, Zadie. *White Teeth* (2000). London: Penguin, 2001.
Spencer, Robert. 'Cosmopolitan Criticism'. In *Rerouting the Postcolonial: New Directions for the New Millennium*. Eds. Janet Wilson, Cristina Şandru and Sarah Lawson Welsh. London and New York: Routledge, 2010, 36–47.
Sutcliffe, Tom. 'Suicide Bombers and a Novel Twist'. *The Independent*, 17 December 2010. Available online: http://www.independent.co.uk/opinion/columnists/thomas-sutcliffe/tom-sutcliffe-suicide-bombers-and-a-novel-twist-2162274.html (accessed 4 March 2011).
Vasileva, Katya. 'Population and Social Conditions'. *Eurostat: Statistics in Focus* 34 (2011). Available online: http://epp.eurostat.ec.europa.eu/cache/ITY_OFFPUB/KS-SF-11-034/EN/KS-SF-11-034-EN.PDF (accessed 13 May 2014).
Wilson, Janet, Cristina Şandru and Sarah Lawson Welsh. 'General Introduction'. In *Rerouting the Postcolonial: New Directions for the New Millennium*. Eds Janet Wilson, Cristina Şandru and Sarah Lawson Welsh. London and New York: Routledge, 2010, 1–13.
Yassin-Kassab, Robin. '*Ours Are the Streets* by Sunjeev Sahota (Review)'. *The Guardian*, 8 January 2011. Available online: http://www.guardian.co.uk/books/2011/jan/08/ours-are-streets-sunjeev-sahota?INTCMP=SRCH (accessed 4 March 2011).
'Zahid Hussain on The Curry Mile'. *The Asian Writer*, 12 November 2007. Available online: http://theasianwriter.co.uk/2007/11/zahid-hussain-on-the-curry-mile/ (accessed 20 February 2012).

Timeline of Works

2000

J.G. Ballard *Super-Cannes*
Iain M. Banks *Look to Windward*
Nicola Barker *Five Miles from Outer Hope*
Niall Griffiths *Grits*
Kazuo Ishiguro *When We Were Orphans*
John King *Human Punk*
Doris Lessing *Ben, in the World*
Toby Litt *Corpsing*
Ken MacLeod *Cosmonaut Keep*
China Miéville *Perdido Street Station*
Alan Moore and Kevin O'Neill *The League of Extraordinary Gentlemen volume 1* (first serialized between March 1999 and September 2000)
Jeff Noon *Needle in the Groove*
David Peace *Nineteen Seventy-Seven*
Philip Pullman *The Amber Spyglass*
J.K. Rowling *Harry Potter and the Goblet of Fire*
Will Self *How the Dead Live*
Kamila Shamsie *Salt and Saffron*
Zadie Smith *White Teeth*
Jeanette Winterson *The PowerBook*

2001

Pat Barker *Border Crossing*
Nicholas Blincoe and Matt Thorne (eds) *All Hail the New Puritans*
A.S. Byatt *The Biographer's Tale*
Jonathan Coe *The Rotters' Club*
Jim Crace *The Devil's Larder*
Sebastian Faulks *On Green Dolphin Street*

Niall Griffiths *Sheepshagger*
Abdulrazak Gurnah *By the Sea*
Gwyneth Jones *Bold as Love*
James Kelman *Translated Accounts*
Hanif Kureishi *Gabriel's Gift*
Doris Lessing *The Sweetest Dream*
David Lodge *Thinks . . .*
Ian McEwan *Atonement*
David Mitchell *Number9Dream*
V.S. Naipaul *Half a Life*
David Peace *Nineteen Eighty*
Philip Reeve *Mortal Engines*
Salman Rushdie *Fury*
Iain Sinclair *Landor's Tower*
Ali Smith *Hotel World*
Irvine Welsh *Glue*
Alex Wheatle *East of Acre Lane*

2002

Iain Banks *Dead Air*
Nicola Barker *Behindlings*
A.S. Byatt *A Whistling Woman*
Maggie Gee *The White Family*
Niall Griffiths *Kelly + Victor*
Stewart Home *69 Things to Do with a Dead Princess*
Gwyneth Jones *Castles Made of Sand*
Jon McGregor *If Nobody Talks of Remarkable Things*
China Miéville *The Scar*
Courttia Newland *Snakeskin*
Jeff Noon *Falling Out of Cars*
David Peace *Nineteen Eighty-Three*
Christopher Priest *The Separation*
Gwendoline Riley *Cold Water*
Will Self *Dorian, an Imitation*
Kamila Shamsie *Kartography*
Zadie Smith *The Autograph Man*

Sarah Waters *Fingersmith*
Irvine Welsh *Porno*
Alex Wheatle *The Seven Sisters*

2003

Monica Ali *Brick Lane*
Martin Amis *Yellow Dog*
J.G. Ballard *Millennium People*
Pat Barker *Double Vision*
John Burnside *Living Nowhere*
Niall Griffiths *Stump*
Gwyneth Jones *Midnight Lamp*
Hari Kunzru *The Impressionist*
Hanif Kureishi *The Body*
Toby Litt *Finding Myself*
Patrick McCabe *Call Me the Breeze*
Jon McGregor *If Nobody Speaks of Remarkable Things*
Alan Moore and Kevin O'Neill *The League of Extraordinary Gentlemen*
    volume 2 (first serialized between September 2002 and November 2003)
Caryl Phillips *A Distant Shore*
Gwendoline Riley *Carmel*
J.K. Rowling *Harry Potter and the Order of the Phoenix*
Graham Swift *The Light of Day*

2004

Nadeem Aslam *Maps for Lost Lovers*
Iain M. Banks *The Algebraist*
Nicola Barker *A Transparent Novel*
Jonathan Coe *The Closed Circle*
David Dabydeen *Our Lady of Demerera*
Maggie Gee *The Flood*
Mark Haddon *The Curious Incident of the Dog in the Night-Time*
Philip Hensher *The Fit*
Alan Hollinghurst *The Line of Beauty*

Gwyneth Jones *Life*
James Kelman *You Have to Be Careful in the Land of the Free*
A.L. Kennedy *Paradise*
John King *The Prison House*
Andrea Levy *Small Island*
China Miéville *Iron Council*
David Mitchell *Cloud Atlas*
V.S. Naipaul *Magic Seeds*
David Peace *GB84*
Gwendoline Riley *Sick Notes*
Salman Rushdie *Shalimar the Clown*
Iain Sinclair *Dining on Stones*
Colm Tóibín *The Master*
Jeanette Winterson *Lighthousekeeping*

2005

Leila Aboulela *Minaret*
Tash Aw *The Harmony Silk Factory*
Julian Barnes *Arthur & George*
Chris Cleave *Incendiary*
Sebastian Faulks *Human Traces*
Maggie Gee *My Cleaner*
Niall Griffiths *Wreckage*
Abdulrazak Gurnah *Desertion*
Stewart Home *Tainted Love*
Kazuo Ishiguro *Never Let Me Go*
Gwyneth Jones *Band of Gypsys*
Hari Kunzru *Transmission*
Marina Lewycka *A Short History of Tractors in Ukranian*
Tom McCarthy *Remainder*
Ian McEwan *Saturday*
Ken MacLeod *Learning the World*
Caryl Phillips *Dancing in the Dark*
J.K. Rowling *Harry Potter and the Half-Blood Prince*
Kamila Shamsie *Broken Verses*
Ali Smith *The Accidental*

Zadie Smith *On Beauty*
Alex Wheatle *Island Songs*

2006

Martin Amis *House of Meetings*
J.G. Ballard *Kingdom Come*
Kiran Desai *The Inheritance of Loss*
Mark Haddon *A Spot of Bother*
Zahid Hussain *The Curry Mile*
Gwyneth Jones *Rainbow Bridge*
Jon McGregor *So Many Ways to Begin*
Gautam Malkani *Londonstani*
Alison Miller *Demo*
David Mitchell *Black Swan Green*
David Peace *The Damned Utd*
Will Self *The Book of Dave*
Sarah Waters *The Night Watch*
Irvine Welsh *The Bedroom Secrets of the Master Chefs*

2007

Iain Banks *The Steep Approach to Garbadale*
Nicola Barker *Darkmans*
Pat Barker *Life Class*
John Burnside *The Devil's Footprints*
Jonathan Coe *The Rain Before It Falls*
Jim Crace *The Pesthouse*
Tan Twan Eng *The Gift of Rain*
Sebastian Faulks *Engleby*
Alasdair Gray *Old Men in Love*
Niall Griffiths *Runts*
A.L. Kennedy *Day*
Hari Kunzru *My Revolutions*
Doris Lessing *The Cleft*
Marina Lewycka *Two Caravans*

Toby Litt *Hospital*
Tom McCarthy *Men in Space*
Ian McEwan *On Chesil Beach*
Jon McGregor *So Many Ways to Begin*
China Miéville *Un Lun Dun*
David Peace *Tokyo Year Zero*
Gwendoline Riley *Joshua Spassky*
J.K. Rowling *Harry Potter and the Deathly Hallows*
Ali Smith *Boy Meets Girl*
Graham Swift *Tomorrow*
Roma Tearne *Mosquito*
Irvine Welsh *If You Liked School You'll Love Work*
Jeanette Winterson *The Stone Gods*

2008

Nadeem Aslam *The Wasted Vigil*
Iain M. Banks *Matter*
Chris Cleave *The Other Hand*
Jim Crace *On Heat*
David Dabydeen *Molly and the Muslim Stick*
Gwyneth Jones *Spirit*
James Kelman *Kieron Smith, Boy*
John King *Skinheads*
Hanif Kureishi *Something to Tell You*
Doris Lessing *Alfred and Emily*
Ken MacLeod *The Night Sessions*
Alan Moore and Melinda Gebbie *Lost Girls*
Joseph O'Neill *Netherland*
Salman Rushdie *The Enchantress of Florence*
Will Self *The Butt*
Joe Stretch *Friction*
Roma Tearne *Bone China*
Irvine Welsh *Crime*
Alex Wheatle *The Dirty South*

2009

Iain Banks *Transition*
John Burnside *Glister*
A.S. Byatt *The Children's Book*
Maggie Gee *My Driver*
Samantha Harvey *The Wilderness*
Marina Lewycka *We Are All Made of Glue*
Hilary Mantel *Wolf Hall*
Simon Mawer *The Glass Room*
China Miéville *The City and the City*
David Peace *Occupied City*
Kamila Shamsie *Burnt Shadows*
Joe Stretch *Wildlife*
Roma Tearne *Brixton Beach*
Adam Thorpe *Hodd*
Sarah Waters *The Little Stranger*
Irvine Welsh *Reheated Cabbage*

Timeline of National Events

2000

UK forces intervene in Sierra Leone to protect and evacuate foreign citizens caught up in the civil war. They subsequently stay on to help train the government army.

The Millennium Dome opens on the Greenwich peninsular in South East London. The Millennium Experience exhibition runs at the Dome throughout the year but fails to attract the anticipated numbers.

First series of *Big Brother* runs on Channel Four.

Tate Modern opens in the former Bankside Power Station in Southwark, London.

Friends Reunited is launched by Steve and Julie Pankhurst.

Sarah Payne, a Surrey schoolgirl, goes missing causing a nationwide search. Her body is found two weeks later and Richard Whiting is eventually convicted of her murder.

Fuel protests in the Summer against the prices of petrol and diesel cause major disruption on the UK's roads.

J.K. Rowling's *Harry Potter and the Goblet of Fire* is published and becomes the fastest selling book ever.

Labour's Human Rights Act (1998) becomes law, bringing into effect in the UK the rights contained in the European Convention on Human Rights.

2001

Foot and Mouth disease outbreak. Many farms across Britain are quarantined and eventually around 10 million sheep and cattle are killed.

General Election, which New Labour under Tony Blair win with a slightly reduced majority, the first ever full second term to be won by the Labour Party. Iain Duncan Smith subsequently wins election to become leader of the Conservative Party following the resignation of William Hague, only to be replaced two years later by Michael Howard.

Al Megrahi is found guilty of the 1988 Lockerbie bombing and sentenced at a court in the Netherlands to life in prison, which he will serve in Scotland. His co-accused is found not guilty.

Provisional IRA decommissioning of weapons begins in Northern Ieland.

Following attacks on the United States on 11 September, Tony Blair supports US-led campaign against international terrorism and Britain participates in bombing of Afghanistan.

2002

Golden Jubilee of Queen Elizabeth II.

Soham killings of two English girls, Holly Marie Wells and Jessica Aimee Chapman, both aged ten. Ian Huntley, a caretaker at their school in Cambridgeshire, is convicted of their murders in 2003.

Thirteen-year-old Milly Dowler is abducted on her way home from school in Walton-on-Thames and subsequently killed. Levi Bellfield was found guilty of her murder in 2011. The case became caught up in the 2011 Leveson Inquiry into the ethics of the British Press, due to allegations that her mobile phone was hacked by journalists during the period after her disappearance.

Northern Ireland Government suspended and direct rule reinstituted.

In September, the government publishes *Iraq's Weapons of Mass Destruction: The Assessment of the British Government*, a report that became known as the 'September dossier', and claimed to show evidence of the existence of weapons of mass destruction (WMD) in Saddam Hussein's Iraq. In the foreword, Tony Blair claimed that the report showed that the military planning of Saddam Hussein's regime 'allows for some of the WMD to be ready within 45 minutes of an order to use them'.

2003

During a debate in the House of Commons in March on the Iraq crisis, the Prime Minister Tony Blair claims that Iraq possesses weapons of mass destruction, a claim later shown to be untrue.

Later in March, the UK joins US-led military campaign against Iraq.

David Kelly, a British scientist and expert on biological warfare employed by the Ministry of Defence, is found dead in July. Earlier in the month he had spoken off the record to a BBC journalist, Andrew Gilligan, expressing misgivings about the claims made in the previous year's 'September dossier'. Gilligan's subsequent report leads to the revelation of Kelly as a source. He is called before the parliamentary Foreign Affairs Select Committee on 15 July to answer questions on the issues, and the Intelligence and Security Committee on the 16 July. He is found dead the next day. The government sets up the Hutton Inquiry (which opened in August and reported in January 2004) to investigate the circumstances of Kelly's death.

England wins the Rugby World Cup due to Jonny Wilkinson's drop goal, scored with twenty-six seconds to go.

2004

The Hutton Inquiry reports. It exonerates the government and criticizes the BBC, leading to the resignation of Director General Greg Dyke and Chair of Governors Gavyn Davies. It concludes that David Kelly had committed suicide.

Following the referendum for Scottish devolution in 1997 and the establishment of a Scottish Parliament in 1999, the new Scottish Parliament building is opened in the Holyrood area of Edinburgh, designed by Enric Miralles.

A devolution referendum is held in the north east of England in November. This was the first of three proposed referenda on the establishment of regional assemblies in the north west and the north east of England, and in Yorkshire and the Humber. The north east referendum voted against regional government by 77.9 per cent of the votes. The subsequent referenda were postponed and then dropped.

In October, the Iraq Survey Group concludes that Iraq did not have weapons of mass destruction.

The Butler Review, the Review of Intelligence on Weapons of Mass Destruction, is set up by parliament to investigate the claims that Iraq had weapons of mass destruction in order to justify its invasion. It concludes that the key intelligence used to justify the war had been unreliable.

2005

The car manufacturer, MG Rover, goes into administration.

In March, the anti-terrorism bill is passed in parliament after vociferous debate. The bill brings in control orders for suspects, including what is effectively house arrest.

In May, New Labour wins its third term in government. David Cameron wins the subsequent election to become leader of the Conservative Party following the resignation of Michael Howard.

In London on 7 July, 52 people are killed and around 700 injured as a result of four suicide bomb attacks on the London Underground and on a bus.

On 21 July, in London, four more attempted suicide bomb attacks take place on the public transport system. A fifth man dumped his bomb before detonating it. The bombs failed to detonate properly, causing only one minor injury, and the bombers fled. CCTV footage of those involved was released, and all four were arrested and sentenced to life imprisonment in 2007. The following day, Jean-Charles de Menezes, a young Brazilian man, was shot dead in error by police at Stockwell tube station in London. They had mistaken him for one of the fugitives from the previous day's failed bombing attempts.

Prince Charles, Prince of Wales, marries Camilla Parker-Bowles in Windsor in April.

Malcolm Glazer, a wealthy American businessman, and his family buy controlling shares in Manchester United Football Club, allowing them to take the club into private ownership for the first time since 1990. A large number of fans protest, and subsequently begin to plan a takeover of the club funded by fans.

The English cricket team wins the Ashes from Australia for first time in eighteen years.

Provisional IRA declares the end of their thirty-six-year armed campaign following the final act of weapons decommissioning.

Following the Civil Partnership Act (2004), civil partnerships come into force in the UK, allowing same-sex couples to enter a similar legal framework as that provided by heterosexual marriage. Heterosexual couples are not eligible for civil partnerships.

As part of the implementation of the Licensing Act (2003), pubs, bars and clubs are able to apply for new licenses that extend opening hours. This becomes known in the media as '24-hour drinking', and sparks a widespread debate on what the effects of such extensions might be.

2006

The *Oxford English Dictionary* includes the verb 'to google' for the first time.

A former Russian security service officer, Aleksandr Litvinenko, an outspoken critic of the Kremlin living in exile in London, dies there after being poisoned by a radioactive substance.

The Government of Wales Act (2006) reforms the National Assembly of Wales, which had been established in 1999 following the 1997 devolution referendum, and extends its powers, including the establishment of the executive of the Assembly as a government rather than a committee. The Welsh Senedd, or National Assembly building, is opened in Cardiff. The building was designed by architect Richard Rogers.

Between October and December five women are murdered in Ipswich, Suffolk. All five women worked as prostitutes in the Ipswich area. The murders were quickly linked, and a suspect was arrested in December and subsequently convicted of all five murders. The murders and investigation sparked a national debate about legal and media treatment of women working in the sex industry.

2007

In January 2007, Clive Goodman and Glenn Mulcaire, who were respectively a reporter and a private investigator working for the *News of the World*, are sent to prison for hacking the telephones of members of the Royal Family in order to access voicemail messages illegally. The phone hacking scandal would subsequently lead to the 2011 Leveson Inquiry into the practices and ethics of the British Press, and also result in the newspaper being closed in 2011 and the imprisonment of its former editor, Andy Coulson, in 2014.

Towards the beginning of the year, Tony Blair announces the first large-scale withdrawal of British troops from Iraq.

Following the election held for the then-suspended Northern Ireland Assembly on 7 March, devolution is restored when the two largest parties following the election, the Democratic Unionist Party (DUP) and Sinn Féin, agree to enter a power-sharing government together. An administration is eventually established on 10 May with Ian Paisley as First Minister and Martin McGuinness as Deputy First Minister.

In May, the Scottish National Party wins forty-seven seats, one more than Labour, in the Scottish election and forms a minority government. Plaid Cymru come second in the Welsh Assembly election and enter into coalition government with Labour on the condition that they agree to seek the devolution of further powers, which, following a referendum in 2011, are eventually gained.

On 3 May, three-year-old Madeleine McCann disappears from her bed in a holiday apartment in the Algarve in Portugal. The resulting missing-person hunt has been the most reported in British history and remains ongoing.

J.K. Rowling publishes *Harry Potter and the Deathly Hallows*, the seventh and concluding volume of the phenomenally bestselling series.

On 27 June, Gordon Brown takes over from Tony Blair as leader of the Labour Party and as Prime Minister, as had long been arranged.

On 1 July, a smoking ban comes into force in England making it illegal to smoke in enclosed work spaces, including pubs and restaurants. Similar bans had already come into force in Scotland, Wales and Northern Ireland earlier in the year.

In December, BBC iPlayer, a system for streaming television and radio programmes on the internet, is launched.

2008

In January, Tower Colliery in Hirwaun, Rhondda Cynon Taf, the last deep mine still working in the South Wales Coalfield shuts, marking the end of an era.

In February, the Northern Rock Bank, which had made news headlines the previous autumn when it experienced the first 'bank run' in Britain for 150 years, is nationalized.

Nine-year-old Shannon Matthews goes missing in February from her home in Dewsbury, West Yorkshire. Following a major police operation, reminiscent of the search for Madeleine McCann, she is found at a house owned by her mother's boyfriend and the case is revealed to be a fake kidnapping.

In local elections in May, the Labour government suffers its worst results in forty years. At the same time, Boris Johnson of the Conservative Party wins the election to become Mayor of London, replacing Ken Livingstone.

In July, the General Synod of the Church of England instigates the drafting of legislation for the ordination of women bishops, which would eventually be adopted in November 2014.

In October, the government establishes a bank rescue package of £5 billion in response to the global financial crisis in order to support British banks and the financial system. The fund was essential for supporting Lloyds, HBOS and the Royal Bank of Scotland, amounting to a partial nationalization.

On 26 November, the well-known high street shop, Woolworths, announces it is entering administration as a result of the consequences of the financial crisis and recession. A number of other chain stores, such as MFI and Zavvi (formerly Virgin Megastores) also go out of business in the run-up to Christmas.

2009

In response to the ongoing financial crisis, the Bank of England sets interest rates at 1.5 per cent, the lowest for 315 years.

In May, the *Daily Telegraph* begins publishing unexpurgated details of MPs' expenses records, which had been leaked to it. A scandal ensued when it became obvious that the system was being widely misused and several MPs were subsequently prosecuted and sent to prison. The scandal as a whole led to a widespread dissatisfaction with elected politicians that has coloured British public affairs ever since.

The establishment of the Chilcot Inquiry into the British role in the Iraq War is announced in June. As of January 2015, the report of the Inquiry is yet to be published.

In July, virtually all the remaining British troops in Iraq return following the handover of responsibilities to the Iraq Government.

Carol Ann Duffy is named the first woman poet laureate.

Salman Rushdie's *Midnight's Children* (1981) wins The Best of the Booker in celebration of the 40th anniversary of the Prize.

Official figures would subsequently show that the Economy emerged from recession in the last quarter of the year, following six consecutive quarters of recession.

Timeline of International Events

2000

Vladimir Putin is elected president of Russia, replacing Boris Yeltsin.

The International Space Station receives its first crew members, after its first module component was launched in 1998. It has become the station with the longest occupancy to date.

Presidential Elections in the US see George W. Bush elected on the narrowest of margins. Controversy surrounds the result in Florida due to the potential miscounting of votes, known as the 'hanging chads' controversy, which refers to the fact that many of the punch cards in the voting system had failed to record votes correctly.

Summit between Israeli Prime Minister Ehud Barak and PLO leader Yasser Arafat at Camp David with US President Bill Clinton. The summit ends without an agreement being reached.

Second Intifada begins in Israel. The conflict eventually results in the estimated death of 3,000 Palestinians and 1,000 Israelis. Although the conflict in the region continues, the Second Intifada is generally agreed to end in 2005.

Al-Qaeda suicide bombers target the USS *Cole*, a US Navy guided missile destroyer as it is refuelling in the Yemeni port of Aden. The attack results in the loss of seventeen American sailors.

A coup against Slobodan Milošević in Serbia ejects him from power.

2001

Wikipedia, a free, open-access online encyclopaedia is launched by Jimmy Wales and Larry Sanger.

The Human Genome Project publishes a working draft of the human genome. This was followed by publication of the complete human genome in 2003.

In March, the dot.com bubble bursts as share prices tumble. Many internet companies go bust.

On 11 September, The World Trade Center in New York and the Pentagon in Washington are attacked by hijacked passenger planes. The attacks cause the collapse of the twin towers at the Center, with the loss of nearly 3,000 people. Al-Qaeda takes responsibility for the attacks. 9/11, as it becomes known, casts a shadow over the whole decade, as George W. Bush's 'War on Terror' results in the military invasions by US and Allied forces of Afghanistan in October, and Iraq in 2003.

War in Afghanistan begins as part of the US government's response to the events of 9/11. Allied forces invade Afghanistan and target the Taliban forces predominantly located in the north of the country.

Warner Brothers release *Harry Potter and the Philosopher's Stone* (2001), the first of what will eventually be an eight film series, and to date, the highest grossing film franchise.

The Lord of the Rings: The Fellowship of the Ring (2001), directed by Peter Jackson, released by New Line Cinema.

Enron scandal leads to the bankruptcy of the Enron Corporation, the largest bankruptcy in US history.

George W. Bush refuses to endorse the Kyoto Protocol, an international agreement on reducing emissions to prevent climate change.

Same-sex marriages are legalized in the Netherlands, the first country to do so.

Timothy McVeigh executed in the US for bombing federal buildings in Oklahoma City, killing over 160 people in 1995.

China is admitted into the World Trade Organization.

2002

New Euro notes and coins are introduced to mark the adoption of the Euro as the official currency of the Eurozone countries with the previous national currencies no longer being accepted as legal tender.

In January, in his State of the Union address, George W. Bush uses the phrase 'axis of evil' for the first time, referring to a perceived, but unjustified, link between the governments of Iran, Iraq and North Korea.

Guantanamo Bay detention camp is established at the US Guantanamo Bay Naval Base in Cuba. Suspected terrorist detainees begin to arrive in January.

Slobodan Milošević goes on trial in The Hague for crimes against humanity and breaching the Geneva Convention. The trial continues until 2006, when Milošević dies of a heart attack while still in detention.

Chechen rebels seize a theatre in Moscow. The consequent intervention of Russian Security Services results in the deaths of 40 of the rebels and around 130 hostages when toxic gas is pumped into the theatre.

The United Nations' International Criminal Court is established in The Hague, The Netherlands. The US, along with forty-five other members of the UN, does not ratify the agreement to set up the court.

The Bali bombings in the tourist district of Kuta kill 202 people. The Islamist group Jemaah Islamiyah are held responsible and three members of the group are sentenced to death, and executed in 2008.

November, Resolution 1441 at the UN, contributed to by US and UK, asking that Iraq disarm or face 'serious consequences'.

2003

Iraq War begins in March when Allied forces, led by the US, invade Iraq without a declaration of war. The 'shock and awe' attack eventually leads to the Ba'ath Party government being toppled and its leader Saddam Hussein being captured in December and executed.

Second Life, an online virtual world, is launched by Linden Lab.

The Space Shuttle Columbia disaster results in the death of seven crew members.

The Human Genome Project is completed.

Aung San Suu Kyi is taken into custody by the ruling junta in Myanmar (Burma).

Protests against Robert Mugabe's regime in Zimbabwe are led by opposition leader Morgan Tsvangirai. In December Zimbabwe withdraws from the Commonwealth.

2004

Facebook, the online social networking site, is launched by a group of college friends from Harvard, including Mark Zuckerberg. It initially only gave access to users who were students at Harvard. This was then extended to college students beyond Harvard, and then in 2006 it was opened to all those over thirteen with an email address.

In March, ten explosions on four commuter trains in Madrid, Spain, kill 191 and wound nearly 2,000. The bombs were the work of an Islamist cell inspired by Al-Qaeda but without direct links to the group. At the general election three days later, Spain's ruling party, Partido Popular, is ousted.

Photos of human rights abuses committed by US military personnel in the Abu Ghraib prison in Iraq come to widespread public attention.

George W. Bush is re-elected for a second term as President of the USA, defeating Democratic Party candidate John Kerry.

On 26 December, following an earthquake under the Indian Ocean, a tsunami kills around 250,000 people, Indonesia being the country worst affected, followed by Sri Lanka, India and Thailand.

Both NATO and the European Union are enlarged to include many former eastern bloc countries.

The Orange Revolution begins in Ukraine, a series of protests and demonstrations following charges of corruption in the general election in November which had been won by the incumbent Prime Minister, Victor Yanukovych. The results of the election are eventually annulled and another election held, which gives victory to the opposition leader, Viktor Yushchenko.

In a school in Beslan, in North Ossetia, Islamic separatists from Chechnya take over 1,000 people hostage, most of them children. On the third day of the siege, Russian security services storm the school. Nearly 400 of the hostages are killed. The events act as a justification for the consolidation of power in the Kremlin, and particularly for a strengthening of the powers of the president.

2005

YouTube, the video sharing website, is launched by three former employees of PayPal. It would be bought by Google in 2006 for $1.65 billion.

John Paul II dies after nearly twenty-seven years as pope. In the same month Pope Benedict XVI is inaugurated as the new pope.

US cyclist Lance Armstrong wins his seventh consecutive Tour de France. He would be stripped of his titles in 2012 after being charged with the widespread use of performance-enhancing drugs.

Hurricane Katrina hits the coast of Louisiana, causing destruction along a wide section of the south east of the United States. Large areas of New Orleans floods when its levee system fails. The city was evacuated just before the storm hit, but many, particularly those in poor areas, were unable to leave. Nearly 1,500 people died. Government preparation for and response to the hurricane was severely criticized, including President Bush's slow return from a holiday following the devastation of the hurricane.

Angela Merkel, leader of the Christian Democratic Union, becomes the first woman chancellor of Germany.

The Second Intifada ends as Israel withdraws from Gaza and Palestinian President Mahmoud Abbas attends the Sharm el-Sheihk summit with Israeli Prime Minister, Ariel Sharon, and other middle eastern leaders.

2006

Saddam Hussein, the former president of Iraq, is executed by hanging after being found guilty of crimes against humanity by an Iraqi Special Tribunal.

Twitter, the online networking service that allows users to send and receive short messages, is launched.

Pluto is reclassified as a dwarf planet by the International Astronomical Union.

Seven bomb attacks on trains in Mumbai, India result in 209 people being killed and over 700 injured. The organization Lashkar-e-Qahhar claim responsibility, although Indian intelligence suspect both Al-Quaeda and the Pakistan intelligence agency ISI.

2007

Beginning with the bursting of the housing market bubble in the US, real estate values decrease, destabilizing financial institutions across the globe. The housing bubble had been fuelled by the granting of mortgages to buy homes beyond the homeowners' financial capacity to repay them: so-called sub-prime mortgages. The collapse of the US housing market was fundamentally destabilizing because so much of the world's financial markets was based on such packaging and reselling of debt. A worldwide financial crisis followed throughout 2008, the most significant since the Great Depression of the 1930s.

Apple releases the first generation iPhone.

Amazon releases its e-book reader, the Kindle, onto the market.

Benezir Bhutto, the first female leader of a Muslim country, is assassinated in Pakistan after returning there from exile to stand in a general election.

Google Street View, an online site that provides street level shots from thousands of locations around the world, is launched.

Anti-government protests in Myanmar (Burma) are crushed.

2008

The Large Hadron Collider, the world's largest and most powerful particle collider, built by the European Organization for Nuclear Research (CERN), is launched near Geneva in Switzerland. It was built to allow the testing of theories of particle and high-energy physics, in particular the testing of the existence of the theorized Higgs boson.

A worldwide economic crash begins in September, caused by the financial crisis that had begun in 2007 and the subsequent global recession. A number of significant financial institutions went bankrupt during this period, including the financial services firm Lehman Brothers, and others, such as Merrill Lynch, were bought at discounted prices.

Barack Obama becomes the first black US President, following his election victory over John McCain.

2009

On 3 January, the Israeli Army launches a ground invasion of Gaza with the stated intention of bringing rocket attacks to a halt. The troops withdrew after three weeks, leaving over 1,000 Palestinians dead.

In May, the Sri Lankan Civil War ends after 26 years following the final victory of Government forces over the Tamil Tigers.

In June, public protests begin in Iran following the announcement that incumbent Mahmoud Ahmadinejad had won nearly 60 per cent of the vote in the presidential election despite several reported irregularities. The protests were eventually suppressed by the Government.

The Boko Haram rebellion begins in Nigeria in July.

In August, it is reported that the population of Africa has reached 1 billion.

3D scanning becomes commercially available.

On 1 December, the Treaty of Lisbon comes into effect, amending the constitution of the European Union in a number of ways, including introducing the principle of qualified majority voting to replace that of unanimity in many policy areas, and placing more emphasis on collective foreign policy. It also established procedures that would permit a member state to leave the EU.

Biographies of Writers

Leila Aboulela was born in Cairo in 1964 and brought up in Khartoum, Sudan, where she attended the American School before studying economics at the University. Following further studies at the London School of Economics, she moved to Aberdeen in 1990, when her husband took a job there working in the oil industry. She began writing while looking after her children and teaching university level statistics, but gave the latter up after six years. Her first novel, *The Translator* (1999), concerned a widowed Muslim mother living in Aberdeen who falls in love with a Scottish secular academic. A collection of short stories, *Coloured Lights* (2001), followed. In her second novel, *Minaret* (2005), a formerly privileged and secular Muslim woman finds herself gradually embracing her faith while impoverished in exile in London. Her third novel, *Lyrics Alley* (2011), is set in 1950s' Sudan on the brink of independence and was the winner of the Fiction section of the Scottish Mortgage Investment Trust Book Awards.

Born in Dhaka, Eastern Pakistan (now Bangladesh) in 1967, **Monica Ali** moved to Bolton with her family when she was three. After attending the Bolton School, an independent school, she studied Philosophy, Politics and Economics at Oxford. Ali was named by Granta as one of their Best of Young British Novelists in 2003 shortly before her first novel, *Brick Lane* (2003) was published. *Brick Lane*, which was shortlisted for the Man Booker Prize, is set within London's Bangladeshi community in Tower Hamlets. It was filmed in 2007. *Alentejo Blue* (2006) marked a change of pace and setting, composed of a sequence of chapters by different characters set in a Portuguese village. In 2009, Ali returned to writing about the lives of London's migrant populations with *In the Kitchen*, set amongst the workplace of the Imperial Hotel, Piccadilly. Her most recent novel, *Untold Story* (2011) imagines the life of a Princess Diana-like member of the Royal Family who has faked her own death and is now living in small-town America.

Nadeem Aslam was born in 1966 in Gujranwala in Pakistan. His family moved to Britain, where they settled in Huddersfield when he was fourteen, because his communist father had to flee the country. Aslam studied biochemistry at the University of Manchester but left before he completed his degree in order to become a writer. His first novel, *Season of the Rainbirds* (1993) is set in Pakistan and won the Betty Trask Prize. It took him ten years to write his second, *Maps for Lost Lovers* (2004), which revolves around members of an immigrant Pakistani community in an unnamed Northern English town. His two subsequent novels are *The Wasted Vigil* (2008), set in Afghanistan, and *The Blind Man's Garden* (2013), which considers the War on Terror from the perspective of local characters in Western Pakistan and Eastern Afghanistan.

Born in 1949 in Swansea, South Wales, **Martin Amis** is the son of the novelist Kingsley Amis. After graduating from Oxford in 1971, where he studied English, Martin Amis worked as a literary journalist until 1979. During this time he worked on his first four novels: *The Rachel Papers* (1973), *Dead Babies* (1975), *Success* (1978) and *Other People: A Mystery Story* (1981). In 1984 he published his most acclaimed novel, *Money: A Suicide Note*. After publishing a collection of essays, *The Moronic Inferno and Other Visits to America* (1986) and a collection of stories, *Einstein's Monsters* (1987), he published the second of an informal trilogy of novels, *London Fields* (1989) (the first being *Money*). His other works include: *Time's Arrow* (1991), *The Information* (1995) (the third novel of his trilogy), *Night Train*, a pseudo-detective story (1997), *Yellow Dog* (2003), *House of Meetings* (2006), *The Pregnant Widow* (2010), *Lionel Asbo* (2012) and *The Zone of Interest* (2014). His other published work includes a collection of stories, *Heavy Weather and Other Stories* (1998), a highly original memoir, *Experience* (2000), a collection of his journalism, *The War Against Cliché: Essays and Reviews, 1971–2000* (2001) and a political essay about Stalin's years of terror, *Koba the Dead: Laughter and the Twenty Million* (2002).

A.S. Byatt was born in Sheffield in 1936 as Antonia Susan Drabble. Her father was a barrister, her mother was a scholar of Robert Browning, and her younger sister is the novelist Margaret Drabble. Byatt graduated from Newham College, Cambridge and went on to study at Bryn Mawr College, Philadelphia, and Somerville College, Oxford, before subsequently working as an academic from 1962 to 1983. Her first novel, *The Shadow of the Sun* (1964), is the story of a girl growing up in the shadow of a dominant father. Other novels include *The Game* (1967), which concerns the relationship between two sisters, *The Virgin in the Garden* (1978), *Still Life* (1985), *Babel Tower* (1996), *The Biographer's Tale* (2000) and *A Whistling Woman* (2002). *Possession* (1990), the story of two academics uncovering the relationship between two nineteenth-century poets, won the Booker Prize and was filmed in 2002. *Angels and Insects* (1992) is set entirely in the Victorian period and was filmed in 1995, and *The Children's Book* (2009) was shortlisted for the Booker Prize. Byatt was awarded a CBE in 1990 and made a Dame in 1999.

Born in London in 1973, **Chris Cleave** went on to study Psychology at Oxford. His first novel, *Incendiary*, which imagined a terrorist attack on London was published by coincidence on 7 July 2005, the day of the suicide bombings in central London often referred to as 7/7. *Incendiary* was filmed in 2008, the same year as his second novel, *The Other Hand* (known in the US and Canada as *Little Bee*) was published. The novel draws on Cleave's experience of having worked briefly during a university vacation as a casual labourer at Campsfield House, Oxfordshire, a detention centre for asylum seekers. Between 2008 and 2010, Cleave wrote a column about his children, 'Down with the Kids', for the Family section of the *Guardian*. His third novel, *Gold*, was published in 2013.

David Dabydeen was born in 1955 in Guyana. He moved to the UK with his family in 1969. During the 1980s he first joined and went on to run the Centre for Caribbean Studies at the University of Warwick, where he is still a member of staff. He has written criticism, novels and poetry. His first book, the collection of poetry *Slave Song* (1984), won the Quiller-Couch Prize and the Commonwealth Poetry Prize. In 1991 his first novel, *The Intended*, won the Guyana Prize for Literature. This and his subsequent novels – *Disappearance* (1993), *The Counting House* (1996), *A Harlot's Progress* (1999), *Our Lady of Demerara* (2004) and *Molly and the Muslim Stick* (2008) – all explore the complex historical and contemporary relations between Europe and those colonized by it and their descendants. He was appointed as Guyana's Ambassador to China in 2010, and as its non-resident ambassador to Japan in 2014.

Sebastian Faulks was born in Donnington, Berkshire, in 1953. His father was a soldier, who became a solicitor and then a judge, and his brother, Edward, became a Conservative Government Minister in 2014. Faulks was schooled at Wellington College before reading English at Cambridge. After a period living in France, and a job as a teacher, Faulks became a journalist, going on to become literary editor of the *Independent* in 1986 and deputy editor of the *Independent on Sunday* in 1989. Following the huge success of his fourth novel, *Birdsong* (1993), which interweaves a story set in the First World War with events occurring in the late 1970s, Faulks left journalism to become a full-time writer. His next book, *The Fatal Englishman* (1996) was an interesting biographical account of the three short lives of Christopher Wood, Richard Hillary and Jeremy Wolfenden, which, collected together, generated an offbeat cultural history of England. Subsequent novels included *Charlotte Gray* (1998), *On Green Dolphin Street* (2001) and *Human Traces* (2005). In 2008, he published *Devil May Care*, a James Bond novel commissioned to mark the birth centenary of Ian Fleming. Five years later, he resurrected another popular literary classic by turning this time to the characters of P.G. Wodehouse with *Jeeves and the Wedding Bells* (2013).

Niall Griffiths was born in Toxteth, Liverpool, in 1966 into a family with Welsh roots. In 1976 the family emigrated to Australia only to return three years later. His non-fiction book, *Ten Pound Pom* (2009), records his experiences of returning to Australia and reflecting on his childhood memories. After gaining a degree in English, Griffiths worked in a number of short-term jobs before starting a PhD at Aberystwyth University. However, he ended up dropping out and accumulating experiences around the town, which fed into his first novel, *Grits* (2000). His second novel, *Sheepshagger* (2001) was a compelling account of the revenge that Ianto from the West Wales mountains takes on those he sees as desecrating his homeland. *Kelly + Victor* (2002), set in Liverpool, describes how a passionate sexual relationship tips into destruction with visceral detail, and was subsequently filmed in 2012. His fourth novel *Stump* (2003) tells the intersecting stories of a one-armed man from Liverpool hiding out in a Welsh seaside town and two men on the way from Liverpool hunting for a one-armed man somewhere in Wales. *Stump* won both the Welsh Books Council Book of the Year and the Arts Council of Wales Book of the Year Award. After two more novels, *Wreckage* (2005) and *Runt* (2007), he wrote the travel guides *Real Aberystwyth* (2008) and *Real Liverpool* (2008). *The Dreams of Max and Ronnie* (2010) was Griffiths' take on *The Dream of Rhonabwy*, a contribution to the Welsh publishing imprint Seren's series *New Stories of the Mabinogion*, in which modern authors rewrote the stories from that Welsh classic. Griffiths' most recent novel is *A Great Big Shining Star* (2013).

Stewart Home is the pen-name of Kevin Llewellyn Callan, who works in a number of forms including fiction, art, film and as an art historian, pamphleteer and political activist. He is associated with avant-garde art, political agit-prop and the punk movement. He was born in 1962 in South London and his mother, Julia Callan-Thompson was a model involved in the radical arts scene in Notting Hill Gate in the 1960s. In the 1970s Home was attracted to the Trotskyist Socialist Youth League, although he never joined. In the late 1970s he was bassist with the punk band *The Molotovs* and produced punk fanzines. In the 1980s he founded the band White Colours and published the art fanzine *SMILE*. He was also involved in a number of art groups and installations during this period in London, including the Neoists, and launched the Art Strike campaign in the early1990s. During this period he produced a number of pulp novels, often as parodies of the 1970s' skinhead fiction of Richard Allen. The first novel that was recognized by the mainstream literary press in Britain was *69 Things to Do with a Dead Princess* published by Canongate in 2002. This was followed by *Down and Out in Shoreditch and Hoxton* (2004) and *Tainted Love* (2005), which is set amidst the counterculture of 1960s' London. He has since produced several novels alongside a wide variety of non-fiction publications. His fiction includes *Memphis Underground* (2007), *Blood Rites of the Bourgeoisie* (2010) and *The 9 Lives of Ray the Cat Jones* (2014).

Kazuo Ishiguro was born in 1954 in Nagasaki, Japan. His family moved to the UK in 1960. Ishiguro graduated from the University of Kent in English and Philosophy. He worked as a social worker for a while, and went on to gain an MA in Creative Writing from the University of East Anglia in 1980. He became a British citizen in 1982, the year of the publication of his first novel, *A Pale View of the Hills*. Both this novel and his second, *An Artist of the Floating World* (1986), are set in Japan, although, after his family's emigration, he did not visit Japan again until 1989. *A Pale View of the Hills* won the Winifred Holtby Memorial Prize and *Artist of the Floating World* won the Whitbread Prize. His next novel, *The Remains of the Day*, won the Booker Prize in 1989. Ishiguro was included in the Granta 'Best of Young British Novelists' in both 1983 and 1993, and was awarded an OBE in 1995. His remaining novels are *The Unconsoled* (1995), *When We Were Orphans* (2000) and *Never Let Me Go* (2005). Two of his novels have been adapted for films, *The Remains of the Day* in 1993 (dir. James Ivory) and *Never Let Me Go* in 2010 (dir. Mark Romanek). He also published a collection of short stories, entitled *Nocturnes: Five Stories of Music and Nightfall*, in 2009.

John King was born in Slough in 1960. His first novel, *The Football Factory* (1996), made an immediate impact on publication for its hard-hitting story of working-class football 'hooligans' in London. It was followed by two loosely linked sequels, *Headhunters* (1997) and *England Away* (1998), which intercut scenes following fans to an England football match in Berlin with those of a pensioner's memories of the Second World War. His fourth novel, *Human Punk* (2000), drew on his memories of growing up in Slough as it switches between scenes set in the present and in 1977 at the height of the punk rock era. It is regarded as the first volume of *The Satellite Cycle*, which also includes *White Trash* (2001) and *Skinheads* (2008). King's other novel, *The Prison House* (2004), has a more existential feel, being set in a prison outside England, but is nonetheless intense and impassioned as all his work is. In 2006, King set up independent publisher London Books with fellow author Martin Knight, and they have since republished a number of out-of-print working-class novels in their London Books Classics series. King has contributed introductions to two of these: Gerald Kersh's *Night and the City* (2007) and John Sommerfield's *May Day* (2010).

Patrick McCabe was born in Clones, County Monaghan, Northern Ireland, in 1955. He was educated at St Patrick's Training College in Dublin and began work as a teacher in London in 1980. He has published novels, short stories and plays for stage and radio. His first novel, *The Adventures of Shay Mouse*, a children's book, was published in 1985. After publishing two more novels, *Cain* (1986) and *Music on Clinton Street* (1989), his breakthrough novel *The Butcher Boy* was published in 1992 and won the *Irish Times* Irish Literature Prize for fiction, and was short-listed for the Booker Prize. *Dead School* followed in 1995 and *Breakfast on Pluto* in 1998, which was also short-listed by the Booker judges. A film adaptation of *The Butcher Boy*, directed by Neil Jordan, was released in 1997. Jordan also directed the 2005 adaptation of *Breakfast on Pluto*. *The Butcher Boy* was also adapted by McCabe for the stage, under the title *Frank Pig Says Hello* and was first performed at the Dublin Theatre Festival in 1992. In 1999 he published the collection of short stories *Mondo Desperado*. He has published five novels in the 2000s: *Emerald Gems of Ireland* (2001), *Call Me the Breeze* (2003), *Winterwood* (2006), which won the Hughes & Hughes/*Irish Independent* novel of the year, *The Holy City* (2009) and *The Stray Sod Country* (2010). McCabe's fiction is renowned for its mixture of violent characters and darkly comic scenarios set against the backdrop of the Troubles in Northern Ireland.

Tom McCarthy was born in 1969 in London. His schooling was at Dulwich College in south London, and he studied English Literature at New College, Oxford. After university he spent time working in Prague, Berlin and Amsterdam. His first novel, *Remainder*, was published in 2005 by a small French publisher, Metronome Press, having been rejected by numerous mainstream British publishers. His second novel, *Men in Space* (2007), was published by the independent publisher Alma Books. His third novel, *C* (2010), was published by Vintage and long-listed for the Booker Prize. McCarthy has also published critical work, including *Tintin and the Secret of Literature* (2006). His work with the philosopher Simon Critchley through their International Necronautical Society (http://www.necronauts.org/), which published its first manifesto in 1999 in the *Times* asserting its central aim to 'bring death out into the world', explores the relation between philosophy, the art world and experiment in writing.

Ian McEwan was born in Aldershot, Hampshire, into an army family in 1948. He spent much of his childhood until he was twelve abroad. He graduated from the University of Sussex in English Literature in 1970, and went on to be one of the first students to graduate from the MA in Creative Writing at the University of East Anglia. His first collection of short stories, *First Love, Last Rites*, was published in 1976, followed by another, *In Between the Sheets*, in 1978. His first two novels, *The Cement Garden* (1978) and *The Comfort of Strangers* (1981), were both short and concerned with dark psychological states, perverse relations and violence. His next novel, *The Child in Time* (1987) marked a change in his work, the novel combining political satire with the possibility of redemption, and won the Whitbread Novel Award. McEwan's nine subsequent novels have generally alternated between historical fiction and narratives dealing with very contemporary concerns and situations. They are: *The Innocent* (1990), *Black Dogs* (1992), *Enduring Love* (1997), *Amsterdam* (1998), *Atonement* (2001), *Saturday* (2005), *On Chesil Beach* (2007), *Solar* (2010), *Sweet Tooth* (2012) and *The Children Act* (2014). McEwan has been shortlisted for the Booker Prize six times, winning in 1998 with *Amsterdam*. He has also won many other prizes and awards, and has written screenplays including adaptations of his own work, an oratorio and children's fiction. He was awarded a CBE in 2000.

Jon McGregor was born in 1976 in Bermuda and was brought up in Norwich and Thetford, Norfolk. He studied Media Technology and Production at Bradford University where his first published fiction 'Cinema 100' appeared in the anthology *Five Uneasy Pieces*. After completing his degree he moved to Nottingham, where he lived for a while on a narrow boat. His first novel, *If Nobody Speaks of Remarkable Things*, was published in 2002. It was longlisted for the Booker Prize, and won the Somerset Maugham Prize and the Betty Trask Prize. His second novel, *So Many Ways to Begin*, was published in 2007. In 2010 he was awarded an honorary doctorate from the University of Nottingham and was made an honorary lecturer of their English Department. His third novel, *Even the Dogs* (2013), won the prestigious International Dublin Literary Award.

He has also published several short stories, including the collection *This Isn't the Sort of Thing That Happens to Someone Like You* (2012). He is currently a writer-in-residence for the charity, First Story.

Gautam Malkani was born in Hounslow, London in 1976. His mother was a Ugandan of Indian descent. He studied Social and Political Sciences at Christ's College Cambridge. Since leaving university he has a pursued a successful career as a journalist working primarily for the *Financial Times* since 1998 both in London and in their Washington bureau. He has worked on the *Financial Times'* Business Life section and as an associate editor for their Weekend Magazine. In 2006 his only novel to date, *Londonstani*, was published by Fourth Estate, a novel about youth subcultures in West London. He has also had work published in the *The New York Times*, *Prospect*, and *Time Out*.

Born in 1952 in Derbyshire, **Hilary Mantel** studied law at the LSE and the University of Sheffield, and then worked as a social worker. Mantel lived in Botswana and Saudi Arabia as a result of her husband's work as a geologist, returning to the UK in the mid-1980s. Her first novel, *Every Day Is Mother's Day*, was published in 1985. This was followed the next year by a sequel, *Vacant Possession*, both of which show Mantel's taut style, its wit, social satire and bleak comedy. *Eight Months on Ghazzah Street*, set in Saudi Arabia, was published in 1988. *Fludd* followed in 1989. Mantel won numerous prizes for these early novels, including the Winifred Holtby Memorial Prize, the Cheltenham Prize and the Southern Arts Literature Prize for the latter novel. In 1992 Mantel published *A Place of Greater Safety*, her extraordinary fictional account of the French Revolution, seen through the eyes of its three architects, Robespierre, Desmoulins and Danton. This was followed by *A Change of Climate* (1994), *An Experiment in Love* (1995) and *The Giant O'Brien* (1998). *Beyond Black* (2005) is the story of a woman, Alison Hart, living in the south east of London in the 1990s and apparently in contact with the dead. Such intersections of those things that are normally assumed divided between different temporalities occur in much of her work. Fittingly the figure of haunting is central to her work, as is clear in her memoir *Giving Up The Ghost* (2003), which explores the legacy of her background and experiences for her fiction – including her family's Catholic faith, her estrangement from her father and her childlessness. Her historical novels *Wolf Hall* (2009) and *Bring Up The Bodies* (2012) – the first two novels in a planned trilogy centred around the sixteenth-century lawyer and courtier Thomas Cromwell – have both been awarded the Booker Prize, as well as numerous others, and have been adapted for television and theatre. Her short story collection *The Assassination of Margaret Thatcher* was published in 2014.

Alan Moore was born in Northampton, where he still lives, in 1953. Moore began writing comics for various independent outlets in the late 1970s before progressing to writing serials for British comics, such as *Warrior*, in which *V for Vendetta* (1982–9; collected 1990) first appeared, and *2000AD*, for which perhaps his best work was *The Ballad of Halo Jones* (1984–6; first collected 1991), the story of a fiftieth-century mall rat who manages to find her way into the wider galaxy, gaining a political education in the process. Moore spearheaded the British invasion of American comics and made his reputation through his 1984–7 run on *Swamp Thing*, which was later credited by Neil Gaiman as inspiring him to write his own comics. This was followed by *Watchmen* (1986–7; collected 1987), illustrated by Dave Gibbons, a ground-breaking story of superheroes with very human problems set in the context of post-Vietnam America. The completion of the dystopian *V for Vendetta*, which had been interrupted when *Warrior* closed down, compounded his status. From the late 1980s onwards, Moore started to consciously step back from the limelight, concentrating on writing for independent outlets again and producing work such as *From Hell* (1989–96; collected 1999) a retelling of the Jack the Ripper story, the sexually explicit *Lost Girls* (1991–2006) and *The League of Extraordinary Gentlemen* (1999–2012). His novel, *Voice of the Fire*, was first published in the mid-1990s but did not appear in a commercial edition until 2004. It is set in Northampton over the period of several millennia. In 2014, the *Guardian* newspaper reported that Moore had finished the first draft, over a million words long, of a novel, provisionally entitled *Jerusalem*, which is set once more in Northampton.

Born in Ossett, West Yorkshire, in 1967, **David Peace** went to Manchester Polytechnic, and in 1991 left the UK to teach English in Istanbul. Between 1994 and 2009 he lived in Tokyo where he also taught English. His first novel, *Nineteen Seventy-Four* (1999), was the first in the Red Riding Quartet series of novels, consisting of this novel and *Nineteen Seventy-Seven* (2000), *Nineteen Eighty* (2001) and *Nineteen Eighty-Three* (2002). The novels are all set in West Yorkshire, and are narrated by various characters involved in the murky relations between the West Yorkshire police and the criminal world. Central to the middle two novels are the crimes of and hunt for the Yorkshire Ripper. Peace's treatment of the Ripper set the pattern for his subsequent work, all of it dealing with specific historical periods, the real events and people (often renamed) involved in them intertwined with fictional characters and events. All of Peace's novels are concerned with the dark underside of social and political life, and are dominated by crime, violence and conspiracy. Peace's next two novels, *GB84* (2004), for which he won the James Tait Black Memorial Award, and *The Damned Utd* (2006) were about the 1984/5 miners' strike and Brian Clough's time at the football club Leeds Utd in 1974 respectively. *Tokyo Year Zero* (2007) and *Occupied City* (2009) returned to the haunted, repetitive, elliptical lyricism of the Red Riding Quartet to depict the immediate post-war devastation of Tokyo. His most recent novel, *Red or Dead* (2013), again uses this form to investigate the fifteen years at Liverpool Football Club of manager Bill Shankly. Overall, Peace's work has returned repeatedly to questions of politics – in the Britain of the 1970s and 1980s and in post-war Tokyo – questions of where power is and how it works, of its darkness and violence. The Red Riding Quartet was adapted as a three-part series for TV in 2009, and *The Damned Utd* was made into a film in the same year. Peace was named by Granta as one of their Best of Young British Novelists in 2003.

Ali Smith was born in Inverness, Scotland, in 1962. She studied at the University of Aberdeen, and Newnham College, Cambridge, where she began a PhD. She lectured at the University of Strathclyde, before becoming ill. Following that she began to write, first publishing short stories collected as *Free Love and Other Stories* (1995) and then *Other Stories and Other Stories* (1999). Her first novel, *Like*, was published in 1997 and the second, *Hotel World*, was published in 2001 and shortlisted for numerous prizes, winning the inaugural Scottish Arts Council Book of the Year Award. She has published four more novels – *The Accidental* (2005), *Girl Meets Boy* (2007), *There But For The* (2011) and *How To Be Both* (2014) – and two more collections of short stories. Smith's work is formally inventive, often narrated from a number of positions, and often suggestive of life and experience as mysterious, with explanations just outside the field of vision. A number of her works have used their formal explorations to think about the identities and possibilities open to women and about the construction of sexuality, and in this she has been seen as reviving and rethinking the experiment of Virginia Woolf. In 2013 Smith published a series of lectures given by her at Oxford University in the previous year, and these, like Woolf's essays, combine literary critical work with fictional scenarios and voices.

Zadie Smith was born in the London Borough of Brent in 1975. She went to Hampstead Comprehensive School before studying English Literature at

Cambridge. Her first novel, *White Teeth* (2000), finished during the final year of her degree, was the subject of much anticipation, having been auctioned before completion. On publication, it quickly became a bestseller and was critically praised, winning many awards including the James Tait Black Memorial Prize and the Commonwealth Writers First Book Prize. A long, complex but often comic tale of post-war London, featuring a cast of characters from different ethnic and class backgrounds, the novel was at first viewed in some quarters as celebrating a multicultural London before further consideration and the author's own statements suggested that it was expressing a more nuanced viewpoint. *White Teeth* was adapted for television in 2002, the same year as Smith's second novel, *The Autograph Man* was published to mixed reviews. During the academic year 2002–3, Smith studied at Harvard and her third novel, the Orange Prize winning *On Beauty* (2005) is set mainly in the Greater Boston area. She published a collection of essays, *Changing My Mind*, in 2009. After teaching at the Columbia University School of the Arts, Smith took up a permanent post at New York University in 2010. Her fourth novel, *NW* (2012), is set in Kilburn and follows the trajectories of several characters who grew up in the same housing estate. It is more brutal than *White Teeth* but also evokes a modernist temporality and a sense, at least, of what is at stake in thinking about the future rather than the past. Press reports in 2013 suggested that Smith's next novel would be a work of science fiction, and a futuristic short story 'Meet the President' was published by the *New Yorker* in August of that year. Since then, she has published a novella, *The Embassy of Cambodia* (2013) and her short story 'Miss Adele Amidst the Corsets' (2014) was shortlisted for the BBC National Short Story Prize.

Alex Wheatle was born in 1963 to Jamaican parents. He spent much of his childhood in a children's home in Surrey. At the age of fourteen he left the home to live in a hostel in Brixton. He was a founder member of the Crucial Rocker Sound System at the age of 16, taking the name Yardman Irie for his DJ sets, and writing lyrics about everyday Brixton life. The Brixton riots happened in 1981 and Wheatle was involved, resulting in him serving a three-month prison sentence. It was in prison that he read many of the authors that would influence his own writing: Chester Himes, C.L.R. James, John Steinbeck and Richard Wright. He performed on the performance poetry circuit in the early 1990s as The Brixton Bard. His first novel, *Brixton Rock*, was published in 1999. This was followed by *East of Acre Lane* (2001), which includes descriptions of the Brixton Riots of 1981, and received the London Arts Board New Writers Award. He has also contributed to BBC Radio programmes about the riots. In 2008 he was awarded an MBE in the Queen's Birthday Honours for services to literature. His latest novel to date, *Brenton Brown*, was published in 2011 and is a sequel to *Brixton Rock*. His other novels are *The Seven Sisters* (2002), *Checkers* (2003), written with Mark Parham, *Island Songs* (2005), which is a prequel to *East of Acre Lane*, and *The Dirty South* (2008), which is a sequel to the same novel. He currently lives in London, and visits various institutions working with creative writing groups.

Index

7/7 London bombings 58, 63, 117, 126, 238
9/11 terrorist attacks
   and British Asian writing 126–40
   and the end of postmodernism 14
   and hybrid identities 118–19
   and *Incendiary* (Cleave, 2005) 135–7
   'Last Days of Mohammad Atta, The' (Amis, 2006) 129–31
   and *Londonstani* (Malkani) 63
   and multiculturalism 224
   and *Netherland* (O'Neill) 177
   and postcolonial literature 117–18, 126–9
   referenced directly in literature 7
   and *Saturday* (McEwan, 2005) 131–5
   as significant event 3, 5–6
   and subcultures 58
   and Zadie Smith's work 184–5

Aboulela, Leila 127, 137–8, 236, 269
Absolute Beginners (MacInnes, 1959) 54, 70, 75
Accidental, The (Smith, 2005) 17, 189–91
actuality and reality 150, 158
Adelson, Leslie A. 227
aesthetics 40–2, 54, 104
Afghanistan 58, 117
African-Caribbean identities 69–72, 75
Agamben, Giorgio 10–12
Akbar, Arifa 238
Alberto Angelo (Johnson, 1964) 180
Ali, Amir 225–6
Ali, Monica
   biography 269
   Brick Lane (2003) 44, 58, 116, 125, 236
   media-friendly 'authenticity' 46
   and the South Asian diaspora 45
   Untold Story (2011) 27
Allen, Richard 65, 74
Allen, Woody 73
All Hail the Puritans (Blincoe and Thorne, 2001) 15

Alma Books 50
Alter, Robert 199
altermodernism 16
Alzheimer's disease 103, 105, 110 n.1
Amis, Martin
   on 9/11 14, 126
   biography 270
   'Last Days of Mohammad Atta, The' (2006) 127–31
   and the literary establishment 15
   Money: A Suicide Note (1984) 129, 180
   Yellow Dog (2003) 110 n.1
anarchism 78 n.27
anti-heroes
   in *Sheepshagger* (Griffiths) 34
   in *Tainted Love* (Home) 74
anti-multiculturalism 226
Antinomies of Realism, The (Jameson, 2013) 10
anti-rebels 210–11
aphasia 86
Appadurai, Arjun 118, 130
Appiah, K. Anthony 128
archaeology 93
Arthur and George (Barnes, 2005) 183, 207–8, 210, 212
artificiality 180–1, 183, 192
'Art of Fiction, The' (James, 1884) 186
Asia
   Asian British writing 123–5
   Asian youth subcultures 53, 60–4
   South Asian diaspora 45–50
Aslam, Nadeem 119, 127, 137–8, 269–70
asylum seekers 122, 138, 139
atheism 90
Atonement (McEwan, 2001) 19, 86, 159–63, 179–81, 201–2, 206, 207, 211
Augé, Marc 12
authenticity
   media-friendly multicultural 'authenticity' 46

and metafiction 50
and performance 27
and subcultures 62, 64, 65, 69–70
Author, Author (Lodge, 2004) 182
author self-insertion into the text 180
autism spectrum 85
autobiography 193–4
Autograph Man, The (Smith, 2002) 199
avant-garde writing 72
Aw, Tash 125

Badiou, Alain 27
Bagnall, Nicholas 38
Baileys Prize, *see* Orange Prize
Baker, Ernest 145–6
Balasubramanyam, Rajeev 225
Ballard, J.G. 28, 165
  Kingdom Come (2006) 59
  Millennium People (2003) 7
banking crisis 4
Banks, Iain 35–6
Barker, Nicola
  Behindlings (2002) 59
  postmodernism and grounded ethics 17
Barker, Pat 7
Barnes, Julian
  Arthur and George (2005) 183, 207–8, 210, 212
  Flaubert's Parrot (1984) 208
  History of the World in 10½ Chapters, A (1989) 180, 183
  and the literary establishment 15
  and modernism 19
  narrative regeneration 216
  Sense of an Ending, The (2011) 183, 212
Barthes, Roland
  'concrete reality' 164, 166
  and David Peace's work 169
  on Flaubert 166
  'Reality Effect, The' 147–8, 150–2, 159
  Writing Degree Zero (1953) 155
Bauman, Zygmunt 9
beauty and postmodernism 19
Beckett, Samuel 86
Behindlings (Barker, 2002) 59
Be Near Me (O'Hagan, 2006) 27
Bentley, Nick 75, 119, 184
Berhman, Mary 201
Berlin Wall, fall of 83, 229

Bernard, André 208
Bérubé, Michael 200, 205, 208
Bible 36
Bichat, Marie François Xavier 89
bildungsroman narratives 54, 58–9, 74, 215
Billy Liar (Waterhouse, 1959) 54
Billy Lynn's Long Halftime Walk (Fountain, 2012) 206
biography 193–4, 210
biological reductionism 104
Birdsong (Faulks, 1993) 86
Birmingham School (CCCS) 54, 60, 68, 77
Black, Shameem 213–14
Black American subcultures 63
Black British writing 120–3
Blair government 1, 3–4, 29, 36, 224, 229
Blake, William 34, 36
Blincoe, Nicholas 15, 16
BNP (British National Party) 128
body–mind separation 85, 102
Bogue, Ronald 47
Bone China (Tearne, 2008) 116
Booker prize, *see* Man Booker prize
Borck, Cornelius 98
Bourdieu, Pierre 56
Bourriaud, Nicholas 16
Boxall, Peter 8–9, 101, 103–4, 160
Boyle, Danny 54
Bradbury, Malcolm 176
Bradford, Richard 116, 124, 200
Bradley, Arthur 135
Bradshaw Variations, The (Cusk, 2009) 27
brain-imaging techniques 97
Brave New World (Huxley, 1932) 211, 213, 214
Brick Lane (Ali, 2003) 44, 58, 116, 125, 236
Bring On the Books For Everybody (Collins, 2010) 146
Bring Up The Bodies (Mantel, 2012) 155–7, 163, 206–7
Brooker, Joseph 42
Brown government 2, 4
Buddha of Suburbia, The (Kureishi, 1990) 54
Bunker Man (McLean, 1998) 34
Burnside, John 193
Burrow, Colin 157, 163
Bush, George (President) 83, 84

Bush, George W. (President) 3
Butler, Judith 55
Byatt, A. S.
   Angels and Insects (1992) 209
   Biographer's Tale, The (2000) 210
   biography 270–1
   Children's Book, The (2009) 208–9, 210
   and the literary establishment 15
   Possession (1990) 208, 209, 210
By the Sea (Gurnah, 2001) 122

C (McCarthy, 2010) 192–3
Café Cyprus (Kara, 2010) 229
Cain's Book (Trocchi, 1960) 76
Call Me the Breeze (McCabe, 2003) 30–4
Cameron government 29, 223
campus novels 85
Canongate 50
capitalism
   and cosmopolitanism 128
   and literacy criticism 12–13
   and postmodernism 16
   and *Saturday* (McEwan) 133–4
   and the temporal crisis 10
   and 'urban tribes' 56
Carey, Peter 187
Caribbean culture 66, 68
Carter, Angela 15
Carter Wood, John 228
Chabon, Michael 206
Chadha, Gurinder 45
Charcot, Jean-Martin 95
Charles, Alec 169
Cheah, Pheng 129
Cheesman, Tom 227
chemical generation 36
Chicago School 54
chicken tikka multiculturalism 224–5
Children's Book, The (Byatt, 2009) 208–9, 210
children's literature 209
Childs, Elaine 234
Childs, Peter 174
Choudhury, Suparna 106
Christianity 139
Chronicles of Narnia (Lewis, 1950–6) 215
cinema and film
   9/11 prefigured by American disaster movies 6

Damned Utd, The (2006) 29
Go-Between, The (film, Losey, 1970) 151
and the historical novel 145
and postmodernism 14–15
and the South Asian diaspora 45, 49
and subcultures 53
Trainspotting (film, Boyle, 1996) 54
Zelig (Allen, 1983) 73
Clarke, Gary 55
Clarke, John 68
Clarke, Susanna 207
'clash of civilizations' 127, 135, 138–9
class, *see also* working-class culture
   and Asian British writing 124
   in David Peace's work 43
   in *Incendiary* (Cleave, 2005) 135–7
   in *Londonstani* (Malkani) 48–9
   and subcultures 55, 56
   and terrorism 127
Cleave, Chris 127, 135–7, 271
clones 213
Cloud Atlas (Mitchell, 2004) 17, 188
Cockin, Katharine 116
Coe, Jonathan
   Like a Fiery Elephant (2004) 183
   Rain Before It Falls, The (2007) 183
   Rotters' Club, The (2001) 57
   What a Carve Up! (1994) 183
'cognitive revolution' 83–110
Cohen, Phil 55, 68
Coles, Nicholas 140 n.5
Collins, Jim 146
Collins, Michael 67
Collins, Wilkie 207
colonialism 12, 35, 39, *see also* postcolonialism
Color Purple, The (Walker, 1982) 208
commercial success
   of Haddon's *Curious Incident* 207
   Hilary Mantel's work 206
   and the historical novel 145
   and *Londonstani* (Malkani) 44, 50, 63
   and metafiction 50
   Small Island (Levy, 2004) 122
   of Zadie Smith and Monica Ali 46, 63
Commonwealth Writers' Prize 122
communist collapse 16
complicitous critique 18
Complicity (Banks, 1993) 35–6

Concise Companion to Contemporary British Fiction (English, 2006) 116
Conrad, Peter 129
consciousness
  in *Atonement* (McEwan) 86, 159, 160–1
  in 'neuronovels' 88, 89, 90–1, 98, 99–100, 107
  and the Red Riding Quartet (Peace, 1999–2002) 168
  in *Saturday* (McEwan) 158
  and third-person narration 153
  in *Wolf Hall/Bring Up The Bodies* (Mantel) 157, 159, 163–4
constructionist approaches 16
consumer culture
  in *Call Me the Breeze* (McCabe) 33
  and cosmopolitanism 128
  in 'Last Days of Mohammad Atta, The' (Amis) 131
  and literary criticism 12–13
  in *Londonstani* (Malkani) 49
  in *Saturday* (McEwan) 132
  and urban tribes 56
'contemporary', definitions 7–11
Contemporary British Fiction (Bentley, 2008) 119
Contemporary British Novel, The (Tew, 2004) 118
Contemporary British Novelists (Macmillan) 203
Contemporary Centre for Cultural Studies 56, 63
Cook, Robin 224
Cooter, Roger 84
Cortiglia, Carlos 128
cosmopolitanism 116, 122, 124–9, 137, 228
country house novels 179, 201, 211–12, 214
Crace, John 205
creative writing courses 13
crime fiction 42, 45, 166, 215
criminality and deviancy 53, 58, 61, 63, 64, 69, 165–6
critical anthologies 116
critical distance 7–8
critical nostalgia 57
cultural capital 56
cultural privilege 48
Cunningham, Michael 153
Cunningham, Valentine 176

Curious Incident of the Dog in the Night-time, The (Haddon, 2003) 85, 207
Curry Mile, The (Hussain, 2006) 239–41
Cusk, Rachel 27
cyberpunk novels 60
cyphers of the author 180

Dabydeen, David 120, 122, 123, 271
  Molly and the Muslim Stick (2008) 127, 138–40
Damned Utd, The (Peace, 2006) 29, 189
D'Angelo, Kathleen 202
Darwin, Charles 95
de Freitas, Michael (Michael X) 75
de Groot, Jerome 145, 146, 160, 165
Demo (Miller, 2006) 58–9
Deresiewicz, William 199
Derrida, Jacques 10
Desai, Kiran 116
Descartes, René 88, 90, 102
desi/rudeboy subcultures 45, 61, 64, 67, 125
devolved government 20, 29
Diana (Princess of Wales), death of 7–8
diasporic literature
  Loh's chapter 115–40
  South Asian 45, *see also Londonstani* (Malkani, 2006)
digimodernism 16
disenfranchisement 27, 43, 48, 126–7, 129–30
Distant Shore, A (Phillips, 2003) 121–2
domesticity 38, 47
Dostoyevsky's holy fool 30, 33
Double Vision (Barker, 2003) 7
dream sequences 35
Drew, Elizabeth 9
Dubliners, The (Joyce, 1914) 158
Duggan, Mark 53
Dumit, Joseph 97
Dyer, Geoff 201, 211
dystopia 214–15

Eaglestone, Robert 133
Eagleton, Terry 176
Eastern Europe 119–20
East of Acre Lane (Wheatle, 2001) 57, 69–72, 121
Edwards, Caroline 186

Eisner, Will 215
Elias, Amy J. 204
Eliot, George 209, 214
Eliot, T.S. 183, 206
embodiment 102–4, 109–10
Empire Falls (Russo, 2001) 208
Enchantress of Florence, The (Rushdie, 2008) 124
end of history 16
Eng, Tan Twan 125
English, James F. 116, 202
Enlightenment 12
epistolary style 31, 127, 135, 208
Equality Act (2010) 2
Erber, Pedro 11–12
erotica 215
ethical functions 42
ethical relativism 16
ethnic minorities 59, 119, 225
European Enlightenment 132
European Union 2
Evans, Gareth 39
Even the Dogs (McGregor, 2010) 185–8
experimental vs. realistic writing 19, 146, 149, 173–9, 181–95, 206

Faber 29
faith and spirituality 90, 110 n.5, 135
fantasy
    and cultural hybridity 234
    Patrick McCabe and the social fantastic 30
    and psychoanalysis 6–7
Farmer, Andrew 4
Faulks, Sebastian
    biography 271–2
    Birdsong (1993) 86
    Human Traces (2005) 85, 86, 94–9, 105–7
fictionality 164–70
film and cinema
    9/11 prefigured by American disaster movies 6
    Damned Utd, The (2006) 29
    Go-Between, The (film, Losey, 1970) 151
    and the historical novel 145
    and postmodernism 14–15
    and the South Asian diaspora 45, 49
    and subcultures 53

Trainspotting (film, Boyle, 1996) 54
Zelig (film, Allen, 1983) 73
financial crisis (2007–8) 4–5
Financial Times 47
Finney, Brian 201, 202
first person narratives 61–2, 85, 100–1, 155–6, 163, 182, 186, 188
Fjorde, Jasper 207
Flaubert, Gustav 147–8, 151, 152, 166, 177
Flaubert's Parrot (Barnes, 1984) 208
fMRI (Functional magnetic resonance imaging) 98
Forster, E.M. 19, 184–5, 199
Fortier, Anne-Marie 226
Foucault, Michel 89, 106
Fountain, Ben 206
Fourth Estate 44
Fowles, John 145, 162, 180
fragmentation 32, 57
Frankenstein (Shelley, 1818) 214
Franklin, Ruth 200
free indirect style 89, 101, 190
French Lieutenant's Woman, The (Fowles, 1969) 145, 162, 180
Freud, Sigmund 93, 95–6, 97
Friction (Stretch, 2008) 59
From Hell (Moore, 1989–96) 215
Fukuyama, Francis 16
fundamentalism 118, 132, 135, 138, 233, 238
Fury (Rushdie, 2001) 124

Gabriel's Gift (Kureishi, 2001) 58
Gaedtke, Andrew 100
Gaiman, Neil 207, 214
gangs 53, 60
Gąsiorek, Andrzej 174, 177, 179, 185
gay subcultures 75
GB84 (Peace, 2004) 28, 29–30, 39, 40–4, 188–9
Gee, Maggie 117
Gelder, Ken 56, 65
gender
    male dysfunctional behaviour 34–5
    masculinity 30, 31–3, 47, 48
    Muslim immigrant women 127, 137–8
    and *Sheepshagger* (Griffiths) 35
    women and the historical novel 146

genre
    and the historical novel 145–6
    Weston's chapter 173–95
    works outside any genre 36
geopolitics 139
Ghost Milk (Sinclair, 2011) 194
Gift of Rain, The (Eng, 2007) 125
Gilman, Sander 95
Gilmore, John 120
Gilroy, Paul 117–18, 122–3, 140 n.1
Glass Room, The (Mawer, 2009) 188
globalization
    and American hegemony 214
    Erber on 12
    and fundamentalism 138
    'global turn' 203
    and masculinity 32
    and postcolonialism 116, 128
    and regional Britain 28–9
    and subcultures 62, 63
    transnational literary scene 203
    working-class marginalization 136
Go-Between, The (film, Losey, 1970) 151
Go-Between, The (Hartley, 1953) 150, 201
Golding, William 63
Good of the Novel, The (McIlvanney and Ryan, 2011) 178, 195
gothic novels 165, 207, 208
Graham, James 28, 44, 46, 48
grammar
    in *Londonstani* (Malkani) 46
    preterite verbal constructions 37, 155
    in *Sheepshagger* (Griffiths) 37
    unprecursed pronouns 156
    in *Wolf Hall*/*Bring Up the Bodies* 156
Granta 29, 124, 174
graphic novels 215–16
Gray, J.A. 199
Gray, John 240
Gregory, Philippa 206
Griffiths, Niall
    biography 272
    Grits (2000) 28, 34, 59
    and Literary London 43
    on *Londonstani* (Malkani) 46
    Sheepshagger (2001) 27, 34–40
    themes 27, 34–40
Guardian 45, 63, 110 n.5, 149, 151, 155, 157
Gunesekera, Romesh 123

Gupta, Sunetra 123
Gurnah, Abdulrazak 122

Hackney, That Rose-Red Empire (Sinclair, 2009) 194
Haddon, Mark 85, 207
Half a Life (Naipaul, 2001) 123–4
Hall, Steven 50
Handbook to Literature, A (Holman and Harmon, 1965) 204
Harlot's Progress, A (Dabydeen, 2000) 122
Harmon, William 204
Harmony Silk Factory, The (Aw, 2005) 125
Harris, Jane 16
Harry Potter 207, 215
Hart, Matthew 165, 188–9
Hartley, L. P. 150, 152, 201
Harvey, Samantha 110 n.1
Harwood, John 16
hauntology 165
Hayes, M. Hunter 202
Head, Dominic 177
Hebdige, Dick 55
Hedgecock, Andy 28
hegemony 193, 214
Heilmann, Ann 16
Henderson, Philip 9
Hensher, Philip 110 n.1
hesitation 176–8, 180
'hindsight' vs. 'insight' 8, 13
hippy subcultures 57–8, 73
history
    and Black British writing 122
    in David Peace's work 42
    'hidden history' 165
    historical fact merged with fiction 73–4, 76–7
    historical fiction 145–70, 179
    'historical importance' 187
    historical metanarrative 183
    historiographic metafiction 15, 74, 146
    neo-Victorian tales 207–10
    prominence of neo-historical fiction 16
    subcultures of the past 57
    'traditional' narrative pleasures 207
    Wilson's chapter on historical fiction 145–70
History of the World in 10½ Chapters, A (Barnes, 1989) 180, 183

Hodd (Thorpe, 2009) 188
Hodkinson, Paul 56
Holcombe, Garan 27, 28, 29
Hollinghurst, Alan 19, 182
Holman, C. Hugh 204
Home, Stewart 57, 72–7, 272–3
Home Truths: Fictions of the South Asian Diaspora in Britain (Nasta, 2002) 123
homophobia 48–9
hooks, bell 15
Hotel World (Smith, 2001) 17, 189
Hounslow 44–50
Hours, The (Cunningham, 1998) 153–4
Howards End (Forster, 1910) 19, 184–5, 199
Human Punk (King, 2000) 64–5
Human Traces (Faulks, 2005) 85, 86, 94–9, 105–7
Huntington's Disease 92, 102
Huq, Rupa 53, 56
Hussain, Zahid 239–41
Hussein, Aamer 123
Husserl, Edmund 101
Hutcheon, Linda 18, 74
Huxley, Aldous 211, 213, 214
hybridity
    cultural hybridity 228, 234
    hybrid identities in Britain 118–19
    and the South Asian diaspora 45
'hypermodernism' 9
hyperrealism 121, 182
hysteria 95–6

IC3: The Penguin Book of New Black Writing in Britain (Newland and Sesay, 2001) 120–1
identity
    in *Call Me the Breeze* (McCabe) 31–3
    and the diaspora 116
    and neuroscience 84
    polycentric identities 227
    and postmodernism 36
    sexual identity 86
    and the South Asian diaspora 45
    subcultural identity 55, 58–9
    transgressive identity 30, 32, 39
    tribal identity 55
If Nobody Speaks of Remarkable Things (McGregor, 2002) 185–7

immigration 117–19, 121–4, 127, 177, 231–5, 240
Impressionism 153–4
Impressionist, The (Kunzru, 2003) 124
Incendiary (Cleave, 2005) 127, 135–7
inequality, rising 4–5, 36
Infinite Jest (Wallace, 1996) 210
Ingersoll, Earl G. 201
Inheritance of Loss, The (Desai, 2006) 116
innovation and invention 182–3, 193–4, *see also* experimental vs. realistic writing
'insight' vs. 'hindsight' 8, 13
intergenerational issues 47, 49, 239
interiority 154–5, 158
intertextuality 19, 35, 158, 207
Iraq war 3–4, 29, 58, 99, 102, 117, 158, 182, 189
Irish literature 28, 30–4, 119, 177
ironic distance 67, 76–7
Ishiguro, Kazuo
    biography 273
    narrative regeneration 216
    Never Let Me Go (2005) 59, 211, 212–13, 214–15
    Nocturnes (2010) 211
    Remains of the Day, The (1989) 211, 213
    return to sincerity 211–12
    When We Were Orphans (2000) 207, 211, 213
Islamophobia 117–18, 127, 134, 138, 224

Jack, Ian 174
Jackson, John Hughlings 97
James, David 19, 182–3
James, Henry 153–4, 182, 186
Jameson, Frederic 10, 15, 16, 170 n.1
James Tait Black Memorial Prize 29
Japan 17
Jay, Paul 200, 205–6
Jencks, Charles 14
Johnson, B. S. 180
Jonathan Strange & Mr Norrell (Clarke, 2004) 207
Jones, Cecily 120
Jones, Owen 67
Josipovici, Gabriel 147, 148–9, 150, 152, 169
Journal of Postcolonial Writing 124

Joyce, James 155, 157, 205, 206
   Dubliners, The (1914) 158
   Ulysses (1922) 158, 163–4

Kafka, Franz 200
Kakutani, Michiko 213
Kara, Yadé 229
Karl, Frederick Robert 9
Kartography (Shamsie, 2002) 116
Kear, Adrian 7–8
Keen, Susan 202
Keen, Suzanne 145
Kehlmann, Daniel 229
Kelly, Adam 16
Kelman, James 119
Kennedy, A. L. 17, 34
Kermode, Frank 200
King, John 273–4
   England Away (1999) 64
   Football Factory, The (1997) 64
   Headhunters (1998) 64
   Human Punk (2000) 64–5
   Skinheads (2008) 57–8, 64–9
Kingdom Come (Ballard, 2006) 59
Kirby, Alan 16
Kongslien, Ingeborg 227
Kowaleski Wallace, Elizabeth 133
Kraken (Miéville, 2010) 60
Kray twins 73
Kunzru, Hari
   Impressionist, The (2003) 124
   My Revolutions (2007) 124
   postmodernism and grounded ethics 17
   Transmission (2004) 124
Kureishi, Hanif
   and Asian British writing 123
   Buddha of Suburbia, The (1990) 54
   Gabriel's Gift (2001) 58
   and the South Asian diaspora 45

Lacan, Jacques 6
Laclau, Ernesto 66
Lane, Richard J. 119
language
   in *Human Traces* 96
   in *Londonstani* (Malkani) 45, 46, 47–8, 61–2, 125
   in *Saturday* (McEwan) 98
   and Scottish/Welsh/Irish literature 119
   text-speak 46
   White Teeth (Smith, 2000) 121
La Rochelle (Nath, 2010) 85
'Last Days of Mohammad Atta, The' (Amis, 2006) 127, 129–31
Lawrence, D.H. 34
Lawson Welsh, Sarah 227
Lazarus, Neil 120, 140 n.2
Lea, Daniel 27
League of Extraordinary Gentlemen, The (Moore, 1999) 215
Leavis, F.R. 216
Leitkultur ('leading' or 'dominant' culture) 224, 226
Lennon, John 73, 74–5
Levinas, Emmanuel 163
Levy, Andrea 122
Lewis, C.S. 215
Lewycka, Marina 119
liberalism 103, 185, 240
Lie About My Father, A (Burnside, 2006) 193
Light of Day (Swift, 2003) 207
Like a Fiery Elephant (Coe, 2004) 183
Line of Beauty, The (Hollinghurst, 2004) 19, 182
Lipovetsky, Gilles 9
'liquid modernity' 9
literary culture
   British vs. international 201–2
   and David Peace 29
   and the historical novel 145
   popularization of literary novels 146
   and Stewart Home 74
   and transnational literature 116–17, 121
   White Teeth (Smith, 2000) 121
   Zadie Smith on 174
Lit-lit novels 146
Litt, Toby 17
Living Nowhere (Burnside, 2003) 193–4
Llewellyn, Mark 16
Lockwood, Dean 165
Lodge, David 85, 100, 173, 174–6, 178, 180
   Author, Author (2004) 182
London
   7/7 London bombings 58, 63, 117, 126, 238
   and Asian British writing 124

Brick Lane (Ali, 2003) 44, 58, 116, 125, 236
East of Acre Lane (Wheatle, 2001) 57, 69–72, 121
Londonstani (Malkani, 2006) 28, 44–50, 58, 60–4, 71, 125
riots 53, 70–2
Tainted Love (Home, 2005) 72–7
White Teeth (Smith, 2000) 231–2
London literary culture 43
Londonstani (Malkani, 2006) 28, 44–50, 58, 60–4, 71, 125
Long Song, The (Levy, 2010) 122
López, José 16, 17, 176
Lord of the Flies (Golding, 1954) 63
Lord of the Rings (Tolkein, 1937–49) 215
Lost Girls (Moore, 1991–2) 215
Low, Gail 122
Luckhurst, Roger 86
Luetzow, Gunnar 229
Lustig, T. J. 110 n.3
Lynch, David 31
Lyotard, Jean-François 15
lyric essays 194–5

MacInnes, Colin 54, 70, 72–7
MacLeod, Ken 60
Macmillan 203
MacPhee, Graham 115, 138
Maffesoli, Michel 55–6, 77
magical realism 97, 127, 138–40, 149
Magic Seeds (Naipaul, 2004) 123–4
Malabou, Catherine 86
Malaysian writing 125
male dysfunctional behaviour 34–5
Malkani, Gautam
  biography 276
  and globalization 29
  Londonstani (2006) 28, 44–50, 58, 60–4, 71, 125
  themes 28
Maltz, Diana 209
Man Booker prize
  Accidental, The (Smith, 2005) 189
  Bring Up The Bodies (Mantel, 2012) 155
  C (McCarthy, 2010) 192
  vs. commercial success 207
  Gift of Rain, The (Eng, 2007) 125
  Ian McEwan 149

Inheritance of Loss, The (Desai, 2006) 116
Line of Beauty, The (Hollinghurst, 2004) 19
Netherland (O'Neill, 2008) 177
Remains of the Day, The (Ishiguro, 1989) 211
Sense of an Ending, The (Barnes, 2011) 186, 212
True History of the Kelly Gang, The (Carey, 1987) 186–7
Wolf Hall (Mantel, 2009) 155, 206
Manchester subcultures 59–60
Mantel, Hilary
  American reception of 206–7
  biography 276–7
  Bring Up The Bodies (2012) 155–7, 163, 206–7
  and the prominence of neo-historical fiction 16, 154–7, 163–4
  Wolf Hall (2009) 154–7, 163–4, 188, 206–7
Manz, Stefan 224
Maps for Lost Lovers (Aslam, 2004) 119, 127, 137–8
Marcus, Laura 202
marginalized groups, *see also* subcultures
  and Black British writing 122
  and the 'chain of equivalence' 66
  and the diaspora 118
  economic marginalization 136, *see also* working-class culture
  and postmodernism 16
Marxism 55–6, 128
masculinity 30, 31–3, 47, 48
Mason, Wyatt 199
Master, The (Tóibín, 2004) 153, 154, 182
Matrix, The (film, Andy and Lana [Larry] Wachovski, 1999) 6
Matz, Jesse 152–3
Mawer, Simon 188
McCabe, Colin 200
McCabe, Patrick 274
  Call Me the Breeze (2003) 30–4
  and globalization 29
McCarthy, Tom
  in America 205
  biography 274–5
  C (2010) 192–3

postmodernism and grounded ethics 17
Remainder (2005) 50, 85, 86, 108–10, 173, 191–2
McCrum, Robert 44
McEwan, Ian
  on 9/11 126, 168
  American reception of 201–2
  Atonement (2001) 19, 86, 159–63, 179–81, 201–2, 206, 207, 211
  biography 275
  On Chesil Beach (2007) 85
  and fictionality 166
  and generic discontinuity 179–83
  and the literary establishment 15
  'Literature, Science and Human Nature' (2005) 107
  and modernism 19, 161, 179–80, 182–3, 202
  narrative regeneration 216
  and postmodernism 179, 183, 207, 214
  and the 'reality effect' 149–52, 157–8, 159–63
  Saturday (2005) 7, 19, 85–107, 109–10, 127–9, 131–5, 158–9, 181–2
  and Zadie Smith 179, 185, 200
McGivering, Jill 238
McGregor, Jon
  biography 275–6
  Even the Dogs (2010) 185–6
  If Nobody Speaks of Remarkable Things (2002) 185–6
  So Many Ways to Begin (2006) 185–7
McIlvanney, Liam 178, 195
McLean, Duncan
  Bunker Man (1998) 34
  and genre 36
McLeod, John 120
McNeill, Dougal 42
media, and subcultures 56, 63, 64–5
memoirs 193–4
memory 42, 50, 87, 183
Mengham, Rod 195
Merkel, Angela 223
Merleau-Ponty, Maurice 102
Merritt, Stephanie 200, 228
metafiction
  and *The Accidental* (Smith) 190
  and A.S. Byatt 208, 210
  and *Atonement* (McEwan) 19, 182, 207

historiographic metafiction 15, 74, 146
  and postmodernism 17, 174
  and *The Raw Shark Texts* (Hall) 50
  and *Remainder* (McCarthy) 50
metamodernism 9, 16, 204
metaphor
  in David Peace's work 165
  in *Saturday* (McEwan) 90, 92–3
Metronome 50
Middlemarch (Eliot, 1871) 209
Midnight's Children (Rushdie, 1981) 145
Miéville, China
  Kraken (2010) 60
  New Weird genre 215
  Un Lun Dun (2007) 214
migration 117–19, 121–4, 127, 177, 231–5, 240
Millennium celebrations 2000 1
Millennium People (Ballard, 2003) 7
Miller, Alison 58–9
Minaret (Aboulela, 2005) 127, 137–8, 236
Miss Herbert (Thirlwell, 2007) 147
Mitchell, David
  Cloud Atlas (2004) 17, 188
  Number9Dream (2001) 17
  postmodernism and grounded ethics 17
modernism, *see also* postmodernism
  and American reception of British literature 203–5, 209–10
  free indirect style 89, 101, 190
  vs. globalism 206
  and historical fiction 145, 147, 152–3
  and Ian McEwan 19, 161, 179–80, 182–3, 202
  and Ishiguro 213–14
  modernist narrative techniques (return to) 17, 19–20, 152–3, 161, 182–3
  vs. postmodernist experimentation 17, 205
Molly and the Muslim Stick (Dabydeen, 2008) 127, 138–40
Money: A Suicide Note (Amis, 1984) 129, 180
Moore, Alan 215–16, 277
moral panic 53
Morrison, Jago 28–9, 116
Mouffe, Chantal 66

Mourning Diana: Nation, Culture and the Performance of Grief (Kear and Steinberg, 2002) 7–8
Mrs Dalloway (Woolf, 1925) 90, 153, 158, 182
Muggleton, David 55
Müller-Wood, Anja 228
multiculturalism
    and Asian British writing 124
    and Islamophobia 118
    in *Londonstani* (Malkani) 44
    Tancke's chapter 223–41
    in Zadie Smith's work 28, 44–5, 184
murder 165–6
Murphy, Neil 123
music 56, 63, 70–1, 103
My Revolutions (Kunzru, 2007) 124

Nabokov, Vladimir 150
Naipaul, V. S. 123–4
Nairn, Tom 203
Namjoshi, Suniti 45
narrative techniques
    anonymous narration 108
    epistolary style 31, 127, 135, 208
    first person narratives 61–2, 85, 100–1, 155–6, 163, 182, 186, 188
    and postmodernism 16–20
Nasta, Susheila 123
Nath, Michael 85
National Book Critic's Circle Award 206
nationalism 37, 39, 42–3, 59, 115, 119, 203, 227
nature vs. nurture 37
Nealon, Geoffrey 16
neo-colonialization 115
neo-conservativism 135
neo-Edwardian literature 209–11
neo-historical fiction 16
neo-modernism 186
neo-phenomenological narrative 101, 102–3, 104
neo-racism 226
neo-Victorian literature 207–10
Nesbit, E. 209
Netherland (O'Neill, 2008) 173, 175, 177–8, 181, 192
neurochemical self 84
neurological disorder 85–6

'neuronovels' 84–110
neuroscience 83–110
Never Let Me Go (Ishiguro, 2005) 59, 211, 212–13, 214–15
Neverwhere (Gaiman, 1996) 214
'New Atheism' 135
New Atheist Novel, The (Bradley and Tate, 2010) 135
New English Library 65
New Labour 1–2, 36, 224–5
Newland, Courttia 58, 120–1
    Society Within (1999) 121
new puritans 16
new sincerity 16
New Weird fictions 215
New York Review of Books 173
New York Times bestseller lists 206
Nietzsche, Friedrich 10–11, 36
Nineteen Eighty-Four (Orwell, 1949) 67, 213, 214
Nineteen Seventy-Three etc (Peace, 1999–2002), *see* Red Riding Quartet
Nobel Prize for literature 123
non-fiction 193–5
Noon, Jeff 60
Northern Ireland 2, 3
nostalgia 212
Novel Now: Contemporary British Fiction, The (Bradford, 2007) 116
Number9Dream (Mitchell, 2001) 17
NW (Smith, 2012) 19, 200, 206

Observer, The 228
O'Hagan, Andrew 27
Oldham riots 53, 224
On Beauty (Smith, 2005) 19, 58, 184–5, 199, 203, 206, 210
On Chesil Beach (McEwan, 2007) 85
O'Neill, Joseph 173, 175, 177–8, 181, 192
Orange Prize 122, 199
orientalism 117, 120, 125
'original trauma' 232, 234–5
Orlando (Woolf, 1928) 194
Ortega, Francisco 100
Orwell, George 67, 213, 214
Osborne, Peter 9
Osgerby, William 56, 65, 74
Other, the
    and Asian British writing 123

and contemporaneity 12
and David Peace 43
and European Enlightenment 132
European supremacy over 12
in *Londonstani* (Malkani) 49
neo-orientalism 120
and Niall Griffiths 43
Ours Are the Streets (Sahota, 2011) 236–9

Pakistani writing 124
Parekh Report 224–5
Passaro, Vince 208
patriotism 128
Pautz, Hartwig 224, 226
Peace, David
   and Ali Smith 190
   biography 277–8
   Damned Utd, The (2006) 29, 189
   GB84 (2004) 28, 29–30, 39, 40–4, 188, 188–9
   Red Riding Quartet (1999–2002) 27–8, 29, 40, 164–70, 188
   and regional fictions 29
Peacock, James 110 n.3
Peddie, Ian 39
Penguin Books 120–1, 207
performance and performativity 27, 55, 62
Perloff, Marjorie 182
Pervez, Summer 45, 48, 49
PET scans 97–8
Phelan, James 202
Phillips, Caryl 121–2, 228
Pickett, Katie 4–5
Pinker, Steven 227
Planet Diana: Cultural Studies and Global Mourning (Re:Public, 1997) 7–8
poetic prose 41
poetry 193
police 70, 71
Possession (Byatt, 1990) 208, 209, 210
postcolonialism
   and America 199
   Loh's chapter 115–40
   and multiculturalism 227, 228, 235
   'postimperial melancholia' 117–18
   and postmodernism 45
postmodernism
   and *Atonement* (McEwan) 179, 181, 207

   and Barnes 208
   in *Call me the Breeze* (McCabe) 31–3
   and grand narratives 139
   and the historical novel 145–6
   and history 179, 187
   and Ian McEwan 179
   and identity 36
   and innovation 176
   and literary style 13–20
   vs. modernist experimentation 205
   and neo-Victorian novels 208
   and postcolonialism 45
   postmodern Impressionism 153–4
   postmodern realism 17, 204
   post-postmodernism 109, 203–4
   and psychological trauma 87
   and subcultures 55
   Žižek on 7
postmulticulturalism 226
postnationalism 211, 212, 214
post-postmodernism 16–17, 109, 203–4
post-subcultural theories 55, 60, 63
Postwar British Literature and Postcolonial Studies (MacPhee, 2011) 115
post-war novels 174, 177, 179, 204
Potter, Gary 16, 17, 176
Pratchett, Terry 207
preterite verbal constructions 37, 155
prize-winning books 122, 123, 125, 155, 174, 184, 206, 207, 208, *see also individual prizes e.g. Man Booker*
Proctor, James 120
pronouns, unprecursed 156
psychoanalysis 6–7, 85–6, 94, 95
psychological realism 87, 109–10, 191–2
psychological shift 84
publishing industry 28, 33
Pulitzer Prize 208
Pullman, Philip 60
pulp fiction 74
puritanism 15

Rachman, Peter 74
racism
   in *The Buddha of Suburbia* (Kureishi) 54
   colonial racism 130
   in *Londonstani* (Malkani) 46, 62
   in *Minaret* (Aboulela) 138
   neo-racism 226

and postcolonial literature 117
and *Saturday* (McEwan) 134
and *Skinheads* (King) 69
in *Tainted Love* (Home) 76
in *White Teeth* (Smith) 232
Rain Before It Falls, The (Coe, 2007) 183
Ranasinha, Rivani 115–16
Randhawa, Ravinder 123
Rastafarian culture 59, 69, 71–2, 76
Raw Shark Texts, The (Hall, 2007) 50
'readability' 207
reader intimacy 42
realism
    American fiction 208
    in Black British writing 121
    in David Peace's work 40–2, 188
    experimental vs. realistic writing 19, 146, 149, 173–9, 181–95, 206
    and the historical novel 147
    and history 150
    hyperrealism 121, 182
    hysterical realism 19, 121
    'lyrical realism' 175–8, 191
    lyrical realism 173–4
    magical realism 97, 127, 138–40, 149
    and modernism 147
    and the neuronovel 27–8
    non-realism in *Londonstani* (Malkani) 46
    postmodern realism 17, 204
    psychological realism 87, 109–10, 191–2
    'reality effect' 147–52, 157–63, 164–70
    in *Saturday* (McEwan) 96, 103, 182
    surrealism 31, 72, 213
    and *White Teeth* (Smith) 184
Reality Hunger: A Manifesto (Shields, 2010) 194–5
recession 4–5
Redhead, Steven 55
Red Riding Quartet (Peace, 1999–2002) 27–8, 29, 40, 164–70, 188
Reeve, Philip 60
refugees 122, 138, 139
religion
    Christianity 139
    faith and spirituality 90, 110 n.5, 135
    Islamophobia 117–18, 127, 134, 138, 224
    'Last Days of Mohammad Atta, The' (Amis, 2006) 130–1

Molly and the Muslim Stick (Dabydeen, 2008) 139
'New Atheism' 135
Remainder (McCarthy, 2005) 50, 85, 86, 108–10, 173, 191–2
Remains of the Day, The (Ishiguro, 1989) 211–12, 213
reportage 69
Richard and Judy Book Club 45
Riley, Gwendoline 59–60
riots 53, 68, 69–71, 224
Ripper murders 29
Robbins, Bruce 140 n.3
Roberts, Maureen 121
Robinson, Alan 16
Robinson, John 53
Robinson, Richard 202
Rose, Nikolas 84, 87
Rose, Steven 98, 104
Ross, Michael L. 133
Roth, Marco 84, 85
Rotters' Club, The (Coe, 2001) 57
Rowling, J.K. 201, 207, 215
rudeboy/desi subcultures 45, 61, 64, 67, 125
rural areas 30–4
Rushdie, Salman
    on 9/11 126
    and Asian British writing 123
    and 'British' designation 205
    Enchantress of Florence, The (2008) 124
    Fury (2001) 124
    and the literary establishment 15
    Midnight's Children (1981) 145
    Shalimar the Clown (2005) 124
    and the South Asian diaspora 45
Russo, Richard 208
Ryan, Ray 178, 195

Saga of the Swamp Thing (Moore, 1984–7) 215
Sahota, Sunjeev 236–9
Said, Edward 120
Salisbury, Laura 96
Salt and Saffron (Shamsie, 2000) 116
Șandru, Cristina 227
satire 33
Saturday (McEwan, 2005) 7, 19, 85–107, 109–10, 127–9, 131–5, 158–9, 181–2

Saturday Night and Sunday Morning (Sillitoe, 1958) 54
Schäfer, Stefanie 234
Schoene, Berthold 186, 227
Schuessler, Jennifer 209
Schwartz, Alexandra 206
science fiction 60
Scottish independence 2
Scottish literature 119
Sebald, W.G. 194
Selam Berlin (Kara, 2004) 229
Selby Jr, Hubert 34
Self, Will
   and modernism 19
   postmodernism and grounded ethics 17
   Shark (2014) 19
   Umbrella (2012) 19
   Walking to Hollywood (2010) 194
selfhood 86, 105, 107
self-improvement 48–9, 67
self-reflexivity 13, 15, 17, 61, 105, 180, 186, 205
Seltzer, Mark 166
Sense of an Ending, The (Barnes, 2011) 183, 212
September 11, *see* 9/11 terrorist attacks
Serpent's Tail 29
Sesay, Kadija 120–1
Seshagiri, Urmila 19
sexual assault 35–6
sexual relationships 33
Shaffer, Brian W. 202
Shalimar the Clown (Rushdie, 2005) 124
Shamsie, Kamila
   and cosmopolitanism 124
   Kartography (2002) 116
   on *Londonstani* (Malkani) 63
   Salt and Saffron (2000) 116
Shamsie, Muneeza 124
Shark (Self, 2014) 19
Shaw, Katy 30, 41, 165
Sheepshagger (Griffiths, 2001) 27, 34–40
Shelley, Mary 214
Shelley, Percy 214
Shields, David 194–5
Shields, Rob 56
Shone, Tom 207
Showalter, Elaine 209
Shultz, Kathryn 206

Shyrock, Andrew 117
Sick Notes (Riley, 2004) 59
Sillitoe, Alan 54
Sim, Wai-chew 123
Simons, Jake Wallis 237
'Simple Heart, A' (Flaubert, 1877) 147–8
sincerity, return to 211
Sinclair, Iain 41, 42
   Ghost Milk (2011) 194
   Hackney, That Rose-Red Empire (2009) 194
Sinfield, Alan 204
Singaporean writing 125
Skinhead (Allen, 1970) 65, 74
Skinheads (King, 2008) 57–8, 64–9
Slaby, Jan 106
slavery 122
Small Island (Levy, 2004) 122
Smith, Ali
   Accidental, The (2005) 17, 189–91
   biography 278
   and David Peace 190
   Hotel World (2001) 17, 189–90
   innovative fiction 189–90
   postmodernism and grounded ethics 17
Smith, Andrew 119
Smith, Zadie
   American reception of 199–200, 202, 205–6
   Autograph Man, The (2002) 199
   On Beauty (2005) 19, 58, 184–5, 199, 203, 206, 210
   biography 278–9
   and Ian McEwan 179, 185, 200
   intertextuality 19
   media-friendly 'authenticity' 46
   and modernism 19
   narrative regeneration 216
   NW (2012) 19, 200, 206
   'Two Paths for the Novel' (2008) 173–4, 175–8, 181, 184, 185, 191–2
   White Teeth (2000) 19, 27, 28, 44–5, 58, 60–4, 118, 121, 184, 199, 205–6, 228–36
social realism 121, 127
Society Within (Newland, 1999) 58, 121
So Many Ways to Begin (McGregor, 2006) 185–7

South Asian diaspora 123
Spencer, Robert 135, 227
Spirit Level, The (Wilkinson and Pickett, 2009) 4–5
steampunk novels 60, 215
Stein, Mark 120
Steinberg, Deborah Lynn 7–8
stereotypes
   in *Brick Lane* (Ali) 125
   in *East of Acre Lane* (Wheatle) 72
   in Malkani's work 44
   in McCabe's work 31–2
   and multiculturalism 230, 233, 235
   national stereotypes 200
   negative Muslim stereotypes 138
   racist stereotypes 233, 235
   skinheads 66
   youth subcultures 72
Sterne, Laurence 205
Stevenson, Randall 189
Stierstorfer, Klaus 16
stop and search legislation 70
Strauss, Darin 206
Stretch, Joe 59
Su, John 203, 212, 214
subaltern groups 16, 70
Subculture (Hebdige, 1979) 55
subcultures
   Bentley's chapter on youth 53–77
   Black American subcultures 63
   in *Londonstani* (Malkani) 48
   Manchester subcultures 59–60
   post-subcultural theories 55, 60, 63
   rudeboy/desi subcultures 45, 61, 64, 67, 125
   skinheads 57–8, 64–9, 74
   'subcultural capital' 56, 63
   urban tribes 56, 77
Subcultures Network 78 n.2
subjectivity 157
subject vs. object of knowledge 12–13
surrealism 31, 72, 213
Sutcliffe, Tom 237
Sutherland, John 200, 203, 204
Swainston, Steph 215
Swift, Graham
   Light of Day (2003) 207
   Waterland (1983) 183
   Wish You Were Here (2001) 183

Syal, Meera 45
'syndrome fiction' 110 n.3

Tainted Love (Home, 2005) 57, 72–7
Tate, Andrew 135
Tearne, Roma 116
Tebbs, Paul 38
teen/young adult novels 44, 75
Telegraph Avenue (Chabon, 2012) 206
television
   and subcultures 53
   TV adaptations 29–30
temporality 7–11
temporal turn 9
Tennyson, Alfred 209
terrorism, *see also* 9/11 terrorist attacks
   7/7 London bombings 58, 63, 117, 126, 238
   Incendiary (Cleave, 2005) 136–7
   'Last Days of Mohammad Atta, The' (Amis, 2006) 129–31
   Loh's chapter 115–40
   and multiculturalism 224, 236–9
   and *Netherland* (O'Neill) 177
   and postcolonial literature 117–18, 126
   and reality vs. the fantastic 7
   and *Saturday* (McEwan) 101, 104, 132
   and subcultures 63
Tew, Philip 118, 119, 184, 195
text-speak 46
Thatcher government 29, 35–6, 42, 76, 116
Thinks . . . (Lodge, 2001) 85, 100
Thirlwell, Adam 147, 148
Thorne, Matt 15, 16
Thornton, Sarah 55, 56, 63
Thorpe, Adam 188
Thus Spake Zarathustra (Nietzsche) 36
Time After Time (Woods, 2007) 9
Tóibín, Colm 153, 182
Tolkein, J.R.R. 215
trade union activity 30, 36, 57
'Tradition and the Individual Talent' (Eliot, 1919) 183
Trainspotting (film, Boyle, 1996) 54
Trainspotting (Welsh, 1993) 28, 54
transgressive identity 30, 32, 39
translation 98, 105, 110
Transmission (Kunzru, 2004) 124

transnational literary scene 115–40, 200, 203, 228
'trauma culture' 86
Treanor, Jill 4
Tresize, Rachel 36
tribal identity 55
Tristram Shandy (Sterne, 1759) 205
Trocchi, Alexander 34, 73–7
True History of the Kelly Gang (Carey, 2000) 187
Twenty-First-Century Fiction: A Critical Introduction (Boxall, 2013) 8–9
Two Caravans (Lewycka, 2007) 119
'Two Paths for the Novel' (Smith, 2008) 173–4, 175–8, 184, 185, 191–2
Tyler, Imogen 53, 67

Ulysses (Joyce, 1922) 158, 163–4
Umbrella (Self, 2012) 19
uncertainty 176
underclasses 39
underground behaviours 64
universalism 226–7
Updike, John 150
urban novels 121
urban tribes 56, 77

van den Akker, Robin 9, 16
Vasileva, Katya 223
Vermeulen, Timotheus 9, 16
vernacular dialogue 45, 46, 47–8, 61–2
V for Vendetta (Moore, 1982–5) 215
Vidal, Fernando 84, 100
violence, *see also* war
  and Alan Moore's work 215
  and multiculturalism 228
  riots 53, 68, 69
  and *Sheepshagger* (Griffiths) 36–7, 39
  in *White Teeth* 232
  and youth subcultures 53, 62
vision 11–12, 72, 101

Wagner, Henry 97
Walker, Alice 208
Walking to Hollywood (Self, 2010) 194
Walkowitz, Rebecca 203, 211, 214
Wall, Kathleen 200
Wallace, David Foster 200, 210–11

war
  Iraq war 3–4, 29, 58, 99, 102, 117, 158, 182, 189
  and psychoanalysis 86
  War on Terror 3, 19, 135, 136–7, 237
Warner, Alan 31
Warwick, Alexandra 164–5
Waste Land, The (Eliot, 1922) 206
Watchmen (Moore, 1986–7) 215
Waterhouse, Keith 54
Waterland (Swift, 1983) 183
Waters, Sarah
  Affinity (1999) 207
  Fingersmith (2002) 207
  Little Stranger, The (2009) 207
  neo-Victorian tales 207–8
  Night Watch, The (2006) 207
  and the prominence of neo-historical fiction 16
  Tipping the Velvet (1998) 207
Watman, Max 200–1
Waugh, Evelyn 212
Waugh, Patricia 101, 108, 158–9, 182
Weinzierl, Rupert 55
Welcome to the Desert of the Real (Žižek, 2002) 5–6
Well, Juliette 201
Wells, Lynn 133, 160–1, 163
Welsh, Irvine
  and genre 36
  hybridity 119
  and Niall Griffiths 34
  Trainspotting (1993) 28, 54
Welsh literature 34–40, 119
What a Carve Up! (Coe, 1994) 183
What Ever Happened to Modernism? (Josipovici, 2010) 147
Wheatle, Alex
  biography 279–80
  Brixton Rock (1999) 69
  Dirty South, The (2008) 58, 69, 118, 121
  East of Acre Lane (2001) 57, 69–72, 121
When We Were Orphans (Ishiguro, 2000) 207, 211, 213
Whitbread Book of the Year 122
Whitbread First Novel Award 125, 189
White Family, The (Gee, 2008) 117

White Teeth (Smith, 2000) 19, 27, 28, 44–5, 58, 60–4, 118, 121, 184, 199, 205–6, 228–36
Wilkinson, Richard 4–5
Wilson, Janet 227
Winterson, Jeanette 15, 205
Wish You Were Here (Swift, 2001) 183
Wolf Hall (Mantel, 2009) 154–7, 188, 206–7
Wong, Cynthia F. 202
Wood, James 19, 121, 181
Woods, David 9
Woolf, Virginia
    and *The Hours* (Cunningham, 1998) 153–4
    and modernism 206
    on modernism 14
    Mrs Dalloway (1925) 90, 153, 158, 182
    Orlando (1928) 194
    referenced in *Atonement* (McEwan) 19
    and subjectivity 157
Wordsworth, William 214

working-class culture
    and globalization 129–30
    Incendiary (Cleave, 2005) 135–7
    and Muslims in Britain 118
    post 9/11 working-class literature 140 n.5
    in *Saturday* (McEwan) 92
    and youth subcultures 56, 64, 67, 72, 76
'writing back' 117
Writing Degree Zero (Barthes, 1953) 155
Wynne-Davies, Marion 122

Yassin-Kassab, Robin 237
Yorkshire 29, 40–4, 164–70
Young Adam (Trocchi, 1957) 76
young adult novels 44, 75
youth culture
    Bentley's chapter 53–77
    in *Londonstani* (Malkani) 44, 47, 49
    and postcolonial literature 125

Zandy, Janet 140 n.5
Zelig (film, Allen, 1983) 73
Žižek, Slavoj 5–7, 14, 135

www.ingramcontent.com/pod-product-compliance
Lightning Source LLC
Chambersburg PA
CBHW051804230426
43672CB00012B/2629